Parasocial Experiences

Parasocial Experiences

Psychological Theory and Application

DAVID C. GILES AND GAYLE S. STEVER

OXFORD
UNIVERSITY PRESS

Oxford University Press is a department of the University of Oxford. It furthers
the University's objective of excellence in research, scholarship, and education
by publishing worldwide. Oxford is a registered trade mark of Oxford University
Press in the UK and certain other countries.

Published in the United States of America by Oxford University Press
198 Madison Avenue, New York, NY 10016, United States of America.

© Oxford University Press 2024

All rights reserved. No part of this publication may be reproduced, stored in
a retrieval system, or transmitted, in any form or by any means, without the
prior permission in writing of Oxford University Press, or as expressly permitted
by law, by license, or under terms agreed with the appropriate reproduction
rights organization. Inquiries concerning reproduction outside the scope of the
above should be sent to the Rights Department, Oxford University Press, at the
address above.

You must not circulate this work in any other form
and you must impose this same condition on any acquirer.

CIP data is on file at the Library of Congress

ISBN 978-0-19-764764-6

DOI: 10.1093/oso/9780197647646.001.0001

Printed by Marquis Book Printing, Canada

CONTENTS

Acknowledgments ix
Acronyms and Definitions xi

Introduction 1
Gayle S. Stever and David C. Giles

1. Parasocial Theory and Psychological Theory 6
   David C. Giles
   Researching the Parasocial 8
   Three Unanswered Questions 10
   Theoretical Perspectives 15

2. Parasocial to Social as a Continuum
   Gayle S. Stever
   Parasocial Interaction 19
   When Is It Parasocial? When Is It Not?
   Scandal, Gossip, and Notoriety 21
   Parasocial to Social Transitions 23
   Differentiating a PSR From Identification
   The Role of Imagination 24
   Narrative Psychology and the Science of Storytelling 25
   PSRs and Distinguishing Actors From Their Characters 27
   Parasocial Breakup 28

3. Multisocial Interaction? 32
   David C. Giles
   Defining New Types of Media Figure 36
   New Types of Parasocial Interaction 42
   Approaches to Studying New Media Figures
   Social Media as Multisocial Interaction 49

vi

4. Parasocial Perception and Para-Communication 50
   Gayle S. Stever
   Parasocial Perception 51
   Para-Communication and Parasocial Perception in Fandoms 52
   Illusion Versus Reality 53
   Case Studies 54
   Conclusion 73

5. Parasocial Aspects of Social Relationships 7
   David C. Giles
   What Is Donald Trump Doing in My Dream? 76
   Media Figures as Family Members and Friends 79
   Parasocial Relationships in Childhood 8
   Self–Nonself Boundary 94

6. Psychoanalytic Theory and the Parasocial 98
   David C. Giles
   Three Unanswered Questions in Media Psychology 98
   In Defense of Psychoanalytic Theory
   Transitional Objects and Media 10
   The Elsewhere and the Other 102
   Identification With the Other 10
   Fantasy . . . and Phantasy 108
   Language 109
   Narrative 111
   Psychoanalytic Theories and Attachment Theories 114

7. Parasocial Attachment and Its Place in Attachment Theory 115
   Gayle S. Stever
   What Are the Essential Elements of Attachment Theory? 115
   Place Attachment 116
   Attachment to Animals/Pets 8
   Winnicott's Object Relations Theory: Attachment to Transitional Objects 118
   Attachment to God 119
   Parasocial Attachment as Mediated Attachment 119
   Parasocial Attachment and the Death of Queen Elizabeth 121
   Attachment and Its Relationship to Evolutionary Psychology 123
   Evolutionary Theory and Arousal 123
   Parasocial Romantic Relationships 124
   Observations on A 127
   What Does All This Mean in the Context of the PSRR? 128
   Exploring Further: The Crush 129
   The Narrative as Related to PSRRs 130
   Aidan Turner and *Poldark* 130
   Conclusion 1

8. The Social and the Spiritual in Fandom and Parasocial Relationships 135
Gayle S. Stever
Social and Emotional Impact of Fandom and Parasocial Relationships in a Variety of Contexts 135
The Sociometer Theory 136
Collective Effervescence 137
Mudita 139
Fandom as Compared to Forms of Religious Expression 139
Charisma 142
Celebrity Worship 144
To Consider 145
Fandom Versus Parasocial Relationships 146
Conclusion 147

9. Fans Meet Celebrities: Cameo and Conventions 148
Gayle S. Stever
Cameo and Parasocial Interaction 149
Talking With Dean O'Gorman 151
Social Media as Self-Help 153
Nana Visitor 154
Robert Picardo 156
Denise Crosby 158
Cameo as a Fan Activity 161
Crossing the Social–Parasocial Line 162
Social Media as Operant Conditioning 163
Conclusion 163

10. Additional Concepts Applied to the Study of Audiences 166
Gayle S. Stever
Role Modeling 167
Vicarious Social Experiences 168
Identification 168
Transportation 170
Conclusion 172

11. Research Methods in the Field of Parasocial Theory 173
David C. Giles
Qualitative Methods 174
Quantitative Methods 180

12. View From the Road and Methods Employed 184
Gayle S. Stever
Participant–Observer Ethnography 184
What Exactly Does It Mean to Do Qualitative Research? 185
Various Kinds of Qualitative Inquiry 186
Autoethnography 187
Quantitative Methods in This Area of Study 190
Conclusion 192

13. Summary and Conclusions 194
Gayle S. Stever and David C. Giles
Parasocial and Social as a Continuum 194
Popular (Mass) Culture or High Culture? 195
Social Media and PSRs 196
Para-Communication and Parasocial Perception 196
The Unconscious and Psychoanalytical Perspectives on PSR 196
Survival and Reproduction: Evolutionary Psychology and PSR 197
A Cautionary Point 198
PSRs and the Spiritual Life of the Audience Members 198
Evolving Forms of Social Media: Cameo and Similar New Platforms 199
Theoretical Avenues to Studying the Audience 199
New Questions for Future Research: The Psychology of Acting 199
Acting and Mental Health 201
Further Examples 205
Another Perspective: Acting as Behaviorism Would See It 206
PSRs and Methods of Inquiry 210

Notes 213
References 217
Index 249

ACKNOWLEDGMENTS

A number of people were instrumental in helping us with the writing of this book.

At the top of the list is Gayle's student from Empire State University, Donna Martini, a recent graduate in psychology who proofread all of the chapters for this book, making suggestions where appropriate. We are certain your future in media psychology is secure should you decide to pursue it! You are very much appreciated!

We also thank both Donna Martini and Holly Hassett for their hard work in the construction of the index for this book.

We appreciate very much the input and support we have received from our various editors at Oxford University Press, and also the reviewers who gave suggestions for our book.

David C. Giles
Gayle S. Stever

Gayle also acknowledges the following contributors to her work.

It is inevitable in fan studies that a number of media fans become interested in the work and read chapters for me each time I tackle the writing of a project like this one. Linda Burnett has been doing this for me for many years, and she has been generous in reading all of every book I've written! A number of other fans read selected chapters for me, and these include Kathy Wang, Christie Zizo, Blairsanne Knoedler, Lisa Holden, and Jan Learmonth.

Marjorie Davis is a good friend and fellow educator who read several chapters for me and gave excellent feedback.

A number of the cast members of *Star Trek* have, for years, been generous in talking with me about various experiences they have had with their fans and what the life of an actor and celebrity is like. For this book, Armin Shimerman and Andrew Robinson answered questions for me over email, and Nana Visitor, Denise Crosby, Robert Picardo, and Alexander Siddig each gave me interviews with respect to various chapters. Armin, Andy, Siddig, and Nana have been friends since *Star Trek: Deep Space 9* began filming 30 years ago, and over those years each has given me numerous interviews in addition to the ones for this book. My gratitude to each and every one of you for your help and insights is endless.

Dean O'Gorman, from the first Cameo question he answered for me to the Zoom interviews we did, shared remarkable insights with respect to his long and distinguished acting career and his extensive experience with audience members for his various projects (which include *The Hobbit, The Almighty Johnsons, Trumbo*, and numerous other film and television roles). I am extremely grateful.

I am privileged to have faculty colleagues who read chapters for me and offer their insights and expertise. Lorraine Lander, Jill Oliver, Suzy Horton, Connie Rodriguez, and Josh Cohen have all contributed in important ways to the development of the ideas within this book.

The first time I emailed David Giles back in 2005 to ask him questions about his groundbreaking publication from 2002, I could not possibly have known that he would become a colleague, a mentor, an inspiration, and a friend. I will always be grateful for the help and guidance you have given me over these years, and for agreeing to write this book with me. Thank you so much!

My family has always been an important source of support and inspiration for me, and my husband John is the wind beneath my wings and the ultimate inspiration for it all.

Gayle S. Stever

ACRONYMS AND DEFINITIONS

IWM—internal working model: This is a term used in the attachment literature to refer to the ways that we come to understand and relate to various kinds of people in relationships. These are the mental representations we have for the possible kinds of relationships we might develop throughout the lifespan.

PSA—parasocial attachment

PSB—parasocial breakup: A term used in the parasocial literature to talk about any time that a parasocial relationship ends, either voluntarily or involuntarily from the point of view of the audience member.

PSE—parasocial experience: This is an umbrella term that includes all of the various aspects of parasocial theory.

PSI—parasocial interaction

PSR—parasocial relationship

PSRR—parasocial romantic relationship: A parasocial relationship that is based primarily on a romantic attraction to or "crush" on a media figure.

parasocial attachment (PSA): If one comes, over time, to experience comfort and a sense of security from the presence of certain mediated figures, that is a PSA. Attachment (the broader construct) is defined as a relationship from which we derive comfort and feel a sense of security from the proximity (real or vicarious) to someone. Infant–caregiver attachment is the best-understood type, but we also talk about adult romantic attachment and other forms of attachment whereby we experience this comfort. PSA is a newer concept in the parasocial literature but dates back to the early 1990s when the term was conceptualized as a merging of PSR with secondary attachment. PSI and PSR date all the way back to Horton and Wohl in 1956, who originated the concept.

parasocial interaction (PSI) is when the mediated message is playing, and one is interacting with it in real time. It may be as simple as listening, but sometimes we do things such as "talk back" (as in a televised sporting event during which we cheer on our team), or sing along, or in some other way express ourselves relative to what we are experiencing. So, this PSI is where it starts. We interact with the person in the media rather than just watch. The interaction can be mental or imagined, or it can be expressed out loud as if talking or responding to the other person. The person to whom we are responding is not aware of the response, although they might be generally aware of an audience who potentially responds; this is the case when the parasocial object is a real person.

parasocial relationship (PSR): The term *parasocial* refers to a relationship in which one person knows the other intimately but is not known in return. The relationship is reciprocal in the sense that the celebrity or media persona is sending out messages, songs, art, or other expressions, and the audience member is responding to the personality, work, and expressions of that persona. This is true for a real person, but parasocial relationships can also be with fictional characters, in which case reciprocity is not possible.

Introduction

GAYLE S. STEVER AND DAVID C. GILES ■

This book is partially the result of a continuing dialogue between the two authors with respect to a number of issues. The first was the disparity in the way different disciplines talk about parasocial experiences (PSEs). In psychology, in places such as the celebrity worship literature (Maltby et al., 2003), parasocial relationships (PSRs) are placed in the realm of pathology, with the suggestion that forming a very close and personal connection to a media figure is a slippery slope to mental illness (Maltby et al., 2006; Shabahang et al., 2019). In cultural studies, prominent figures in the study of fandoms have expressed the belief that the entire parasocial construct pathologizes fandom (Duffett, 2013; Groszman, 2020; Jenkins, 2006; Jensen, 2002). Similarly, some sociologists consider that fandom and PSRs should be treated as something troublesome and problematic (Ferris, 2005; Rojek, 2015).

Contrast this with communication studies, where the idea that PSRs imply pathology is anathema to many of those scholars (Erickson, 2022; Tukachinsky Forster, 2021). Our collaboration and resulting book attempt to shed some theoretical light on these issues by applying traditional and well-developed theoretical perspectives, specifically psychodynamic, ethological, and developmental theories.

CHAPTER 1

Chapter 1 recognizes that with the diversity of both theoretical perspectives and methods involved in the study of parasocial experiences, developing a unified approach to such research is a challenge. Because shared points of reference with respect to these things are critical in understanding media, trying to do cross-disciplinary research in an area such as parasocial experiences is difficult at best. This chapter explores these challenges involved in research on parasocial theory. The field to date has relied heavily on psychometrics and quantitative approaches to research, and the weaknesses in this singular approach are introduced. Taking

Parasocial Experiences. David C. Giles and Gayle S. Stever, Oxford University Press. © Oxford University Press 2024.
DOI: 10.1093/oso/9780197647646.003.0001

a reductive rather than an inductive approach to understanding parasocial experiences is fraught with peril.

CHAPTER 2

The authors' discussions for a number of years have also centered around the idea that many things that are presumed to be social actually have many elements of parasocial imbedded within them. Conversely, relationships that begin as purely parasocial have the potential to transform into relationships that are reciprocated in minor ways (e.g., responses on social media) such that around the time Twitter and Facebook began to be popular, the question "Is this still parasocial?" emerged (Paravati et al., 2020; Stever & Lawson, 2013; Tsiotsou, 2015). We began to realize and discuss what we were observing in our own work—that parasocial to social is more of a continuum than a dichotomy. This topic is discussed at various points in this book, particularly in Chapter 2, in which it is introduced in some depth. Chapter 2 elaborates on the parasocial–social continuum and discusses the various aspects of parasocial theory, beginning with parasocial interaction (PSI), PSRs, and parasocial attachment (PSA). This chapter introduces the concept of identification by contrasting it with PSRs, and then in Chapter 10, identification as a construct is developed in more detail. Vicarious experiences and transportation are also introduced and further developed in Chapter 10.

CHAPTER 3

In Chapter 3, we discuss the impact of social media on PSRs in the present century. New technologies afford different types of media figure–audience interaction, as well as new types of media figures. The challenges for parasocial theory are discussed in relation to these. This chapter introduces the universe of new types of media figures that have come into being as a result of interactive social media platforms such as YouTube, TikTok, and livestreaming platforms. Continuing to reinforce the idea of parasocial to social as a continuum rather than a dichotomy, these newer forms of PSI and ways of exploring these newer types of media figures are discussed. The term *multisocial interaction*, as introduced by Hills (2015), is recognized as a way to describe such newer social media platforms.

CHAPTER 4

Within the study of PSE, there has been a decided lack of attention to the celebrity side of PSRs when the PSR is with a living person. Although we observe that PSRs with fictional characters are, of necessity, never reciprocated, the social interactions that celebrities have with their fans as a group and the response those fans make to those interactions develop into a social relationship that has para-communication on one side and parasocial perception on the other. Para-communication recognizes that the experience of PSI is fueled by audience members recognizing that celebrities intentionally reach out and communicate directly with them (Hartmann, 2008). Parasocial perception (Riles & Adams, 2021; Wiemer et al., 2022) then involves the ways that audience members react to that para-communication. Chapter 4 is specifically dedicated to these constructs and case examples that illustrate the ways that this develops within the parasocial realm. The parasocial-to-social transition is supported with research data from the authors and also from the literature (Riles & Adams, 2021; Wiemer et al., 2022).

CHAPTERS 5

Chapter 5 develops one of the core themes of the book, which is how we make sense of the difference between the social and the parasocial. It examines the ways in which social relationships are always "parasocial" and how the imagination is involved even with our closest companions, partners, and family members. It attempts to chart the development of PSRs in childhood by comparing them with other kinds of nonsocial relationships, such as imaginary companions.

CHAPTER 6

In Chapter 6, some of the themes from Chapter 5 are developed in relation to psychoanalytic theory, considering what can be learned from the work of Freud, Winnicott, Lacan, and Klein. The chapter then moves toward the importance of language and narrative in making sense of our relationships more generally. Although previous literature has developed some aspects of psychoanalytic theory and how that theory connects with PSEs, Chapters 5 and 6 specifically address the ways that dreams and the unconscious can figure prominently within the parasocial realm. Winnicott's object relations theory is applied here and additionally is applied in the subsequent chapter on attachment. The case is made for a parasocial object qualifying as a transitional object as defined in that literature.

CHAPTER 7

With respect to developmental psychology, one of the most prominent theories in lifespan development is attachment theory (Bretherton, 1992). Within our fieldwork, we have observed that when a PSR progresses to the point where the connection offers the audience member a degree of comfort and safe haven and has elements of both proximity seeking and separation distress (Stever, 2013), the PSR can be called a PSA. Chapter 7 develops this construct in the context of evolutionary psychology. Although some might have believed that attachment requires a direct and real-world in-person relationship, the literature clearly reveals cases in which the attachment construct has been applied to other than child–caregiver or adult partner relationships (the two areas most traditionally considered in the attachment literature). To illustrate how this principle is more widely applied, attachments to pets, places, and God are discussed in the context of the research literature on these topics. The chapter goes on to develop, in some depth, physiological aspects of parasocial romantic relationships (including literature on "crushes" with information about the mechanisms of such attractions). Also recounted is research exploring the stigma of having a parasocial romantic relationship for women in middle age and old age.

CHAPTER 8

Chapter 8 brings in concepts from social psychology and fan studies, applying those to PSEs. Both the individual and collective impact of fandom are described through concepts such as the sociometer, collective effervescence, Mudita, fandom as a spiritual or religious experience, charisma, and celebrity worship. The chapter concludes with a comparison of the concepts of PSR versus fandom. This chapter addresses the intersection between parasocial theory and fan studies, connecting the social with the parasocial in the collective and spiritual aspects of fandom.

CHAPTER 9

No discussion of PSEs would be complete without addressing PSI, the sense a viewer gets that a distant parasocial object is addressing them directly and personally. While writing this book, Gayle discovered the relatively new social media platform called Cameo. She dedicated much time to studying its mechanisms and impact, realizing that Cameo exemplifies exactly what we define as PSI, specifically the use of direct address and eye gaze. These features have been identified as prominent aspects of parasocial interaction in previous literature. To develop this area of inquiry, four actors with Cameo accounts were interviewed extensively for their views on the role that Cameo has played in their careers and has affected the ways they interact with audience members. In these interviews, actors related in an experiential way how their own connections with fans sometimes transitioned from parasocial to social. Part of that transition involves the fan coming to know the actor as a person rather than just as the characters they portray, a point brought up specifically by both Dean O'Gorman and Nana Visitor.

CHAPTER 10

Although this is a book about parasocial experiences, there are a number of related constructs that are introduced, particularly for the reader who is unfamiliar with them. These include vicarious social experiences, identification, transportation,

Introduction

and role modeling. The roles of producer and consumer have become more fluid, and the person who is sometimes the audience member, viewer, or fan might tomorrow become the blogger, video creator, fan fiction writer, photographer, visual artist, or musician. This chapter recognizes this overlap in concepts and roles.

CHAPTERS 11 AND 12

The methods for researching parasocial experiences that we have used through the years are described, along with alternative approaches that could be applied constructively. We encourage researchers in the field to explore beyond the psychometric approach that currently dominates the literature and has considerably restricted the conceptual development of parasocial theory.

CHAPTER 13

We summarize the main points made in this volume and close with a few research questions that can potentially move parasocial theory forward. Noteworthy was the discovery that very little, if anything, has been done in previous literature on connections with media personae to investigate a specific relationship between actors and their characters. The chapter concludes with a discussion with three prominent and successful actors as they share their perspectives on this relationship and how characters are created for media. Future research in this area is encouraged.

1
Parasocial Theory and Psychological Theory

DAVID C. GILES ■

While you are reading an academic publication, does it matter whether the author is a psychologist, a sociologist, a communication scientist, or a media scholar? We would like to assume we are all discussing the same phenomena, with little more than a change of perspective: different references or differently named theories, perhaps. When academics apply for research funding, there is a modern preference for proposals that are "multidisciplinary" or "interdisciplinary," based on the concept of "triangulation," as if the psychologist, sociologist, and communication scientist are all looking at the same research object through different colored lenses. We will put trivial differences aside to hold hands and agree to disagree in the name of objectivity.

That's what we like to think. The reality is somewhat more complicated. For a start, each of those academic disciplines encompasses huge diversity in theoretical and methodological perspectives. You could put together a team of psychologists who would effectively constitute a multidisciplinary panel because their ideas about what they are researching, how they conduct the research, and what they can conclude from their data are so radically different that they may as well be from completely different disciplines. The same is true of sociology, communication, and pretty much any other social science. At the same time, the psychologists will share some common background: They will have all been exposed to the same topics, authors, and studies in their training. They may not all agree on Piaget's theory of child development, but they will all know it and acknowledge its significance as a reference point. This perspective will not necessarily be shared by sociologists and communication scientists. Somewhere along the line, these diverse and shared reference points may become crucial to the project's outcome.

The central goal of this book is to try to bridge some of these interdisciplinary gaps that exist within the study of human behavior in relation to media, with

Parasocial Experiences. David C. Giles and Gayle S. Stever, Oxford University Press. © Oxford University Press 2024.
DOI: 10.1093/oso/9780197647646.003.0002

specific reference to what has become known as "parasocial" theory. On the face of it, this would appear to be a classic "multidisciplinary" topic: You just get the psychologists in as experts on behavior and team them up with people with expertise across the many different aspects of media (traditional and social), and they will, depending on their perspectives, agree on a variety of suitable methods—survey, experimental, qualitative—that generate a "rounded," comprehensive data set that will address whatever intellectual question is deemed important to the funding body or publisher.

This is, of course, thinking about research as a one-off, here-and-now activity that can achieve some "impact" on wider society. But theories, paradigms, and so on develop over a much longer period and are not driven by the immediate interests of the wider society. Theories evolve because researchers in different disciplines find them useful, often for non-theoretical reasons: Think of the incredible success of the "Big Five" personality theory of Costa and McCrae (1988) that is routinely dropped into any multivariate study in which individual differences are thought important to the outcome. Unless it acquires a dubious or notorious reputation, a theory of this sort will just grow and grow so long as researchers (across disciplines, perhaps) find it useful.

This brings us to parasocial theory. Gayle and I have been using the concept of the parasocial for several decades because, as psychologists interested in media influence, we find it useful as a framework for exploring the relationship between media and behavior. We call things "parasocial" because they are beyond the social and yet have impacts that are clearly social. Advice is a good example. A first-time mother might seek out advice from her mother or a friend who is already a mother on a topic like breastfeeding. She might change her approach in the light of this advice. This is clearly a social impact. If the same mother changes her strategy again after hearing the accounts of a "sharenting" influencer on her YouTube channel, the social impact would be exactly the same, but the communication channel would be completely different. It would involve accepting advice from someone she does not actually know (and trusting them more than her own mother), mediated through some form(s) of technology. She could even change her breastfeeding behavior after watching a film or TV drama based on the experience of a fictional character with whom she identifies as a fellow mother. This "person" does not even exist as anything other than a cultural representation, but again the social impact is the same.

How would the average psychologist make sense of this seemingly irrational social behavior? In most cases, they would probably draw one of two possible conclusions. The first is to ignore the media context completely. So what if the "mother" is a YouTuber or fictional character? The psychological processes are the same. They might draw on a cognitive model such as the theory of planned behavior (TPB; Ajzen & Fishbein, 1980) to trace the decision-making path the mother has taken. The input is largely irrelevant. (The TPB, used heavily in health psychology, largely glosses over where health "information" comes from because it is concerned with cognitive processes that are fundamentally biological, even though this is not explicitly stated or even accepted by its adherents.)

The second explanation is that the mother's decision to accept the breastfeeding advice of mediated figures is based on wholly unreliable information and can only be explained through defective decision-making. In other words, she has been somehow "duped" or tricked into believing that something is true (that the influencer is reliable, that the fictional character is "real"). A sensible, rational person would be cognitively robust enough to reject both sources of information and stick with the "real" social advice from family and friends or, better still, seek the advice of professionals (from the worlds of health, parenting, and nutrition). So, this would be a simple matter of individual dysfunction: Perhaps the stress and trauma of first-time motherhood have addled her brain and caused her to drop her guard.

The problem with the first explanation is, of course, the precise reverse of the second. By ignoring the nature of communication channels, we make little allowance in human behavior for selecting between different sources of information. But the second explanation errs in assuming that this selection process is uncomplicated and is simply a matter of paying attention and applying conventional reasoning. Despite this, both explanations are firmly rooted in the belief that human decision-making is essentially rational. (The TPB grew out of an earlier model, Ajzen & Fishbein's [1975] theory of reasoned action.)

However, many of our responses to media are not rational at all. How many tears, for instance, have reasonable, intelligible viewers wept over fictional tragedy? Clearly, some further level of explanation is needed to account for these and other similarly illogical reactions. A central goal of this book is to propose ways we can incorporate the irrational into parasocial theory without pathologizing media users.

RESEARCHING THE PARASOCIAL

The concept of parasocial interaction (PSI), as communication students know, was first elaborated by Horton and Wohl (1956), a truly multidisciplinary partnership of sociologist and psychiatrist, respectively. But it was only intermittently referenced in the subsequent two decades before being picked up by communication scientists Mark Levy and Alan Rubin (Levy, 1979; Rubin et al., 1985), who between them turned it into a measurable construct—the Parasocial Interaction Scale—that could be comfortably accommodated, typically as one of several psychometric measures, in multivariate studies of media influence. Publications multiplied, and a small literature emerged in which the Rubin scale (henceforth, the PSI scale) was used as a predictor of various affective and behavioral responses to media stimuli.

But this is where the disciplinary tensions start to be felt. Just what does the PSI scale measure, and what exactly does it tell us about media audiences? Summatively, it is a measure of the "strength" of PSI between the respondent and one specific media figure, typically a favorite. "I miss X when they are not on the show" is one typical item, derived (like most of them) from Levy's (1979) focus group discussions with viewers of TV news bulletins. In the context of, say, TV news presenters, this would constitute a meaningful and relevant variable. But the PSI scale has been used across all manner of contexts and types of media figures with few attempts to generalize from one topic to media use more generally. At the same time, it is practically the only way PSI had been studied at the turn of the century. We had reached a point where, as I discovered at my personal cost, a research paper on the topic could be rejected because the author had declined to use the PSI scale and therefore was unable to claim he was studying something called parasocial interaction.[1]

Two decades later, the situation has improved. Researchers have attempted to disentangle PSI from parasocial relationships (PSRs) more generally. As media psychology has evolved as a discipline, a bridge has crossed the gap between communication and psychology, albeit at a single crossing point, with a fairly predictable traffic flow (the psychometric obsession in psychology complementing that in communication science). Ultimately this has simply resulted in yet more psychometric scales, measuring slightly different constructs, resolving some issues but leaving others wide open. More bridges are needed, less well-trodden but serving different crossing points, connecting a range of communities embracing different theories and methods. We hope that this book will constitute one of those bridges.

What is lost in parasocial research by relying solely on psychometric scales? I outlined many of the shortcomings in a literature review more than 20 years ago (Giles, 2002). The fundamental problem with the PSI scale and its derivatives is that they are essentially, perhaps necessarily, reductive measures. For convenience, parasocial experience (PSE) is boiled down to a positive engagement with a single figure. This is fine for studying fans of a specific figure, but the majority of parasocial studies ask respondents to select a "favorite," often from a very broad catchment (sometimes "celebrity" or "media personality," often barely defined). While this may be all that researchers need to capture some kind of broad engagement with the media product under investigation (news, soap, YouTube, or whatever), the trail left behind in the literature is patchy, to say the least. We get very little idea of how the research participants' lives have been affected by these relationships.

There are also certain assumptions in the literature around parasocial theory that have remained unexplored—largely, I suspect, because they do not contribute directly to the hypothesis under investigation, which usually derives from a communication or media research question. One of the ways in which the limitations of the PSI scale have been addressed is by breaking the parasocial down into specific elements—cognitive, behavioral, and so on (Tukachinsky & Stever, 2019). Communication scientists have also begun to differentiate between aspects of the parasocial, distinguishing PSRs, which are really what many items in the PSI scale measure, from PSI, the moment-by-moment response of the media user to a specific media figure, and parasocial attachment (Dibble et al., 2016). (These developments of parasocial theory are discussed in more detail in Chapter 2).

Hartmann and Goldhoorn's (2011) original measure, the Experience of Parasocial Interaction scale, explores the intensity of this real-time encounter, assuming no previous (parasocial) relationship between user and figure. It attempts to isolate the cognitive and behavioral elements of encounters by asking respondents to rate statements relating to their feelings about the media figure (in their study, an experimental video featuring a single presenter). Although this measure addresses the issue of "normal social interaction," it does include a rather strange item, which asks respondents to indicate their level of agreement with the statement "the media figure was aware of me." Given that this is clearly an irrational belief (they are in a laboratory watching an original video), it would seem to be measuring a degree of irrationality in the PSE. But this fundamentally very interesting proposition is not followed up, here or elsewhere, in the literature.

Maybe all this is nothing more than a psychologist's frustration with literature generated largely in a cognate discipline. If communication is only interested in behavior during the act of media use, it may never wonder what goes on the rest of the time. As a result, the parasocial part of human experience is left behind in the interface. But it's clear—from the behavior of fans, in particular—that those experiences are influential, if not necessarily in the pathological sense implied by some of the research on "celebrity worship" (McCutcheon et al., 2003). Other researchers have documented the role that fandom plays in the lifespan development of individuals (Harrington et al., 2011; Sandvoss, 2005; Stevenson, 2009; Stever, 2021), where the media figure becomes a significant other, even a lifelong guide, without the fan ever harboring any wish to meet the figure (i.e., turn a PSR into a social one). Either way, it's time to bring a bit more psychology into the picture, to find ways of incorporating PSE into psychological experience, to fulfill Horton and Wohl's (1956) original aim "to learn in detail how these parasocial interactions are integrated into the matrix of usual social activity" (p. 225).

THREE UNANSWERED QUESTIONS

What is there left to find out about the parasocial experience? I'm going to try and narrow the field of interest down somewhat. By concentrating on three specific unanswered questions, I hope these can act as points of convergence between the parasocial and the social.

The first question is really an ontological one with respect to media figures, the "other" in the PSR. Of course, this starting point rests on an assumption that in a parasocial dyad, one is an "other," and the "I" is either you (the reader) or I (the author), and that neither you nor I happen to be the media figure in the relationship. If you (the reader) are any kind of "media figure," this does not, of course, preclude you from enjoying PSRs with other media figures. But already, I am questioning exactly what a media figure is and where the boundary lies between media users and media figures.

Let's return briefly to the vexed topic of celebrity worship, where, as with PSI, the field is dominated by a single psychometric instrument, the Celebrity Attitude

Scale of Maltby et al. (2002). This scale includes items such as "If I were to meet my favorite celebrity in person, he/she would already somehow know that I am his/her biggest fan," predicated on the idea that my favorite celebrity is alive and well and that fans are worshipping them largely as compensation for not having actual contact with them. Stever (2009, 2016) points out that fans often do have contact with celebrities through fan organizations, often quite regular and extensive contact, albeit not with the degree of intimacy that some might desire. There is no allowance for the fact that the celebrity might be dead, as in the case of a celebrity like Elvis, who is often said to be worshipped in a quasi-religious fashion (Wise, 1984).

Some parasocial researchers have addressed the ontology issue by adapting the items of the PSI scale by rewording them for use with specifically fictional figures—for example, in Perse and Rubin's (1989) study of soap opera audiences. Since the PSI scale was initially devised to study relationships with news presenters, clearly, items such as "I miss X when he or she is on holiday" will not be appropriate for a fictional character. But what are the implications for grafting one construct (our attachment to living media figures) to another (our attachment to made-up, obviously fictional dramatic characters)? This has been described as the narrative enjoyment of a fictional PSR in retrospect and using imagination as contrasted with a PSI in the present, clearly making the distinction between the two constructs (Slater et al., 2018).

All that remains, once items have been reworded and omitted, might be a simple measure of liking. Ultimately, the much less problematic construct of "liking" may have done the job perfectly well that communication and media researchers have long allocated to the parasocial.

The reason the ontology question is important to parasocial theory is that we need somehow to connect our attachment to media figures with our attachment to non-mediated figures—family, friends, neighbors, colleagues, and so on. Perhaps this question is of no interest to media researchers, but for media psychology, and for psychology in general, it allows us to understand the important forces shaping human behavior in the 21st century. Does our attachment to Elvis spring from the same universal psychological needs as our attachment to our grandfather, dead or alive? Or a close friend, dead or alive? Therefore, could the same universal needs be fulfilled by an attachment to a fictional figure? How do these things work? We will explore this issue in Chapter 5 on evolutionary theory and attachment (Stever, 2020).

The second unanswered question concerns the context in which media users encounter media figures. I touched on this previously in the discussion on PSI versus PSRs, but this is really only the tip of the iceberg. An obvious hurdle here is the nature of the media themselves. Parasocial theory was devised and developed for use with broadcast media, predominately with television. In the same way that some communication researchers believe that it can only be studied using the PSI scale, and (therefore?) can only be a positive experience, it could be argued that it is only relevant to a media landscape in which a gulf separates users and figures, where media use is contained within discrete episodes (turning on the device;

consuming a specific product; switching it off again) and where there is no opportunity for reciprocity.

I'll return to the reciprocity/social media issue again shortly, but in the meantime, it is worth wondering whether this perceived gulf between users and figures ever existed in the way it is assumed in the literature. As I suggested earlier, we have to assume that the media user cannot be mistaken for a media figure, but clearly, some of the time, this has never been true. What I mean to say is that the parasocial has always had leaky boundaries: Some fans become celebrities in the end and, even as celebrities, continue to have PSRs with other celebrities. But is it fair to say that these relationships are slightly "less parasocial" than the relationships you and I have with those same celebrities? And how do we incorporate these differing degrees of parasociality into our theory?

In Chapter 9, we discuss some of the alternative constructs that have been proposed to address these obvious flaws in parasocial theory. An important figure in the literature is Matt Hills, a media scholar specializing in fandom, who has sought to refine parasocial concepts in ways that make them more suitable for studying fans without pathologizing them (Hills, 2016, 2019). He makes the point that the social–parasocial boundary is somewhat arbitrary when we consider what kinds of social information are assumed to be absent in PSRs. For example, an essential criterion for PSRs is that the media user does not know the figure; we have to rely on a mediated performance or presentation. Off-camera (only the act of viewing is ever really assumed), that figure may behave in a completely different manner. But how do our closest social acquaintances behave when they are not in our company? Much of the time, we only have their word to rely on.

Why is this important? As Hills argues, the role of imagination—which is sometimes reduced to the level of "fantasy" in relation to PSRs—plays an essential part in our social relationships too. We imagine that our romantic partner is faithful to us, sometimes as a result of optimism rather than rational belief, when the evidence mounts up to suggest the contrary. We assume that they are consistent in their interactions with other people out of view. And then we learn things about them through other people, who act as mediators much in the same way as television and other media offer us a partial view of our favorite celebrity. So, the encounter itself, whether mediated or otherwise, is just one of the psychological building blocks in any relationship. Once we start to break down the elements of relationships and attachments by going off-piste and thinking beyond the (mediated) encounter, the social–parasocial dichotomy starts to look less convincing. Should this spell the end of parasocial theory? In Chapter 3, and in this book as a whole, we argue that it is more like a beginning.

The third and final unanswered question concerns the actual definition of parasocial. For many researchers in the humanities, whose concerns are with cultural activity in a broad sense, the concept of the parasocial as outlined in the communication literature is "pathologizing" because it implies that media users engage in PSI because they have a defective awareness of reality, an impression not banished by test items such as "the media figure was aware of me." There is also a widespread assumption, among critics as well as some proponents of parasocial theory, that PSRs function as substitutes for social ones, leading, as with popular assumptions about fandom, to the suggestion that they are engaged in largely by individuals who, for whatever reason, are unable to form satisfactory social relationships. As discussed in Chapter 2, most of the empirical research on the subject does not support such an interpretation.

With the advent of the internet, the definition of parasocial has been subject to a different kind of challenge, specifically the gray area between the parasocial and the physically remote. Some researchers in areas such as computer-mediated communication and marketing have latched on to parasocial theory in the quest for a construct that describes online relationships in which the participants have not physically encountered one another. This has led the term to be occasionally confused with distance relationships (e.g., pen friends) and online relationships in general. A further gray area concerns relations between game players and their avatars (self-generated or otherwise), where parasocial theory has also been tentatively adopted. There is something parasocial there, no doubt.

This is why Gayle wrote an introduction to her article on parasocial attachment that clearly defined the differences between PSRs and computer-mediated relationships/communication (CMC) as it is discussed in the literature (Stever, 2013). The reviewers of the article wanted to know about "parasocial relationships people have with their cell phones." Editor Stuart Fischoff agreed that the introduction to the article was necessary because of the general confusion concerning the two terms. The literature on CMC dates back to the 1980s (Kiesler et al., 1984; Siegel et al., 1986), which means it was an area that was being developed parallel to PSRs, but much like other topics in parasocial theory, these differences were well understood by communication scholars but not familiar to psychologists.

Ultimately, the one single feature that distinguishes parasocial from social relationships is the degree of reciprocity. This is what makes distant pen friends and never-encountered email/social media correspondents social. They are social because they correspond. The loop is closed; the relationship is consummated. Parasociality, leading from this criterion, emerges out of the lack of awareness on the part of the "other" who has not closed the loop, either because the relationship is fundamentally unequal (the user is one of the millions of fans whose communication goes ignored) or because they can never reciprocate (because they are fictional or dead). The loop can remain open for many years and then be closed (many fans eventually get to meet, or even marry, their idols), but until that happens, the relationship remains on a parasocial level.

Social media have, as mentioned previously, problematized the reciprocity criterion. Twitter,[2] in particular, has provided direct action to famous people who once would have been shielded by gatekeepers such as record companies and fan clubs. As it has turned out, some celebrities are willing to respond directly to their followers or retweet positive messages, and these communications are sometimes received with delighted surprise (Giles, 2018; Stever & Lawson, 2013). At the same time, celebrity–follower communication can even be unwelcome (see Stever and Hughes's [2013] reported account of a celebrity "trolling my timeline").

For some media scholars (e.g., Marwick & boyd, 2011), these new communication patterns spell the end of the parasocial, making the concept redundant. This reading arises partly out of the problem discussed previously, whereby the social and parasocial are subject to too rigid a differentiation, an issue that will be tackled shortly. It also assumes too rigid a differentiation between media. Much as communication context is important, in psychological terms, the separation between, say, fans and celebrities is more than just physical. The differences in social roles and social capital existed long before social media began to chip away at the boundary. And these social differences have always transcended the physical means of communication. Marwick and boyd (2011) might have just as well pointed to a mid-20th-century fan convention as evidence for the redundancy of the parasocial.

Three Potential Avenues for Resolving Some of These Problems

In the final part of this introductory chapter, we discuss ways of addressing these and other issues arising from the limited theoretical treatment of parasocial phenomena.

We begin by returning to the two "archetypal" explanations for parasocial theory. They are Explanation 1, the "media equation" position in which (social) information is uncritically received and acted upon and the source is irrelevant, and Explanation 2, the "pathological" position in which PSI is an irrational response to an unambiguously "unreal" source. I've called these "archetypal" with a nod to Jung because I believe these are ideas that persist in the collective unconscious ("culture" if you prefer) and shape both lay and academic responses to media phenomena. But largely, I'm using them as a frame for the following suggestions of how to resolve the issues outlined so far in this chapter.

Avenue 1: The Dimensional Approach

Explanation 1 is tackled by taking a dimensional approach to the parasocial in which many social encounters are neither fully "social" nor "parasocial." I first presented this idea in Giles (2002), where I suggested that we can broadly classify encounters along three dimensions: the number of individuals involved, the physical distance, and the constraints imposed by the social situation (relative status, and so on). At the "social" end of the dimension, we have intimate encounters, either physical (in person) or distant (mediated; e.g., a phone call), where the relative status of the individuals defines the outcome of the encounter (compare, say, a date to a job interview). At the "parasocial" end, all the encounters are mediated, but if they are with real, living people, there is a theoretical chance of reciprocation, depending (perhaps) on relative status. Once we factor in these elements common to both social and parasocial encounters, we can tackle the gray areas and start to consider parasocial as an extension of the social rather than an irrational, potentially pathological response to media.

AVENUE 2: INTRODUCING THE DISCURSIVE

Explanation 2 is tackled by introducing a discursive or narrative angle to research, where relationships are generally viewed as concepts that can be understood as partly or wholly discursive events. Media psychology has always struggled with some of the more bizarre audience responses, such as the fans of a TV hospital drama who wrote to its protagonist for medical advice and fans of a soap opera sending raincoats in the mail to a character who had lost hers in one episode (Giles, 2003). In purely cognitive terms, we have to classify these behaviors as irrational or even delusional, but in some respects, they are no more irrational than weeping over a romantic film or hiding behind the sofa to avoid an onscreen serial killer.

Those latter responses are sometimes explained as involving the suspension of disbelief, but maybe this concept has a longer reach, stretching well beyond the immediate viewing context. Perhaps the best way to understand such behavior (assuming that it exists independently of any other obvious psychological dysfunction) is through a narrative lens. Audiences are "transported" (Green & Brock, 2000) by a good story, real or fictional, and, in the same way that PSRs are incorporated into the everyday social experience, those stories become interwoven with our more immediate personal stories. This way, we become emotionally involved in big news stories even if they do not have any direct impact on us as individuals. This takes us back to Matt Hills's ideas, discussed previously, about the way that imagination contributes to our social relationships as well as our parasocial ones, and allows us to become entirely deceived about an intimate partner. Indeed, fantasizing about potential relationships with real people in our immediate environment is scarcely grounds for concern about our mental health. The idea that social relationships are "true" and media ones "false" is surely due for an overhaul.

AVENUE 3: THE PARASOCIAL ACROSS THE LIFESPAN

Finally, we need to bring the person into parasocial research, not just as a disconnected member of a media audience but as someone with a personal history, perhaps crossing an entire life, for whom relationships with media figures might be as significant and influential as their family and friends. This way, we can avoid pathologizing lifelong fans who have followed a specific figure (or figures) since childhood without losing their sense of reality. More generally, it enables us to see the parasocial as an everyday part of the many social influences that form our individual characters and life stories. This avenue does require drawing on psychoanalytic and psychosocial theory, and ways in which we can do this are outlined in Chapters 3 and 4.

THEORETICAL PERSPECTIVES

Unlike some scholarly treatments of a topic, we have chosen to approach parasocial experiences from a multiplicity of perspectives, believing that each one offers different information that illuminates aspects of interest to an overall understanding of the topic.

Key theoretical approaches included in this book are the psychoanalytic approach, discursive psychology, evolutionary psychology and the ethological approach, and a neuroscience approach. In addition to these, we also consider the idea that much of what is pleasurable in our consumption of media involves operant conditioning, wherein certain kinds of behavior are reinforcing and thus liable to be repeated with increasing frequency.

Sometimes these paradigms are seen as being in competition with one another, but layered on top of one another, each contributes a different type of understanding to fan behavior as well as the parasocial experience. For example, if I tweet to a celebrity and my tweet is acknowledged, this reward reinforces my tendency to tweet them again. As Thorndike suggested, behaviors that have satisfying outcomes will be repeated (Waters, 1934).

Our methods include aspects of interpretivism, multiperspectivism, and social constructionism, all forming the philosophical foundations for approaches taken over the past 30-plus years.

2

Parasocial to Social as a Continuum

GAYLE S. STEVER ■

In academic discussions concerning parasocial experiences (PSEs), there is some controversy regarding what the line is between the parasocial and the social. A parasocial relationship (PSR) typically has meant it was nonreciprocal, with no contact whatsoever between the parasocial object and the individual experiencing such a relationship. It is worth noting that before the advent of social media, this debate did not exist in research literature. The division between celebrities and fans was considered to be fairly clear. If a fan came to be known by a celebrity in person well enough to be recognized and responded to, the relationship ceased to be parasocial.

Twitter (X), Instagram, Facebook, and similar platforms have changed all that. In 2009, with a study of Twitter (Stever & Lawson, 2013), clear instances were found in which social media interaction was crossing that parasocial–social line. Celebrities (the ones who manage their own social media accounts) were responding to fan tweets by clicking the like button or even sending replies, and when they met these fans in person, they remembered them from Twitter! This observation was made, in part, as a result of an in-depth case study of the fans of Josh Groban (Stever, 2016) in which Groban, a fan-friendly person, was recognizing his active Twitter followers at in-person signings. *Star Trek* was another fandom in which the parasocial line was being crossed fairly regularly, as many *Star Trek* actors are both active on social media and also highly interactive at science fiction conventions. That combination increased the frequency of the parasocial line being breached.

Despite this transformation in media, there are still media realms that remain purely parasocial. The most obvious one of these is the PSR with a fictional character. This has been observed in many fandoms, including *The Lord of the Rings* (*LOTR*). The release of the three blockbuster *LOTR* films in 2001, 2002, and 2003

Parasocial Experiences. David C. Giles and Gayle S. Stever, Oxford University Press. © Oxford University Press 2024.
DOI: 10.1093/oso/9780197647646.003.0003

put a face to the characters that Tolkien created in his extremely popular books, written and published in 1954, although the love of these characters did not begin with the films, as many fans had interacted parasocially with them much of their lives. However, giving face and voice to the characters outside of the interactions with the book characters conflated the PSR so that it was both with the fictional characters and often with the actors who portrayed them. If a fan has a romantic attraction to Aragorn, King of Gondor, or Legolas, Prince of Mirkwood, or if these characters personify heroic archetypes, is that attraction to the character, to the actor, or both? This is where visual media introduced new complexities to the PSR, although, as previously noted, PSRs with these characters happened long before fans had visual representations.

Much has been studied and written about the parasocial romantic relationship (PSRR) in particular (Erickson, 2022; Erickson et al., 2018; Tukachinsky Forster, 2021). Being "in love" with someone from a distance is a phenomenon that elicits particularly passionate and intense feelings for the person engaged in that PSR. Although there are many other types of PSRs, this kind of "crush" is prevalent and studied in depth. This is particularly true as it involves adolescents who often use romantic PSRRs to "practice" their romantic feelings and relationship skills from a safe distance, with the object of those feelings not being in a place to make any demands or to reject the attention. Evolutionary theory predicts that the familiarity of the face and voice of another person is the basis for the ultimate attraction that is felt for that person (this is discussed further in Chapter 7).

Parasocial friendship, also explored by Tukachinsky (2011) and differentiated from a PSRR, recognized that sometimes when we love a favorite character or celebrity, that love is not romantic at all. The Greeks did a better job of distinguishing different types of love than happens in English. *Eros*, or romantic and sexual attraction, was quite different from *storge*, deep affection, or *philia*, brotherly love, characterized by the affection associated with friendship. Research has shown that having social connections is one of the most reliable ways of ensuring health and longer life. Adult friendships, in particular, predict well-being, mitigating the tendency to be either anxious or depressed (Abrams, 2023). Thus, understanding this kind of PSR and the ways it might imitate the effects of in-person friendship becomes even more important than it might initially seem.

PSRs are basically imagined relationships. Interaction occurs with people who have not been actually encountered, either because they are fictional (do not exist) or because they are distant (not in our everyday lives and too far away or otherwise inaccessible). But it is important to remember that interaction also occurs in the imagination with people who are known socially. We imagine our next conversation or practice what we want to say in anticipation of an important discussion.

Each time you read a book, you imagine characters interacting with each other. Every time you watch a movie, a play, or a television show, you have mental representations of other people or characters who relate to one another in the various ways that human beings relate to one another. Every kind of relationship imaginable can be a part of the parasocial realm.

PARASOCIAL INTERACTION

At the heart of PSEs is parasocial interaction (PSI). This simply refers to the individual consuming media and hearing the messages in a way that both personalizes them and also responds to them. While watching a favorite sports team on television (or even in person), a viewer will often find themself yelling at the team, statements such as "Why did you do that?" or "You dropped the ball again?" In these cases, the person on the sports team cannot hear the viewer. So why do they do it? The answer is that it is human nature to respond to the social messages of others. We respond to the things other people do and say, and before visual media, everything we saw them do or heard them say was in our physical presence. It was not until the early 20th century that we could watch a sports figure play a game and react to their performance without being there in person. However, the in-person relationship with the sports star was still parasocial, particularly with respect to professional sports.

So, the audience watches a talk show, and when the host asks a question, they answer it, either out loud or, at the very least, in their minds. Even in fictional dramas, they tend to interact mentally with those who are on their screens.

For the purposes of the discussion in this chapter, "the audience" refers to viewers, both individual and as a collective. However, PSI and PSRs most often deal with individual audience members, so it is important to keep that in mind during this discussion. Also, to be clear, it is not media that makes a PSI or PSR but, rather, the lack of reciprocity between the individual audience member and the parasocial object. This can happen in person as easily as it can through media, as discussed further below.

WHEN IS IT PARASOCIAL? WHEN IS IT NOT?

Parasocial experiences have come to be associated with the media. By definition, a PSE is one with another person who is known but does not know you back. There are many instances when we have PSIs with people that are not mediated. Picture the member of a very large church. Any church larger than perhaps 1,000 members probably has a pastor who does not know every single member. At some point, it becomes impractical to know every member of a large group. But week after week, the parishioners sit in church and hear sermon after sermon, and in this process, they get to know that pastor quite well. But if they encounter the pastor in another setting, the pastor is possibly not going to recognize them.

Picture a university setting with a large lecture hall of 300 or more students. The professor lectures in front of that class from one to three times a week, and those students take notes and (it is hoped) listen carefully. The students know the professor but are most likely not known back, particularly if their grades are managed (as often happens) by a teaching assistant.

Picture the mayor or council representative in a city or town. The town's citizens most likely know those elected officials fairly well, but the officials are unlikely to know each person in the town. At a large town rally, those elected officials give speeches and even shake hands but are unlikely to recognize every individual.

Each of these is an example of PSI that is not mediated. In the continuum of social to parasocial discussed in Chapter 1, this might be closer to the middle of the continuum because, in each of these examples, there is the possibility of real social interaction. But two characteristics of PSI are present: the absence of reciprocity and a difference in social status.

However, the PSI that leads to a PSR happens more frequently when engaging with others through mediated channels. Media has such a long reach that a media figure comes to be known well by those who are not at all in their own immediate circle.

Recently, I experienced a sense of PSR with two people I know through the media. Chasten and Pete Buttigieg just posted pictures of themselves holding their new twin babies on social media. Pete Buttigieg is well known as first the mayor of South Bend, Indiana, then as a candidate for president, and now as the secretary of transportation in the executive branch of the U.S. government. He has gotten unusual publicity for such offices because he is the first prominent person at this level of government in a same-sex marriage. But for my sense of a PSR, as I thought about these two young men with two new babies, I wondered if they would get baby gifts and who might crochet baby blankets for them. My thinking did not progress enough to consider sending a blanket (I crochet quite a bit), but the fact that the thought entered my mind points to the notion that I feel like I "know" these young men.

Part of the reason is that I listened to Chasten Buttigieg's self-narrated memoir on audiobook. This is an area of newer media that is growing exponentially in popularity. With a self-narrated memoir, the listener is not only privy to the storyteller's private thoughts but also exposed for hours to their voice. We talk in parasocial theory about the "illusion of intimacy." Nothing can promote an illusion faster than believing someone is speaking directly to you about their private life. As discussed in Chapter 7, attachment theory talks about the infant being attached to the familiar face and voice of the parent. That personal connection with the speaking voice of another is a part of the functioning of our brain that is present from birth and, as a result, is a very strong influence in creating relationships.

Much of the PSI/PSR literature focuses on admired media figures of whom we are fans or whose work we enjoy. It is possible, however, to have a PSR with someone who is disliked or who is negative in some way. For example, elected officials, such as the president or a governor, become an unavoidable/inevitable part of our social lives. We do not seek out these people, and we may or may not vote for them, but once in office, we have to deal with them. If these officials do things that are distasteful, distressing, or even criminal, their presence in our lives can create the same level of inordinate stress as is created by a family member or a troublesome next-door neighbor.

Then there are media characters who might be comical, viewed as inept, bumbling, or otherwise less than admirable, such as Homer Simpson, Fred Flintstone, or Betty White's character on *The Golden Girls*. We might identify with some of that or perhaps just enjoy having a laugh at their expense. These are examples of PSRs with characters when the relationship is not positive and when we do not admire the media figure. But we might still know them quite well. It is important to recognize that PSRs can run the full range of positive to negative relationships (Tukachinsky Forster & Click, 2023).

We might know people in our real lives who play these comic or bumbling roles, perhaps in a family or community group. Maybe we would not laugh at them, but we might gossip about them. Some people are annoying or kept at a distance. Social groups are full of people who are less popular and less sought out. Their media counterpart would be characters who are dull, pedantic, or wearisome (think Sheldon Cooper in *The Big Bang Theory*).

In both social and mediated settings, it is difficult to avoid people who annoy us or whom we do not like or admire but still engage with. The only difference between the two is whether in knowing them, we are known back, yet these types of PSRs are not usually studied (Oliver et al., 2019; Tukachinsky Forster & Click, 2023).

SCANDAL, GOSSIP, AND NOTORIETY

In both the parasocial and the social realms of life, there are times when a person becomes the object of ridicule or scorn. People's reactions to these times are similar regardless of whether or not that relationship is social or parasocial.

In my own work, I did a 4-year case study of Michael Jackson fans from 1988 to 1992, and at that time, I moved on to other case studies and somewhat lost touch with Jackson and his fan base (although I had several friendships that I have maintained over the years since). Jackson went through a period of time beginning in 1993 when he was investigated for various crimes, including molesting of minors. In 2005, after many years of allegations and purported victims, Jackson was acquitted of all charges during a trial in Santa Barbara, California. Some issues muddy the waters in this case, including extremely large sums of money changing hands. It was alleged that witnesses on both sides were pressured and paid off to testify one way or the other to the point where it was seemingly impossible to distinguish truth from fiction. But in the parasocial realm, it was significant to me that most of the fans I knew, some of whom had a good deal of mediated contact with Jackson and had followed him for many years, never lost faith in him and believed, to the end, that he was not guilty of the charges. This is not unlike a social relationship in which someone is accused of bad conduct or even crimes, and the family member, friend, or acquaintance continues to defend the accused. It is also noteworthy that since Jackson died in 2009, most of the publicity surrounding him has been positive, with a few exceptions. (Again, some were driven by monetary profit—for example, the film released in 2019, *Leaving*

Neverland, which was a clear attempt to gain from Jackson's notoriety after his death.) Attempts to sue his estate were unsuccessful, and with Jackson no longer alive to defend himself, such cases faded away into obscurity (Tsioulcas, 2019).

A 1994 article in *GQ* magazine put forward the theory that Jackson was framed by one of the parents of an alleged victim to obtain a large payoff, an attempt that appeared to have succeeded. This is one in a long succession of "he said, she said" stories and exploitations of the situation (Curry, 2010).

Research examining the connection between both PSIs/PSRs and scandal has found that scandal has a negative influence on both PSIs and PSRs. In addition, scandal is positively related to parasocial breakup (PSB). This is a similar finding to that of research on personal relationships and how they are affected by negative events that are similar to scandals. People have been found to respond to parasocial figures in the same way they respond to similar behavior in their interpersonal relationships (Hu, 2016).

Typically, PSR research measures people's attraction to media personalities who are attractive, admirable, or act as positive role models in some way—for example, celebrities who participate in philanthropy. My research on fans of Josh Groban found that committed fans were as admiring of his philanthropy as they were of his musical ability. The same could be said for some *Star Trek* actors I know who have worked hard to raise money for various important causes, such as Doctors Without Borders, Save the Children, Amnesty International, and The Heifer Project. Groban's charity, the Find Your Light Foundation, supports and sponsors arts education programs in poorer areas where funding is unavailable.

It is not necessary for the celebrity persona to have any particular talent or skill or even exhibit admirable behavior to be the object of a PSR. They can be appealing for a number of reasons, ranging from good looks to a great personality. There are media personalities such as the Kardashians or Zoella who are simply well-known for being who they are without any particular ability separating them from the crowd. Sometimes wealth separates that person from others, as in the case of those who grew up in a wealthy family, such as Paris Hilton. Zoella is an example of a social media influencer who developed a brand and an image through her YouTube channel, amassing enough followers to be sought out by advertisers.

This is a common phenomenon on YouTube, and sometimes the YouTuber has a particular skill, sometimes they do not. Davie504 is a bass guitarist with approximately 12.9 million followers on YouTube. He built his popularity by initially posting videos of himself playing his electric bass. He is possibly not the best bass player on YouTube, but in 10 years, he has become one of the most well-known, creating an online personality and style that are individual and unique.

David Letterman hosts a show for Netflix called *This Person Needs No Introduction*. In 2020, he did a segment with Kim Kardashian, and during their interview, he questioned the assumption that she was simply known for being well-known and did not have any particular skills. He noted that she was very accomplished at managing her social media account (Instagram) and that this was something he himself was unable to do. He disagreed with the idea that she had no skills to distinguish herself. Indeed, when talking about being famous for being famous, the go-to example seems to be the Kardashians, but maybe Lettermen is right. Lack of familiarity with a celebrity can translate into lack of appreciation for whatever that celebrity might be good at, but the fans usually know these things.

Similarly, Zoella, with 10.7 million YouTube subscribers, has managed her YouTube account and clearly has skills as both a makeup expert and an entrepreneur. These examples bring attention to the changing landscape of skill sets and what it is that is worthy of being admired. There are doubtless generational and cultural differences to be considered here as well. Similar arguments have been made by Giles (2018) and Bennett et al. (2011). They agree that skill in managing media, both in image and presentation, must be evaluated in the context in which it is found. Two other considerable aspects for future research are deciding who has good skills and how such skills would be evaluated.

PARASOCIAL TO SOCIAL TRANSITIONS

One of our main points is that each of these PSRs has counterparts in our social lives and that PSRs can transition into social relationships through other means. In my own life, I can think of several celebrity public figures who started out at a distance but through various encounters, I came to know them quite well. The first time I heard actor Rene Auberjonois speak at a *Star Trek* convention, we had obviously never met. I was studying *Star Trek* fandom and became involved in *Star Trek* charity efforts. That was in 1993, the first year *Deep Space Nine* (his program) was on the air. Flash forward to a charity event in 2001, the Galaxy Ball, hosted by Robert Beltran of *Star Trek Voyager* for Down syndrome in Los Angeles. Auberjonois appeared that night, and I accompanied him. We reminisced about that first convention when I saw him and thought, "He seems like a nice man. I'd like to meet him someday." At that point, he whirled around and said, "And now you're one of my closest friends!" This may seem like an unusual turn of events, but I could direct you to at least 25 fans of *Star Trek* who developed personal friendships with Rene and were close with him right up until his death in December 2019. *Star Trek* actors in particular offer many examples of the parasocial becoming social, in part because the conventions where one can meet these actors are frequent and well attended.

Both social and parasocial connections are fluid and changeable. I saw an example of social becoming parasocial (again, think of it as a continuum and not a dichotomy) when I heard fans talking about being at a backstage meet and greet at a Josh Groban concert. Standing in line were women who had been Groban's teachers in high school, right alongside fans hoping to get a photo and quick hello with the famous singer. Here is a case in which status and social distance have flip-flopped so that the teachers have become fans. We frequently hear stories from people who knew a famous person when they were younger. Maybe they were in school together or were co-workers. At some point, one person crosses the line into celebrityhood, leaving behind some of the people they knew when they were a "regular" person. These examples point to the fluid nature of social interaction. What starts out social can become parasocial, and what starts out parasocial can become social.

DIFFERENTIATING A PSR FROM IDENTIFICATION

Identification differs from PSRs in that rather than relating to the character in some role that is parallel to real-life relationship roles, the audience member relates to the character as if they were themself. The reader or viewer adopts the character's perspective and becomes a part of the story through that character. Identification has been divided into three components: cognitive, emotional, and motivational (Cohen & Tal-Or, 2017). Although PSRs are different from identification, it has been suggested that they also have cognitive, emotional, and motivational components (Stever, 2009; Tukachinsky & Stever, 2019).

There are interactions with media that are similar to identification which are predicted by social cognitive theory. Imitation, modeling, vicarious reinforcement, and vicarious punishment are all part of this theoretical model (Bandura, 1986; Browne Graves, 1999). With all of these processes, the viewer inserts themself into the story and experiences things that they then take out of the story and into day-to-day life. One of my students recounted to me that the main character in the film *Working Girl* became a model for her own work relationships and was instrumental in causing her to challenge an abusive boss and then leave to start her own company.

Again, each of these has a cognitive component, an emotional component, and motivational component. When I watch the story, what do I think is happening? But also, what does that make me feel, and what am I motivated to do as a result? All of these aspects are part of analyzing the effects of a story on the viewer (Stever, 2009) and the resulting PSR that might be formed. This topic is explored further in Chapter 10.

THE ROLE OF IMAGINATION

In the final analysis, PSRs are fueled by imagination. Caughey (1984) originally coined the term *imaginary social relationship* to describe a similar phenomenon. Consider the role of the imagination in any social relationship. A critical component of social relationships is deciding what to say in the next conversation or interaction. Imagining these conversations for the purpose of making them go and flow better in the future is a critical aspect of social success in relationships. Without the imagined element, perhaps more real relationships would fail.

The major component of storytelling is imagination. PSRs are like telling stories in your head about characters you admire or find attractive. Just like in a real relationship, a story is a way to spend time with a character, and just as in a real relationship, this interaction brings pleasure to the storyteller. Internal storytelling is a major component of the PSR. For this reason, fan fiction writing is a prominent form of the PSR made accessible to someone else.

Narrative psychology is the branch of psychology that examines the role of storytelling in human thinking and uses those stories to ascertain the inner functioning of the mind. From the narrative emerges the internal working model (IWM), in that a person's stories center around themes from that person's current life and past memories. Attachment is based on a person's IWM of what relationships should look like and how those relationships provide a sense of safety and security in their day-to-day experiences. Attachment style, then, can be argued to be revealed through the narrative of one's life.

The quality of a parasocial attachment (PSA) is directly tied to the IWM and is affected by not just the actual attachment relationships a person has but also the kinds of attachment relationships that the person desires. If a secure relationship is missing in someone's life, creating one through imagined interactions with a distant figure (whether real or fictional) provides a new IWM for the desired relationship. Whether or not that leads to an actual secure relationship would be an important area of inquiry for future research. Furthermore, it must be acknowledged that the PSR is pleasurable within itself without any need to apply it to real life, just as reading stories is pleasurable.

NARRATIVE PSYCHOLOGY AND THE SCIENCE OF STORYTELLING

Eder (2006) has discussed various ways that the audience and audience members can feel close to fictional characters. He brings together disparate parts of the literature in an attempt to define five different ways this happens. One of the five is parasocial interaction and relationships (PSI/PSR). A second one, affective closeness, is very similar to what is described as PSA.

To understand how relationships with fictional characters can be similar to those we have with real people, the process of how we interact with those we know must be analyzed. Cognitive psychology has held that in our real-life interactions, we develop IWMs that consist of the stable characteristics associated with that person. We then interact with these models in our imagination to better understand and plan how to conduct real interactions. This is the foundation of social cognition, the idea of understanding others and making attributions about them using these imaginal processes. Interaction is shaped by the roles those people play in our lives: parent, child, lover, partner, co-worker, and so on. It has been found that in the parasocial realm, all of these same relationships experienced in real life are duplicated so that a parasocial connection is felt with those who might be lovers, partners, co-workers, parents, or children.

The attachment literature has much to say about developing IWMs for our attachment objects that elicit a sense of safety, security, and safe haven. PSA recognizes that attachments are formed based on stable mental models that have been created in response to individual needs for such security. If I need someone to believe in me, I have people in my real life who do believe in me, but I can also imagine a fictional character who might believe in me as well. I will base my IWM of this imaginary champion on how their character has been created in fiction.

How much stronger would the connection be if that fictional character had been created by me in the first place? Authors have a special bond with the characters they create. They sometimes even have a character in the story that represents them in a real sense. For example, J. R. R. Tolkien recounted that in his *LOTR* stories, Faramir was the character he saw as himself. In fan fiction circles, a name is given to the fan placing themself in the story. The "Mary Sue fan fiction" stories are so named because the largest percentage of fan fiction writers happen to be women. In short, the foundation of PSR and PSA is found in the author–character relationship, but the truth is that many typically "write" these stories only in their imaginations. The trend to co-opt characters that have been created by someone else is at the foundation of this fan fiction story writing that is central to many media fandoms.

In interacting with a fictional character, it is often true that one knows things about them that cannot be known about the people in real social interactions. In a story, one often hears the thoughts of the character. As such, it could be argued that the PSR is more intimate than at least most real face-to-face relationships, which may be a good part of the appeal of PSI and PSRs. Knowing a character intimately, particularly a type one could never meet in real life, offers not only entertainment but also a psychological satisfaction that comes from knowing and feeling represented, especially if we are the ones writing the story. This is a good explanation for why superheroes, elves, and other fictional beings are so very popular in contemporary stories. *Harry Potter*, *Star Wars*, and *LOTR*, popular story franchises in today's Western world, contain supernatural characters with supernatural powers and abilities.

Using magnetic resonance imaging, researchers Broom et al. (2021) studied the brain activity of viewers watching their favorite characters in the popular television series *Game of Thrones*. They reasoned that identification with a fictional character can cause changes in attitude, behavior, and belief about the self. Identification has been described as a merging of the self with the admired fictional character (Cohen, 2001; Kaufman & Libby, 2012; Oatley, 1995), and data from this study support that theory. Previous work that focused on behavioral changes rather than neural changes came to similar conclusions (Djikic & Oatley, 2014; Kaufman & Libby, 2012; Sestir & Green, 2010). Although the viewer and/or author might choose to identify with a character, it is not a given that they will do so (Cohen, 2013), so the reading process may or may not include identification or PSRs or both, depending on the reader's motivations.

Character attachment is common in role-playing games, in which the character in-game and individual outside the game move in parallel ways, in turn increasing the player's focus and loss of self-awareness or flow (Raney et al., 2020).

In visual media, the audience might experience a sense of para-proxemics (Eder, 2006), the illusion that a character is physically close. This can enhance the illusion of intimacy with that character. While reading, the illusion of proximity is created entirely in the reader's mind and the character can be as close or distant as desired. In both film and printed fiction, the audience member can go along on a journey with a character, vicariously experiencing what the character experiences.

Vicarious experiences go hand in hand with PSEs (Shackleford et al., 2022). The concept of transportation is also related to both PSRs and vicarious experience, as once someone is transported into a story realm, the experience of that realm as "real" is greatly enhanced. This is at the heart of the appeal of not only fiction but also video games. Vicarious experiences and transportation are discussed further in Chapter 10.

A stable IWM is at the heart of PSRs. Having a consistent perception of a character means that interactions with the model incorporate all aspects of the character, including the physical, social, and cognitive aspects (Eder, 2006). The same kind of stable mental model is at the heart of attachment relationships in real life, which is why the likelihood of a PSR becoming an attachment relationship is greater in the presence of such stable mental models.

PSRS AND DISTINGUISHING ACTORS FROM THEIR CHARACTERS

Much is made in the parasocial and fan studies literature about the audience's challenge in distinguishing actors from characters. However, in my study of *Hobbit* fandom, I came across books that were marketed to promote the films (Weta, 2015). Here, the actors talked about both the characters from the movie and also the actors who played them. As one reads, it soon becomes clear that the lines between actor and character also become blurred for those who are playing those parts. Just a few examples will be enough to make this point.

Dean O'Gorman (Fili, the Dwarf) talked about one of the other actors, Ken Stott, who played an older dwarf, Balin:

I always thought of Balin as the sympathetic, compassionate voice of someone who had been through a lot and seen a great deal in their long life. . . . Like Aidan [Turner] and me, I think Fili and Kili were sometimes a bit irreverent and would have some fun with a few of the older Dwarves, playing a prank or giving them some well-meant cheek, but not with Balin or Ken. There was a respect there that just came out of who he was and who the character was. (Weta, 2015, p. 65)

Jed Brophy, an experienced actor who had played multiple roles in the *LOTR* films, played Nori the Dwarf in *The Hobbit*. He talked about Richard Armitage (who played the Dwarven King, Thorin Oakenshield) and the dwarves' final charge out of the mountain and into battle at the end of the third film:

I think Richard was no more our King than in the very moment when he looked at me and said, "I know you've been waiting for this for two years. Let's get it done." He was amped. He was King Thorin. (Weta, 2015, p. 167)

And O'Gorman again, this time talking about Graham McTavish, who played the dwarf Dwalin, stated,

Dwalin was the fun uncle. He was the warrior who was always up for some swordplay. Part of that dynamic was a result of who Graham McTavish was and how we related to him as a person. Graham is like a big kid. (Weta, 2015, p. 173)

In each of these examples and countless more that could be recounted, it becomes clear that who these actors were in real life became a significant part of the characters they played. It could be argued that this is a feature of the acting profession itself (see Chapter 13 for a further discussion on this subject). For this discussion, however, it is enough to observe that the same sense that fans have when they meet an actor, and it feels like they are meeting a beloved character, is certainly one that the actors would relate to and identify with as well. This then becomes a factor in the way actors meet fans and understand the fan experience. This subject is discussed further in Chapter 9.

PARASOCIAL BREAKUP

In the context of the need to create and maintain social connections, where does the concept of PSB belong? In general, PSB refers to the loss of a PSR. Does this happen because it is imposed on the audience member, or do viewers choose to break up with parasocial objects? Arguably both things need to be included in a complete conceptualization of PSB.

Recognizing that PSRs can be with either a character or a real-life celebrity, the possibilities for PSB include the death of a character on a show, the death of a real-life celebrity, scandal around a celebrity (already mentioned with respect to Michael Jackson) that causes an audience member to no longer want to follow them, cancellation of a media program such as a television series, or the maturing of an audience member such that the character or celebrity no longer appeals to them. The study of PSR dissolutions or PSBs finds its foundation in the study of interpersonal relationship dissolutions. Hu (2023) explained that the three kinds of PSR dissolutions most studied are the death of personae (either celebrity or fictional), the removal of personae from the air, and the circumstances in which audience members outgrow in some way their need for the PSR.

When looking at a PSB, two potential hypotheses seem to come into play. One is the "love more, hurt more" (Hu, 2016, p. 227) idea that the more you love someone, the more painful it is to lose them. In the parasocial context, this manifests itself in either the cancellation of a beloved program or the death of a beloved character or celebrity (or both). A second is the "love more, forgive more" (p. 227) hypothesis, which basically states that the more commitment you have made to someone, the more likely you are to forgive transgressions (Hu, 2016). This may have come into play with the Michael Jackson case (discussed previously), in which fans had followed him for many years.

Meyrowitz (1994) examined the behavior of audience members concerning the deaths of John Kennedy, John Lennon, and Elvis Presley. Using qualitative methods, one key observation was that because the relationship has its foundations in the media, it never really dies, as the mediated work will always be part of the life of audience members. A rather eerie reminder of this occurred when, in 2021, Peter Jackson released his documentary, *Get Back*. It was based on original footage shot in early 1969 of the Beatles' last live performance from the roof of the Apple Building in central London and on their work on the album *Let It Be*. For major fans of Lennon, watching this brand new and previously unseen material depicting him hard at work and alive and well was emotional to process. Despite still having the work of the artist or celebrity who has died, the grief over the loss of such a person is enormous in almost all cases (see the discussion in Chapter 7 concerning the death of Queen Elizabeth II in early 2023).

Using inductive methodology, Meyrowitz (1994) concluded that grieving the death of a celebrity has both personal and social elements. Much of the expression of grief manifests itself in public gatherings and rituals. He observed that despite the continued availability of media content, which was the primary way the audience member "met" the celebrity, the grief and sense of loss are still deep and profound. Of course, one of the elements of "loss" for the fan is the lost potential or future work the artist or public figure might have generated. I remember vividly the day in 2008 I learned of the death of Heath Ledger at age 27 years. Showing great promise from the very beginning of his career, I felt a deep sense of sadness that we would have no more new films from this truly great actor. In the same way, fans grieved the loss of Michael Jackson, Prince, Whitney Houston, and so on.. The list of lost artists would be endless.

Difficulty in processing the death of their favorite character was a recurring theme in my study of fans of *The Hobbit*. At the end of the third film, three of the most beloved dwarves die at the hands of the antagonist, and one of the ways fans deal with their sense of loss is by writing what are known as "alternate universe" fan fiction stories. Visit Tumblr and read the myriad of stories written about the Tolkien universe, or Middle Earth as it is called, where the dwarves all live, and their story continues. This is a common mechanism used in fan fiction to counter or deal with the loss of a character.

From interviews with the actors, it is clear that they were affected by the deaths of the characters they had portrayed. As recounted by Dean O'Gorman, Fili the Dwarf (Weta, 2015),

My mom always joked that if I ever died on screen, she wouldn't look. I used to brush it off, "Mum it's just acting!" but after seeing Aidan die on screen,

I was really affected. . . . And then seeing Thorin go as well, and even my own character's death, I was surprised by how affected I was. (p. 223)

So, even actors are not immune to the deaths of their own characters. After the death of Captain Kirk in the film *Star Trek: Generations* (1994), William Shatner wrote a series of novels bringing Kirk back to life and creating new stories for him. *The Return* (1996) featured a plot whereby Kirk was brought back to life and continued his service in Starfleet.

Another common situation involving PSB is the cancellation of a favorite television program. Cohen (2004) found that those with anxious attachment styles (see Chapter 7) had the most difficulty dealing with the cancellation of a program when they had a strong attachment to its main characters. Eyal and Cohen (2006), examining specifically the end of the sitcom *Friends*, concluded that viewers form close ties with their favorite characters. Based on their measures, however, losing those PSRs will not generate the same level of distress as losing a regular social relationship. As such, PSRs rank higher than acquaintances but lower than close friends in the hierarchy of social significance for important relationships. The death of Matthew Perry (*Friends*; Chandler Bing) in 2023 and the extensive grief reactions by viewers reported in the media point again to the power of PSRs and PSB.

One variable not covered in the literature is the impact of the cancellation of a show with respect to how long the show had been on the air and whether or not principal storylines had been resolved. *Friends* was on the air for 10 seasons (1994–2004), and at the end of the last show, the story arcs of the main characters were resolved. Likewise, *The Big Bang Theory* ended after 12 seasons (2007–2019) with a similar satisfying end to continuing storylines. By contrast, the UK television drama *Poldark* aired for 5 seasons and ended on a cliffhanger, with 5 of the 12 books (the series was based on) not having been filmed. Fans on the fan websites and Facebook pages have been campaigning to bring back the show since it went off the air in 2019, and as of the writing of this book in 2024, #BringbackPoldark or #Poldark6 still trend on Twitter (now known as X) in the top 20 every weekend. This is for a show that has been off the air for 4 years! Clearly, further study is needed to understand the different factors at work in PSB for characters from a television series when it ends.

The final major factor in PSB is audience members who outgrow their interest in a character and are ready to move on. This often happens with children who, as they mature, find a different level of character to be engaging (Hu, 2023). Sometimes in the case of PSRRs, the intensity of the initial crush runs its course, and the fan moves on to a different PSR or even a regular social relationship (Tukachinsky Forster, 2021).

A study in which parents were asked to evaluate and rate the characteristics of their children's PSRs was a follow-up to studies done on these same children 3 years earlier (Aguiar et al., 2019). Several factors in this study support the idea that as children mature, they seek out PSRs with characters that are more consistent with their enhanced maturity. Social realism was an important dimension of this study, as in the 3 years since the previous study, children were more likely to understand that their favorite characters on television were not real people. In fact, social realism was the only significant age-related difference from the younger samples to the older ones. One finding was that 76.9% of children had different favorite characters from those identified in the earlier studies (Bond & Calvert, 2014a; Richards & Calvert, 2016). On the other hand, 11% did identify the same favorite character, indicating that not all children move on in the same ways with respect to PSRs. The other 12.1% had no favorite character in the first study but did have one in the later study. These studies reinforced research evidence that PSRs are an important factor in children's social development overall.

An earlier study specific to PSB (Bond & Calvert, 2014b) found that gender was an important factor in choosing favorite characters, with boys choosing more females when they were younger but moving to males as they matured. Girls showed no such age difference for males versus females. Boys chose more masculine figures as they matured, whereas girls chose more feminine characters overall at the 6- to 8-year-old age range compared to younger samples. The factors most often identified in this study for PSB were the child's maturation, the influence of other media characters, and habituation to newer characters. More work is needed to enhance our understanding of these kinds of PSR dissolutions.

3

Multisocial Interaction?

DAVID C. GILES ■

There are two arguments underpinning this book that seem inherently contradictory. The first is that parasocial relationships (PSRs) are largely benign, predictable phenomena that one would expect to occur in a mediated environment. Call this the "media equation" argument if you like. The second argument is that context is everything. This is effectively an updated position reflecting Marshall McLuhan's philosophy, represented by that immortal maxim "the medium is the message" (McLuhan, 1964). Never lose sight of the mediated nature of the phenomenon in question. This is essentially where the present chapter is coming from. From this perspective, audience comments on YouTube are not necessarily comparable with similar-seeming 20th-century phenomena such as letters to the fan club or conversations in front of the television at home. We can only understand the YouTube comments in the context of the unique medium that is YouTube, with its unique affordances for audience involvement.

So, how do we reconcile these two positions? How can we equate media with everyday life if the medium is the message? The important thing here is not to get trapped into a position where "effects" researchers could use the media equation as a way to justify censorship (i.e., if media content is represented in the brain as indistinguishable from direct social experience, 1,000 on-screen homicides are represented as personally witnessed massacres).

Psychology is often concerned, for better or worse, with the search for timeless universals, the fundamental qualities of "human nature" essentially unchanging across time and place and largely unaffected by history and culture save for the random mutations of biological evolution. A good example of this would be something like the digit span capacity of short-term ("working") memory, long said to be somewhere between five and nine pieces of abstract information, such as a random string of numbers (Miller, 1956). Cognitive capacity ought, one would think, to be constrained by the physical nature of the hardware—the human brain. In all its various manifestations, it should only be able to process a finite amount of abstract information. And yet even this type of psychological "fact"

Parasocial Experiences. David C. Giles and Gayle S. Stever, Oxford University Press. © Oxford University Press 2024.
DOI: 10.1093/oso/9780197647646.003.0004

Multisocial Interaction? 33

has been found to be susceptible to cultural influence (Naveh-Benjamin & Ayres, 1986) and has been challenged in terms of what the information consists of, how it is represented, and how it is remembered (Cowan, 2015). The flaw consists in reducing the problem to that of the hardware itself, as if the pure brain can be somehow recovered, uncontaminated by its owner's social and cultural habitat.

With media psychology, we are dealing with something even more elastic than the cognitive capacity of the brain. Since media, like society itself, are in a continuous state of flux, their influence on human behavior is correspondingly a work in progress. What holds for one generation will not necessarily pass to the next. Broadcast media limited our worldview in the late 20th century; digital media have made different ways of behaving possible in the current century. This process was clearly identified by Marshall McLuhan, who used the example of the electric light as a mass medium that extended human possibilities in ways unimaginable to previous generations (McLuhan, 1964). Where sunset was once simply a cue for Wee Willie Winkie to retire upstairs to bed with a dripping candle, the electric light brought into being the entire nighttime economy, reconfiguring our concept of time itself and what is possible to cram into those previously lost hours. In other words, history, technology, and culture do not change human behavior, but they generate opportunities for human behavior that end up changing society in unforeseen ways.

But psychology and history make uncomfortable bedfellows. Psychology seeks to nail human behavior down to a set of fundamental principles: *The brain does this, people do that, it's human nature . . . now that we've worked it all out, let's see what we can do with it.* History never sits still in this way. Its very nature means that it is constantly on the move, rethinking itself. Even the Stone Age isn't safe. And it could all be changed between the time this book is written and the time you read it. Hopefully for the better!

However, when it comes to media psychology, there is simply no excuse for drawing a line under what we (think we) know about human behavior. When Horton and Wohl published their seminal paper on parasocial interaction (PSI) in 1956, the media available to the public was limited to print (books, magazines, newspapers), tightly regulated and scheduled broadcast media (radio and television—with a limited number of channels), and audio/audiovisual entertainment (cinema and the early record industry). Scientific interest in television was as much concerned with its effect on children's eyesight as anything psychological.[1] Audiences were still naïve: It was barely two decades since the famous Orson Welles *War of the Worlds* broadcast[2] (Schwartz, 2015), and the phenomenon that sparked Horton and Wohl's curiosity, Jean King's late-night 15-minute slot as *The Lonesome Gal*, also troubled the boundary between imagination and reality. King's character broke the "fourth wall" by addressing the audience in the singular second person (*tu* rather than *vous*, for French speakers):

> I know more things about you because I take the trouble to find them out: I know how sweet you are, and how sentimental you are, because those are the things about you that I want to see, and I do understand you.[3]

The servicemen whose letters and marriage proposals poured in to the WING studio in Dayton, Ohio, were effectively just continuing their side of the dialogue.

If it took another two decades before PSI was to be picked up by communication researchers, it might be due to the nature of media as anything else. There was simply nothing quite like *The Lonesome Gal* to inspire slavering devotion. Media violence had been the obsession of the 1960s and 1970s, fueled by the postwar experimental tradition in social psychology, and here (as discussed in Chapter 4), "identification" was the principal psychological mechanism that explained audience–media figure responses. The "hysteria" displayed by fans of the Beatles and 1970s boy bands did not evidently warrant serious attention from academics. Perhaps the collective nature of pop fandom failed to register with the sender–receiver communication model. When PSI did return to the academic literature, it was initially focused on media figures who directly address the audience, such as newscasters (Levy, 1979; Rubin et al., 1985). Subsequently, it was drawn on by other researchers as an explanatory mechanism for audience response to soap operas, sitcoms, and other drama media formats in which audience interaction with the figures resembled friendship rather than moment-by-moment "interaction." This resulted in an expansion of the parasocial concept into the field of relationships (Rubin & McHugh, 1987).

In the relatively early days of social media, some media scholars suggested, rather hopefully, that it could sound the death knell for the whole notion of the parasocial project. Marwick and Boyd (2011) claimed that

> while parasocial interaction is largely imaginary and takes place primarily in the fan's mind, Twitter conversations between fans and famous people are public and visible and involve direct engagement between the famous person and the follower. The fan's ability to engage in discussion with a famous person de-pathologizes the parasocial and recontextualizes it within a medium that the follower may use to talk to real-life acquaintances. (p. 148)

Leaving aside the question of why something cognitive and "imaginary" should necessarily be pathological, this statement posed a serious challenge to the idea that PSRs are defined by the lack of reciprocity. Of course, this was always nonsensical if one considers the many media figures who enjoy PSRs themselves, with one another, not to mention the ordinary fans and media users who interact with famous people in their actual social environment, either deliberately or accidentally. Nevertheless, this was the assumption of Horton and Wohl (1956, p. 215), who argued that the TV viewer lacks "effective reciprocity" and that any interaction with a media figure is "not susceptible of mutual development." In their very limited conceptualization of media use, we can now see how inadequate this definition is within the contemporary media landscape. But we are arguing throughout this book that, even in 1956, it was inadequate to capture the psychological experience of the whole television audience unless we restrict our definition of media figures solely to those that are fictional, nonhuman, or dead.

Meanwhile, social media have created an environment in which reciprocation is not only "effective," but fundamental to the whole enterprise. From the word go, Facebook, Twitter, and others sought to democratize the media landscape by removing any kind of media user–figure distinction. On Twitter, everyone is simply a "member," and unless stated explicitly on the user profile, there is no way of distinguishing between "users" and "figures" other than by analyzing the textual and paratextual information provided. Similarly, one can only infer that "followers" are fans in the absence of any other contextual detail. In Giles (2017), I attempted to do this by studying a small sample of crime writers who had recently published their first novel and were each building a small following of several thousand, the kind of people who have been described as "microcelebrities" (Marwick, 2013). I found that it was only possible to identify followers as fans if they could not be classified in terms of their profile (as fellow writers of various kinds, publishers, or ancillary professionals such as journalists, academics, or legal experts interested in crime fiction). Even then, I needed to sift through people who were following the author because they were long-standing friends or relatives. And, within the remainder, there were aspiring authors, creative writing students, and fellow microcelebrities such as book bloggers, who had a substantial following of their own.

Of course, as far as the full-blown celebrity is concerned, star status is conferred by the weight of follower numbers alone. Mr. Beast, an American YouTuber famous for his various stunts, has 231 million subscribers to his channel at the time of writing (January 2024). In addition, certain indicators, such as "verified" blue ticks (ostensibly to demonstrate the authenticity of the Twitter profile but clearly treasured as a status symbol), have been incorporated into profiles on some media that perform the function of demarcating an elite set of users. Inevitably, reciprocal interaction will be limited by the sheer size of each elite user's audience. (If you are followed by 3 million people, how could you possibly respond to every single tweet?) For this reason, some media scholars have claimed that social media interaction between celebrities and fans "is not in practice taking place" (Kehrberg, 2015, p. 93). Nevertheless, for celebrities with more modest followings, a substantial amount of reciprocity can be observed (Stever & Hughes, 2013), and even big stars can generate considerable excitement among their followers by retweeting and "quote tweeting" material they have received (Giles, 2018).

Not only have social media platforms reshaped the communication between media users and media figures but they have also introduced new types of media figures that afford different types of relationships with their audience. How parasocial are these relationships, and do we need to reconfigure our understanding of what "parasocial" actually means as a result? As we go on to argue in subsequent chapters, the conceptual framework already exists, but I will use the remainder of thepresent chapter to apply this framework to the contemporary situation, exploring new types of media figures, new types of communication affordance, and the intellectual demands imposed by these changes on parasocial theory and particularly on research.

DEFINING NEW TYPES OF MEDIA FIGURE

Definitions of PSI tend to vary according to the research interests of the people studying it, and this is particularly true when it comes to identifying media figures and the types of relationships we might expect to have with them. For example, Tsay-Vogel and Schwartz (2014) identified four dimensions of media figure: (a) depiction or appearance, (b) "story" (effectively reality status; i.e., fictional or nonfictional), (c) form (human or otherwise), and (d) traits (human or otherwise; e.g., superhuman). Inevitably, this taxonomy lends itself more to studying PSRs with fictional creations than those with human figures. For the latter, we are limited to taxonomies of fame and celebrity, such as Giles (2000), where I suggested (a) role-based fame (e.g., president or monarch); (b) fame on merit (e.g., sports stars); (c) culturally specific fame (e.g., singers or actors); and (d) accidental fame, where people become newsworthy in fields not normally associated with celebrity, such as criminals or victims of crime, "have-a-go" heroes, or a figure at the center of a scandal, court case, or other big news story.

Note that Giles (2000) was effectively a way of accounting for fame itself rather than just creating categories of celebrity. For the latter, Rojek (2001) and Turner (2004) are recommended, even if they map fairly closely to Giles (2000). For example, Rojek has "ascribed celebrity" for role-based fame (my category 1); "achieved celebrity," which covers my category 2 and (some of) category 3; and "attributed celebrity" for category 4 and, potentially, the rest of category 3. It is category 3 that splits the models: Rojek refuses to discriminate between fame that is indisputably merited and that which derives largely from media exposure. But this is only to be expected if we think of fame as a social process (where the fastest runner will be more famous than the others) and celebrity as a cultural one, typically dependent on media (so if running has very little cultural capital in a society, nobody cares who is fastest). A fourth category of celebrity, according to Rojek, is the "celetoid." This type of figure, which also maps onto the fourth category in Giles (2000), refers to a specific type of attributed celebrity that is very short-lived, largely because the people involved are unable to support the attribution of celebrity in the longer term. So, it covers those types of figures listed above under "accidental fame" but also includes people in more conventional fields such as music (described by Rojek as "one-hit wonders") whose careers fail to build on their brief moment of glory.

Within only a couple of decades, these taxonomies already appear well past their use-by date. Social media has revolutionized the ways in which people can become famous and the outlets they achieve fame within. Who "attributes" celebrity to whom in digital culture? Ascribed and achieved fame cling on tenaciously, largely via the legacy media, while one might argue that the celetoids have, via social media, emerged as the dominant form. Some celebrity researchers have more or less abandoned the traditional field in order to account for the new digital order, moving toward the study of "persona" rather than celebrity (Marshall et al., 2020). I will discuss this literature in more detail later in the chapter.

An alternative approach is to define emerging types of media figures in relation to the specific media that afford them, which I attempted to do in Giles (2018). Not all social media platforms possess the same celebrity-producing affordances. Facebook and Twitter, for example, tend to rely on their users achieving fame in other domains (whether traditional, such as music, or digital), whereas one can become famous solely because of one's YouTube channel, which affords the creation of audiovisual material just like television and cinema. Instagram, with its visual affordances, has enabled people, even in unlikely categories such as poetry, to become famous largely through their accounts in that medium. TwitchTV, the gaming platform, has generated its own celebrity category in a way that vaguely resembles sports stardom. Finally, one can identify short-lived "celetoid"-type figures that attain fame through their (often unwitting) association with memes and other viral material.

At the same time, as Marshall et al. (2020) argue, it is almost impossible to isolate one social medium from digital culture more generally. Even thinking of these platforms as media may not be helpful. "Where there was once a clear division between what was considered media and what was described as communication," Marshall et al. (2020, p. 39) write, "a new hybridity has occurred" (p. 39). This they describe as "intercommunication." For example, a YouTube video may be linked in a tweet, and the creator may be best known for their blog on a stand-alone website (not to mention live shows, occasional TV appearances, and a column in an online newspaper). Up to a point, this has always been the case and is probably why traditional celebrity taxonomies were not made up of "radio stars," "pop stars," and so on. However, "TV personality" had considerable currency as a celebrity type for many years, and as Bennett (2011) has argued, there are certain unique skills associated with this type of performer that do not always carry over into other media. So, I think it is legitimate to acknowledge the source of fame, even while we accept that it is practically impossible to avoid that fame spilling over into other domains.

In the following section, I want to discuss a handful of uniquely 21st-century media figures with whom we can enjoy PSRs as well as the specific impact digital culture has on those relationships.

(Social Media) Influencers

This is undoubtedly the broadest and most extensive category of modern celebrity, but it is probably the most difficult to gain any firm conceptual grip on. Like celebrity itself, no two authors have ever agreed on the same definition of the 21st-century "influencer." To begin, I have selected three sources by way of illustration. Crystal Abidin is a media researcher who has published extensively on the topic of influencers and would seem a reliable place to start. For her (Abidin, 2016, p. 86), social media influencers (SMIs) are people who "accumulate a following . . . through the textual and visual narration of their personal, everyday

[life], upon which paid advertorials—advertisements written in the form of editorial opinions—for products and services are premised." The important criteria here, then, are (a) the maintenance of some kind of blog or vlog that documents the individual's day-to-day lifestyle and experiences and (b) a commercial imperative. Someone pays the influencer to promote their products.

An alternative definition is provided by Delbaere et al. (2021, p. 102): "SMIs are third-party users of social media who have achieved micro-celebrity status in the form of large followings on social media platforms and who have a position of influence on their audience." The "third party" reference here is a marketing term relating to people who are positioned neither as (primarily) consumers nor producers, which allows them to maintain an air of objective neutrality, unlike Abidin's influencers, who are effectively producing advertising copy. However, they need a *large* following (despite being only microcelebrities) and—as one might expect—exert some unspecified influence on their audience.

Rather, and more specifically, Stoldt et al. (2019, p. 2) provide a list of criteria for defining an SMI. First is that, as in Abidin (2016), they "document their lives." Second, unlike the other two definitions, they suggest some subtypes, namely "bloggers, activists, comedians," among others, inferring that influencers are not just advertisers. Third, they sum up the commercial status succinctly: "Influencers are sellers, buyers, and commodities: They consume products and services; promote products and services; and sell themselves as a brand to be consumed by audiences." Fourth, importantly, they "produce social media content to serve niche audiences" (fashion, gaming, travel, etc.). Finally, they are not always paid for their promotions, and much of their labor is aspirational. Nevertheless, there are obvious gaps here. What size following is necessary? Where does "influence" occur?

One of the few publications to attempt a full-blown classification of SMIs is Ouvrein et al. (2021), which attempted to define (social) influence as "informational" and "normative" following the social psychological literature, but with the crucial additional characteristic of "ordinariness." As with Delbaere et al. (2021), this is important to maintain a degree of what we might consider "stake inoculation," a discursive device that effectively distances the speaker from the charge that they have a vested interest in the claims they are making. Or, in contemporary social media, a stake in any product they are promoting. Unlike the figures studied by Abidin (2016), many influencers take great trouble to deny direct marketing connections with brands or find ways of circumventing accusations of bias (for some in-depth analysis of this practice, see Giles, 2018).

In Ouvrein et al. (2021), we also tackled the issue of audience. In terms of sheer size, one can distinguish "mega influencers" with more than 1 million followers from "macro influencers" (between 100,000 and 1 million) and "micro influencers" (1,000–100,000). These cutoffs will vary according to certain limitations on the audience, such as national and linguistic reach, as well as domain, denoting that the scope of mega influencers may extend well beyond a specific field, such as beauty or gaming. Finally, we identified five types of influencers based partly on their appeal to the audience:

1. *Passionate influencers*: These are performers whose content is driven initially by a passion for the field, whether it be food, fashion, or travel. This does not stop them from eventually becoming mega influencers or being sponsored by multiple brands in their domain.
2. *Passionate business influencers*: The main difference between this group and the first is that their commercial intent is evident from the start. These figures set out to court brand sponsorships, set up their own clothing lines, and enjoy a different, often more remote, relationship with their audience.
3. *Celebrity influencers*: These individuals have achieved celebrity in a traditional domain, such as television or music, and have used their celebrity capital to engineer influence, sometimes in multiple fields (fashion, health, and even social issues), attracting sponsors easily through their existing audience reach.
4. *Dreaming business dormants*: These are essentially failed Category 2 figures, striving to exert influence on a modest audience but only achieving limited success. It is suggested that these figures lack the "storytelling" appeal of top influencers; their content lacks sufficient appeal to build a substantial following.
5. *Passionate topic enthusiasts*: These are Category 1 figures who have not attracted a sufficiently large audience to interest brands, largely because this is not the primary purpose for content creation.

Naturally, the practice of defining and surveying the field could use up the rest of this book, but we have plenty of other things to talk about. The one thing lacking in these definitions is a clear sense of where we find these people, so we also need to consider figures in the context of specific social media.

YouTubers

If an influencer is active on YouTube, does this make them a YouTuber? Answer: of course. You can be a YouTuber and an influencer at the same time. Technically, anyone with a channel on YouTube is a YouTuber, which limits it to potentially 2 billion people, although only a mere 38 million of them have active channels (Hayes, 2023). Unfortunately, the academic literature is barely more helpful for defining YouTubers than influencers: Martínez and Olsson (2019) simply describe them as "microcelebrities," yet another floating signifier, Tolbert and Drogos (2019) as "YouTube personalities" in the tradition of TV personalities, and most other authors simply classify them as content creators who have amassed a significant number of subscribers to their platforms or channel(s). Ultimately, the defining quality of a YouTuber is that they owe their fame to their work in the medium rather than anywhere else, although for performers who have emerged in the "intercommunicative" world of digital culture, this is increasingly difficult to ascertain.

The main point to make about YouTubers as a media figure type is that, like TV personalities before them, they demonstrate familiarity and a certain degree of skill with regard to how they utilize the affordances of the medium. Just as Bennett (2011) talks about the "televisual skills" of people like chat show hosts and game show presenters, we can specify certain features of YouTubers that help them build their subscriber numbers. First and most obvious is the relentless creation of new material. Gamer Stampylongnose is, or was, reported to have uploaded a new 20- to 30-minute video every day (Newman, 2016). Most successful performers quickly adopt a standard stratification of videos and playlists and, eventually, separate channels in which they portion out different types of material (one channel for the daily or weekly vlog, another for pranks, another for haul videos, or whatever). They adapt to the latest trends on the medium, whether it be a particular "challenge" or a recognizable format such as a "reaction" video (where, for example, friends and family members of the vlogger appear to provide spontaneous emotive reactions to old videos), or even the latest graphics for decorating thumbnail tiles (the images representing each video) (Giles, 2018). Then there are the typical presentational details: "the sign-ons, sign-offs, and key phrases that help to construct narrative unity, thematic cohesion, and a shared language that can be readily deployed by fan bases" (Betancourt, 2016, p. 199).

It is, of course, possible to divide YouTubers into subcategories based on their broad fields of activity: Almost all of them will present some kind of regular vlog, perhaps supplemented by partners, family, pets, and friends. There are those who are primarily orientated in beauty or fashion, offering make-up tutorials, reviewing "hauls" of High Street shopping, or reviewing the latest products. There are gamers offering "playthroughs" of popular games like *Minecraft*, reviewing new releases. There are channels devoted largely to comedy: sketches, pranks, stunts, and challenges. A few provide more traditional celebrity fare, such as music, although this rarely works abstracted from the conventional industry. Other successful performers offer an audiovisual complement to a stand-alone blog, dealing, for example, with food, books, or travel. Apart from a few exceptions, fiction is not well presented in the medium.

TikTok(k)ers

Whereas YouTube is not far from completing its second decade, TikTok is a much younger phenomenon, dating from 2018, and there is a certain amount of overlap between the platforms. Nevertheless, TikTokkers[4] can be defined in largely the same way as YouTubers in that they are content creators who owe their fame to the specific affordances of the medium, chief among which are the various time limits imposed on the length of the videos. Although these have varied through its short life,[5] in 2023, it was limiting creators to 3 minutes, although it seems most users prefer considerably shorter ones, finding anything more than a minute "stressful" (Stokel-Walker, 2022). This naturally rules out some of the characteristics of

YouTube videos, rewarding creators who are able to reduce their material to a brief presentation of catchphrases, musical motifs, or visual gags.

Although TikTok lacks the scope for patiently building an audience of subscribers through following regular vlogs, its creators still manage to recruit substantial followings. As of early 2023, the Senegalese-born Italian Khaby Lame was the most-followed on the medium, with 161 million, fast approaching Mr Beast's YouTube tally.[6] The fact that Lame's voice has never been heard in any of his videos illustrates the quality that TikTok best affords: the global language of satirical, humorous visual communication.

Livestreamers

One outcome of the massively expanded gaming industry this century is the popularity of online gaming videos and livestreams, initially on Facebook and YouTube but increasingly on dedicated sites. Most notable of these is Twitch, a community that attracts more than 10 million viewers a month, and in May 2023 boasted 17.25 million[7] "livestreamers" (Clement, 2023) who generate content for the platform. A typical livestream features game action with the player's webcam feed appearing in a corner of the screen. To the right of the screen is a chat stream in which viewers, and occasionally the players, post content. While most livestreams consist of gameplay, over time, as in other social media, the content has diversified somewhat so that many streams and videos are dedicated to people doing other things,[8] such that a specific genre of stream is labeled "Just Chatting" (Leith, 2021).

Twitch streamer follower numbers are not quite as impressive as those on YouTube or TikTok, but in June 2023, the most popular, Ninja, had 18.5 million. According to the very helpful website TwitchTracker (2023), most of the top streamers (nine have over 10 million followers) are players of very popular games like *Minecraft*, *Fortnite*, and *Grand Theft Auto*. Nevertheless, it is noticeable that, even for these figures, some of their most-watched material comes in the "Just Chatting" genre.

Avatars

Whereas livestreaming allows gamers to interact with one another as well as with new types of celebrity, a different game-related phenomenon has generated a new form of media figure, the avatar. Whether an avatar can genuinely be classified as a "media figure" is questionable because it is, in most cases, co-authored by the player, who may be able to give it a bespoke name, appearance, and various characteristics. Furthermore, the relationship between the player and avatar differs entirely from that between media users and figures, even contemporary online celebrities. Effectively, the avatar is the player's direct representative in the game world, is controlled by the player, and enjoys no autonomy beyond the textual confines of the game itself. Some researchers have applied the parasocial concept to gameplay with avatars (Banks & Bowman, 2016; Jin & Park, 2009).

Conversational Agents

In recent years, our homes have been host to a variety of artificial intelligence–generated virtual assistants, perhaps most famously the disembodied voice belonging to "Alexa" or "Siri" (associated with Amazon and Apple, respectively) that responds to queries by retrieving the same kind of search information as a search engine and converting it into natural-sounding speech. The ability to hold a "conversation" with the assistant gives them a human-like quality even if the limited range of potential responses soon becomes evident, even to small children. Nevertheless, some researchers have claimed that users are able to form meaningful relationships with the assistant, even referring to Alexa as their "friend" (Ramadan et al., 2021). This is particularly the case for people who are isolated or disabled and have come to rely on Alexa (or several Alexas stationed around the home) to operate appliances or summon help. As users form a dependency relationship with the assistant, it or "she" assumes an importance similar to that of a carer, going beyond simple companionship. This is an example of a 21st-century "media" figure (like robots, to be discussed later) that extends the concept of the parasocial into new territory. So much so that some researchers in this field have suggested that new theories might be necessary for capturing contemporary human–technological interaction (Lim et al., 2022).

NEW TYPES OF PARASOCIAL INTERACTION

In addition to the many new types of media figures, the present century has seen the emergence of many new media environments that afford different types of interaction between users and producers. So blurred has the distinction between these last two groups become that for a while, it was customary to talk of "produsers" (Bird, 2011), although this term seemed to fade away as the old star system of traditional media began to reassert itself in a digital guise.

Perhaps the most striking difference between traditional broadcast media and digital culture is the ability of audiences to contribute directly to the environment by posting comments on the same platform where they encounter the creators. On Twitter or Instagram, you can send anyone a message that will potentially be seen by the recipient and their followers. On YouTube, Twitch, and TikTok, comment streams allow users to post "below the line," thereby generating an interactive thread with conversational potential. The same format has been adopted by more traditional media, such as online newspapers. To some extent, these opportunities simply ramp up long-standing features of print media such as the letters page, except the interaction happens instantaneously, and there are more opportunities for interaction among the audience itself, not to mention the creators who have uploaded the content in the first place.

Regarding PSI, the contemporary media environment is quite different from the one typically envisaged by Horton and Wohl (1956), where the solitary army conscript sits glued to the transistor as the Lonesome Gal purrs into his ear. It is hard to fantasize about a private relationship with a YouTuber when there are several thousand comments on the list, and many of them will be gushing over their personal attributes. This makes contemporary audience–media figure interaction more like the experience of a fan community than the one-on-one dyads studied by Rubin et al.'s (1985) scale or Hartmann and Goldhoorn's (2011) Experience of Parasocial Interaction (EPSI) instrument. In the latter, the user is assessed on their answers to questions about a single actor on screen watched in isolation. At the same time, audiences have always consumed media in groups, watching TV with family or friends, commenting on the shows, and potentially influencing one another's perception of the onscreen figures. This is a limitation of parasocial research that has never truly been addressed (Giles, 2002).

It is not, therefore, surprising that fan scholars have dismissed parasocial theory as unsuitable for explaining audience behavior (Duffett, 2013; Jenson, 1992). As even Freud (1922) observed (see Chapter 4), fans of performers will tend to bond together and share their appreciation rather than disintegrating into a vicious mass of bitter rivalry. Some studies of online fandom suggest that the fan community may effectively be as important to its members as the fan object itself (Giles, 2013). It is evident in these cases that PSI can spill across individual boundaries and take place at a group level. Hills (2016) has proposed treating such instances as "multisocial interaction." He argues that among fans, PSI is always social, with fans sharing their parasocial encounters as "[resources] within their self-narratives" (p. 471).

The idea of PSRs as narrative resources reminds us that in digital culture, interaction is fundamentally discursive. Social media platforms afford audiences the opportunity to approach media figures in print and to discuss them with one another in print. The interaction is archived and can be available on the site and easily searchable for many years subsequently. As discussed in previous chapters, we use many of the same words and concepts to construct PSRs as we do for social relationships. For instance, although the use of terms such as love and hate may be partly metaphorical or even tongue-in-cheek, when applied to people we do not know personally, the relationship itself is built from the same blocks.

How do we go about incorporating these new ways of thinking about the parasocial? One obvious outcome is the way it is researched. Although the PSI scale is intended to capture private cognitive processing on the part of the individual audience member, it still requires respondents to consciously reflect on their experiences and, like most psychometric scales, is subject to social desirability bias. Given some of the stigma around fandom and the long-standing "third person effect" in media research, one would imagine that asking direct questions about respondents' parasocial experiences is not the optimum method. Meanwhile, there are vast reserves of "data" stored online that enable us to observe online communities interacting with media figures (who are effectively part of that community). As the archaeologist William Rathje noted, you can learn much more about people's consumption behavior by examining the contents of their rubbish bin than from their answers to a survey (Rathje & Murphy, 1992). By saying this, I am not implying that social media content is necessarily rubbish, but—and this is essentially Rathje's point—it constitutes "material culture." Media audiences have gone from passive, mostly silent consumers to active participants in content creation, and psychometric instruments are less capable than ever of capturing this important aspect of media user experience.

In a recent study (Giles, 2024), I examined the comment threads associated with YouTube videos in which the creator disclosed their experiences of depression. I chose to study these modern-day "celebrity confessions" partly because they open up a space where highly intimate details of the creator's life are shared with the audience. One would expect such content to reinforce the private experience of being immersed in vloggers' lives and being a privileged member of their extended social circle. Had YouTube not allowed users to post comments underneath the videos, this content would be little different to broadcast media such as television, and we could have easily filed the user experience under "parasocial interaction." But the videos in our sample had generated, in some cases, hundreds of comments, many of them hearably addressed to the creators themselves. And in many cases, a creator had responded, either by thanking them personally for the comment or posting a heart symbol to register their approval of the message.

One goal of the study was to determine if the comments could be interpreted as either "social" or "parasocial." If a user addresses the creator as "you," for example, does this mean the user thinks they have a direct connection to the creator? Indeed, many comments were formulated this way. On one Spanish video with a religious theme, one user posted, "I admire very much that you are a yutuber [sic] and speak in this medium about what a relationship with God is." Another posted, "I like it when she reads the Bible." Which comment is "more parasocial"? One might conclude that the use of the second person "you" equates to the belief (as tested by the EPSI scale, perhaps) that the media figure is aware of the user. However, in this particular instance, the media figure replied directly to the user saying, "You don't know how happy I am to know that my trials can be a blessing to other people, I'm sending you a big hug!" *Not* very parasocial, then.

Given the limitations of this particular strategy, I moved on to examining the community as a whole. What sort of interaction can we observe between the creator and the audience? Qualitative analysis of the comments suggested that there were four distinct types of communities[9] associated with these particular videos. Clearly, size (number of comments/number of subscribers to the vlogger's channel) imposes limits on the interactional style, although it is undoubtedly not a determinant, as some vloggers with relatively small subscriber numbers did not reply to any comments. Another factor was the extent to which subscribers interacted with one another. In one or two large communities, there was considerable interaction with much discussion about the vlogger in the third person. These seemed more like fan forums than anything else (it is not unusual for fan objects to contribute directly to these, either). This goes somewhat against the finding from livestreaming research that large communities do not foster as much sense of community as smaller ones (Sherrick et al., 2023) (even though some of these vloggers had well over 1 million subscribers), but it may reflect a different type of interactional environment. Then there were communities in which the creator themself was highly interactive, responding to numerous comments, but without any interaction between the subscribers. It seemed in these communities that users had sufficient confidence in making direct contact with the creator, and they did not need to bond with fellow users.

My conclusion from this study was, perhaps not surprisingly, that dividing relationships between media figures and media users along a strict social–parasocial boundary is now more challenging than ever. Clearly, the experience of subscribers to popular channels is "more parasocial" because of the low probability of making direct contact with the creator, however interactive and responsive they may be. Those subscribers settle, like Freud's (1922) fans, for (mostly) amicable discussion among themselves. If you want the satisfaction of reciprocation, follow a less popular channel, but don't bank on getting a reply. The overall picture, then, is not that incompatible with the social–parasocial continuum of Giles (2002), in which audience size—online or offline—is an important determinant of how intimate and "social" an encounter can be.

APPROACHES TO STUDYING NEW MEDIA FIGURES

How has the academic/scientific community responded to the new challenges posed by digital culture in the first three decades of the present century? At first glance, one might think it is by simply recycling all the old methods. There are now numerous studies in which communication scholars have run the old PSI scale (and other, newer variants) on audiences of social media influencers (e.g., Lou & Kim, 2019), YouTubers (e.g., Rihl & Wegener, 2019), and livestreamers (Sherrick et al., 2023). In some respects, the assumptions of these measures have not changed. If the PSR is what goes on inside the media user's head outside specific episodes of media use, what difference does it make if the media figure has been able to reply to your comment? Relatively little, claim Rihl and Wegener (2019), who asked YouTuber fans how often they received replies to their comments. Decidedly, other, more traditional factors were better determinants of high PSI. But this is traditional PSI, based on broadcast media, in which reciprocation should not take place to begin with. The question itself seems illogical.

At the same time, a number of studies have drawn on alternative methods to try to capture the observable data. Faced with the torrent of verbal information on Twitch, Leith (2021) used natural language processing to study, among other things, the "verbal immediacy" of messages addressed to livestreamers compared with those addressed to the audience as a whole. These were found to involve shorter words and be more present-focused, implying that the user imagines themselves in direct contact with the streamer. Likewise, Thelwall et al. (2022)

analyzed personal pronoun use cn YouTube and found that it tended to be associated with less popular channels, perhaps those where the creator is more likely to respond. He also found it was more likely on channels with high "parasocial potential," measured by things like the visual focus on the presenter and their eye contact with the camera.

Other researchers, without necessarily abandoning the parasocial concept, have explored different ways of thinking about media and celebrity. As discussed briefly earlier in this chapter, the blurring boundary between users and creators in social media has prompted some authors to stop treating media figures and media users as meaningful categories, focusing on "persona" instead (Marshall et al., 2020). A new field, persona studies, has been established to examine this phenomenon, and, as one might expect, psychoanalytic theory has played a significant role in its conceptualization. Jung's theory of "persona"'—the "mask" that we use to interact with other people—directly applies to the creation of profiles in social media and the strategic fashioning of the user's identity (Marshall et al., 2015).

The main principle of persona studies is that it focuses on *performance* as much as people: This is not to say that YouTubers and other digital media figures are "inauthentic" but that audiences are interacting, albeit across different media, with multiple personas that constitute different performances by the same social actor. This is supported by accounts from influencers and other contemporary figures that they use different social media to manage separate aspects of their celebrity— for example, Instagram for formal presentations, Twitter for "backstage" material (Abidin, 2017), or even two separate accounts on the same platform for "private" and "public" content (Wedgwood, 2017).

Although persona studies offers an interesting perspective on media and celebrity, what does it mean for parasocial theory? In truth, its literature has not really touched on the interaction between personas and audiences because the concept effectively disregards the distinction. In social media, we are all various personas performing a kind of celebrity, only some personas are just more popular than others. Ultimately, social media's affordances are the same for all its users, so the social–parasocial distinction is unnecessary. Marwick and boyd (2011) effectively made the same point by declaring social media as "context collapse." If everyone on Twitter has a follower, then everyone on Twitter has a fan. This is borne out to some extent by the various findings discussed in this chapter which suggest that the interaction between social media users reflects little more than the size of each user's following.

For all this literature is convincing, it is nonetheless important not to become too distracted from our broad psychological goals by focusing too closely on the experiences of media content creators. Of course, the actual number of highly successful influencers and YouTubers remains relatively small, and the audience activity around a performer with more than 1 million followers is not all that different from that surrounding Hollywood icons and global pop stars. Many of the biggest 21st-century celebrities re-enact all the clichés derived from broadcast media stardom (Giles, 2018).

Navigating the Uncanny Valley

As the media–audience distinction breaks down and we start to explore different ways in which the parasocial manifests itself, we might want to consider other related phenomena as relevant to the phenomenon, such as pets and children's imaginary friends. Neither of these objects meets the traditional definition of a media figure: Imaginary friends, like the fictional creations of authors, are surely under our cognitive control to some extent, whereas pets are fully flesh-and-blood companions who reciprocate our communication toward them. Our relationship with companion animals is, one would argue, entirely social.

Voice assistants, like Alexa and Siri, might also be considered media figures with whom we can develop PSRs, but in some respects, these figures, like pets, are in our homes and—while disembodied—within our physical environment. They are not "broadcast" to us from far away. The same might be said of *robots*, which again are rarely thought of in parasocial terms yet are no more or less "mediated" than Alexa and Siri. This is probably another example of how parasocial theory has been driven by the demands of communication and media researchers rather than psychologists, where what counts as "mediated" is less important than the user experience. Robots (and pets, for that matter) can easily fit into the social–parasocial continuum (Giles, 2002), where they are physically proximate but less human, so therefore "more parasocial" than interacting with actual humans. And at times, the interaction resembles that with media figures. If we receive a letter supposedly from our favorite Hollywood film star but really from the fan club secretary with a forged signature attached, in what way is this different from an obviously programmed response from a robotic dog or chatbot?

Research on human interaction with robots has taken place in scientific fields not seemingly familiar with the parasocial literature, so there is a certain sense of reinventing the wheel here. But in an earlier communication study (Lee et al., 2006), the authors hypothesized that the psychological tendency to form PSRs with media figures would be the impulse for human–robot relationships. They studied this in relation to a robotic puppy developed by Sony called AIBO that responds in a physically dog-like fashion to verbal instructions (stroking and non-verbal gestures), although rather than eliciting dog-like sounds, it communicates using melodies. In an experimental design with a convenience sample of undergraduates and using a somewhat scaled-down version of the PSI measure, the researchers found that stronger PSI with media figures predicted high levels of social attraction toward AIBO. This suggests that the two constructs have roughly similar psychological roots.

Subsequent literature has focused more on human relationships with pets as predictors for whether AIBO would suffice as a companion for a human. Konok et al. (2018) reviewed this work and concluded that dogs constituted a promising template for developing companion robots because of how humans perceived them, attributed personalities, etc. However, in the authors' own research, participants had broadly negative attitudes toward the idea of a robot companion compared to an animal, and the authors' conclusion was that in the future, robotic dogs should incorporate more of the qualities of real animals. This was largely because the participants stated that real dogs would not be perfectly obedient and would manifest personality through autonomy (disobeying owners, being "imperfect"). This is reminiscent of some of the imaginary companions reported by children that we will discuss in Chapter 5 (Taylor, 1999).

Would our attitudes toward robotic dogs improve if they *looked* more like dogs, though? For many years, there has been a tendency in the industry to refrain from making robots resemble humans (or animals) too closely because it is believed that this would ultimately deter people from trusting them. This was described in an essay by Mori (1970/2012) as the effect of the "uncanny valley." The closer a robot resembles a human, he argued, the more we are likely to reject it as "eerie," reacting even with revulsion if the object we perceive as a human turns out to be nonhuman. Rather than basing this on any actual research, the idea stems from his own reaction to seeing a lifelike artificial limb performing, convincingly, the action of a real hand. One might be tempted to wonder if the "uncanny valley" is nothing more than a realism bias, rather like the end of a sci-fi film in which the villain, on receiving a fatal wound, is revealed to consist not of blood and bones but of wires and circuit boards. After all that time, our hero was being pursued by a machine?

The "uncanny valley" theory has informed development in the field of "ethorobotics" (Miklósi et al., 2017), where designers are urged to refrain from developing humanoid robots—at least in appearance—and to allow them to evolve "naturally" as if they were a separate species. Instead of trying to deceive humans into thinking the robots are really human, the emphasis is more on "social competence." So, rather like the (occasionally) disobedient robotic dogs recommended by Konok et al. (2018), robots *behave* like real humans, at least verbally, with their own original utterances and the ability to detect the moods and desires of their human companions. Perhaps for this reason, there has been more interest recently in developing chatbots as companions, which avoids the need for visual simulation.

With chatbots and possibly verbally interactive robots, we are moving into new territory for parasocial theory because we have to incorporate the role of reciprocation. It is perhaps notable that a model of how human–chatbot relationships might develop (Skjuve et al., 2021) was based not on PSI but, instead, on social penetration theory (Altman & Taylor, 1973). According to this theory, relationships develop through increased self-disclosure on the user's part, although this was based on the assumption of mutual self-disclosure. The formation of human–chatbot relationships, on the other hand, requires the user to acquire trust in the companion, which, in Skjuve et al.'s (2021) model, is largely about accepting the chatbot, given its obvious limitations, as socially useful. Again, chatbots—along with robots—can easily be fitted into the social–parasocial continuum (Giles, 2002), so parasocial theory is perfectly capable of absorbing such relationships into its explanatory power.

SOCIAL MEDIA AS MULTISOCIAL INTERACTION

In Chapter 9, we explore a brand-new social media platform, Cameo, that continues the discussion of how PSI and parasocial theory relate to the newest forms of mediated communication among fans, celebrities, and other audience members. Using Cameo, an audience member sends a request to a celebrity and, for a fee, receives a video that was created just for that audience member (or occasionally a small group of audience members).

Already suggested is the idea that fans share their PSIs/PSRs with each other within social media platforms. One interesting aspect of Cameo is that the Cameo videos created by (usually) traditional celebrities and sent to individual users become a part of the social media zeitgeist as fans share, indeed are encouraged to share, their Cameos with other fans.

What results is a much more personal connection that fans feel with that celebrity. And, as the sharing of these Cameo videos grows into a larger conversation among fans and celebrities, all of this becomes part of para-communication and parasocial perception (described in more detail in Chapter 9).

4

Parasocial Perception and Para-Communication

GAYLE S. STEVER ■

Because parasocial relationships (PSRs) are defined as lacking reciprocity, how can they in any way be considered reciprocal? This question neglects to consider fundamental factors of para-communication and parasocial perception, which are discussed in this chapter. Hartmann (2008) defined para-communication as a playful interaction between media personae and audience members but later used the term "experience of parasocial interaction" (EPSI) to discuss this phenomenon more specifically (Hartmann & Goldhoorn, 2011). At the heart of PSI is the understanding that the interaction creates the illusion of reciprocity where none typically exists. To experience this is to participate in the mediated illusion that one is part of the other half of a mutual social communication. As such, the literature has focused on the "illusion of intimacy," which is particularly accurate if the mediated persona is a fictional character.

But what about when the mediated personality is a real and living person who is making a conscious attempt to communicate with the audience members? In this case, para-communication represents one-half of the PSI created by the media celebrity to forge a connection and understanding with an audience. Hartmann (2008) noted that "para-communication also occurs with interactive characters who establish a real give-and-take. Nonreciprocity is regarded as just one possible mediator of a perceived distance towards an encountered media character" (p. 186) (see also Konjin et al., 2008).

A major tenet of parasocial theory has been that a PSR is, by definition, not reciprocated. What this means when talking about real people in the media is that the celebrity is known by the individual audience member quite well, but that audience member is not known in return. But this focus has always been on the individual audience member. Indeed, psychology is the study of the individual in a social and behavioral context. However, in both sociology and social psychology,

Parasocial Experiences. David C. Giles and Gayle S. Stever, Oxford University Press. © Oxford University Press 2024.
DOI: 10.1093/oso/9780197647646.003.0005

the perspective of the collective is more central. It is in this context that PSRs with real people have an element of reciprocity. Although the celebrity does not know much, if anything, about individual fans, they usually know quite a bit about the collective group of their fans. It is important to distinguish here between the PSR with a real and living person from the PSR with a fictional character. PSI and PSR in each of these cases can be very different.

The literature on PSRs, dating back to Horton and Wohl (1956), talks about how any perception an audience member has that the PSI is, in some way, reciprocal must be an illusion (Hu, 2023). Indeed, the wording on items for scales measuring PSI and PSR presumes that such interactions and relationships are illusory (Dibble et al., 2023).

A key factor in this discussion hinges on the celebrity knowing the fan as an individual versus knowing fans or the audience as a group. Ask an actor or musician, "Who are your fans?" and they can most often give a cogent and concise answer with respect to age, gender, and other key demographics. The actors I interviewed for this book were able to describe many things about their fans. They all engaged in para-communications, which are ways that a celebrity chooses to communicate with the audience about things of importance with respect to their work and life. This feature must be carefully distinguished from a PSR with a fictional character because, in that case, the illusion of being "known" by the fictional media character is, of necessity, imagined.

PARASOCIAL PERCEPTION

A newer term in the parasocial landscape, parasocial perception, has been proposed by Riles and Adams (2021): "A concept from interpersonal relationship literature (i.e., interpersonal perception) is developed within a parasocial relationship (PSR) framework as a means of drawing additional parallels between parasocial and interpersonal relationships" (p. 792). It was further developed in the context of audience members' PSRs with musicians (Wiemer et al., 2022). Interpersonal perception is when one forms inferences about behaviors and attributes of others that are signals for interest or reciprocity. This is a key aspect of attribution theory, wherein one attributes the behavior of another person to imagined attitudes, preferences, and interests of that other person. Attributions are part of the underlying process whereby one tries to understand the social world around them. We use thought and language in an attempt to understand the behavior of another person. We process information in order to understand the role of other people in our own lives (Manusov & Spitzberg, 2008).

Applying this concept to the parasocial realm means that now the person engaged in a PSR is using real-world information in order to draw inferences about how a distant person perceives those admirers or "fans" who are known to them through various elements of typical fan/celebrity interaction. This interaction is most often mediated. In fact, when it is no longer mediated, as when a fan meets a celebrity and becomes known to them, PSRs can transition to the realm of more ordinary social relationships. But mediated interaction is a key element of the PSR when it involves a real person (but not a fictional character).

This concept builds on the foundation of our understanding of PSI as a form of communication in which the mediated person communicates as if they do know that audience. When talking or performing in front of a camera, actors and television personalities behave toward the audience much as they would for interpersonal interactions. An example of this is *The Late Show with Stephen Colbert*, where each night when Colbert comes into the Ed Sullivan Theater, he greets the studio audience while looking right into the camera, saying things such as "Hey there, so glad to see you here" and similar remarks. Understanding this form of direct address has been a hallmark of PSI research (Dibble et al., 2016).

In this context, mutual awareness of each entity for the other forms the basis of this kind of PSI that involves real people. In the above example, although Colbert has not met all of his audience members, he is aware of their presence, experiences the reactions of a subset of those audience members (presumably through fan mail and social media), and also sees a sample of them in his studio audience each evening. Although there is no direct communication between each audience member and Colbert, the awareness of each for the other is consistent with this concept of para-communication which, again, later came to be known as EPSI (Hartmann & Goldhoorn, 2011).

PARA-COMMUNICATION AND PARASOCIAL PERCEPTION IN FANDOMS

There is a repartee between many celebrities and their fan bases that constitutes a reciprocated relationship in the broadest sense of the concept, and this para-communication leads to parasocial perception. Parasocial perception is the "investment they believe these figures orient towards them in return" (Wiemer et al., 2022, p. 1), something I have observed in multiple fan community case studies during a period of more than 35 years. Although Wiemer et al., in their discussion, referred specifically to musicians and their fans, the same phenomena have been observed in television and film fandoms as well. And to take the concept a bit further, it isn't just the perception of reciprocity on the artist's part but, rather, the observation of actual reciprocity by artists. PSRs of this type do not happen in a vacuum; indeed, they do not happen just in the imagination. Celebrities are real people with real behaviors and real expressions of their attitudes toward not just the audience but also the subset of the audience that has been called "the fans." This is a largely overlooked aspect of parasocial experiences (PSEs) and one that is critical with the rise of various forms of media that are conducive to increasingly more personal and intimate communications from celebrities (see Chapter 9 and the discussion on Cameo as an example).

Clearly, the described phenomenon is limited to a very specific type of PSR, the one that a viewer has with a real person as opposed to a character in fiction, an avatar, or a digitally created persona.

Again, from Wiemer et al. (2022),

> Whereas scholarship on parasocial relationships has routinely focused on how audience members invest and have concern for media figures, it has not focused as closely on how audiences perceive media figures to invest and have concern for them, in return. (p. 2)

The fact is that many media figures do invest in and have concern for their fan communities, and this chapter offers specific examples of this.

ILLUSION VERSUS REALITY

In discussions of parasocial phenomena, one assumption is often that every aspect of the PSR is the result of fantasy, projection, and a secondary attachment, not to the celebrity themselves but, rather, to one's own internally created image of that celebrity, referred to as secondary attachment (Greene & Adams-Price, 1990). There is evidence that in some cases, this is true—for example, this fan talking about her favorite celebrity on Tumblr:

> During the course of this summer, I read so many accounts of people meeting him, so much speculation about his personality and private life, and I must conclude that I love my fantasy version of XXX so much that I don't really care about who he really is. My version is mine, and it makes me happy.

However, other fans are equally clear that they admire their favorite celebrity and emulate their behavior, values, and choices. Wiemer et al. (2022) discuss media content creators and the choices those content creators make regarding how to distribute their creative endeavors. The audience perceives that through those choices, the artist is expressing reciprocal care for the audience. When audience members draw inferences from choices made by artists, they are no longer engaging in a secondary attachment but, rather, are developing their understanding of PSIs by looking at the actual behaviors, choices, and words of the celebrities they follow and not their imagined behaviors.

This is contrary to the belief that when fans indicate that they feel the celebrity reciprocates the relationship in some way—for example, by answering positively on items such as the one in the EPSI process scale (Hartmann & Goldhoorn, 2011) that states, "The media figure was aware of me"—the assumption is that the audience member has somehow been deceived into believing the interaction is individually reciprocal. If one were to take such self-report data out of a real-world context such as the ones presented here, the potential error is that one reads into a response on a questionnaire item in a way that is narrowly constructed and outside the contexts of both active fandoms and 21st-century digital media interactions. Also, in the above-mentioned item, does "me" mean the individual, or could it mean the individual as part of a larger group? These are important questions to consider when interpreting such data.

CASE STUDIES

When one engages in case studies, a problem is that findings for an individual case are not generalizable to the universe of similar cases. However, when one has done many case studies of the same phenomenon, patterns begin to emerge, and it can be proposed that those patterns become the basis for a credible theory as to the nature of the phenomenon of interest.

This is the foundation of this chapter, my 35-plus years of individual case studies in multiple fandoms. Beginning in 1988, I observed, both in person and through the internet, fan–celebrity interactions. As a result of these opportunities, one conclusion is that a single meeting or interaction with the real target of interest is not enough to move the relationship from the parasocial to the social realm. Although PSRs are defined as lacking in reciprocity, most celebrity encounters offer very limited information to the celebrity about the fan and change very little about the fan's relationship with the celebrity. This chapter proposes that fans with limited interaction with a favorite celebrity still have a relationship with that celebrity which is largely parasocial in nature.

That interaction can be a quick autograph or selfie, a single tweet, or a wave or single acknowledgment in passing. For most fans, the line from a PSR to a social relationship is not crossed until the fan is recognized and known, either by face or by name, and this typically takes multiple encounters. I have written extensively about the social relationships that fans have with celebrities (Stever, 2016), and I still maintain that this is not as uncommon as one might think. Realistically, however, the parasocial–social line is not easily breached, and most fans do not achieve it.

In a Digital Age, Intimacy at a Distance Is Less and Less an Illusion

When Horton and Wohl (1956) wrote about PSRs and PSI as an illusion of intimacy, they probably couldn't have imagined where media would be by the 2020s. To discuss this topic, it is necessary to consider how intimacy is defined. Horton and Wohl were using 1950s television as the benchmark for constructing mediated intimacy. Even using television, it was still possible to get to "know" someone as well as one might know neighbors or distant (but probably not close) family members.

Tukachinsky Forster (2021) documented the history of PSRs, particularly those of the romantic variety, building the case that having romantic feelings for a media persona (real or fictional) is far from being a new phenomenon. In addition, she has documented with research evidence the fact that having romantic feelings for a media figure is a very common phenomenon across the lifespan.

It could be argued that having romantic feelings for someone sets that person up for an intimate connection with the object of those feelings. Dictionary definitions of *intimate* (dictionary.com) include "closely acquainted and familiar" or "private and personal." In an age of digital media, the opportunity to become closely acquainted and familiar with someone one has never met is greater with the increase in both the quality and quantity of various kinds of media available. Parasocial attachment (PSA) theory (Stever, 2013, 2017; see Chapter 7, this volume) makes the case that human beings are hardwired to be attracted to familiar faces and voices, and the availability of the faces, voices, and words of one's favorite celebrity persona makes it increasingly easier to form an attachment to that persona. Attachment affords safe haven and comfort in both primary attachments and also in PSAs.

Parasocial perception is the belief on the part of the audience member that the celebrity object, in some sense, cares about audience members and may even have affection for the audience. By this, we are not talking about erotomania (Tukachinsky Forster, 2021), when the audience member has a delusional belief that they are actually in a relationship with the celebrity. In a real-world sense, then, how does an audience member develop a sense of the care and support of their favorite celebrity? And how does this perceived care contribute to intimacy at a distance?

The sweeping power of imagination and particularly of shared stories is at the heart of the PSE and the reason PSRs are such a universal experience. There is no finer example of this than the work and life of J. R. R. Tolkien. That human cultures commit such a vast amount of time, energy, and money to the sharing of these fantasies is evidence that this is true. Originally shared via the printed word, his stories have been made into epic motion pictures at a price tag of millions and millions of dollars. The imagination of Tolkien yielded a rich, complex, and detailed fantasy world complete with varied races, languages, and a fictional history so compelling that the stories are told over and over again. Dozens of examples are possible, but one in this instance should suffice.

The 21st century has changed the benchmark for how well audience members can come to know their favorite celebrities and fictional characters. When Peter Jackson produced and directed the *Lord of the Rings* (*LOTR*) films (2001–2003), in addition to making those films, he did extensive "video blogs" containing behind-the-scenes information about how the movies were made and cast, and he included extensive interview footage with the cast and crew of the films. In addition, he afforded a small group of fans early access to the sets on a limited basis, and those fans had the opportunity to get to know various insiders. Those experiences were shared on a website called "The One Ring Dot Net." TORN (as it came to be known) was another window into the intimate world of *LOTR*.

Fans of these films were now afforded the opportunity to gain intimate knowledge about their favorites in a way that Horton and Wohl (1956) could hardly have imagined. Now with the presence of YouTube, any fan, new or old, can watch hundreds of hours of footage about the making of *LOTR* and, subsequently, the making of Tolkien's *The Hobbit* (2012–2014).

Parasocial perception is the reciprocation that an audience member senses, coming from the object of the PSR. In an example such as this, the belief that the actors and crew care about the fans and appreciate the loyalty and relationship the fans have with the Tolkien universe is reinforced by constant messages from the "making of" videos and press interviews given by every person who was involved in the making of these six films. The cast members then become recipients of the support that many actors would envy, as the PSR with an actor from these films often translated into support for the entire rest of that actor's career.

A specific example of how parasocial perception works is the case of fans of *Fellowship of the Ring* (*FOTR*, the first *LOTR* film) and a character called "Figwit." The character came into being when a fan who lived in Israel was watching a scene in *FOTR* and saw an extra (nonspeaking) elf character who was particularly nice-looking. The joke was "Frodo is great. . . . Who is that!?!" thus the acronym, Figwit. There is a long journey that began from that moment when a fan created an acronym for a character who only appeared on film for 3 seconds. For the purposes of this discussion, where the argument is made that fans perceive the interest of distant parasocial figures in a way that reinforces their fan interest and support, suffice it to say that during the next 12 years, director Peter Jackson, solely because of the fans' interest in this extra (played by Bret McKenzie of *Flight of the Conchords* fame), brought him back for *Return of the King* (the third *LOTR* film) in a speaking role, and then brought him back as another elf character for *The Hobbit* again in 2012. In a documentary made in 2004 about Figwit (*Frodo Is Great, Who Is That?* by Midnight Films), Peter Jackson was interviewed and made it clear that these cast and film decisions were made principally as a nod to the fans who had adopted this character and created fan websites and an entire fan base for him. In addition, McKenzie, an actor and celebrity in his own right (and Oscar winner for songwriting), also appeared in this documentary, meeting and socializing multiple times with these same fans. In a post on the YouTube upload of this documentary (Part 5), one fan posted, "That shows a lot of love for the fans that they gave Bret his role as Figwit back JUST so the fans could see him again after the first movie." This is a clear example of how "audiences perceive media figures to invest and have concern for them" (Wiemer et al., 2022, p. 2).

Another example from the cast of *The Hobbit* further illustrates the phenomenon of parasocial perception with the fan–celebrity relationship around actor Richard Armitage. Remember that the point of this newer concept in the realm of PSEs alleges that fans base their perception of reciprocity on the part of their favorite actor by looking at the actor's actual real-world behavior, challenging the assumption that fans who report that their favorite actor cares about them are somehow deluded or out of touch with reality.

The Armitage Army: The Fan Base of Richard Armitage

Richard Armitage (Figure 4.1) is a British actor with a long and illustrious career. In July 2022, the University of Leicester in the United Kingdom honored him with a Doctor of Letters for his work in film, theater, and television. He is a graduate of the London Academy of Music and Dramatic Arts and has appeared in well over 200 television episodes, films, and plays. He is best known for his role in *The*

Figure 4.1 Richard Armitage.
Source: Tinseltown/Shutterstock.com.

Hobbit films (as Thorin Oakenshield) and also for a number of prominent roles in television shows such as *MI5*, *Berlin Station*, and *North and South*.

Armitage, prior to *The Hobbit*, doubtless already had fans who had a PSR with him. However, entering the world of Tolkien fans, who already had been established as a huge media fan base during the 2001 to 2003 release of the *LOTR* films, his potential fan base increased exponentially. These films were shown in more than 30 countries throughout the world, and active fan groups developed in many of those countries. While searching for Richard Armitage on YouTube, you will find hundreds of videos, many of which were created by fans. There are endless iterations on various themes, from the individual programs in which he has appeared (including *The Hobbit*) and also the many Audible books he has narrated to interviews that have been given to numerous media outlets. It would be a challenge to watch them all, and one could watch one video after the next for days or even weeks and still not have seen them all, a task I attempted during the summer of 2022. After 3 months of an almost daily search, I was still coming up with new videos that I had not yet seen. Saving them in a list, I had well over 200 videos when I stopped counting.

This is a major way in which PSRs have changed in the past 20 years. In the 1990s, if a fan wanted to find material on their favorite artist or celebrity, they had to network with other fans who often had a supply of videos to exchange, something I experienced first-hand during my study of Michael Jackson fans from 1988 to 1992. Back then, the VHS videocassette was a common medium for sharing. Before the VHS tape, audio recordings were really the only medium available for sharing fan material, along with endless photographs.

Today, there are Web pages. Type "Richard Armitage" into Google, and more than 8 million results are generated in a manner of seconds. "Richard Armitage *The Hobbit*" generated well over 600,000 internet hits. For the fan feeling a parasocial attraction to the character or the actor (or both), this is an amount of material so vast that it literally could not all be viewed. Note that this 2022 search was for an actor appearing in a movie 10 years prior (2012–2014), and it still generated over 600,000 hits.

If PSRs are "intimacy at a distance" (Horton & Wohl, 1956), and if observing the face and voice of the target celebrity increases the sense of knowing the person, then it is no wonder that PSRs have become so very commonplace. The Armitage Army, the name many of the Richard Armitage fans have given themselves, is just literally that: a sizeable army of followers who can meet online, network with each other, and collectively reach out to their favorite actor as was done in 2013. At that time, *The Anglophile*, an internet-based program, voted Armitage the most popular British star for that year and had him on their program to interview him and present him with an award and myriad of fan-made videos from fans proclaiming undying devotion, this from all over the world. If Armitage looked a bit overcome during the presentation, it's not difficult to understand why, as any person might find that level of attention to be overwhelming.

It is tempting to decide that being a fan at that level of devotion surely must be a sign of a troubled mind, but research into fandom (Stever, 2009, 2011a, 2011b,

Parasocial Perception and Para-Communication

2013, 2016, 2017) suggests that fans of this type actually tend to be respectful and supportive of artists rather than meeting negative stereotypes that the media would ascribe to all manner of fans. This is not to say that there are no "celebrity worshippers" for whom the connection is troubling, but data suggest that celebrity worshippers are as common in the general population as they might be in any individual fan club (Stever, 2011b). Listen to media interviews with actors from *The Hobbit*, and their accounts are that the fans are not troubling or "crazy" at all (as a group) and are driven by a passionate interest in Tolkien's creative works and, more than anything, the creative work of the actors. I have viewed such interviews with actors from *The Hobbit* where the question asked directly is, "Tell me a crazy fan story," and one after the other said they haven't really had any. In 2017, Dean O'Gorman (Fili the dwarf in *The Hobbit*), in an interview done for MagicCon, was asked if he'd had a "really, really weird fan experience." His reply reflects answers given by other actors (including Richard Armitage, Lee Pace, Aidan Turner, Orlando Bloom, Evangeline Lily, and others from *The Hobbit*) during similar interviews. His response was, "No, not really. Most of the fans are really lovely and enthusiastic and very generous with their time and presents and things."

Take this interview of Richard Armitage with Marilyn Denis on December 3, 2012, on her television program in Toronto, Ontario, Canada. Toward the end of her interview, she asks, "I know you have followers, and they call themselves the Armitage Army. What kind of fan mail do you get?" His response:

They are the most lovely supportive fan base I could possibly wish for, and they have been there for 8 years. I can't thank them enough because they really do follow my work, and I often don't know what my schedule is. I just go on the website, and they tell me where I'm supposed to be.

From this interview, Armitage dates the "birth" of his fan group to approximately 2004, which would be when he was cast for his first major television series in the United Kingdom, a program called *North and South*. He is always respectful when talking about his fans in media interviews, but clearly, a journalist crossed the line into disrespect at a point in 2009, prompting Armitage to post this letter to the fans on various websites created by fans dedicated to him and to his work (the letter is edited because the original was longer):

3rd August 2009
It has come to my attention that offense may have been taken by some comments made about the AA in various print interviews. I have to apologize for this offense, it was only ever my intention to be positive about any group or forum that is kind enough to offer their support to me in my work. I believe this is how I have presented myself to journalists although I cannot control the bias they might wish to "spin" regarding their opinion of such forums.

So, I hereby categorically, and hopefully for the last time say to all fans on any board discussion group or forum:

Any amount of support, any gesture of appreciation is never underestimated or dismissed. Every letter is read and whenever a response is requested an attempt is made to do this, I understand the commitment of fans and the way I chose to return that compliment is to continue to produce work which will be of interest to as many as possible.

Ps. I also hate the word "fan."

This is one of a series of communiques posted through his spokesperson on various online fan forums, although most of them were holiday greetings or other more straightforward types of communication. (See https://richardarmitagenet.com/ramessages for further examples).

The important point here is that Armitage has an apparent pattern of interaction with his fan base. He values what they do for him (the numerous gifts he has been given by fans are acknowledged during his messages to fans) and appreciates their support of his career.

Individual celebrities take many steps to enhance the parasocial perception that they are attending to individual fans. In an interview with Audible, in which questions were taken from Twitter, Armitage began each answer by repeating the name of the person who posed the question (Audible on YouTube, 2016). In fact, two fans in the comments after the interview specifically mention the connection they felt because he said their names. Other actors from *LOTR* and *The Hobbit* have done similar recognition of individual fans on social media or at conventions.

An important resource for information about celebrities and their fans is found on YouTube, where I found five basic categories of videos. The first was "red carpet" events for new programs where one can see actors interacting not only with media but also with various fans. A second was "behind the scenes" videos about filming on the various projects represented. A third was fan-made videos using source material from a variety of projects worked on by the actor. Fourth was appearances on talk shows, a different type of interview from the red carpet or news media interviews. The final type was stage-door appearances after theater events, where it is common for stars, even big-name "A-list" stars, to come out and autograph and/or pose for selfies with fans.

It took several weeks to develop any kind of working knowledge of Armitage's career as he has the aforementioned vast catalog of work he has done. Because of streaming services, it is fairly easy to look at the previous work of an actor, even work that was done some time ago. Armitage offered the additional bonus in that two of his theater roles for which he had received the most accolades had been filmed and were available to watch online (*Uncle Vanya* by Chekov and *The Crucible* by Arthur Miller). As another bonus, Armitage had done a large amount of voice acting vis-à-vis Audible, where he is a popular audiobook narrator. Then, in 2022, he wrote his own novel for Audible (*Geneva*), and it later appeared in hardback in October 2023. In short, there was no lack of available material from which to become familiar with the work of this artist.

It was his role as Thorin Oakenshield that offered up a great wealth of interviews and behind-the-scenes glimpses into things such as the acting process. As already mentioned, Peter Jackson is well known for offering extensive DVD extras showing how his movies are made, and those include interviews, brief reactions to various situations, and a chance to watch the actors work together on the film. Recall that one of the goals of this chapter is to explore the potential for "intimacy at a distance," and glimpses into the working life of actors are one window into that world. Indeed, Jackson's behind-the-scenes offerings originally were a primary reason for my choosing to look at the fandoms of actors in his movies.

Having traveled to many fan events and watched numerous celebrities signing autographs and posing for photos, one recognizes that there is a skill set for doing this. Some celebrities are very good at it, some are just adequate, and some really don't want to do it and aren't very good as a result. Armitage (based on many videos posted on fan websites) appeared to be very accomplished at meeting fans in a way that presented him to the fan base as authentic and engaged. Many fans described him as shy, and one friend of mine who met him more extensively at a press party concurred that he seemed to be a bit uncomfortable in a crowd. Again, the argument comes around, "But how can you tell what a celebrity is really like?" My answer to that is to say that this is true of any person you meet anywhere, celebrity or not (Babcock, 1989). But when talking about parasocial perception—the belief, for example, on the part of an audience member that they have just met a "good person, if someone who is a bit shy"—this perception would be based on evidence that is not much different from the evidence on which one might base attributions about anyone. If you meet your next-door neighbor and report later to someone that the neighbor seemed "shy," that is based on one initial encounter. Might the impression change with time? Sure! But it's based on one real-life encounter, and the fact that a person is a celebrity doesn't change that. If the real-life encounter is filtered through media, it still makes an impression that is potentially as authentic as any other one-time encounter.

Another thing that can happen is that audience members base their evaluation of the actor on the character (or characters) that the actor plays. This is also somewhat common, but in the case of Armitage, he has played so many characters over a period of almost 20 years that it would be difficult to maintain a parasocial perception of this particular actor that wouldn't change completely with every role he plays. Contrast this with the section below about Alexander Siddig, who played the same character on *Star Trek* for 7 years.

When considering motivations for attraction to a celebrity, the big three (Stever, 2009) are task attraction, romantic attraction, and hero/role model attraction. Armitage appeared to be the recipient of all three types of attraction. The task attraction is based on him being an accomplished professional actor. The hero/role model attraction would be based both on real-life philanthropy (he is very active in a number of causes) and on his having portrayed heroic characters such as Thorin Oakenshield. Romantic attraction seems to be a given for nice-looking actors who are within 20 (or even more) years of the age of audience members. Interviewers on more than one occasion tried to make something of the "middle-aged" nature of Armitage's largely female audience. My observations and data collected over 35 years have supported the notion that fans tend to be the artist's age, plus or minus 15 years. So, for Armitage, that would be 37–67 years. Yes, that would be middle-aged fans, and what one would expect.

As I read through internet accounts by fans who had met Armitage, I was struck by several things. First, a good number of these fans (at least a dozen) reported that when they met him, they were either accompanied by their husbands or boyfriends or had been assisted by those same partners in some way in their endeavors to meet their favorite actor. One husband suggested his wife make a sign of some type to get Armitage's attention, which might give her a greater chance of success. Overall, this speaks to the thesis that this fan activity based on PSRs is a normal social activity that, in most cases, is not perceived as a threat by real-life romantic partners. In many instances, the husbands were just as excited to meet Armitage as were their wives, many of these during *The Hobbit* (suggesting perhaps that they were also Tolkien and Armitage fans).

This chapter makes the case that parasocial perception is based on real and accurate information that a fan gleans from many sources, such as the internet, media interviews, and other fans. It is important to note that although it is nice when these various celebrities appear to be good and authentic people, for the purposes of analyzing parasocial perception, it is not critical that this be the case. People meet each other all the time and assess those people based on social cues that are part of a repertoire of social skills one obtains throughout life. Sometimes, others are judged to be a certain way, and they turn out not to be that way. That this is just as true in the parasocial realm as it is in the social realm highlights yet one more way that the social and parasocial are similar.

Armitage is active on social media, with verified accounts on Twitter/X and Instagram. He posts quite frequently and is interactive with the fans who post there, although most of his posts are directed at the public at large and rarely to individual fans. On November 2, 2022, with Twitter having been purchased by Elon Musk and the future of the platform in question, Armitage tweeted,

> I regard the blue tick as a way to ensure you know it's me. [Note that Twitter, at that time, was suggesting it would eliminate the feature, which authenticated the identity of a celebrity from the platform.] There are a number of fakes out there. I see it as a way to protect you from unscrupulous people. Not for one second do I think I'm better than anyone else for having verification. It's looking increasingly likely that, like many others, we may have to find another platform to converse. I'll let you know, and we will find our own way to verify. If that happens, I will likely leave this account open but perhaps will leave it alone. Let's see how things go.

The next day, he tweeted,

> There may be new platforms set up in the coming months and I will let you know here if I choose to open one.

Then, having set up a new account on Mastodon, a newer social media platform, his message was,

Twitter still active, it's going to take a bit of time to find out how to use Mastodon, but we'll work it out together. Once again, as a rule, I urge everyone to support each other in a positive way, to remember that there may be little ones here and older peeps who might find strong language offensive. I use social media mainly to let you know what I'm up to, but I tend to do more listening than talking.

These Tweets reveal several aspects of Armitage's relationship with his fan base. He shows an eagerness to communicate, particularly about new projects he has coming up, and refers to doing "more listening than talking," suggesting that he reads what the fans post to him. In addition to participating on Twitter/X and Instagram, Armitage gives frequent media interviews and speaks to his fans and the public about his work and approach to various roles. He also talks about his work on Audible, where he is a frequent reader of various novels.

Overall, Armitage is a good example of a celebrity who engages extensively in para-communication, fostering the parasocial perception that he cares about his audience and is interested in maintaining a positive relationship with them.

The Grobanites: "I Am Theirs, and They Are Mine"

When thinking about parasocial perception, the case of Josh Groban (Figure 4.2) and his extensive fan base comes easily to mind for me. Groban, in 2024, is a 43-year-old singer who has adopted a signature "classical" style for what is still popular music. He has a "big" operatic-sounding voice and tends to sing a lot of love songs, although recently he has departed from those somewhat and sings about other subjects as well. I have done participant observation ethnography in this fandom beginning in 2005 and up until 2020 at the beginning of the pandemic when fieldwork was, of necessity, somewhat curtailed.

I have written elsewhere about this fandom (Stever, 2011b, 2016), but for this discussion, note that Groban's quotes about his fans are well known among the fans and reflect his love and respect for the fan group. The fact that these quotes are recognized and often repeated among fans is a testament to that. In addition to the one in the heading of this section, here are two more that are representative of things Groban has said about his fans:

I try to have a real close connection with my fans. That's extremely important. They are the ones that have been there from the beginning and proved everyone else wrong. (*Inside Connection*, February 2004)

I still like to keep all the love songs for the Grobanites, I like to make sure that they know those are just for them.

Figure 4.2 Josh Groban.
Source: lev radin/Shutterstock.com.

More recently, in 2020, an interviewer observed, "The 39-year-old year Groban has a deep connection with his fans and has been open with them about his struggles with anxiety" (May 24, 2020, on *Sunday Morning* on CBS). In addition to comments such as these in interviews from the beginning of his career, Groban has done things that speak to his devotion to and connection with the fans. One example here should suffice.

Groban starred on Broadway in *Natasha, Pierre, and the Great Comet of 1812* beginning in October 2016 and ending on July 4, 2017. The musical was nominated for a Tony award for best musical, and Groban was nominated for the best male actor in a musical. I attended several of the shows, including two in October 2016 and two at the end of the run, on July 3 and 4, 2017. In addition, I attended two shows in February of 2017. Fans I know who attended other shows and internet fan boards I follow attest to the fact that what I observed at the shows I attended generalized to almost all of the shows during its 9-month run. Groban came out after almost every show to sign autographs and take selfies with fans. He had conversations with fans and recognized repeat attendees, many of whom were known to him from other fan events. In 2023, he began his Broadway run as the lead in the Sondheim musical *Sweeney Todd* and continued his pattern of meeting fans after the show, signing autographs, and posing for photos, again something I was able to personally experience and observe.

But this discussion is about parasocial perception, and clearly, those fans who met him repeatedly and were known to him had crossed the line from parasocial to social. However, in the parasocial realm of his fandom, those who have not met him and are not known to him had access to a vast amount of information via the internet. It was easy, then, to know that he was doing this for the fans who could attend the shows. Thus, if you asked a fan if he cared about his fans, was aware of his fans, and responded to his fans, the "yes" answer would be based on a wealth of real-world information from those who attended and reported back to the fans who could not be there.

This is an important aspect of PSI and PSRs, the reports, and the credibility of fellow fans who have had first-person encounters. Parasocial perception, the belief that the celebrity cares about or has a positive relationship with their fans, is reinforced by reports from other fans, the ones lucky enough to have had personal encounters with the favored celebrity.

A recent news report and concert review had this to say about Groban, describing the essence of para-communication (Johnson, 2022):

> Some artists take the stage solely to perform. Fans pay good money to hear them sing, and that's what they're going to do. But Groban puts continual effort into forming a connection with his fans, crafting stories, and painting as vivid a picture through his words as he does through song.

SidCity.net: The Sid City Social Club and Alexander Siddig

Alexander Siddig (stage name; Figure 4.3), also known as Siddig El Fadil (birth name), is an actor who came to fame in his 20s for his role in *Star Trek: Deep Space Nine* (*DS9*). Beginning in 1993, I began a longitudinal ethnographic participant–observer study on the newly developed *DS9* by doing interviews with actors and fans and collecting a variety of kinds of qualitative and quantitative data on that fandom (Stever, 2009).

The history of *Star Trek* fandom predates that study by decades, beginning with the original series show that aired from 1966 to 1969. Communities of fans have emerged from *Star Trek* fandom and engaged in a variety of activities common to fan groups everywhere that included (but were not limited to) writing fan fiction (Verba, 2003), attending conventions, participating in mail-out newsletters, having local fan groups that met on a regular basis, raising money for various charities, and engaging in pen pal networks. All of these are pre-internet forms of social engagement for fans, and principally it was conventions that gave access to the stars themselves.

Siddig began his history of interacting with the fans of *Star Trek* in 1993 by attending the conventions that were standard fare for the fandom. He had been doing those for about a year when, in frustration with the lack of chances to actually visit with and get to know fans, he contacted those who had started an

Figure 4.3 Alexander Siddig.
Source: DFree/Shutterstock.com.

individual actor fan club for him and asked if they could arrange and organize something more personal where he could actually get to know fans and talk with them. Thus was born a series of events called "Lunch with the Doctor" (Siddig's character was Dr. Bashir on the show) during which anywhere from 60 to 120 fans gathered on a yearly basis to visit with and get to know Siddig. This began a shift in Siddig's fandom where dozens of fans crossed the line from parasocial to social.

All of this is offered by way of background for the purpose of understanding that this actor had a history of reaching out to fans and wanting to get to know them beyond the superficial meetings that were typical of ordinary conventions. By the time the COVID-19 pandemic emerged in early 2020, there was a firmly established network of fans who had come to know Siddig over a period of more than 25 years. One of those fans is Melissa Lowery, who in 1998 was invited to host the official fan club website for Siddig. She is part of a group of perhaps a dozen or more fans with whom Siddig had developed significant friendships over the years of *Star Trek* and beyond.

Given this background, Siddig, or "Sid" as his friends call him, reached out to Lowery and asked her to help him organize what came to be known as the Sid City Social Club (Sid City being the website that Lowery had produced and moderated over more than 20 years). The premise was that by using Zoom, Sid would meet with as many as 100 fans at a time to just chat about what was happening in the world. Using a model that he had developed at the earlier luncheons, he would have conversations with fans, one after the other. This was not unprecedented for him. At each of his fan club's annual events beginning in 1994 and ending in 2003, he would sit and chat with every fan who attended, signing autographs and posing for photos, such that, for example, in 1998, during a 2-day event (which by that time included other *DS9* actors as well) he spoke one-on-one with each of 100 fans for a total of 9 hours.

For the Sid City Social Club, Sid met on Zoom with fans twice a week for 2 hours at a time and would spend 10–20 minutes per fan having conversations about whatever occurred to them. Doing this weekly for a period of more than 2 years, most participants had multiple chances to have these conversations, and just as with the in-person events, Sid came to know the individuals in the Sid City Social Club quite well. Some of these fans were long-time participants in the fandom who had been attending events with him from the 1990s. Others were brand new younger fans who had just found the show on streaming services or DVD and were attracted to the social club after hearing about it on social media. However, there was still a significant subset of "lurkers" who never spoke with Siddig and never became known to him. Because of this, the club ran the gamut from social to parasocial, with all gradations in between. Even those who came to be known by Sid during these times were still in a quasi-parasocial relationship with someone they only knew through these meetings and with whom they had no ongoing access or relationship.

As the pandemic began to subside and people began going out, the meetings went from twice weekly to once a week. As of summer 2022, the social club had been going on for 2½ years and was still meeting regularly. In late 2022, because he was getting extensive acting work, the social club meetings ended, although there was an in-person meeting May 4–6 in 2023 at a convention in Philadelphia, Pennsylvania, where approximately 100 of the social club members attended a 2-hour session with Siddig and his various guests (mostly from the aerospace industry—guests he interviewed for the group and with whom he had the kinds of conversations that had been characteristic of the social club Zoom calls). A subsequent Zoom meeting happened in January 2024, and more will doubtless happen in the future.

In discussing parasocial perception, there is still the vast majority of Siddig's fans for whom the relationship is parasocial. Already mentioned was that some people who attended the Zoom meetings of the social club never interacted with him but, rather, played the role of lurkers, simply watching and listening to the interactions. For those participants, this became yet one more example of mediated social activity on which to base an opinion of Siddig. This would be in addition to his ongoing body of work that includes more than 30 years of television series (in addition to *DS9*, he has had regular roles on *24*, *Gotham*, *Peaky Blinders*, *Game of Thrones*, *Shantaram*, and *Foundation*) and numerous feature films (*Syriana*, *Kingdom of Heaven*, *Cairo Time*, and others).

In addition, the Sid City Social Club meetings are posted on YouTube, where anyone can watch them. As in the other cases described here, YouTube is part of a vast amount of information on which this actor's fans can base their opinions. Martin and Cohen (2023) referred to this kind of interaction, watching individual fans interact with a celebrity, as vicarious social interaction.

Siddig's investment of time and energy into the social club speaks to a person who cares deeply about others. In a recent discussion we had on this topic (personal communication, July 23, 2022), he noted that he strives for authenticity at the club meetings, self-correcting when he finds that something he has said in a previous meeting was wrong in some way. He has been truly astounded at the impact the social club has had on individual members. A number of groups have broken off from the larger group and started their own Zoom and Discord groups based on special interests. In a recent publication by Sidcity.net, 16 social club members have written essays about the impact of the social club on their lives. In the book, Lowery recounted the formation of the group and Siddig saying, "I guess the thing I most want to do is help generate a community of people who risk becoming depressed right now" (e.g., in the midst of the pandemic; Lowery & Lloyd, 2022, p. 9).

Within the essays in this book, one fan recounted that she "fell head over heels in love with him" after seeing his work (Lowery & Lloyd, 2022, p. 12), a parasocial romantic relationship at its classic best. One essay recounted with respect to Siddig and some of his *DS9* costars who attended social club meetings, "They [the fans] were treated with respect and as equals, as were we all" (p. 98).

The following is another quote that reflects the spirit of the Sid City Social Club (Lowery & Lloyd, 2022):

> It began with getting to know people as they spoke with Sid: the stories, the wisdom, and the inspiration from around the world. The quality of those conversations has grown and deepened over time. The demonstrations of care and concern for members, especially their health and well-being, are ongoing. Our conversations about identity and what it means to respect one another embody friendship in its highest form. (p. 126)

It is outside the scope of this chapter to report in any more detail the content of the meetings of the Sid City Social Club. The point of this discussion is to again highlight an example of parasocial perception, where fans were basing their opinions of and respect for a favorite celebrity based on their mediated interaction in a setting that was both personal and yet at a distance. The Sid City Social Club might be the ultimate example of "intimacy at a distance." (For further information on this group, see Knipe, 2022).

It is also not possible to know which other celebrities might have done events with fans similar to the Sid City Social Club on Zoom, although I had a report from a fan that Nancy Grahn (Alexis on *General Hospital*) made a similar use of Zoom with her fans during the pandemic, also without remuneration.

Aidan Turner: *The Hobbit* and *Poldark*

Aidan Turner is an actor who is best known for a number of roles, such as Kili the dwarf in *The Hobbit* (2012–2014) and John Mitchell, a vampire in *Being Human* (2009–2011). He has appeared in numerous other films and television series, including *The Suspect* (2022), in which he portrayed Dr. Joe O'Loughlin, a psychiatrist; *15/Love* (2023), in which he played Glenn, a tennis coach; and *Rivals*, a 2024 miniseries. The role Turner might be best known for is Ross Poldark in the BBC period drama *Poldark* (2015–2019; see Chapter 7 for an extended discussion of this program).

Turner is an interesting example because unlike many other contemporary celebrities, he completely avoids social media of any kind. As such, one might be tempted to think that he does not engage in para-communication and that fans have no basis for a valid parasocial perception.

But in place of the usual social media avenues employed by many celebrities, he communicates directly with his audience through numerous television, radio, and print interviews, and those interviews most often end up on either YouTube or other media and program websites, such as the ones he did for the BBC. This allows the actor to say exactly what he wants to say in his own voice, again lending credibility and authenticity to the communication. Fake social media accounts (of which there are many) and scams are circumvented by this more direct approach to para-communication, but fans have to be savvy to this to avoid being fooled by the scam accounts.

In an example from early 2023, Turner was preparing to do a play at the Harold Pinter Theater in London called *Lemons, Lemons, Lemons, Lemons, Lemons*. Several radio and television interviews were a means to communicate what the work involved, what the character was like, who was being portrayed, and the overall nature of the project. By speaking directly with the audience, an actor can convey their values, work ethic, and motivation for a current project. In turn, the fans develop the perception that they are the valued recipients of such communication. Fans outside the studios where these interviews were given were greeted warmly, and resulting selfies were posted on social media. After most of the shows, photos and videos of fans meeting Turner inevitably showed up on social media following play nights, further conveying a sense of respect and care.

I had the opportunity to attend this play in March 2023, and everything I had seen in videos on the internet turned out to be reflective of the actual experience I had at the play.

Like Armitage, there were hundreds of YouTube videos of Turner, of the types already discussed. When Turner appeared in 2018 in the West End play *The Lieutenant of Inishmore*, he appeared at the stage door after the play each night and signed autographs for fans. There are dozens of videos that one can find showing him doing this, most of them having been taken by fans on their own cell phones. In this way, a viewer can watch Turner interact individually with numerous fans, and in the same manner, many videos of him signing autographs at science fiction conventions portray a similar picture of personable and caring interaction with the public. Parasocial perception is enhanced not only by the actual activity wherein an actor meets and interacts with individual fans but also by the subsequent and easily accessible postings of these videos.

At the end of the 10-week run of the *Lemons* play, composite videos of the stage door meetings were posted by fans on Facebook fan websites and also on YouTube, with each video running continuously for 45 minutes to an hour. These consistently showed an artist who spoke with fans and signed autographs for them with a great deal of respect, care, and kindness.

Dean O'Gorman: *The Hobbit* and *The Almighty Johnsons*

In a global media economy, actors who are from the far-flung reaches of the earth, or in this case New Zealand, get a chance to build a more international fan base. Dean O'Gorman (Figure 4.4) played one of the main characters in *The Hobbit*, and although he is a television favorite and prominent star in New Zealand, his fan base was extended through the reach of Tolkien and *The Hobbit*, playing Fili, son of Thorin Oakenshield and heir to the crown of Erebor. His Internet Movie Database (IMDB) page lists more than 200 film or television episodes that he has appeared in during his extensive career thus far.

O'Gorman is another actor who uses social media to communicate with a fan base and yet maintains his personal life as quite private. He is a contrast to Armitage and Turner in a number of ways, and with respect to his social media use, he is somewhere between his two *Hobbit* co-stars. He is somewhat active on Instagram, and although he has an official Twitter/X account, he has not used it in several years. However, in 2021, he opened a Cameo account (discussed in detail in Chapter 9). In these ways, O'Gorman is accessible via social media.

With respect to para-communication, O'Gorman has participated in science fiction conventions and, through his appearances there, has established the kind of person he is with fans who follow him. The question-and-answer sessions at conventions allow fans to interact socially with their favorite actors, but it is still only in rare instances that the parasocial-to-social line is crossed.

One fan had this to say (posted on a public blog): "I've met him, and he is very humble and sweet, remembers fans' names, he's a bit cheeky and very lovely. He

Figure 4.4 Dean O'Gorman (left) with Aidan Turner.
Source: Jaguar PS/Shutterstock.com.

has beautiful eyes, and I adore him. He is fun to be around and made me laugh." A second fan told me (personal email) the following:

> I met Dean O'Gorman, along with a few other male actors from the new show *Young Hercules* when I attended a *Xena* convention in Burbank in the late 1990s. It was 20 years ago, and he must've been in his early 20's at the time. I don't remember exactly his responses when I spoke to him, but I was left with a feeling of friendliness and intelligence. I was also struck by the idea that these guys were gobsmacked that anyone actually watched the show! I am still a fan of Dean's decades later.

These fan quotes represent parasocial perception, the impression the individual fan has that the celebrity is engaged in a positive and interested way in the fan base, and these quotes are representative of the ways fans talk about him on public Facebook message boards dedicated to his career. In the interview with O'Gorman presented in Chapter 9, he indicated he is well aware of the part he plays in creating beloved characters, recognizing his need to "stand in" for the character when he realizes what the fan really wants is to meet that character. Hartmann (2008, 2023) talks about "authenticity," and it reflects authenticity for an actor to recognize the desire of the audience member to "meet" a beloved character and step in for that character, in a sense, extending the original performance. This is part of what happens when actors create their half of the PSI. Bob Picardo (*Star Trek: Voyager*) mentioned something similar with respect to his *Star Trek* character and received requests to re-create him on Cameo (interview in Chapter 9).

All three of these *Hobbit* actors (Armitage, Turner, and O'Gorman) have a positive parasocial perception, meaning that those who post on actor-specific message boards believe that the actor behaves in a way that reflects care and respect. O'Gorman has a quote on his IMDB page, similar to one already mentioned: "To be honest, I really enjoy the chance to meet the fans because I've found with '*The Hobbit*,' the fans are all really lovely and enthusiastic."

Also discussed in Chapter 9 is O'Gorman's participation on Cameo, a media service that reaches out to fans. Cameo is a way that a fan or audience member can send a message to a celebrity for a fee (fees range from $5 to $1,000) and receive a personal video response. Always eager to learn about new ways of para-communication, I sent O'Gorman a question on Cameo and asked him his preferred way to interact with fans. He responded that he really likes the conventions and being interpersonal with fans but that during the pandemic, Cameo had been a good way to talk to fans when international travel was not possible. He indicated that social media was not a very interpersonal way to interact with fans and something he did in limited amounts.

Another unique service that actors can provide via Cameo was suggested to me by O'Gorman. Someone can send him a request for a birthday greeting, pep talk, or special message, and by virtue of his familiarity as a celebrity, he is able to greet the fan in a way that is personal to that fan without having to know the individual personally. Particularly if it is the favorite character that the fan wants to "meet," the celebrity can fulfill that request in a fun and individual way. The message is special and exciting because it comes from someone with whom the fan already has a PSR. The irony is that the relationship is still parasocial. The fan is no more "known" after the video exchange than before, but the greeting is still intimate and tailored to the fan and, therefore, special.

Chapter 9 has a much more extensive discussion of Cameo and also science fiction and fantasy conventions and the ways that fans can use these to connect to their favorite artists.

All three *Hobbit* actors Armitage, Turner and O'Gorman, have stated that it is a personal goal to keep their private lives separate from their public celebrity lives, and they make decisions about social media use with that goal in mind. For Turner, that has meant no social media at all, and he quite articulately explained his reasoning on the subject on Sky News (United Kingdom) on January 30, 2023:

> I don't have social media; I don't do Twitter or anything like that. I would give myself a wide berth on a lot of things like that, sharing ideas instantly online about things like that, I don't think I've ever really done it. So yeah, I avoid that kind of thing at all costs. I think the more you share, the more people know you, the harder the job gets to convince people that you're these characters. You're very very exposed to everyone and everyone knows intricate details about your personal life. It gets a little bit hard. Some air of mystery might be a good thing with actors.

O'Gorman has the already mentioned occasionally active Instagram account, as does his wife, and they have shared some personal items, such as pictures from when their daughter was born or photos of trips they've taken, but his activity overall on social media is very minimal. I have already discussed Armitage's social media use, but he is active on both Twitter and Instagram, where he regularly updates fans on his professional activities, using social media in a manner common to public figures who use it to share about their work (Stever & Lawson, 2013).

CONCLUSION

Parasocial interaction, parasocial relationships, and parasocial attachment are all concepts that historically have been explored more thoroughly from the point of view of audience members than the point of view of the media figures who have been engaged as parasocial objects (Hartmann, 2008). In this chapter, I have presented several examples of artists' engagement with the audience in a way that speaks to the possibility of authentic parasocial perception on the part of audience members. This is important because it challenges the notion that audience members who engage in PSRs are somehow "out of touch" or that parasocial theory represents audience members in a derogatory way, insinuating they are deluded or living with an illusion of an engagement that is not real.

In the area of audience studies, occasionally there have been conflicts among scholars who view fan behavior as a natural kind of participation in a normal creative community (e.g., Jenkins, 2012). This is in contrast to some psychologists and sociologists who have talked about fans in terms of celebrity worship, erotomania, or stalking (Ferris, 2001, 2007; Maltby et al., 2003; McCutcheon et al., 2003), putting forth the idea that even fan letters represent a form of abnormal behavior (Dietz et al., 1991). That PSRs the fans have with artists are more typically represented by the former rather than the latter description is important when assessing the impact of artistic and entertainment media on the audience. That is not to say that people with problematic interests don't exist, as they certainly do. It is rather a matter of a balanced perspective and an understanding that PSRs and related concepts describe the majority of the audience who are using entertainment media as a normal social activity that enhances the day-to-day lives of participants.

Understanding the cultural impact of this kind of social activity going forward, parasocial perception and para-communication (or EPSI) are important constructs that need to be added more extensively to the body of research on PSEs.

5

Parasocial Aspects of Social Relationships

DAVID C. GILES ■

Once upon a time, communication scholars divided the world into two groups: media producers and media consumers. Unless you believed that television was populated entirely by an alien race, you would be willing to concede a small, shaded crossover patch in the Venn diagram, but the patch was never large enough to significantly influence communication theory. The notion of the parasocial fitted this model well—well enough for communication scholars and social psychologists to rarely critique the concept of "media figures" lined up on one glamorous side of the divide and "media users" permanently exiled on the other.

With the arrival of digital culture, the shaded crossover patch has expanded to a point where the overall model of producers and consumers is no longer fit for purpose. To be fair, the patch was growing before social media arrived. The "ordinary" stars emerging from audience participation media such as makeover shows (Giles, 2000, 2003) were already troubling the boundaries by the 1990s. And then came reality TV. In the first decade of the present century, media scholars were talking about the "demotic turn" (Turner, 2010): "the increasing visibility of the 'ordinary' person as they have turned themselves into media content through celebrity culture, DIY websites, talk radio and the like" (p. 2).

After that came, respectively, Facebook, YouTube, and Twitter. The fusing of the producer and consumer in social media has even led some scholars to argue that *persona*, rather than celebrity, is the key concept for contemporary culture (Marshall et al., 2020). The emergence of the microcelebrity (Marwick, 2013), a figure that occupies a liminal position somewhere between traditional celebrity and popular socialite, has broken open the divide to the extent that the original definition of microcelebrity (typically, a tech expert with approximately 50,000

Parasocial Experiences. David C. Giles and Gayle S. Stever, Oxford University Press. © Oxford University Press 2024.
DOI: 10.1093/oso/9780197647646.003.0006

Twitter followers) has had to be radically extended to capture the enormous range of different positions that new forms of celebrity now occupy (Giles, 2018).

The impact of digital culture on audience theory is discussed more generally in Chapter 7, but here I focus specifically on its implications for parasocial theory. If parasocial relationships (PSRs) were really only unreciprocated psychological constructs, one obvious response would be simply to abandon the concept of the parasocial altogether in light of recent technological developments. This is pretty much what Marwick and boyd (2011) had in mind when they declared the parasocial "redundant." What practical use is a concept devised in line with an archaic communication model?

In this chapter, I make a case for keeping the parasocial at the forefront of media psychological theory in the 21st century. This is partly because it addresses the general phenomenon of audience–media figure relationships more adequately than any rival concepts (identification, celebrity worship, and so on, which are really just subconcepts within the parasocial). But it is also because digital culture has drawn attention to the shortcomings of the way the parasocial has been conceived in the literature, hampered by the obsession with psychometric testing and measurement. It has been further constrained by the assumptions of long-standing sender–receiver models of media, and in relation to the psychological literature, these are typically explained as social cognitive events expressed in individual behavior.

I argue here that parasocial interaction (PSI) constitutes a fundamental aspect of social psychology, of more interest to social science than simply a "media effect." Through the work of John Caughey (1984), we can identify throughout history the importance of largely unreciprocated relationships with distant figures that play an important function in society. With reference to social psychology and cultural studies, we can rethink the role that imagination plays in ordinary social relationships, even intimate ones, and rethink some of our taken-for-granted assumptions about the boundary between the self and the other. I start by considering a little-explored topic, the presence of media figures in our dreams, before moving on to more general ideas about the role of cultural materials in psychological life.

WHAT IS DONALD TRUMP DOING IN MY DREAM?

I was in a bar having a drink with a couple of school friends when we were approached by a familiar-looking older man who invited us to his apartment to meet some women. We accepted the invitation (out of character, I hasten to add . . .) and wound up back at his place, where the promised women failed to materialize. Or maybe the alarm clock went off at an inopportune moment. The most memorable thing about this dream was that the sleazy character was none other than the (then) President of the United States, Donald Trump.

As an English academic with only a handful of stateside visits, mainly for conferences and doctoral supervision, I have never had the pleasure of meeting

Mr. Trump in person, and so he remains for me a media figure, someone whom I have seen on numerous occasions in pictures and on video, and whose voice I have heard on news bulletins and documentaries. I feel I know enough about him to have a broad assessment of his character, worldview, beliefs, and values. Combined with his status as the leader of the world's most powerful nation, it is fair to say that Donald Trump is a significant, albeit minor, figure in my waking life. In accordance with Michael Schredl's continuity hypothesis of dreaming (Schredl, 2018), which states that dreams are mostly consistent with waking experience, he is an eligible candidate for an appearance in one of my dreams.

Dreaming is a good laboratory for the investigation of PSRs. It is beyond the conscious control of the individual. Therefore, seemingly rational distinctions between the people we "know" and those we "think we know" are not available, and the dreaming brain can select randomly from the assortment of faces and identities stored in memory across the lifespan (Grenier et al., 2005; Vallat et al., 2017). Continuity theory would predict that the more meaningful the media figures are in our waking lives, the greater the likelihood they will be represented in our dreams.

Despite a large amount of dream research in recent years, there remains little exploration of media content, still less of media figures in particular. In a general sense, media consumption influences dreams in that frequent usage of specific media and media content is reflected in the content of dreams (Moverley et al., 2018). With specific reference to the characters populating the dreamworld, a single case study of one dreamer found that celebrities were present in 4.7% of that individual's dreams and constituted 2.7% of the overall dream characters reported in their dream diaries (Schredl & Schweickert, 2022). Celebrities usually appeared in isolation from other characters, suggesting that they might be represented cognitively as a different category of person.

However, this reading would not be supported by two older studies specifically focused on celebrity dreams. One is reported by Caughey (1984) and consisted of a qualitative analysis of dream diaries compiled by American adults involving different kinds of figures. Media figures appeared in more than 10% of the dreams recorded and often assumed different roles from the ones they occupy in reality. While in one dream, for example, The Who singer Roger Daltrey invites the dreamer on tour with the band, in another, Ronald Reagan is a mere passenger in a car who vanishes unaccountably, and in still another, a woman who may or may not be Goldie Hawn ends up having sex with the dreamer. Caughey argues that dream figures, whether or not they conform with their actual roles, "seem to have internalized American social structural expectations and rules" (p. 92) in that their interactions with the dreamer "are meaningfully patterned by the dreamer's enculturation into a particular system of knowledge" (p. 92). This suggests that the details belonging to dream figures (whether faces, bodies, roles, or identities), unless shaping the dream's narrative, may be largely superficial, perhaps plucked randomly from our store of remembered persons of all kinds. So, Goldie Hawn's face and figure were selected from any possible number of desired figures in the dreamer's memory for the purpose of a sexual desire fulfillment dream.

Similar findings were obtained in a study of dreams carried out by Alperstein and Vann (1997), who began by asking their sample of undergraduate students (also in the United States) whether they had ever dreamed of media figures. More than half of the participants reported doing so, although in a separate analysis of their dream diaries, media figures were only mentioned in 8% of the dreams recorded, slightly lower than Caughey's (1984) figure. Irrespective of the sex of the dreamer, these figures were overwhelmingly male, although females tended to dream about actors and musicians, whereas males often dreamed of figures from sports and politics. In a few cases, the dreamer actually *was* the media figure in question (because these were mostly male dreams, in accordance with their prevalent figures, they were perhaps dreaming of being a top footballer or president).

Like Caughey (1984), Alperstein and Vann (1997) found that media figure status is often altered in dreams, making the point that PSRs are experienced as social ones: "Rather than keeping their social distance or becoming involved in media centered interactions, the media figures represented in the dream reports become a part of the dreamer's everyday social world and in that, their everyday social interactions" (p. 150). They also echoed Caughey's claim about media figures conforming to the interests and expectations of the dreamer so that a young celebrity might give advice to a young dreamer in a way that would seem inappropriate for an older one. An example from my own dream history would seem to fit this pattern. At the time of the dream, Joe Root was the captain of the England cricket team, although as a young sportsman, he would perhaps be unlikely to feature in my social circle. Instead, I dreamed I was giving his mother a lift in my car. (It is not entirely unlikely I would know someone whose child was a successful sporting figure.) I have not knowingly seen Joe Root's mother on television or in a picture (notably in the dream, she was in the back seat), but indirectly, Root himself, one of several players whom I have enjoyed watching play cricket on television, worked his way into the dream via a socially congruent narrative.

Alperstein and Vann (1997) cautioned that there might have been an element of expectancy bias in their survey results. (Wouldn't we likely agree that we dream of celebrities but then fail to report them in our actual dream accounts?) Perhaps most of us have *had* a media figure dream at some point, albeit not many. If the random selection theory holds, then perhaps we would only expect to retrieve a parasocial figure now and again. They also suggested that people may be more likely to report media figure dreams because they are memorable or distinctive. Or possibly they are more likely to *remember* them in the first place, which might account for the high incidence in the survey?

The dreamworld is important for the other theories of human relationships discussed in this chapter precisely because it is beyond cognitive control and therefore allows access, as Freud himself might have argued in today's language, to the unregulated cognitive representational system in which PSRs are coded indistinguishably from social ones. We might think of this as a simple "media effect," but in dreaming, we can see how mediated and immediate experiences are unseparated so that media figures slip seamlessly into the dreamer's social memory.

MEDIA FIGURES AS FAMILY MEMBERS AND FRIENDS

Given that media figures are significant social presences in our lives, how do we make sense of them? This is a topic that has rather foxed media psychologists over the years because if we adopt a purely rationalistic standpoint, PSRs are illogical and potentially embarrassing. This embarrassment emergences at certain points where we are "found out," notably when experiencing bereavement emotions following the death of the media figure. After the death of Princess Diana, the BBC website set up a forum ("message board" in the techspeak of the era) on which visitors could post personal tributes, and a number of them expressed surprise at the psychological impact. "I am a fairly hard-nosed cynic," wrote one, "but tears came despite that." Another described herself as "a happy, well-adjusted woman," and yet "I couldn't stop crying and I didn't know why" (Giles, 2003).

Other people seem to experience little discomfort in forming close PSRs. Most notably, self-confessed fans are those who happily embrace the meaningful presence in their life of a distant "other" who is not a friend, acquaintance, or relative. As I will argue later in this chapter, it is a psychological commonplace to incorporate remote figures into our lives and to grant them a status equivalent to that of our other intimate relationships. They range from imaginary childhood friends to the objects of adolescent "crushes" and to fantasy role models that can shape our decision-making throughout the lifespan, either overtly (as fan objects) or, more subconsciously, as "social ghosts"—inner voices advising the self (M. Gergen, 2001).

I start by considering the work on fandom that has explored the meaning of celebrities (typically musicians) on fans at different stages of their lives because these studies give an insight into the positions in our social network that media figures can potentially occupy. The first point to make is that fans, contrary to various stereotypes often perpetuated by the media themselves, encompass all manner of different types of people. Erika Doss's (1999) study of Elvis Presley fandom focused in part on the extraordinary diversity of Elvis fans. As with Henry Jenkins's (1992) work on *Star Trek* fandom, one of the tasks confronting early academic studies of fandom was the deconstruction of media (and traditional academic) portrayals of fans as irrational, disturbed, and socially inadequate. One of Doss's interviewees commented, "I often wonder why the media take pictures of the people who wear all these Elvis buttons and take it to excess but bypass the professor of law who's also an Elvis fan" (Doss, 1999, p. 53).

Fan Objects as Family Members

Although Doss (1999) dwells on the tireless collectors of Elvis memorabilia and those who perform their fandom within a quasi-religious frame, the most interesting comments from our perspective come from those fans whose relationship with Elvis is expressed "in familial terms—as kin, as blood" (p. 12). "It just seems like he was part of my family," says one. Another describes her extended bereavement reaction to Elvis's death, while Doss suggests that for many fans—and this may well extend to other celebrities—the bonding experience of Elvis signing autographs, talking to fans, and posing for pictures with them felt like being drawn into his broad family circle, as "one big Elvis family" (p. 12).

The question of whether fandom and PSRs might fulfill individuals' social needs is a slightly vexed one, in part because it can be used to reinforce the old stereotypes of fans as socially inadequate. Nevertheless, we can scarcely regard the bereaved, the childless, or the single as "inadequate," and it is these individuals who are perhaps most likely to attach to media figures to compensate for those missing or incomplete parts of the social network. In this way, fandom reflects voluntary kin networks in the way that extended families "adopt" members in order to plug perceived gaps (Braithwaite et al., 2010). One fan of the singer Morrissey described him as "the brother I never had, the father figure I always longed for and the friend I always wanted" (Maton, 2010, p. 185).

The compensation function of the parasocial also applies to situations in which life changes result in either the individual or their relatives moving away from one another. In a study of Michael Jackson fans, one middle-aged woman described her passion for Jackson explicitly in these terms: "I . . . see Michael as . . . a replacement for the children I miss so much. Michael is another child . . . I can't mention Michael and my children in the same sentence without crying" (Stever, 2009, p. 23).

Fan Object as Soulmate or Kindred Spirit

In the same way as the fan object might substitute for absent kin, they may provide the fan with a close friend when, for whatever reason, it has been difficult to form that kind of relationship. Singer–songwriters often appeal to fans in this way not only because of the intimacy of the recorded voice, but also because their lyrics allow them access to deep-rooted values and feelings that often resonate with the listener. Through these, the musician/poet communicates directly with the fan. "It was so comforting to know that I wasn't the only shy, awkward person in the world," wrote one Morrissey fan. "I felt Morrissey really understood me" (Maton, 2010, p. 184). For a Bruce Springsteen fan, the singer "seems to ask many of the same questions I find myself asking about the world" (Cavicchi, 1998, p. 40).

Of course, media figures are much more than just soulmates. They are successful people and often give the impression of having succeeded against all the odds. Although not personally identifying as a member of a sexual minority, one David Bowie fan was inspired by the artist's unusual step of coming out as gay to the music press early in his career. "He has the sort of image that says, 'Come on, stand up for yourself. Be yourself.' He gave me confidence. He was brave, in 1972, to do what he did and has always been one step ahead" (Stevenson, 2009, p. 92).

Some of the Bruce Springsteen fans interviewed by Cavicchi (1998) express their admiration for the artist transcending his working-class roots to become a global superstar, even if they do not identify directly with his background. One said,

> He's definitely been in a process, as we all are in our lives, of growth. . . . He's older than I am, he's from a different socioeconomic background than I am, and he's certainly in a different one now, in many ways, but nonetheless, there's this connection. (p. 142)

An interesting retrospective case of kindred spirit fandom comes from Sue Wise (1990), a teenage Elvis fan who rejected him as an adult in the context of her lesbian sexual identity but subsequently acknowledged that he constituted an important link to her teenage years:

> As an adolescent I had been a very lonely person, never feeling that I fit in anywhere, never "connecting" with another human being. . . . Elvis was . . . another human being to whom I could relate and be identified with. When I felt lonely and totally alone in the world, there was always Elvis. He was a private, special friend who was always there, no matter what, and I didn't have to share him with anybody. He was someone to care about, to be interested in, and to defend against criticism. (p. 397)

Although she had moved on from Elvis by the point of his death in 1977, Wise nonetheless "was surprised at how much his death touched me" (p. 394), and in revisiting her adolescent "scrapbooks . . . clippings, cuttings, and photos . . . the overwhelming feelings and memories were of warmth and affection for a very dear friend" (p. 395).

Fan Object as Friend

Our lives are populated with figures who, without necessarily ever being close companions, enrich our social experience. Friends come and go for all manner of reasons. Even after decades of absence, we can still find ourselves thinking about them, and if they loom back into view, we can rely on our memories of their former selves to evaluate them and compare ourselves with them. Media figures play a similar role. A Bowie fan says, "It's interesting to watch how he's grown. You know he had his second child. You can tell he is happy, but not always. You can watch him through different periods" (Stevenson, 2009, p. 84). This could be an old friend with whom we swap cards at Christmas. There is continuity without any particular strength of feeling.

Just as we remain loyal to former friends, long-term fandom relies on a degree of trust. "I'm sort of ambivalent about the Greatest Hits album," states a Bruce Springsteen fan questioning the wisdom behind what might be regarded as a cynical commercial venture. "On the one hand, it does not say anything artistically, but on the other hand, I look at Bruce as an old friend whom I trust and grant a lot of latitude. So, I say if he wants to do this it is fine with me" (Cavicchi, 1998, p. 85). But trust has its limits, even with PSRs. Morrissey has divided his large fanbase over the years, not only due to the merit (or otherwise) of his later work but also because of repeated controversial statements on race and his apparent support for certain far-right political groups or figures (Giles, 2013). For many, it is simply unacceptable, and after one particular incident, a member of his online fan site compared Morrissey to a "friend who I had once loved [who has] betrayed me." Another expressed their growing alienation from the singer: "After 25 years of being a fan, it's a bit like a marriage that slowly disintegrates over time. You just slowly stop caring" (p. 125).

Fan Object as Mentor or Adviser

Finally, there are fan objects who perform a role that is analogous to a former teacher or mentor. Because of the trust implied through fandom, the figure becomes a reference point to guide one's reactions to a particular phenomenon (a current news story perhaps) or toward a personal dilemma. This was particularly noticeable in Cavicchi's (1998) interviews with Springsteen fans. One claimed that the singer, being a few years older, was "a little bit ahead of me and providing me with some important information" (p. 129). Another, on hearing Springsteen sing about a failing marriage, "taught me a lot of some of the pitfalls that I ought to be looking out for" (p. 129).

And the guidance may not necessarily be for the fans themselves. A female Springsteen fan was able to relate to his negative experiences in the workplace and then advise her partner accordingly:

> I dated my husband for four years while he worked there [*an arduous factory job*] and "Factory" [*LP track*] clearly prophesied his future if he stayed there hating every minute of his job. The image invoked by the song was all too real. Anyway, when my husband (fiancé) confided that he wanted to be a cop, I decided we'd do whatever it took to get him out of that hellhole. And that's what we did. (Cavicchi, 1998, p. 130)

These various accounts from the fandom research demonstrate that fans discuss their heroes as if they were a significant part of their wider social circle, exhibiting at the same time the functions of close relations (such as family members, with whom we may not always agree but to whom we are nonetheless tied permanently) and remote friends (who may no longer be part of our social network but still exert a long-term influence for the qualities we value in them). But at what stage in our lives do these physically distant figures acquire these meanings for us?

PARASOCIAL RELATIONSHIPS IN CHILDHOOD

Children are an important sounding board for studying parasocial phenomena because, like dreaming adults, they lack the inhibitory rationalizing biases that constrain our conscious behavior. In addition, the contemporary child's social relationships emerge in parallel with their initial encounters with media, and this offers an interesting test case for the negotiation of intimate and remote interaction. They are not the best population for psychometric research, however, and probably for this reason, they have been somewhat neglected in the parasocial literature.

One of the earliest studies to explore children's relationships with media figures was by Hodge and Tripp (1986), who took a semiotic approach in which "modality"—the apparent reality of a message—was a central concept in explaining children's understanding of television. Children between the ages of 6 and 8 showed a preference for "low modality" figures on television, such as cartoon characters, whereas those in the 9- to 12-year-old age group were more likely to select "high modality" figures, with more than half of these choosing characters from TV drama (i.e., fictional humans). For the authors, modality judgments are made by identifying which characteristics of a character or situation are naturalistic, so a voiceover, or "canned" laughter, reduces the modality of a show, as do obviously artificial processes such as animation.

This work closely parallels the more general research on children's understanding of media within a developmental psychology framework (e.g., Wright et al., 1994). For example, following the stages in cognitive maturation proposed by Piaget (Piaget & Inhelder, 1969), changes in PSRs reflect the child's increasing sensitivity to the psychological complexities of people in general (Bearison et al., 1982). The shift from one-dimensional cartoon characters to human figures with more fully realized personalities is commensurate with the increased social cognitive abilities of the older child.

One might argue that these shifts in preference are largely dictated by the range of media figures that are offered to children at different ages. There is a chicken–egg conundrum here in that media producers would no doubt argue that age-appropriate figures are generated in response to the "natural" preferences at different stages of cognitive development. However, the settings and plots in which those characters are embedded will also be influenced by the perceived interests and abilities of the developing child. The plot (and other features) of a short cartoon allows for much less character development than a 20-minute drama episode, irrespective of "modality." Market segmentation also influences things like broadcasting schedules so that school-age children will watch a different selection of programs than preschoolers, potentially losing touch with earlier favorite characters (Bond & Calvert, 2014). Therefore, changes in preference for media figures may be hard to disentangle from other aspects of media usage.[1]

It is worth considering some of those aspects in more detail, especially in television aimed at the youngest audience. Preschool shows have long been designed specifically to engage audiences directly, such as the BBC's *Play School*, which, when introduced in the 1960s, took the deliberate step of using human presenters who addressed the viewer as an individual (Jackson, 2010). In most preschool programming, the viewer is invited to say hello, wave, dance, sing, and generally imitate the presenters and characters on the screen. As Briggs (2007) claimed of the 1990s BBC show *Teletubbies*, "The text is structured to encourage parasocial interaction" (p. 15).

It has been suggested that the earliest PSRs emerge from this direct interaction (Bond & Calvert, 2014). Not only are toddlers addressed directly by figures on the screen but many popular characters are reproduced and widely sold as puppets, or "plush toys," thereby maintaining the PSR away from direct media use as the toy enters into the personal play sphere in the child's home (Briggs, 2007). This is by no means a recent phenomenon. My favorite toy as a young child was a glove puppet representing the popular UK children's character Sooty, who not only appeared weekly on TV in the 1960s but maintained a double existence in my imaginative games. He had his own modest home (in the town of Sootyville, no less) and enjoyed relationships with other toys and puppets in the same subjective play world.

I couldn't say that I necessarily *learned* anything from Sooty, who was habitually rather poorly behaved, yet the idea that early PSRs might be instructional has been investigated by U.S. developmental psychologist Sandra Calvert and colleagues for more than a decade, with some interesting results (Calvert, 2017). The typical study paradigm in her work involves a media character carrying out some kind of "seriation" task (e.g., putting different-sized cups in a specific order) and testing how well the watching children perform the same task when provided with the materials. An early study in this series found that children younger than 2 years were able to reproduce the task when they had seen it performed on screen by a well-known character (Elmo from *Sesame Street*, correctly identified by 90% of the sample) (Lauricella et al., 2011). When the same task was modeled by an unfamiliar puppet, performance was significantly worse.

Might there be something special about Elmo that encourages children to follow his instructions? Certainly, some of the study participants had cuddly Elmo toys at home and had clearly built a PSR through watching him regularly on TV, and this prompted Calvert's team to try to manipulate a relationship with the unfamiliar puppet. In a second study, the children were given a representative cuddly toy to play with for 3 months, encouraged by parents, and at the end of this period, they saw the same task performed by the character on screen (Gola et al., 2013). However, overall, the children did not perform significantly better on the task than a control group. Only when footage of the children's play with the cuddly toy was analyzed did any single variable predict better performance, and this was the demonstration of "nurturing" behaviors with the toy (putting it to bed, feeding it, etc.). The authors concluded that these activities allowed the children to form an emotional bond with the character that made them more receptive to its instructions in the test phase.

Parasocial Aspects of Social Relationships

These findings suggest that it is quite hard work for researchers to engineer PSRs with children. An alternative explanation for the apparent superiority of Elmo in these studies is that the unfamiliar puppet lacked a context that was provided by regular viewing of *Sesame Street* and, in some cases, repeated encounters with Elmo in other media, such as games, books, toys, and websites. Another important factor is parental encouragement, which Bond and Calvert (2014) found to be the strongest predictor of strong PSRs for younger children. Briggs (2007) has argued that PSI involves more than simply responding to the onscreen figure and that media figures are integrated into a "play frame" by the children along with co-viewing adults and siblings, who may also encourage responses like waving and even kissing the onscreen character. He argues that this play frame sets children up for a lifelong engagement with fiction (which might relate to the phenomenon of "transportation") and is further reinforced by parenting literature encouraging joint participation in children's media (Briggs, 2006).

Parental influence has also been identified as a factor contributing to the breaking up of childhood PSRs, especially when an early PSR is no longer deemed appropriate for the child's current age (Bond & Calvert, 2014). In addition to parents and older siblings, peers begin to influence PSR choice as media figures enter into playtime conversations. As the child develops a more sophisticated understanding of human relations, social realism becomes an increasingly important factor. This is the extent to which media figures resemble people in "real life" or could potentially exist in the child's actual social network because they possess realistic qualities (Aguiar et al., 2019). Eventually, children may also begin to select media figures that represent an idealized self or aspirational role model, and "wishful identification" has been identified as a significant determinant of PSR intensity in the 7- to 12-year-old age group (Hoffner, 1996).

The Fantasy–Reality Distinction: A Blind Alley?

Much of the literature on children's understanding of television has been based around the idea that there is a gradual and linear relationship between cognitive maturation and the ability to distinguish between "real" media content and that which is clearly unreal or "fantasy." In many ways, Hodge and Tripp's (1986) "modality" concept follows in this tradition, whereby color is always more "real" than black and white. Children's explanations of television have often been dismissed as fantastical. For example, there were claims made about people onscreen being miniatures who were lowered into the set on a rope (Gunter & McAleer, 1990) or that an onscreen box of popcorn would spill out of the set if tipped upside down (Flavell et al., 1990). Notably, adults are never asked how the images are generated, nor how the electronics work to produce moving pictures, and it is likely that our own accounts are scarcely more sophisticated, at least for those of us with limited expertise in physics.

In recent years, however, there has been an increasing awareness among researchers of the limitations of the fantasy–reality distinction, especially given the implications it carries for pathologizing religious belief. As with God and other divine figures, we have to consider the importance of ritual in media use (Kapitány et al., 2020), as well as the child's (and adults') commitment to the fantasy narrative. This latter point is most pertinent in relation to the persistence of belief in culturally endorsed figures such as Santa Claus, the Tooth Fairy, and the Easter Bunny, along with many other such mythical figures in different parts of the world.

Santa Claus is a particularly interesting figure because so many elements of the Santa narrative are inherently contradictory, from flying reindeer and the significance of fully operative chimney stacks to the ubiquitous presence of department store or shopping mall Santas. Although these phenomena may be far removed from children's personal experience, research tends to put the "discovery" of Santa's ontological status at consistently more than 7 years old (Kapitány et al., 2020; Prentice et al., 1978). One might argue that this is the age at which parents are most likely to expect children to grow out of their childish beliefs, yet Bunce and Harris (2008) found that belief seemed to persist even in children as old as 12 years, irrespective of parents' promotion of the Santa myth. They concluded that cognitive maturation might be a better predictor at this stage, although two other possibilities exist: peer influence and sheer dogged determinism. Maybe the allure of the myth is powerful enough to resist the pressure to conform to adults and even to peers.

A further interesting feature of the Bunce and Harris (2008) study is the children's assessment of store Santas, who were widely dismissed as "not the real Santa" even when the child believed in the basic tenets of the Santa myth. This apparent contradiction is only surprising from the point of view of a realist ontology. Like the inner workings of TV, the believing child does not feel compelled to provide a formal logical explanation for how their presents get from the North Pole to their 10th-floor apartment. Clearly, the store Santas are usurping interlopers, mere Elvis-style impersonators whose inspiration, indeed like Elvis, need not be physically encountered to be fully authentic.

Imagined Others and Imaginary Relationships

The literature on imaginary friends has a surprisingly long history, suggesting that it is a robust psychological characteristic and is little influenced (at least in Western cultures) by cultural and technological changes over time. Perhaps partly for this reason, it has rarely been studied in conjunction with parasocial phenomena, with one exception (Gleason et al., 2020), which I return to later in this section.

There is some ambiguity in the literature about what constitutes an imaginary friendship, and most researchers prefer to use the term imaginary companion (IC). But this umbrella term often fails to differentiate imaginary friends, or invisible friends (IFs), from puppets, "plush toys," or "stuffed animals," which are in turn labeled "personified objects" (Taylor, 1999; Yamaguchi et al., 2023). In the latter instance, the companion itself is a tangible object that the child invests with imaginary characteristics, such as speech or personality. The overall prevalence of ICs varies according to the definition used by researchers and by the characteristics of the research population, but a British study using an unambiguous definition of an IF ("a friend that nobody else can see") found that almost half of their sample of 5- to 12-year-old children reported having had one at some point (Pearson et al., 2001). When the same question was asked of young adults, the incidence was slightly lower, but at 41%, this still exceeds earlier studies focusing on younger age groups (Fernyhough et al., 2019). When toys and other figures are included as ICs, the incidence can be as high as 60% (Majors & Baines, 2017).

What psychological function is carried out by imaginary figures in childhood? The literature suggests as diverse a range of benefits as actual friendship. Imaginary figures are cultivated, it seems, for just about everything other than reciprocal activity. Early studies tended to dwell, like much PSR research, on the compensatory, or "deficit" hypothesis (Seiffge-Krenke, 1997), which argues that IFs usually emerge after some kind of loss, typically an actual friend or family member, and may vanish when suitable "real" companions become available (e.g., Myers, 1979; Nagera, 1969). However, these studies were based on clinical samples rather than the general population, and when explored in a wider population, the picture becomes more complicated, again mirroring parasocial research. A more recent study (Yamaguchi, 2023) found no correlation between having an IC and loneliness. As with PSRs, the IC may well be a supplement as much as a substitute.

The most commonly cited function of an IF is to provide the child with a "very special friend" (Seiffge-Krenke, 1997) who may take on a number of different roles depending on the age, imaginative skill, circumstance, or specific psychological needs of their creator. For younger children in particular, IFs are valued for their support in difficult situations—for instance, keeping them company in the dark (Davis et al., 2023; Majors, 2013). They are, above all else, trustworthy companions who are unable to betray secrets (sometimes, they are secrets themselves) and can serve as an outlet for voicing concerns that would be difficult to divulge to other family members or actual friends (Majors, 2013). They may act as advisors or mentors in times of uncertainty (Hoff, 2004–2005). This was certainly the case in the diary-writing study of Seiffge-Krenke (1997), in which many of the adolescent participants addressed their diaries to an imaginary figure, typically female (irrespective of diarist gender). And many entries in one the most famous diaries of all time—Anne Frank's diary—were addressed to "Kitty," particularly when discussing awkward topics such as sexuality (Dalsimer, 1982).

Certainly, IFs take the form of a great variety of different figure types. In Majors' (2013) interview study of 5- to 11-year-olds with ICs (some based on actual toy figures), the small sample included invisible versions of actual friends, a selection of horses that had been previously encountered on holiday, a whole imaginary family, and even the spirit of a late grandmother. More generally, IFs may take on the child's characteristics (age, gender, social background) or act as a complete contrast (Hoff, 2004–2005). Some are inspired by fictional figures, even exotic ones (Jalongo, 1984). Despite the diversity of figure types, they all seem to fall roughly into the company/adviser role discussed above.

The lack of any longitudinal research on IFs makes it difficult to say whether the IFs take on these roles over time or are specially created to address existing needs. One recent exception is Davis et al. (2023), in which a group of 4- to 6-year-olds was encouraged by the researcher (and the children's parents) to generate IFs over a period of several months. No child resisted this proposal, and over the course of the 36-month study, the IFs gradually assumed the same functions as those of a comparison group of children who had previously existing IFs. The one main difference between the groups is that the researcher-elicited IFs were mostly animal in nature. As with the similar PSR-generated study mentioned previously (Gola et al., 2013), one must note that the role of the parents in encouraging and interacting with the respective generated figures could be a significant factor (and, of course, the design rules out the potential for creating fully secret IFs, whose typical creation may reflect family dynamics). One of the few studies of IF prevalence in non-Western populations suggested that parental discouragement may explain some of the cultural differences observed, both within and between different parts of the world[2] (Wigger, 2018; see also Taylor & Carlson, 2000, on opposition to IFs in some religious Western families).

In the same way that PSRs sometimes function as glamorous or exaggerated alternatives to real friends, IFs offer their creators a playmate who cannot challenge their proposals, violate rules, or simply spoil the child's games or activities (Hoff, 2004–2005). However, they may be far from perfect, suggesting the need for a degree of social realism to maintain the authenticity of the relationship. Imaginary horses can be just as stubborn and noncompliant as real horses (Majors, 2013), and Taylor (1999) reports some very interesting cases of IFs who stalk their creators, turning up when least welcome and causing trouble. These case studies suggest that IFs can be more than just useful foils for discussing personal matters and may (at least in some instances) have some other kind of psychological function. Some authors have suggested that IFs are simply imaginative devices for accomplishing some of the "developmental tasks" of childhood (Majors, 2013). These include the development of self-knowledge (particularly around interior aspects such as dreams, feeling ill, and having fun) and the development of private speech (Davis et al., 2011, 2013).

Given the great diversity of different imaginary companions, it might be difficult to identify a precise developmental function that they perform. The function may simply vary according to the needs of the individual child. In this way, IFs or ICs do not seem to be all that dissimilar to PSRs. However, the direct relationship between the two phenomena has been little studied. One exception is Gleason et al. (2020), who asked a sample of adolescents about their childhood imaginary activities (friends, companions, among other things) and found only minimal associations with PSI scores relating to a favorite celebrity or character. Furthermore, high levels of imaginary practice in childhood were characteristic of stable parental attachments (at the time of the study, i.e., in adolescence), whereas PSI scores were, as in some other adolescent studies, associated with anxious attachment. From this result, given the type of data collected, one can only conclude that people do not, as a rule, cultivate one special imaginary figure as a young child and then replace them, like for like, with one special media figure on entering adolescence.[3]

But why do children eventually abandon their imaginary companions? Again, the data are somewhat limited, with earlier clinical studies following the deficit hypothesis, suggesting that the IF disappears along with the psychological need that inspired it in the first place. For example, a lonely child will instead acquire a real friend (Nagera, 1969). Some more recent research suggests that ICs may still be present even in adulthood. Fernyhough et al. (2019) found that 7.5% of their adult sample reported having imaginary friends, although few details are provided. In a study of Japanese undergraduates, Yamaguchi et al. (2023) found that up to 14% of young adults reported some kind of IC, most of these "personified objects" (toys), but that 3% had imaginary friends with human-like appearance.

The company of a teddy bear or other childhood figure is not entirely unusual in adulthood, although often associated with eccentricity, as in the case of Evelyn Waugh's Sebastian Flyte in *Brideshead Revisited*. A recent article in the British newspaper *The Guardian* (Linton, 2022) contained the reports of several adults who were firmly committed to their cuddly toys, mostly childhood companions that had clearly not outlived their social roles (including even a blue ribbon), although one 64-year-old man had purchased his current favorite teddy while in his 20s. As with imaginary diary addressees, there are clearly some functions of imaginary figures that cannot simply be attributed to development unless we argue that the "task" itself has gone unaccomplished.

In terms of individual differences in ICs, one suggestion is that people with ICs are more likely to have "anthropomorphic tendencies" than others (Tahiroglu & Taylor, 2019; Yamaguchi et al., 2023). This is an interesting idea, not least because research on children's evolving PSRs with conversational agents seems to suggest that anthropomorphism plays a significant role in the degree to which children bond with voice assistants like Alexa and Siri (Hoffman et al., 2021). However, the measures of anthropomorphism in these studies are somewhat limited. (For example, the participants in Tahiroglu and Taylor's [2019] study took part in a task in which anthropomorphism was built into the design rather than spontaneously generated by the children.)

Probably the most well-known recent theory of anthropomorphism is that of Epley et al. (2007), which argues that it is a cognitive tendency resulting from certain conditions. Young children anthropomorphize freely after they have acquired knowledge about human nature generally (e.g., emotion concepts), so all kinds of nonhuman and inanimate objects will be ascribed to human characteristics. This tendency diminishes over time and might seem to map onto the findings of Hodge and Tripp (1986) and others that children gradually shift from fantasy and animal PSRs to human ones. In older children and adults, according to Epley et al. (2007), anthropomorphic thinking tends to resurface in times of social need and in relation to the characteristics of the nonhuman object (i.e., the more human-like the animal, the more likely they are to invite human comparison).

90

That ICs are more generally a characteristic of early childhood than adolescence or adulthood would seem to be consistent with Epley et al.'s (2007) theory. However, the association with social need is rather more contentious. Epley and colleagues have tended to use loneliness (typically a psychometric scale) as a measure for social need, and indeed, in an undergraduate sample, they found that people rating high on the loneliness scale were more likely to use uniquely human concepts to describe their pets (Epley et al., 2008). Other studies (e.g., McConnell et al., 2011) have not replicated this finding. Another found that anxious attachment was a better predictor of anthropomorphism than loneliness (Bartz et al., 2016). And, according to the literature on IFs, neither loneliness nor anxious attachment seems to be a necessary condition for their creation.

What does seem to be the case with both ICs and PSRs is that they serve a variety of very specific social needs that cannot necessarily be captured in psychometric research in a general population. Unfortunately, much of the recent literature on anthropomorphism stumbles, once again, into the "deficit hypothesis" trap by treating it as what the critic John Ruskin (1857) referred to as the "pathetic fallacy" of ascribing human emotions to nonhuman objects. Ruskin's original usage targeted the overly sentimental tendencies of Romantic poets such as Wordsworth, but he did not suggest that the practice arose as the result of cognitive deficit. Clearly, poets, when referring to clouds as lonely, are not doing so for any of the reasons specified by Epley et al. (2007). And, maybe, neither are IF-creating children or doting pet owners, however sentimental.

The most profitable application of anthropomorphism to the current discussion is perhaps an older theory in which Fisher (1991) distinguished two different types: situational and imaginative anthropomorphism. The former is perhaps closer to what Epley et al. (2007) are describing: an unconscious attribution made either through naivete (childhood labeling of nonhuman objects) or, indeed, genuine deprivation (an older adult, perhaps, lacking all company, save for a dog or cat). Imaginative anthropomorphism is a different matter. It may be inspired by social need. A recent trend in Latin America is for child-free adults to refer to their pet dogs as *perrhijos* (a blend of *perro* and *hijo*[4]) (Moctezuma, 2019). Alternatively, it may just be a creative form of play or, in the case of Wordsworth, wordplay. Even in Epley et al. (2008), anthropomorphic "cognition" was fundamentally a matter of which adjectives participants selected to describe their pets. We return to these issues in Chapter 6, in which we consider the significance of narrative and storytelling in relationship building.

The Role of Fantasy and Imagination in Social and Parasocial Interaction

A reader writes to *The Guardian*'s agony aunt, saying she has been married for 20 years but has recently discovered that her husband was unfaithful to her within a year of their relationship (Barbieri, 2015). She concludes, "I am devastated, not just about the infidelity . . . but more about the careful deception that persisted for so long . . . all this makes me doubt the whole basis of our relationship."

In this section, I shift the emphasis from using the imagination to generate new or alternative relationships toward the role it plays within traditional, face-to-face social relationships. We tend not to think of these as, in any way, "imaginary," but the number of cases of deception and betrayal reminds us that our everyday social interaction relies heavily on what we *think* about the people around us, including—perhaps especially—those we love and have loved for many years.

And we are more than happy to feed those fantasies. In (U.S.-based) studies of everyday lying, more than 90% of participants admitted to having lied to a romantic partner (Cole, 2001), and all of us tell one or two lies every day (DePaulo et al., 1996). Lies may be self-serving, making one appear something one is not, or they may be "other-oriented," enhancing or protecting others (from embarrassment, disappointment, and so on). They may simply amount to the omission of certain details or exaggeration (of remorse, etc.). The latter type of lies is most typically told in female circles and might be thought of as "kind lies" to spare others' feelings (DePaulo et al., 1996), although as Goffman (1959) argued, lies are an integral part of the liar's self-presentation. Kind lies may be fundamentally a way of presenting oneself as kind.

In close relationships, lying has been described as a "social lubricant . . . between partners and their thoughts" (Cole, 2001, p. 108), but interestingly, we tend to believe it is we who are the liars: In Cole's study, most of the participants considered their partners to be less deceptive than they were. Of course, we may never know how true this is. What the lying research fails to consider, however, in focusing largely on the liars and the nature of the lies themselves, is that lying works in close relationships because the imagination plays such an important part in holding them together. We do not believe the other is as good a liar as we are because if we did, we would probably end the relationship. Like *The Guardian* reader quoted above, it would undermine everything we have hitherto believed about our partner.

IMAGINED INTERACTIONS

While a lie might arise spontaneously from the lips of a practiced liar, most of the tactical lies described above are the product of careful planning. To craft a kind lie, we need a script, an imaginary dialogue in which we rehearse our lines as well as anticipate the responses of the other person. This kind of social cognitive imagery has been discussed for some time as part of the planning function of social relationships, what Duck (1986, p. 83) describes as "out-of-interaction fantasy." In recent decades, this kind of cognitive work has been extensively studied by James Honeycutt and colleagues as "imagined interactions" (Honeycutt, 2003).

Imagined interactions (IIs) have been found to address a number of functions: compensation (for absent friends, partners, and so on); catharsis (as a way of relieving anxiety); relational maintenance (just thinking about the absent partner and potential conversation with them); and conflict linkage, where people ruminate about past grievances in relationships (Honeycutt, 2008–2009). As with tactical lying, IIs enable us to prepare for significant conversations—proposals of marriage or separation, the introduction of problematic material, or simply projecting potential reactions to suggestions. Although the research has tended to concentrate on the individual cognitive functions of IIs, they do appear to be associated with relationship quality in that people with high relationship satisfaction report having more and higher quality IIs and people high in loneliness tend to have poorer quality IIs (Honeycutt, 2003).

These findings suggest that maintaining a relationship may rely substantially on the imagination. When separated from our loved ones, we are often imagining how they would react to the things we are seeing and doing. I might see a beautiful sunset and think how much my partner would appreciate it, so I send her a photograph. If we have had an argument, I might think about the most tactful way of apologizing (even if I don't think it's my fault) or what kind of gesture might restore the peace. When I read a news story, I wonder how she (or any other friend with an interest in the topic) might react and send them the link. In each case, this requires some form of II, not necessarily a fully fledged conversation but some kind of hypothetical exchange between myself and the other person.

If IIs are important for maintaining relationships, one might suggest they fall into the broad realm of "social skills" that are learned during childhood. And indeed, it is argued that young children are more likely to develop imaginary companions if they have siblings (Honeycutt et al., 2011–2012), implying that it is through the mental rehearsal of sibling interactions that the imaginative skills are developed that enable the creation of the IC. The same researchers found that ICs of all kinds were more likely in children who play with dolls and other personified objects, likewise suggesting a creative function in the rehearsal of imaginary conversations. It has also been argued that these imaginary activities allow young children to plan successful conflict resolution at an age when their negotiation skills are undeveloped (Gleason, 2017).

The application of II research to parasocial theory seems obvious, although there is surprisingly little of it in the literature. One exception is the work of T. Phillip Madison and colleagues, who have adapted the Rubin et al. (1985) PSI scale to reflect II (typical item: "I imagine interacting with X"). Madison and Porter (2016) gave this scale to an American undergraduate sample and found that the most common type of II with a favorite TV character was "retroactive," which they interpreted as viewers reflecting on dialogue from the show involving that character and inserting themselves into the text. Subsequent research focused on IIs with specific media figures: Donald Trump and right-wing conspiracy theorist Alex Jones (Madison et al., 2021, 2022). IIs with Trump seemed to have a cathartic function, whereas conflict-linkage interactions with Jones were associated with low credibility: Those who found themselves arguing with him were less likely to endorse his beliefs, which is hardly surprising.[5]

Another aspect of IIs, not seemingly visited in its literature, is the interaction we have with figures from our past, some of whom may no longer be alive. These are not necessarily "retroactive" IIs like the ones reported above or rumination of the conflict-linkage type but, rather, "compensation" IIs of various types. I often think

Parasocial Aspects of Social Relationships

about how my parents, both long dead, would behave in certain situations: how they might interact with my son or react to stories in the news. They flit about my subconscious like benign spirits—which brings us to another concept, that of social ghosts, discussed in the next section.

Social Ghosts and Other Spectral Entities

The idea of "social ghosts" (M. Gergen, 2001) partly derives from the work of Mary Watkins (1986), whose "invisible guests" consist of "imaginal dialogues" conducted with any number of addressees—a photograph of a lost loved one, God, a pet, a movie character, or even with other facets of the self. These dialogues are *imaginal*, not imaginary—they are not immature, pathological, or superstitious; indeed, some of my contribution to this book is the product of dialogue with my own imaginal conversational partner (typically, a radio or TV interviewer: "So how's the book coming on, David?") before finding its way into prose. And what is the act of writing but a dialogue with you, the imaginary/imaginal reader?

M. Gergen (2001) has taken this idea a step further in her theory of social ghosts and studied how these dialogues function in a sample of young adults. Of the 76 participants in her study, only one was unable to identify a social ghost of any kind. For the remaining 75, 37% of these "ghosts" were former partners or friends, 23% were relatives (the largest group being fathers, but covering a full range of relations), 11% were former teachers, but 29% were figures that the participant had never actually met, and the large majority of these (80%) were described as "entertainers."

In terms of the functions of these dialogic partners, many of them acted as social models that the individual used in order to deal with a particular situation: "I try to face the problem as he did, despite criticism from others" (M. Gergen, 2001, p. 138). Contrary to claims that such figures simply substitute for "real" interaction, Gergen found that these social ghosts tended to improve people's social competence rather than hinder it. At other times, they help us form attitudes (although typically reinforcing attitudes already held) or provide emotional support ("My grandmother seems to be watching me and showing that she loves me even if I am not doing so well" [p. 139]). In only a small minority of cases did the ghosts perform a negative role, typically inducing guilt (What would Dad think of my behavior?, etc.).

It is striking, in many ways, how closely this account resembles those of PSRs, particularly Alperstein's (1991) qualitative study of celebrities appearing in advertising, where people made similar comments regarding the significance of media figures in their own lives. One participant described how he tried to make his character like Bill Cosby's; another how she relied on TV presenter Joan Lumsden for advice on pregnancy and childcare. It is unfortunate that such rich studies of parasocial encounters are scarce in the literature and that even these tend to be based around the immediate act of media use, but they point the way forward.

SELF–NONSELF BOUNDARY

In the final section of this chapter, I bring together the various practices of fantasy and imagination with various theories of the self that have articulated the role that other people, real and imaginary, play in constructing our self-concept. The idea of the bounded, unitary self has long been critiqued from an epistemological point of view as a concept peculiar to the industrialized West and contrasted with the relational, socially embedded self of traditional societies such as Java and Bali (Geertz, 1973; Sampson, 1988). As Kenneth Gergen (1991) has pointed out, technological developments do not necessarily reinforce the idea of the bounded self; indeed, devices such as voicemail (a relatively recent development in the 1980s) have enabled us to exist in several different spaces simultaneously, and recording technology, in general, allows our unitary, bounded self to split into many different representations across time and space. Harré's (1983) earlier concept of "file selves" made a similar point about print culture, seeing, for example, a job application as performing a representative function for the self in absentia (i.e., while our prospective employer is reading it, they are effectively interacting with us at the same time as our bounded, physical self is out shopping or sitting around waiting for that hoped-for invitation to interview).

Of course, Gergen and Harré wrote in the 1980s and 1990s, and since then, global society has undergone one or two changes. In Chapter 3, we focused on the historically unique challenges of social media, but we must not forget the similarly unique impact that audio and visual recording in the 20th century would have had on human psychology. And nobody will have felt its impact more keenly than global superstars, who found themselves, through the various media of vinyl, magnetic tape, and digital reproduction, splintered into millions and millions of tiny pieces and disseminated throughout the world for years to come.

The profound consequences of recording were discussed in an essay on Elvis by cultural scholar John Frow (1998), who, in the context of religious parallels with fandom, examined the way that recording techniques, such as dubbing one vocal track onto another in the studio, immortalize their subjects by taking them far away from the original performance. "The real person of Elvis is always and from the beginning a copied person, the authenticity of which derives from the fact and the extent of copying, of representation, rather than anything that precedes it" (p. 205). The proliferation of Elvis impersonators, Elvis sightings, and Elvis shrines makes perfect sense in this light. "The absence of the recorded star, their presence as recording, is the reason why the worship of stars is a cult of the dead" (p. 205).

Other concepts from social psychology relate to the idea that, if not quite on the scale as an Elvis figure, our "selves" contain rather more than the standard set of body parts and personality traits that tend to make up the individual subject of much scientific enquiry. First is the suggestion that the self contains significant others, typically romantic partners but potentially anyone who has made a substantial psychological impact on us (Aron et al., 1991). Evidence for this claim, including its cross-cultural validity, rests largely on the inevitable panoply of psychometric instruments, but the central principle is that we actively seek out relationships which expand the self or at least have the potential to explore new horizons (Aron et al., 2022).

This idea fits comfortably with sociologist Cornel Sandvoss' (2005) description of fandom as an extension of self. He argues that the fan object is not an external entity but, rather, "intrinsically interwoven with our sense of self, with who we are, would like to be, and think we are" (p. 96). As one Bruce Springsteen fan said of his relationship with the singer, "I feel very much like it's a shared journey" (Cavicchi, 1998, p. 40). The concept of the extended self embraces all kinds of fan objects, typically texts (e.g., movie franchises, TV series) rather than individual people. It is not always clear whether the psychological attachment of a fan to an individual is different from that toward a film or series, a sports club, or even a musical group. While each fan object will contain at least one significant individual, such as a favorite character, sporting hero, or musician, the primary attachment is to the unified object itself.

If we consider the fragility of the boundary between self and other, the distinction between the social and the parasocial continues to blur. Just as our future selves are invested in the close relationships we take up, particularly in early adulthood, so they determine the parasocial attachments. This is not a simple matter of fame by association (although that undoubtedly enters into it as well) but is about the use of other people—known and remote—to fashion the persona. We see this in a number of the studies discussed previously in the chapter in relation to imaginary friends and dreams of celebrities, in which the imaginary or external figures merged with the self so that the imager or dreamer became one with the figure. This was particularly true of the children studied by Taylor (1999). Unlike the girls, who created their imaginary companions for company, the boys tended to "impersonate" theirs, including media figures such as Batman, especially where the imaginary figures possessed different characteristics to the child. This kind of fantasy play enables the child to experiment with an alter ego, effectively trying out different possible selves (Hoff, 2004–2005).

Later in life, we are able to incorporate these alter egos into our personal identity. We *become* our media interests and fan objects. In Nick Hornby's autobiography *Fever Pitch* (1992), in which he tells his life story in parallel to the fluctuating fortunes of his favorite football team, Arsenal, there is a very telling passage. Near the book's end, he reflects on his fandom and its meaning to him. He comes to the conclusion that his connection to Arsenal operates as a kind of fame-by-association through which people from his past are permanently anchored to him:

I like the thought of people remembering me on a regular basis . . . you know that, on nights like the '89 championship night, or afternoons like the afternoon of the Wrexham 1992 disaster, you are in the thoughts of scores, maybe even hundreds, of people. And I love that, the fact that old girlfriends and other people you have lost touch with and probably will never see again are sitting in front of their TV sets and thinking, momentarily but *all at the same time*, Nick, just that, and are happy or sad for me. (pp. 194–195, emphasis in original)

The same point could be made by fans of all manner of other kinds of objects, including people. And as well as providing a touchstone for distant friends and acquaintances, the fandom also connects you to your immediate social network, so someone might call or message you to see how you are feeling in the wake of an Arsenal game, a favorite TV show, or news story featuring your favorite celebrity. One of Cavicchi's (1998) Springsteen fans discusses how the singer is incorporated into his identity in the same way as a sports team or any other hobby or pastime, without being treated as an irrational obsession:

My friends accept my affection for Bruce's work and my interest in his life. They know I have other interests, and my world in no way revolves around the life of a popular musician I have never met. My coworkers know that he is my "hero" in many respects, and they accept "The Shrine" as part of the "Far Side" cartoons, *Star Trek* trinkets, and pithy quotations that decorate my work space. (p. 141)

In *The Culture of Narcissism*, Lasch (1991) talks about how the mass media era has produced a "theatre of everyday life" in which ordinary individuals perform as if on stage for an imaginary audience. We select our most flattering characteristics and parade them in front of other people in order to create the best impression (Goffman, 1959). If doing so involves incorporating the verbal tics and gestures of famous people, it is no different from modeling ourselves on admired members of our immediate social circle. If it involves direct reference to famous people or objects—as in explicit and deliberate expressions of fandom—this can also enhance the impression, as long as the audience holds a favorable attitude towards the fan object.

A number of authors have investigated the way in which we perform for imaginary audiences. In one experiment (Baldwin & Holmes, 1987), participants were asked to generate images of known individuals (either peers or older family members) before reading a "sexually permissive" story, and those in the peer-imagery group gave the story significantly higher ratings. The authors concluded that their responses were unconsciously fashioned with the primed audience in mind, assuming that the older family members were likely to disapprove of the "permissive" content. Both Bakhtin (1986) and Shotter (1995) have argued that all our spoken utterances are designed with a third party in mind, who "stands above all the participants in the dialogue" (Bakhtin, 1986, p. 126).

Who is this "third party"? We know that the fashioning of the self has a long history. Foucault (1988) talks about the "technologies of the self"—those activities we undertake in order to "transform [ourselves] in order to attain a certain state of happiness, purity, wisdom, perfection or immortality" (p. 18). He traced this back to Christian practices, the cultivation of the self that would be judged most positively by God. I am not going to suggest that something—the mass media, or any part of it—has simply come along and replaced God as the "imaginary audience," but the practices live on. We are forever finding new materials for fabricating a better self.

6

Psychoanalytic Theory and the Parasocial

DAVID C. GILES ■

THREE UNANSWERED QUESTIONS IN MEDIA PSYCHOLOGY

I want to begin this chapter by revisiting some psychological assumptions that underpin much research and discussion in media psychology yet have not really been opened up to scrutiny and so hover unseen in the background, inviting accusations of "pathologizing" from skeptical fan scholars and others:

1. *Fantasy–reality confusion?* When people sent raincoats to Granada Studios, asked for the Lonesome Gal's hand in marriage, berated a show's actor for their character's scripted behavior, or requested medical advice from an actor portraying a doctor in a soap, were they mad? Is it fair to see celebrity bereavement experiences as the result of a failed ability to distinguish fantasy from reality?
2. *Source monitoring dysfunction?* The illusion of knowing: "Springsteen was reading my mind." Do EPSI respondents really believe that the girl in the video is aware of them?
3. *Where do parasocial relationships (PSRs) come from?* The emergence of PSRs in childhood is part of the child's initiation into media culture, but at the same time, as discussed in Chapter 5, they are shaped by relationship development more generally. Far from being toxic aliens poisoning vulnerable minds, media figures are understood in the context of the child's social awareness, which in turn will depend on their existing model of relationships.

Parasocial Experiences. David C. Giles and Gayle S. Stever, Oxford University Press. © Oxford University Press 2024.
DOI: 10.1093/oso/9780197647646.003.0007

I will argue that these assumptions persist in media psychological theory because we lack the theoretical tools to do them justice. Communication has relied for too long on correlational methods, the legacy of individual differences research in psychology, which, powered by the technological wizardry of SPSS, has outpaced our understanding of tricky, less measurable phenomena such as emotions, language, and relationships. Today, it seems that the only level of explanation that is necessary is a fiendishly complicated network of boxes and arrows linked together by coefficients that boast significant "fit" with a predicted pattern of boxes, arrows, and coefficients. Rather than having a basis in theory, however, the predicted pattern typically derives from the existing literature, which is amassed on the various components of the model and based mainly around box/arrow/coefficient patterns than any coherent psychological theory.

For this reason, communication science has often reproduced the problems of personality science, where theory follows data, a process that qualitative researchers would call "grounded theory" (Glaser & Strauss, 1967). Yet the latter tradition at least relies on raw data—interviews and field notes—rather than psychometric scales, themselves already abstracted and refined to the extent that they no longer capture actual behavior but, rather, a set of truncated and idealized "statements" that respondents have no option other than to evaluate on the researchers' chosen dimension (typically, "positive/negative," "true/untrue," and so on). Finding the way home to actual media experiences through this labyrinth of statistical operations is near impossible, so we are mostly forced to travel in a perpetual loop, forever developing psychometric scales that promise to improve or diversify unsatisfactory existing scales instead of stopping, reflecting, and, if necessary, restarting the whole journey.

The point I am making with this very broad assault on contemporary research methodology is to identify the reason for the blockage in the literature on these unanswered questions in media psychology. So, let's stop, reflect, and perhaps go back a bit. How can we find a way out of the labyrinth?

IN DEFENSE OF PSYCHOANALYTIC THEORY

I am sure that some contemporary psychologists, browsing the contents of this book, might balk rather on seeing that there was a chapter on psychoanalytic theory. In the era of neuropsychology, structural equation modeling, and the theory of planned behavior, a psychologist went back to Freud to try and explain media audiences, for goodness' sake? Penis envy, Oedipus complex, and all that unscientific, speculative, outdated rubbish? Clearing their throats, they put the book to one side and wonder why we didn't just come up with a new psychometric scale instead. . . .

. . . And yet, it is striking how often one ends up going back to Freudian ideas and their subsequent modifications and extensions because there is really nothing in the psychological canon, neurocognition and all, that takes us to the places we want to go. We can't ask babies what it's like to enter the world. If behavior is driven by unconscious desires and motivations, how far can we rely on the self-report methods of social cognitive theories, which currently account for the vast majority of research in social psychology? Sure, you can't open up the brain and look at the psyche or the superego, but try finding the mind . . .

Outside academic psychology, in which the twin doctrines of experimental methodology and multivariate statistics constrict notions of what counts as "science" and "research excellence" (not to mention "impact"), psychoanalytic theory is still where most scholars find their answers to psychological questions. Researchers in the humanities find it baffling that it is not the cornerstone of academic psychology, never mind a discredited chunk of its past that has largely been phased out of the undergraduate curriculum (Redmond & Shulman, 2008). Film, media, and cultural studies programs all typically offer courses in Freud or Lacan while simultaneously railing at psychology's penchant for "pathologizing" eccentric, colorful, or otherwise inexplicable behavior. It is also undeniable that outside the academy altogether, Freud remains the sole identifiable figure who has made any kind of impact on popular culture, to whom we owe such everyday practices as the symbolic interpretation of dreams, the "Freudian slip" or unguarded comment revealing hidden ("unconscious") truths, the identification of defenses such as "denial" and "repression" and of personalities that are "anal," never mind the entire therapy industry. Freud's fingerprints are everywhere in our language and belief system—everywhere, that is, apart from psychology itself. I appreciate that a record does not necessarily become a number-one hit on merit, but in Freud's case, there is no real chart to top. Even as late as the present century, no other psychologist had generated as many citations in either journal articles or introductory textbooks, Freud leading the list by a long way (Haggbloom et al., 2002). Research scrutineers seeking "impact" would do well to consider how little public awareness is achieved through measurable, short-term "interventions." Real impact that takes root in the culture and shapes our belief system takes time. Freudian theory has percolated slowly through the 20th century, while thousands of massive panel studies with structural equation models showing significant fit have whizzed below the radar of everyone except the scrutineers.

There is, of course, intransigence on both sides. The supporters and proponents of psychoanalytic theory have not helped the situation by insisting on the rigorous interpretation of the sacred, original texts and on the absolute purity of the therapeutic process. That's not what Freud/Lacan/Klein said! You've misread/misinterpreted them. Lacan is difficult because he's difficult, don't try and water him down! Stuck in a perpetual labyrinth of their own, the ideas of most of the post-Freudians have resisted appeal beyond their fetishization in cultural studies and certain obscurantist quarters of critical theory (Billig, 2006).

In the remainder of this chapter, I investigate what psychoanalytic theory has to say about the social and psychological life of the individual that could make a contribution to the parasocial literature. In doing so, I intend to deliberately misread, misinterpret, and water down Klein, Lacan, and other difficult writers in order that their ideas can reach beyond small, esoteric circles and be adapted to form new theoretical pathways that connect with the parasocial literature as it currently stands. While the psychometric test creators continue their peregrination around the statistical labyrinth, are there concepts that offer us a glimmer of hope in making sense of the unanswered questions about fantasy, reality, imagination, and experience?

TRANSITIONAL OBJECTS AND MEDIA

The concept of the transitional object (Winnicott, 1971) has informed much of the more serious academic work around fandom, and so this would seem a good place to start in applying psychoanalytic theory more specifically to parasocial phenomena. Of course, fandom is a broad field, and most of the fan objects that scholars have investigated are primarily textual objects rather than social ones. There is, nonetheless, considerable overlap. Most of the texts that generate intense fan followings are fictional (think of a cult TV series here), and so there will be many character relationships embedded in the fandom. It seems reasonable to assume that one's fascination with, say, the Harry Potter franchise will incorporate a few PSRs, not least with Harry himself.

The transitional object (TO) is, for Winnicott (1971), a material entity, jealously possessed by the child in its first 2 years of life, which seems to represent something, typically the absent caregiver. The archetypal TO is a "comfort blanket" or teddy bear—not just any old blanket or teddy at hand, but a cherished object into which considerable emotion and attachment are invested to the point where its disappearance causes great distress. Winnicott suggests that all kinds of objects can fulfill the same psychic function, even pieces of string or the child's own thumb. The core idea is that the object represents a "third area" in the child's experience that is both "me and not-me" and constitutes a mechanism by which the child can enter into the "whole cultural field . . . the external world as perceived by two persons in common" (p. 5). It is transitional because, at some point, the TO will lose its meaning. The favorite teddy will be cast aside as the child begins to invest their emotional energy in cultural pursuits (which might include art and religion, for instance).

Winnicott's ideas, following the earlier work of Klein, were based almost entirely on the observation of play with toys provided by the clinicians, and there is little, if any, consideration in the psychoanalytic literature of how media might fit into the picture. This is where the fan scholars and cultural scholars come in. One of the earliest applications of the TO concept to media was made by British media sociologist Roger Silverstone, who suggested that in infancy, the television set functions as a TO, especially when used as a "babysitter" while the caregiver is otherwise occupied (Silverstone, 1993). Here, the TV is no longer a mechanism for entering the cultural field; it gives direct entry to it. And, importantly, it is no longer transitional; it is permanent.

Television, at least in the broadcast tradition, bound us into a lifelong series of rituals and relationships that connect us to the broader society. News bulletins and weather forecasts function as essential processes for monitoring the social and physical environment. Like the child's lost teddy, our inability to procure a signal back in the broadcast era was a source of distress. On the road or in a TV-free setting, we felt lost, out of touch. The feeling of returning home, switching on the set, and reconnecting with the cultural field reflected a lifelong dependency that has, of course, now been upgraded to a continuous dependency on mobile media. The smartphone is the contemporary, nontransitional object whose disappearance is the cue for existential agony.

Silverstone's use of Winnicott was later developed by fan scholar Matt Hills, who suggested that the Winnicottian TO is gradually exchanged for more mature TOs as the individual moves across the lifespan and that fan objects are best thought of as secondary TOs in the way they occupy the "third area" (Hills, 2002). In this sense, Hills updates Winnicott's relationship between the individual and the cultural field in a way that levels culture out, allowing fandom to perform the same psychological function as more supposedly lofty cultural pursuits. (Naturally, Winnicott did not have cult TV series in mind when formulating his theories.)

At this point, one might wonder how this relates to PSRs, given that Winnicott's TOs are, first and foremost, physical objects as opposed to relationships. Alternatively, they might symbolize relationships (typically, the absent caregiver). But Winnicott, following Klein, sees all relationships as extensions of objects, modeled on the template of the infant's earliest encounters with, most important, the caregiver's body (the mother's breast[1] and the nourishment it supplies). This is the object relations tradition of psychoanalytic theory (Frosh, 2012). Because object relations theory collapses all people and their component parts into a single category of objects and allows one type of object (say, a thumb or rag) to stand for another (the absent caregiver), it offers us a potential way out of the fantasy-reality binary that has constrained thinking around the parasocial.

In this way, PSRs can themselves be thought of as both primary and secondary transitional objects. Over time and in most cases, children outgrow their initial PSRs and embark on new, more age-appropriate PSRs, with the process continuing on in this vein through adolescence and into adulthood. As the seminal work of Hodge and Tripp (1986) found, children have a tendency to proceed from an interest in fantasy or animated media figures toward real people or fictionalized human characters, and this maps closely to the suggestions of both Winnicott and Hills in explaining how children use this "third area" of the "me-and-not me" as a means of entering the cultural field of the external world.

THE ELSEWHERE AND THE OTHER

One of the cognitive challenges young children face in forming PSRs is the ability to negotiate "the elsewhere" (Jovchelovitch et al., 2017). Psychoanalytic theory has focused on the child's immediate relationships, partly because most of its core ideas evolved before the era of mass media but also because the concept of a relationship, beyond that of simple dependency, needs to be acquired through the experience of family life and other childcare settings. Relationships are formed by repeatedly encountering the same individuals and establishing patterns of regular and predictable interaction with them. Although similar patterns emerge through media use, these need to be assimilated into a context that the child is able to recognize (at least in relation to TV) as a process known as "tele-literacy" (Bianculli, 2000).

Jovchelovitch et al. (2017) define "the elsewhere" as a core element of the child's developing representation of the public sphere and their awareness of how they fit into wider society and culture in the broadest sense. Although surprisingly overlooked in their work, media clearly play a significant role in this process, and the emergence of attachments to remote figures, from fantasy characters to young YouTubers, reflects a growing awareness of how media occupy a third area. A television set or iPad is experienced initially as part of the home environment, as part of the household furnishings even, but over time the child soon learns to make the connection between the images and their ontological existence (e.g., that an anchor on BBC children's TV is a real person in another, external, place that is somehow captured by the digital image and made locally available).

So deeply engrained are media devices in the contemporary home environment, one is tempted to put them on a par with mirrors as significant domestic objects in helping children—and even perhaps adults—form their sense of self. The mirror has long been featured in developmental theory for its affordance as a self-recognition tool (e.g., Bertenthal & Fischer, 1978), enabling the child to demonstrate visual familiarity with their body as part of a general cognitive maturation process. In psychoanalytic theory, it is most commonly associated with the writing of Lacan (1949/2006), for whom the "mirror stage," from 6 months onwards, constitutes a significant process in the child's (illusory) developing concept of the integrated self. Although the passing of the "rouge test" (typically around 18 months) is often taken to be the point at which self-recognition occurs, subsequent research has suggested that the infant is capable of self-recognition as early as 4 months (Rochat & Striano, 2002), casting doubt on the "Aha!" notion of sudden enlightenment.[2]

For Lacan (and others), the reflection in the mirror functions as an external representation of the individual self, making them aware of their socially embedded nature and reinforcing the idea that their selfhood is essentially an external phenomenon. The person, or ego, is constituted by its relation with others, formed through language (as I will go on to discuss), and the sense of integration that one receives through the mirror image is fundamentally different from that which I perceive as the subject. This is how *others* see me. In this way, the external image in the mirror can be equated with the child's ego (Frosh, 2012).

Of course, even in the postwar decades when Lacan was writing, there were plenty of other externalizing technologies available to proliferate images of the self, the photograph being a notable example. And today, the ability of any smartphone owner to produce multiple high-quality video recordings means that infants have a vast array of self-representations available to them that could fulfill the same purpose as a mirror. Research on children's self-recognition on video (Bahrick et al., 1996) supports the later mirror findings, suggesting that children as young as 3 months are able to distinguish themselves from peers (or at least, they seem more interested in video footage of peers than themselves, and this is interpreted as familiarity with the self-image). In the many microcomputers operated by parents and siblings in contemporary daily life, this self-recognition process takes place among video footage of many other individuals, known and unknown offline, all of whom are available as models for self-comparison and, potentially, instruction.

One of the problems with most of the standard developmental research on mirrors and self-recognition in infancy is that, as with parasocial interaction (PSI), it generally treats the individual as entirely disconnected from the social world. It is perhaps no coincidence that the rouge test, usually not passed until well into the second year of life, has attained the status of a pivotal moment in self-recognition because it is at this stage that the child is able to draw themselves up straight and observe themselves alone in the mirror. During the first year, mirror recognition can only be done with the assistance of the caregiver. Inevitably, the first face recognized will not be that of the child but of the parent or person who is holding them up to the mirror. This point was made by Lacan when he suggested the image of the parent constituted what Freud called the ego-ideal, whereas the image of the child becomes "the root stock of secondary identifications" (Lacan, 1949/2006, p. 76) or the "ideal-ego."

These two constructs are fundamental to the development of the self in Lacanian theory. They represent two forms of the Other: the ideal-ego, which grows out of the externalized image of the self, roughly corresponding with Freud's ego, and the ego-ideal (Freud's superego), which grows out of the externalized image of the parent, the model to which the child aspires. Lacan represented these as two objects, one small (*objet petit a*, where "a" stands for *autre* or other), and one big (*A*), what we might call the big Other (Lacan, 1973/1994). As the child grows, these objects can be "embodied" by other subjects through the process of identification, in most cases, figures that are appropriate for each function of the ego. So, the "small other" might be an elder sibling whose habits are worth adopting, whereas the "big other" is the parent we are trying to impress by doing so. As we grow older, the big other expands to include institutions and practices beyond the home—laws, religion, ideology—that regulate and constrain our growth as an individual. Meanwhile, the small other will incorporate any number of potential models from different parts of society.

The basic idea of the elsewhere, or the Other, is not so different from Winnicott's "third area." In each case, there is an attempt to explain how the infant starts to form a sense of themselves as part of a culture or wider society that transcends the immediate domestic sphere of early childhood. Clearly, we need to upgrade these concepts with reference to technological development, as even radio or television barely gets a mention in the original work.[3] It is at least a starting point for formulating theory around the origins of the parasocial and its incorporation into our social life. At this point, however, we need to think about how the process of *identification* might operate in the generation of PSRs.

IDENTIFICATION WITH THE OTHER

In Chapter 10, we consider identification as a rival explanation of audience–media relationships by considering its application in the media and communication literature. As with celebrity worship, however, one might also consider it a contingent process in relation to the parasocial: PSRs emerge out of initial identifications (and in a handful of cases go on to involve "worship"). It is not as if some media figures remain permanently "identified with" in the absence of any kind of PSR. Ultimately, it is a matter of endurance. In the humanities, identification has long been treated as the primary process by which spectators form relationships, albeit temporary ones, with film characters, and before parasocial researchers started drawing distinctions between PSI and PSR, it was the interaction itself that was being distinguished from identification in TV viewing (Cohen, 1999; Giles, 2002).

But what *is* identification exactly? Most definitions derive in some part from Freudian theory, citing concepts like the Oedipus complex, where the (male) child is expected to "identify" with the father because of sexual jealousy toward its mother (and end up hating/fearing the father as a consequence). But there are various versions of identification in Freud's work, and it seems he primarily settled on what we typically understand as identification, as taken from his 1922 work, *Group Psychology and the Analysis of the Ego*, in which he argued that it arises out of any kind of jealousy. The mechanism is essentially rivalry, whether it is competing against father for mother, other children in the schoolroom, or even, in one example, fellow fans of a musician. Yes, we find the first psychological analysis of fandom in Freud (1922)! How do we come to "identify" with rivals in the heat of jealousy? Freud argued it was a matter of not losing face; that, given the hopelessness of attaining the desired object (mother, teacher's praise, the musical star), hostility would be counterproductive. Female fans of a male performer (this being Freud's example) "act as a united group, do homage to the hero of the occasion with their common actions" (Freud, 1922, p. 16).

At the same time as identifying yourself with rival others, identification plays an important role in creating the superego, or ego-ideal, around the time of the Oedipus complex. Here, the identification is with parental virtues and their expectations of the child. Later, the parent can be replaced by other individuals, namely teachers, other relatives, and important authority figures. But the form of identification is different here. Freud (1922) gives the example of the army, in which the ordinary soldier takes his general as his ego-ideal, although his immediate identification is with his fellow soldiers. As stated, "he becomes ridiculous if he tries to identify himself with the general" (p. 134). These two positions correspond, more or less, to Lacan's later distinction between the ego-ideal (big Other) and ideal-ego (small other) as captured in the mirror of infancy.

Ironically, when identification was picked up as a mechanism for explaining media–audience relationships in the postwar era, it was through the lens of behaviorism, specifically observational learning. Maccoby and Wilson (1957) argued that "the viewer, in fantasy, puts himself in the place of a character, and momentarily feels that what is happening to that character is happening to himself" (p. 76). Significantly, they go on to claim, "He does reproduce covertly many of the elements of the behavior including the *emotions* he attributes to the character" (p. 76). This echoed popular concerns of the time that movies were triggering an increase in violent crime in the United States, particularly among adolescents, and therefore identification with film protagonists was a worrying trend. As the authors claim, however, this mechanism is only able to explain temporary identifications (and, presumably, refers to fictional characters rather than the actors who portray them).

A hugely influential essay by film scholar Laura Mulvey (1975) made a somewhat different reading of identification in order to develop a feminist account of the way cinema reproduces predominantly male desire. Here, Mulvey drew explicitly on Lacan's (1949/2006) mirror theory (in which the infant identifies with the [false] specular image) to explain how the spectator's gaze is captured by the camera itself, selecting which parts of the visual scene to attend to (Marilyn Monroe's legs, for example), typically privileging the standpoint of the (presumed heterosexual male) director. *Who* identifies with *what* depends on the viewer, of course, but the idea of the cinemagoer captured in the projector's beam has proved an irresistible image for generations of film scholars trying to explain the seductive power of film.

In addition to these two approaches, communication researchers have distinguished between *similarity identification*, where we identify with a media figure because of shared similarities with them, and *wishful identification*, where we identify with someone we would like to become. Cohen (2001) has criticized these positions as misinterpretations of identification, viewing them largely as the "chance for vicarious experience" and distinguishing identification from PSI, in which the media figure is *responded to*, not identified with, more in the manner of a friend or romantic partner. For Cohen, similarity identification is mere "judgment." Wishful identification is better thought of as "imitation." As with PSI, both of these processes position the favorite character as external to the media user rather than a position we take up from where we imagine ourselves in the shoes of the character. Cohen argues that this position is adopted unconsciously through "the loss of self-awareness" (p. 160) as we merge with the character.

Martin Barker (2005) is also concerned about inconsistent definitions in his own critique of Cohen's (2001) paper, although his solution is simply to scrap the concept of identification altogether. It is, he argues, a slippery construct that defies definition. Indeed, it "benefits by remaining unclear" (Barker, 2005, p. 354), and is largely a rhetorical device used to attack media as being responsible for violence. As counterevidence, he reports the findings of an audience survey of a *Lord of the Rings* screening in which fans' "favorite" characters were rarely mentioned in relation to those aspects of the film they most enjoyed or that made the most impact on the experience of viewing. He argues that audiences (at least audiences of this type of film) are too aware of the paratextual details (e.g., the relation between the film and the book) and the conventions of cinema to be captured unconsciously by the process of identification that Cohen claims is necessary for full absorption with the identified object. Barker concludes that the variety of spectator positions on option makes a mockery of the importance of identification with a single character.

As with much audience research, the problem with both Cohen's (2001) and Barker's (2005) work on identification is its limited potential for explaining audience-media figure relations more generally. While justifiably criticizing film theory as being limited to the experience of the spectator in the movie theater itself, Cohen admits that he is mainly interested in "comedy and drama" and that his own theory of interpretation may be harder to generalize to other contexts (such as sport). Barker's data, convincing as they are in relation to a fantasy film adapted from an already well-known book, may have limited explanatory power in most of the relationships we have discussed in this book so far. Like much of the fan studies literature concerned with cult TV, we need to be skeptical about its further application to other types of text, fan object, and medium.

Nevertheless, the criticism leveled at inconsistent definitions of identification does undermine its usefulness as a rival concept to the parasocial. But this is if we assume that one process explains the whole PSR. Perhaps all the processes labeled "identification" that have been identified by Cohen (2001) simply apply to discrete stages of the whole parasocial process. Initially, we select figures to relate to vicariously, perhaps on grounds of similarity. Wishful identification may take some time to develop (for a minority of figures). We can move from one position to another (from identification to PSI and back again, even). As Barker (2005) argues, one can take up any number of positions in relation to a film text, and this holds, perhaps, for other media figures too.

I want to conclude this section by returning to psychoanalytic theories of identification in order to discuss the work of Melanie Klein. Klein's (1946) theory of "projective identification" has not, to our knowledge, been drawn on in the media research, but it would seem to address some of our caveats about the existing literature. Kleinian theory is dense and difficult and relies on all manner of conjecture about infant cognition. But, importantly, she sees identification as variegated. Through fantasy (always *phantasy* in Klein; see next section), the infant projects part of itself into the desired (or hated) object, and these parts can be either returned or retained. "The processes of splitting off parts of the self and projecting them into objects are . . . of vital importance for normal development" (Klein, 1946, p. 103). While the initial target of projection is the mother's breast (a "good" object when it provides food), it then becomes the mother herself (or equivalent caregiver), and later on, the process extends to other significant objects.

In this way, then, the kind of "similarity identification" might be thought of as the projection of positive attributes into another individual. If, for example, we are proud of our national identity, we will identify positively with another person from the same country (essentially the basis of Tajfel and Turner's [1979] social identity theory). If the good parts are returned, we form a positive bond with that person, enabling friendship. When those good parts of the self are not returned (perhaps because the object is too remote to identify with, as in Freud's general, or is unable to reciprocate), we are left with the desire to become the object, thereby eliciting "wishful identification." This would allow us to have a PSR with a media figure that we admire.

At the same time, Klein's theory explains some of the more puzzling parasocial phenomena. Why are we so interested in "baddies" (Konijn & Hoorn, 2005)? PSRs with evil and malign fictional characters have long troubled communication researchers, but through Kleinian theory, we might understand these as instances in which the bad parts of the self are projected into media figures and retained by them. Essentially, those bad parts are expelled from the ego in the process. In most of the Kleinian literature, this tends to happen in therapy, with the therapist retaining the analysand's negative projections, which is considered a problematic outcome. But if the object is parasocial, this is not necessarily the case. Given the appropriate narrative context, it enables us to enjoy the performance of a thoroughly unpleasant character.

FANTASY . . . AND PHANTASY

> The child does not think that a stick is a horse; she uses the stick as a prop to imagine the horse.
>
> *—Jovchelovitch et al. (2017, p. 128)*

One of the goals stated at the outset of this chapter was to explain certain audience behaviors that are typically considered "irrational," suggesting media users have lost a grip on their senses and are slipping into the realms of fantasy. The charge is sometimes brought by the media themselves but is not uncommon in academic literature. Celebrity worshippers are (if "extreme") described as "delusional" for believing that they have a "special relationship" with the celebrity (McCutcheon et al., 2002, p. 81). PSRs are often referred to, even in the literature, as "fantasy relationships" (for a recent example, see Scherer et al., 2022). The connotations are described as make-believe, fantastic, unreal, and airy-fairy. For this reason, many media and cultural scholars have long resisted any reference to the parasocial, believing it to pathologize fans and media users, specifically as "delusional" (Holmes et al., 2015) or "illusory" (Nolan, 2021), and thereby incapable of capturing what media figures mean to their audiences.

Naturally, "fantasy" plays a significant part in psychoanalytic theory, although it is more often represented as "phantasy," a practice largely attributed to Melanie Klein. Although Freud was inconsistent in his use of the terms, the distinction between fantasy and phantasy is typically held to refer to the degree of conscious control that the individual has over their cognitions (Lear, 2010; Spillius, 2001). *Fantasy* is the deliberate imaginative production of an alternative reality, such as an aspiring footballer (or even me) scoring the winning goal for their country in the World Cup final. Or maybe having a romantic liaison with a desired other as an aid to masturbation. Because these are under our conscious control, they are often dismissed as idle daydreams (the implication being that the daydreamer

Psychoanalytic Theory and the Parasocial

is wasting their time rather than doing something productive). It is not hard to see why, labeled as fantasy, PSRs might be seen as indulgent and unprofitable, a lazy substitute for a "real" relationship. Wishful identification, as discussed in the previous section, arises out of this process, although how realistic the fantasy is will depend on personal factors. The great Argentinian footballer Lionel Messi undoubtedly fantasized about scoring in a World Cup final many years before he eventually did, by which point he was already a great Argentinian footballer.

When Klein talks about *phantasy*, on the other hand, she is referring to imaginative thought that has origins in the unconscious. The young infant cannot tell apart (visual) memories and phantasy: They are both images of something not present. She saw these as essentially creative—one might say, the building blocks of cognitive development. One of Klein's examples from her practice is of a young boy learning to write, who saw the lines in his exercise book as roads and the letters riding onto the roads by motorbike as he wrote them (cited in Spillius, 2001). Since he was able to express it, the boy was clearly conscious of this phantasy, but he would not be able to explain its origins, unlike, say, a daydream about emulating Superman. If, on the other hand, he attempted to perform a superhuman feat of strength and was unaware that it arose out of thoughts about Superman, this would constitute a phantasy.

Taking the idea of phantasy forward to the parasocial, then, I would argue that the majority of PSRs that we have are essentially phantasies. We are not consciously aware of entering into a relationship with a media figure, so ubiquitous are they in our hyper-connected society, but they lodge in our unconscious, and it is only at certain moments that they leak out. I was once approached by a very familiar-looking middle-aged man while walking through Cheltenham,[4] where, at the time, I was doing my PhD. My first thought was that he might be one of the senior staff members at the college, but he did not seem to recognize *me*, and only as he asked for directions to his hotel did I realize he was the internationally famous cricket umpire, David Shepherd. I had spent hours watching televised cricket with close-up shots of his face, so I was probably more (visually) familiar with him than most of the college staff. Moreover, I had some idea of what he was "like"'—a bit of an eccentric but mostly affable, and scrupulously fair as an official. I was ignorant of the whereabouts of his hotel; we went on our separate ways. But I retained the phantasy of "knowing David Shepherd," now a tiny bit less parasocial than previously.

LANGUAGE

Language is so made as to return us to the objectified other, to the other whom we can make what we want of, including thinking that he is an object, that is to say that he doesn't know what he's saying.

—*Lacan (1954–1955/1988, p. 244)*

What can we make of this difficult statement in one of Lacan's seminars? In what sense is our objectification a "return"? Is not knowing what you're saying a good thing or a bad thing? The next idea I want to pick up from psychoanalytic theory is arguably the one that poses the biggest challenge to the traditional concept of PSRs, which is that all relationships, social and parasocial together, are fundamentally constituted from words. They are effectively talked into being. At the level of language, it doesn't matter whether we "really" know the other figure or not. By thinking of relationships as primarily discursive, we lose the fantasy–reality boundary that has so troubled researchers over the years and led to the claims that the idea of the parasocial "pathologizes" media users.

Lacan made several important points about the role of language across his work. The first is that the language we speak is not our own. When a child comes into the world, it may already recognize one or two strings of phonemes, but the concept of language has to be learned. The language itself is already there in the child's environment. The child has no choice but to speak it (eventually). The second point is that the child exists as a discursive object long before birth: "A message is written on his head, and he is entirely located in the succession of messages" (Lacan, 1954–1955/1988, p. 283). The child slots into a child-shaped space that has been created by its parents (and perhaps by other relatives, too, not to mention the wider culture). Gender is simply one of many ways in which the nature of this space constrains the possibilities for the later development of the ego. The child is named soon after birth (although the name may have been long established); its place in the family is non-independent. Reaching the milestones of "normal"/ "successful" development is, in many cases, just a case of buying into those plot elements that have been scripted for us in advance.

And as we acquire language, we discover our relationships are scripted in advance too. We discover that Mummy loves us, which is presumably a good thing, and that our siblings (or cousins, aunts, grandparents) are important, along with other significant adults and children. We are told what we are like (naughty, clever, adorable, etc.) and even what we like ("You don't like dolls, do you, Sally?"). It is quite a long time before we can make these choices for ourselves, although modern media give us a much more extensive selection of potential relationship objects—real and fictional—than was ever available to the children of the pre- and postwar psychoanalysts. And, of course, there are always the objects of our imagination, as discussed in Chapter 5.

The idea that relationships are fundamentally discursive is not entirely new. Romantic couples share a common relationship story: how they met, fell in love, negotiated difficult events or periods, formed a family, and so on (Baxter, 2004). Sternberg (1996) has argued that love itself is best understood as a story constructed from the available cultural material: "Through the stories we bring into the world about love and other things, we partially create the world to which we then react, often as though things 'just happened' to us" (p. 71). Stories are powerful, seductive, and difficult-to-revise forces that structure our understanding of our own lives (Sarbin, 1986). Falling in love, then, is about finding the right character to slot into the role in our personal drama, in the same way

Psychoanalytic Theory and the Parasocial

that Don Quixote elevates a peasant girl into "Dulcinea," an idealized woman for whom he is performing his chivalrous acts.

Given the power of these organizing structures, we could say that we talk ourselves into PSRs in the same way, by drawing on precisely the same repertoire of language that we apply to our immediate social relationships. If our feelings for a media figure are intense because we find them so beguiling, so admirable, or so hateful, then they generate the same emotions and cognitions as the "real" people that surround us, and we can ascribe them equal status in our life stories. Personal construct theory (Kelly, 1955) argues that we compare people in our lives according to a set of constructs based on our own personal values and beliefs (that intelligence is important, empathy less so, or vice versa). Studies using Kelly's repertory grid technique with both social and parasocial relationships have found that there is consistency across the categories of relationships. For example, two of Löbler and Raschpichler's (2009) participants positioned fictional or media figures close to "real people" in their lives.

From a research standpoint, the idea of PSRs as discursive constructs forces us to reconsider methodology. The communication literature has worked on the assumption that they are fundamentally cognitive phenomena, requiring indirect methods that tease them out as dependent variables in multivariate designs. Ways we might consider them as language events are discussed in Chapter 11, along with the (essentially cognitive) technique of repertory grids.

NARRATIVE

In this final section, I want to extend the discussion of PSRs as discursive phenomena by considering the role of narrative in constructing and facilitating them. To begin with, I will return to the long-standing challenge of the fantasy–reality boundary that is typically drawn on to explain seemingly baffling and irrational audience behavior and consider whether narrative might provide an answer to this puzzle.

In Chapter 5, we discussed how the fantasy–reality distinction was typically assumed, in the communication and developmental psychology literature at least, to represent a developmental milestone that children reach at some stage in their first 5 years, rather like theory of mind. Passing the test effectively requires children to demonstrate awareness of both social conventions and media conventions. In order to say whether a media portrayal is "realistic" but not "real," one needs to be aware of acting conventions and have a general knowledge of the social "reality" that they are trying to simulate.

However, this is not a straightforward matter because much of children's entertainment, not to mention adult entertainment, consists of convincing portrayals of "real" emotion in the context of quite unrealistic, even magical, circumstances that have no correspondence with any social reality that the children would have experience of. And this is just drama involving human actors. Although the distinction between human actors, cartoons, puppets, and other nonhuman media figures might be based on "modality" judgments (Hodge & Tripp, 1986), such nonhuman characters often demonstrate the same kinds of behaviors as humans. Cartoon dogs do not always perform the role of real dogs. Anything is possible in fantasy media.

Some studies have suggested that the "social realism" of the portrayal is the factor that allows children (at least those aged older than 5 years) to differentiate fiction from real life (Wright et al., 1994), but the various influences on this judgment are rarely unpacked. (For example, whether a drama is realistic or not may depend very much on the viewer's personal circumstances and experiences.) And, as the authors themselves acknowledge, reality judgments are highly contextual. If a cartoon goat speaks English like an adult human, in what way is this realistic? Here, the "reality" exists in the language itself: We can therefore talk of "narrative realism" rather than "social realism."

A sophisticated example of the way narrative realism works to bridge the fantasy–reality divide was provided in a pair of studies by Michael Emmison and Laurence Goldman (1996, 1997) in which they analyzed *The Sooty Show*, a children's series that was broadcast on UK television between 1955 and 1992. The characters are glove puppets who interact with, in most cases, a single male adult presenter. Although the puppets represent animals (a bear, a dog, and a panda), they rarely exhibit animal characteristics (other than things like food preferences) and sometimes adopt human roles (as waiters and diners in a restaurant or as hotel staff in one series). Of the three principal characters, only one speaks; the other two communicate either by squeaking (the dog, Sweep) or by seemingly whispering into the ear of either the human presenter or the other puppets.

The sophistication of this interaction defies rationalist cognitive explanation. If understanding drama requires the piecemeal analysis of all the various transformations that the puppets undergo (from inanimate objects to animate ones, from animal forms to human-like English speakers, and from dogs and bears to waiters and diners), it would require a high level of abstract reasoning. Yet preschool children constituted *The Sooty Show*'s audience (I was a big fan) and had no trouble unraveling these knots. Emmison and Goldman's (1997) explanation for this apparent paradox is that it is the narrative itself that glues the parts together. The puppets are "linguistically constituted as children" and the presenter as a parent, and together they act out scenes that are typical of parent–child interaction that would be instantly familiar to most young viewers.

The contemporary equivalent of this kind of program can be found in *Daniel Tiger's Neighbourhood* (2012–2018), in which the child puppet characters act out typical situations from their daily lives, such as a first visit to the doctor, a first day of school, or being separated from parents and staying with babysitters. Daniel is a tiger, and his friends are other animals. Children connect easily with these characters and the real-life situations that are portrayed on this animated TV show.

As children develop further, their understanding of story frames and character types increases, partly through cognitive maturation (an ability to cope with more sophisticated and complex structures) and partly through sheer exposure. Our memories become organized within the framework of a life narrative through conversation with parents and older siblings (Nelson, 2003), and this slots into broader cultural narratives about the social world and local and global histories, which contain all the archetypal story elements: causes and effects, goodies and baddies, comedy and tragedy, turning points and subplots (Propp, 1968). It is no coincidence that news stories reproduce the same format and that their impact is strongly related to the character-building work that goes along with the gradual unfolding of events (Giles & Shaw, 2009). Where the characters are already known to the viewers or readers, existing PSRs intensify this impact so that the stories are as gripping as those involving our close friends and relatives.

Our psychological relationship with narrative has often been interpreted by communication scholars from a cognitive perspective: We become absorbed in a story to the extent that the events and characters become real, and our imagination allows us to be "transported" into the story world (Green & Brock, 2000). It has been suggested that absorption in a story may activate a "default network in the brain" (Dill-Shackleford et al., 2016, p. 639) that results in "social processing" irrespective of the reality status of the narrative. A similar effect was demonstrated in a study by Konijn et al. (2009), whereby readers were more likely to believe a fictional text was real when they were emotionally involved in the story and the characters.

Although these experimental effects are relatively short term, they deal with largely artificial stimuli, and it could be argued that our day-to-day emotional involvement with narratives has even more enduring effects. The literature on soap opera, particularly in the pre-internet era, has documented a number of incidents in which the fantasy–reality boundary has been seemingly breached. These include applications for work at the fictional Crossroads motel, viewers sending in new raincoats to replace one lost in a long-running soap plot,[5] and sackloads of letters asking for medical advice from a fictional doctor (Giles, 2003). Here, the audience has been captured by the narrative to such an extent that some of its members have attempted to enter the story world, potentially for a variety of different reasons (perhaps sheer desperation, lack of alternative sources of information, or jobs, in the Crossroads example).

Whatever the explanation for individual transgressions of the fantasy–reality boundary, it has been argued that this supposed developmental milestone is never quite reached, and plenty of highly intelligent and successful adults continue to weep over fictional events, avoid walking under ladders, and swear by lucky numbers, amulets, and other fantastic devices (Woolley, 1997). If we understand our lives through narrative structure rather than rationalist logic, this is hardly surprising. So, it is not a huge step from incorporating new friends and colleagues into our life narrative to finding a role in the plot for characters that we do not know personally, whose plots and settings are usually more exciting and dramatic than our own.

PSYCHOANALYTIC THEORIES AND ATTACHMENT THEORIES

In many ways, Freud was the precursor to current thinking about evolutionary psychology, the connections between biology and models of mental illness, and cognitive development (Marcaggi & Guenolé, 2018). It was observed that "nowhere was the impact of Darwin, direct and indirect, more exemplary or fruitful outside of biology proper than within Freudian psychoanalysis" (Sulloway, 1979, p. 275).

Attachment to the primary caregiver, most often the mother, was a central focus of Freud's theory. Freud thought this relationship fueled the development of various behavioral patterns throughout life, which were based on manifestations of unconscious thought. In Chapter 7, we propose that the inborn propensity to be attracted to the face and voice of familiar others is at the heart of parasocial attachment and, by extension, PSRs as well. That this mechanism for development of relationships would exist both in unconscious and conscious thought is at the heart of this argument, and although the discussion so far on the unconscious and on psychoanalysis might feel very different from the arguments in the next chapter, they are fundamentally connected both theoretically and historically.

7

Parasocial Attachment and Its Place in Attachment Theory

GAYLE S. STEVER ■

As a foundation for arguing that parasocial attachment (PSA) is a form of attachment that belongs next to more traditional forms (infant–caregiver and adult romantic attachment), the first part of this chapter discusses the research literature on forms of attachment that do not involve two people in close physical proximity to one another. The argument is made that psychological proximity is a prominent feature of all forms of attachment and that the "partner" in an attachment relationship does not have to be a real person, indeed, does not have to be a person at all.

WHAT ARE THE ESSENTIAL ELEMENTS OF ATTACHMENT THEORY?

One of the most prominent theories in developmental psychology is attachment theory. In its broadest form, attachment theory is behaviorally identified by proximity seeking. Proximity-seeking behavior is present at birth and is relative to all the things in life that give us comfort, safety, and security. It could be argued that without such behavior and interaction, an infant would not survive. John Bowlby (1969) is credited with originating both the term and the concepts of attachment theory based on his observation and study of infants and young children with their caregivers.

The defining features of attachment theory are proximity seeking, safe haven, secure base, and separation distress. These are easily recognizable as a part of the infant behavioral system present from birth. In addition, they are believed to persist into young adulthood and continue throughout the lifespan (Stever, 2023; Trinke & Bartholomew, 1997).

Parasocial Experiences. David C. Giles and Gayle S. Stever, Oxford University Press. © Oxford University Press 2024.
DOI: 10.1093/oso/9780197647646.003.0008

Attachment theory has a long history of success in predicting the development of relationships and resulting adaptive behaviors (e.g., Banchero, 2000; Bates et al., 1985; Solomon & George, 1999). Mary Ainsworth (1978), an important contributor to the development of attachment theory, sought innovative ways to empirically test the attachment styles observed between infants and their first caregivers. Her work resulted in the idea that all humans form attachments, some secure and others insecure. Insecure attachment was either anxious or avoidant. Anxious attachment is associated with inconsistent care, whereas avoidant attachment is associated with less-than-optimal care. Throughout life, various strategies are employed to consistently seek the same goal of finding comfort, security, and safety. Drawing on Piaget's (1954) work, Bowlby (1969) conceptualized how sensorimotor infants interacted with their environment for the purpose of organizing schemas (networks of ideas) that make sense in the context of their interpersonal interactions.

Young children will develop schemas or internal working models (IWMs) based on their early experiences with caregivers and how consistently or inconsistently their needs were met (Bretherton, 1999). As the child grows, IWMs are applied to other relationships. IWMs encapsulate the idea of self in relation to various attachment figures. A key aspect of IWMs is that they are constantly used to gauge and test new experiences and situations. It is a "working" model because it changes and evolves throughout one's lifetime (Bretherton, 1999). As such, developing an IWM is a process unique to every individual, although the resulting models are likely to resemble one another. In an effort to explore the results of IWMs and other types of attachments humans will develop, researchers began applying these models to the realm of mediated relationships, including parasocial relationships (PSRs) (Cohen, 1997; Stever, 1994, 2013).

Attachment theory initially focused on the proximity-seeking behaviors in infants that are used to foster a sense of security, safe haven, and comfort. These behaviors are present at birth. As already stated, without them, it could be argued that the infant would not survive. Throughout our lifespan, whether children or adults, various strategies are employed to seek the same goal of finding comfort, security, and safety.

PLACE ATTACHMENT

Counted (2016) shared that "an attachment bond to a place could be linked to attachment behaviors and internal working models that originate from early bonding experiences with parental attachment figures or caregivers" (p. 8). Because attachments to early caregivers can be transferred to transitional objects such as a blanket or stuffed toy (Winnicott, 1953), they also can be transferred to the places associated with those caregivers. Counted argued that the needs of individuals can then be met by these places.

Place attachment has been defined as an "environmental locus in and through which the actions, experiences, intentions, and meanings" of an individual or community are drawn together spatially (Seamon, 2014, p. 11). A place attachment is a powerful emotional bond that forms between an individual and a place of significance. In this context, a safe haven is a particularly fitting aspect of place attachment. Place attachment has been recognized and discussed in scholarly articles in comparison with PSA (e.g., Pimienta, 2023).

Just as in traditional attachment, where attachment to multiple persons is common, place attachment to multiple places is also frequently found (Scannell & Gifford, 2017). Just as attachments to people begin in infancy but grow in complexity over time as children develop more complex mental schemas for their relationships, so also do place attachments grow and become more complex. It is theorized that as children develop a secure base with their parents, the home serves as an extension of that secure base and comes to represent a secure base in and of itself (Scannell & Gifford, 2017). It is further proposed that there is a synchronicity between interpersonal attachment and place attachment and that these attachments reinforce one another as the child grows and develops (Morgan, 2010). This is an example of a completely inanimate entity (a location) offering the essential elements of comfort, safe haven, and security that are the hallmarks of attachment theory.

One aspect of place attachment that has been developed is the idea of attachment to places that are held as sacred. This could be a church, temple, mosque, or synagogue but also could be a place associated with faith, even if that association is only held by the individual (Aslam, 2023). This combines place attachment with a concept described below, attachment to God (Counted, 2019; Counted & Watts, 2017; Counted & Zock, 2019). Attachment overall shapes our need for security and emotional meaning in our lives. Attachment to sacred places combines this need for security and meaning with a need to have mental representations that anchor the attachment. In the absence of the physical presence of God, the place becomes the anchor for the attachment to the sacred.

In the context of place attachment, also consider the concept of parasocial place attachment. This would be an attachment to a place that only exists in fiction or imagination. Fans identify numerous places that hold appeal, from the Starship Enterprise in *Star Trek* to Hogwarts in *Harry Potter* and Middle Earth in *The Lord of the Rings*. Research is needed to explore the idea that imaginary places are respites offering a safe haven that provides comfort and security to those who feel a connection to them.

Parasocial experiences (PSEs) have elements of both the cognitive and the emotional. Thinking about *Star Trek* fans, some are entirely into the concept of the show (the universe, the ships, the blueprints, and the technology), and others are more into the characters. The Starship Enterprise is an example of a parasocial place attachment object. Whereas some fans are entirely about one of the main characters, others connect with places in the *Star Trek* universe. Both groups are devoted fans of the franchise, but in one case, attachment is more cognitive, and in the other case, it is more emotional.

ATTACHMENT TO ANIMALS/PETS

A number of theorists have addressed the subject of pets as attachment objects (Beck & Madresh, 2008; Meehan et al., 2017; Mikulincer & Shaver, 2020; Sable, 1995; Zilcha-Mano et al., 2012). Beck and Madresh (2008) examined relationships with pets, comparing them to adult relationships with romantic partners. They found that relationships with pets tended to be more secure according to every measure taken in their study. They concluded that pets are a source of attachment security for those who have close relationships with their pets.

Meehan et al. (2017) also found that pets were a source of consistent social support at a level comparable to family and friends. In their study, in which they rank-ordered relationships, pets ranked higher than siblings but lower than romantic partners, parents, or close friends. With respect to four identified attachment behaviors—proximity seeking, separation distress, safe haven, and secure base—pet owners exhibited these behaviors in relation to their pets consistently.

In a study examining the ability of pets to act as either a safe haven or a secure base, participants engaged in either a distress-eliciting task or a goal exploration task using three conditions: physical presence, cognitive presence, or no presence of the pet. Pets in this study were found to help alleviate insecurity as well as provide both a safe haven and a secure base with respect to the experimental tasks (Zilcha-Mano et al., 2012).

Sable (1995) reported that pets contribute to positive well-being in their owners in a multiplicity of ways, including less psychological distress, fewer doctor visits, better recovery from heart incidents, as well as increasing "feelings of happiness, security, and self-worth" while reducing "feelings of loneliness and isolation" (p. 335).

WINNICOTT'S OBJECT RELATIONS THEORY: ATTACHMENT TO TRANSITIONAL OBJECTS

A prominent tenet of psychoanalytic theory is the idea that transitional objects can provide security in the absence of primary caregivers for children (Winnicott, 1953; see also Chapter 5, this volume). These are recognized as blankets, teddy bears, or other comfort objects to which a child becomes attached. Unseen others as attachment objects might also include imaginary friends, which are common in childhood (Granqvist & Kirkpatrick, 2013).

Unlike Freudian psychoanalytic theory, object relations theorists believe that human contact and the need to form relationships are the prime motivation for human behavior and in personality development rather than sexual feelings, as was proposed by Freud (Klein, 1932).

Ball and Tasaki (1992) presented evidence that attachment can be felt for personal possessions. Those possessions play an important role in both self-concept and sense of identity. They relate this to increasing interest in Erickson's (1959) development of identity in current theorizing about possession ownership. A consistent schema with respect to the self is important in the establishment of identity. Such schemata are established by individuals in order to evaluate behavior and fix a sense of self-worth. The importance of an object to the individual is tied to its place in supporting a sense of self-worth. An example of ownership of a possession that involves attachment is owning a certain kind of house or vehicle. The relationship between the object and the self-worth it supports for the individual means that the object can become a source of comfort and safe haven, just as any attachment object might be.

A more recent example of attachment to an object is attachment to one's smartphone or another technological device (Fullwood et al., 2017; Roy et al., 2017). Within these studies, the idea of "app attachment" is explored, particularly with respect to apps that help one manage one's life. Explored is the tendency to anthropomorphize or develop sentimental feelings toward one's phone.

ATTACHMENT TO GOD

One of the most well-developed concepts in attachment literature is the connection between attachment theory and religious forms of expression. At the heart of this is attachment to God, whomever you might conceive Him or Her to be (Cherniak et al., 2021; Granqvist & Kirkpatrick, 2013; Kirkpatrick, 1992, 2012).

Caughey (1984) wrote about this extensively, referring to imaginary social relationships as including those that non-Western Indigenous people had with their various gods: "Among the Ojibwa Indians, it is taken for granted that additional 'persons,'—thunder gods, fabulous giant monsters, and deceased ancestors—not only exist but interact with human beings" (p. 17). It has been argued elsewhere (Stever, 2017) that Caughey's imaginary social relationships are similar to PSRs and PSAs.

Granqvist and Kirkpatrick (2013) speak of symbolic attachment relationships that provide "surrogate attachment figures" (p. 139). The role of the safe haven and secure base essential to attachment is thought to be potentially fulfilled via a relationship with God. The attachment figure is viewed as stronger and wiser than the attached person, and as development progresses, the attached person develops the ability to maintain proximity through psychological rather than physical proximity to the attachment figure. God then becomes this symbolic attachment figure and unseen other who is relied on by the attached person. As an attachment figure, God is always available as (s)he is omnipresent and eternal.

PARASOCIAL ATTACHMENT: MEDIATED ATTACHMENT

Parasocial attachment, as a manifestation of the evolved proclivity to be attracted to familiar faces and voices, is a foundational principle in the understanding of this concept (Stever, 2017). Although attachment is most often to someone or something that is physically present for the individual (whether a child or adult), the above review has developed the idea that attachments that offer comfort and a safe haven are frequently developed with objects as varied as one's concept of God, a place rather than a person, or a pet/animal.

In a study that examined fan attachment to *manga* anime (Pimienta, 2023), all four of the attachment markers—separation distress, safe haven, secure base, and proximity maintenance—were found in a sample of manga readers. The avid readers had stronger attachment than did occasional or moderate readers (Pimienta, 2022).

Primary PSA refers to an attachment that a viewer forms with the actual celebrity in their real life (Stever, 2013). Secondary attachment refers to the viewer who forms an internal working model of a persona (often a fictional character who has been portrayed by the favorite actor) and then forms an attachment to that internally created persona (Adams-Price & Greene, 1990). Attachment is defined as proximity seeking in order to experience a sense of comfort and safe haven. In PSA, the proximity is vicarious or mediated in almost all cases. Looking at posts on social media illustrates the point that these attachments can be with either primary attachment objects or secondary ones. For example, one fan of a popular actor, posting on Tumbler, said the following:

> During the course of this summer, I read so many accounts of people meeting him, so much speculation about his personality and private life, and I must conclude that I love my fantasy version of XXX so much that I don't really care about who he really is. My version is mine, and it makes me happy.

This is a clear case of secondary attachment. Contrast this with attachments to the actual person, as exhibited by a fan making Herculean efforts to meet the celebrity in real life. Many accounts on social media are similar to the following, an account from a woman who traveled to Central London one early morning when she knew her favorite celebrity would be giving a radio interview:

> So yesterday morning I struck gold! I live just an hour outside London by tube, so thought I'd take a chance and go to the XXX Studios. When I arrived, there were a few people waiting, and they had seen XXX go in; we waited until he came out after his interview, and he was happy to have a picture with us! He was lovely, he then got into a waiting car, ready to go on to his next interview. A fabulous morning, so lucky.

From observations and discussions with many fans, the first important point is that the approach is most often respectful and is made in a place where the celebrity's appearance has been advertised. I make this point rather carefully because I have seen accounts of fans exhibiting this kind of behavior where the fan is accused of "stalking" the celebrity. Approaching a celebrity in a public place where their appearance has been advertised does not in any way meet the definition of stalking.

When a person is active in a fan group long enough, the person learns the artist's habits and is able to predict, as did the person in the previous example, when they are likely to be successful in making an approach and getting the desired photo or autograph. When I began my studies in the late 1980s, the desired memento was an autograph. It wasn't until the proliferation of cell phones with sophisticated cameras was the status quo that the "selfie" or photo with the celebrity became the new desired souvenir.

In years of fan studies, I have seen this activity play out hundreds of times. The desire to meet the celebrity in person and get a photo or an autograph is the exact illustration of proximity seeking. What has the person accomplished by doing this? In most cases, they have simply realized a desire to make a real-world connection with someone who is important to them. (For a further discussion on this idea, see Chapter 9 and the discussion about meeting celebrities at conventions or having parasocial interactions with them via Cameo.)

The contrast between primary and secondary attachment is well illustrated by the previous two examples that are at opposite ends of the spectrum. The first fan has her own internal fantasy about the celebrity and is content with it. Proximity to that self-developed image makes her happy. In the second case, the fan has gone to extreme lengths to meet the real person and obtain a photograph. This is primary attachment or attachment to the real person.

It is equally clear that both fans have obtained comfort and pleasure from their encounters. In the first case, "My version is mine, and it makes me happy." In the second case, the fan recounted that she'd had a "fabulous morning" and considered herself lucky. From social media posts, I could tell this story several dozen more times, with photographs to back up the accounts.

In doing participant observer fan research, I saw these encounters in person hundreds of times. The places where fans easily met celebrities in person included fan conventions; red carpet events for film or television debuts; autograph sessions, often with the release of a new product (book, DVD, or CD); sites of media interviews (such as the one recounted above); as a part of studio audiences; after concerts or plays; or on location shoots where the filming had been advertised in advance. This list is non-exhaustive but is representative of the ways that fans, respectfully and non-invasively, met their favorite celebrities. Certainly, there were fans who were stalkerish in their behavior, but they were the exception rather than the rule.

PARASOCIAL ATTACHMENT: THE DEATH OF QUEEN ELIZABETH

There is no better example of a distant figure known primarily through the media who afforded those who knew her a sense of security, safety, and comfort than

Figure 7.1 Queen Elizabeth II and Duke of Edinburgh.
Source: Simon Ward Photography/Shutterstock.com.

Queen Elizabeth II (Figure 7.1). This became evident on the day following her passing when social media was flooded with those who expressed their profound sense of loss for this public figure whom most of them had never met face-to-face. The following is a tweet sample:

> It is so strange, this emptiness I feel—just so unexpected. A great role model for her duty, constancy, and hard work. My thoughts are with her family at this, the saddest of times.
>
> I'm still in shock I'm waiting to wake up from a really horrible dream— Her Majesty was my namesake and always found her to be a very strong and courageous lady to say she'll be sorely missed is the understatement of the millennium.
>
> RIP Your Majesty. You have shown us all how to remain dignified and to put duty before one's own needs.
>
> no matter how old you are, you grew up with her! almost to our own family. a part of it! I will miss her!
>
> She was an awesome lady. A true, great Queen. The likes of her come only once in a generation, if ever. I admired her deeply & I'm going to miss her like a beloved old aunt who I didn't see often, but whom I loved sincerely. My condolences to all the UK and Commonwealth citizens.
>
> Thank you! I can't speak for anyone but myself, but I feel as though I've lost a third parent. I honestly did not know it would affect me like this.

ATTACHMENT AND ITS RELATIONSHIP TO EVOLUTIONARY PSYCHOLOGY

Attachment theory is part of the ethological perspective on human development. This perspective alleges that human beings have biological predispositions that guide their behavior, and the brain is an important, perhaps the primary, organ when considering the mechanisms of attachment and other forms of interpersonal connections. This is all part of a larger theoretical perspective that describes attraction and its place in the two evolutionary imperatives for humanity: survival and reproduction. It has already been noted that attachment behaviors in infancy are critical to an infant's survival. If infants are not cared for by adults, they die.

The instinct for survival and reproduction is discussed in this next section, tying attachment theory and PSEs to principles of evolutionary psychology.

EVOLUTIONARY THEORY: DESIRE AND AROUSAL

According to experts in this area, men and women have very different agendas with respect to the evolutionary imperative to reproduce. Mating and attraction are strategic when considering the survival of our species, with men and women employing different strategies with respect to this agenda. Potential mates are desired for their ability to increase the likelihood that our genes will be passed on to the next generation. For men, the goal is to find as many partners as possible with whom to mate to optimize the passing on of one's genes. Certainly, other aspects of socialization and culture mitigate this behavior, but men have the capacity to produce offspring with multiple partners if they so desire. Women, on the other hand, have a long-term and high-cost investment in each offspring they produce. For this reason, finding a partner who possesses characteristics that promote the success of raising an offspring to reproductive age is the goal. Aspects of modern culture have affected the likelihood of survival of infants in each generation—for example, advances in health care make it more likely that weaker individuals will still survive to reproduce. However, changes in behavior as shaped by natural selection take far longer to adjust to changing conditions, and thus, there is a tendency to behave "as if" conditions are as they have been for thousands of years. Women are not as dependent today on a mate in order to ensure the survival of their children; however, it is still true that survival and the ability for those children to flourish are enhanced by the right partner (Buss, 2003).

Thus, women who seek a partner for a committed relationship, one who will help them raise their children, are biologically but also culturally inclined to seek a mate who is healthy and will offer the optimal benefits and minimize costs with respect to what resources the man has to offer within the role of child-rearing. As such, economic capacity, social status, and ambition all become important factors when considering a mate (Buss, 2003). The reason the focus here is on women is that these factors offer a partial explanation for why women are more likely to have a romantic fixation on a high-status, affluent celebrity than are men with respect to comparable female celebrities. This is not to suggest that men never have parasocial romantic relationships (PSRRs) but, rather, is offered as a partial explanation for why this type of PSR appears to be more frequent in women than in men.

PARASOCIAL ROMANTIC RELATIONSHIPS

Of all of the observed categories of PSRs, a prominent one in women who follow celebrities is the PSRR. Some commonly identified motivations for fan behavior and PSRs are task attraction, identification, hero/role model admiration, and romantic attraction (e.g., the PSRR) (Stever, 1991, 2009). In observations in a number of online fan groups for various actors on Facebook, Twitter, YouTube, and other social media, indications of romantic attraction were the most common and most persistent. This mirrors past findings of other fan groups investigated, such as the pop stars of the late 1980s and early 1990s; fan groups for individual *Star Trek* actors; the fandom of Josh Groban; and, most recently, fans who follow various actors from *The Hobbit* films (Stever, 1991, 2009, 2019, 2022). (See discussion below on *Poldark*.)

Developing the theoretical link between observed fan behavior, in this case with respect to women, and the science of evolutionary psychology and the study of desire for, arousal by, and attachment to media figures is the goal of this section. For this purpose, it is important to discuss the biology of sexuality (Sherwin et al., 1985).

Fisher et al. (2002) have proposed that there are distinct areas of the brain that have evolved to respond to cues in the environment that signal romantic attraction. The goal of romantic attraction is to promote the survival of the human species, and to that end, lust, romantic love, and attachment are different emotions that are processed in the limbic and mesolimbic systems in the brain. Several areas in these primitive parts of the brain serve to direct attention to potential romantic partners.

Restak (1991) has proposed that the brain has a mind of its own, meaning that these more primitive areas of the brain process all cues equally, whether they are in a face-to-face environment or in a mediated environment. The limbic and mesolimbic areas of the brain evolved to ensure our survival as a species. However, evolution proceeds very slowly, and the era of visual media has not been a long enough period of time to allow for any fundamental changes to brain structure that would mitigate this tendency to process everything that is visual as if it were physically present (Stever, 2020). Thus, the attractive male who is the subject of the female gaze on television, film, or the internet is processed as if he actually were an available mate for the viewer. The brain processes images of the potential romantic partner, and in moving from lust to romantic love, the preference for a single potential romantic partner is solidified. Lust looks for suitable sexual outlets but processes all attractive visual potential partners as equivalent. It is in the romantic love stage of attraction that a preferred partner is identified. In the long term, that romantic love shifts to an attachment bond that will last long enough to raise a child into adulthood if the desired connection with the romantic figure is successful.

As previously discussed, in *The Evolution of Desire*, Buss (2003) made the argument that the human mating system has evolved according to the needs of women to find a mate who will care for them and for their offspring by protecting and providing for them. Along the same lines that Restak (1991) proposed, Reeves and Nass (1996) also presented the theory that human perceptions do not effectively differentiate between those from the physically present world and those that come from media. A woman who is primed by evolutionary biology to search for a suitable mate and procreate with him is often attracted to men in a mediated world who are unavailable to her. But the brain is fooled by the apparent proximity of the attractive potential mate and responds to him as if he were available.

Lust or sexual desire, the motivation to seek a sexual partner, will be triggered by cues in the environment and be fueled by androgens, particularly testosterone, which is central to sexual desire in both men and women. The mediated presence of an attractive face or sexy body results in the viewer having a desire that has been triggered by that face and/or body. By recognizing that the progression of affection audience members feel for a fictional character or other distant attractive people can mimic and be very similar to the same romantic feeling for a real person in one's day-to-day life, it becomes easier to understand why so many women "fall in love" with parasocial romantic figures in the media (Tukachinsky Forster, 2021).

What this means is that women often are attracted to a man who is desirable even if he is not available because desire is distinct from arousal (Regan & Berscheid, 1999). Women find enjoyment in gazing at an attractive male even when they do not actually want to have sex with him. Fantasizing about it in a romantic sense is often pleasurable without any actual sex act being involved. And counter to intuition, this romantic attraction with an increase in desire may grow stronger as women age because the balance of estrogen versus testosterone shifts, creating this increase in sexual desire (Hällström & Samuelsson, 1990). Brain scans show that lust activates androgens through the hypothalamus and pituitary (Karama et al., 2002). High levels of testosterone stimulate the sex drive, and low levels dampen it. As women enter menopause, their estrogen levels decline, and the effects of testosterone may increase (Hällström & Samuelsson, 1990).

Chivers and colleagues (2004) found that sexual arousal patterns play fundamentally different roles in male versus female sexuality. One of their conclusions was that "female sexuality, in general, might be more motivated by extrinsic factors, such as the desire to initiate or maintain a romantic relationship, than by intrinsic factors, such as genital sexual arousal" (p. 743). Thus, it might be expected that the desire for romance is more important for women when choosing the object of a PSRR than the goal of satisfying a specific sexual need. As previously stated, desire is different from arousal and, for women, is likely to be more influential in this kind of situation.

The feelings associated with romantic attraction include craving, intrusive thoughts of the beloved, increased energy, separation anxiety, butterflies in the stomach, and a pounding heart. Neuroimaging studies show activation in areas of the brain associated with the "reward" chemical dopamine, such as the caudate nucleus and the ventral tegmental areas. Dopamine from these areas "helps us detect and perceive a reward, anticipate a reward, and expect a reward" (Fisher, 2004, p. 69). In addition, dopamine stimulates the release of testosterone, triggering sexual desire. Other brain areas release epinephrine, norepinephrine, and phenylethylamine. These amphetamine-like neurotransmitters stimulate the feelings of giddiness and excitement that many will associate with passionate love. In addition, brain scans reveal low levels of serotonin, most likely responsible for the obsession a person has for their lover.

As the audience member focuses her gaze from multiple attractive males to a single preferred male, the sense that one has "fallen" for him becomes very real. She knows the celebrity very well, indeed in an intimate way, but the celebrity only knows her as a member of the group, sometimes referred to as a fandom. Celebrities often focus their energy on the group as a whole, a process defined as para-communication (Hartmann, 2008; see also Chapter 4, this volume). Audience members respond to the para-communication by allowing it to become part of the belief they are appreciated and, perhaps, even the object of the affection of the celebrity. In this way, a PSR develops that although not reciprocated, is still a process of give-and-take between the celebrity and the group fandom.

Just as happens in a face-to-face relationship, over time, the intense passion, longing, and obsession of romantic love transform into the calm, comfort, and security of a long-term relationship called PSA. This is when the celebrity fantasy object becomes a source of comfort and security for a fan who has followed that celebrity over a longer period of time (Stever, 2013). Just as in real romantic relationships, a "crush" evolves into a more settled relationship. In PSRR, the lust one might feel for an attractive celebrity early on can smooth out into a more settled, less intense, but still satisfying attraction that manifests itself not only as *eros* (sexual attraction) but also as *storge* (affection), *phileo* (friendship), and even *agape* (charity) (Lewis, 1971).

Dopamine is not the only aspect of brain chemistry that could be a factor in PSRs. Oxytocin has been shown, in numerous studies, to be associated with positive social interactions, social rewards, and even brand loyalty (Fürst et al., 2015; Hung et al., 2017; Uvnäs-Moberg, 1998), all aspects of mediated social activity. In a particularly important study, intranasal oxytocin administration reduced the acceptance of online celebrity bashing by study participants (Rudnicki et al., 2020). Although further research in this area is needed, clearly, levels of both dopamine and oxytocin can have an effect on the feelings one associates with distant social objects such as celebrities.

This discussion focuses on females being attracted to male celebrities, but other combinations (men to women, women to women, and men to men) likely respond to similar mechanisms with respect to brain chemistry; however, further work is needed to hypothesize these connections. The one presented here is an

OBSERVATIONS ON ATTRACTION

example of how this attraction works with respect to the viewer in response to an attractive person who is not physically proximal.

OBSERVATIONS ON ATTRACTION

Swami (2016) noted that attraction is based primarily on four factors: proximity, physical attractiveness, perceived similarity, and mutual liking. These factors have been found to influence those who develop real-life relationships. It is not difficult to see how these four might also be factors in PSRRs.

PSRs are based in large part on extensive virtual proximity. This is simply another way to say that the more one watches a media figure, the more likely one is to develop a PSR with them (Bond, 2021; Bond & Drogos, 2014; Perse & Rubin, 1989; Rubin & McHugh, 1987). Physical attractiveness also makes sense in the realm of PSRRs, although other questions on that point have to be considered and will be shortly. One of the best predictors of PSRs, in general, is homophily or perceived similarity (Bu et al., 2022; Cortez, 1991; Eyal & Rubin, 2003; Schmid & Klimmt, 2011; Turner, 1993; Zhang et al., 2021).

Mutual liking is less obvious, but in discussions of para-communication and parasocial perception (see Chapter 4), it is recognized that celebrities communicate to their audience members through various chosen channels, and audience members base their parasocial perception of those celebrities on those communications. If celebrities are kind, accepting, and warm toward their fan followers, and clearly fans like them in return, this mutual liking would foster an enhanced connection that, arguably, could be on both sides of the relationship.

Although it is true that physical attractiveness plays a primary role in the formation of PSRRs, how is it that various celebrities who appear at first glance to not be classically "good-looking" will still have a wide fan base of loyal followers, many of whom profess to PSRRs with those who do not exhibit prototypical good looks?

One possible explanation already mentioned is that perceived similarity is one of the major components of attraction (Swami, 2016). Swami cited multiple studies dating back as far as the observations of Leonardo da Vinci, which showed that when looking at married couples just after they had married, couples tend to resemble one another. If this is true in the realm of real-life relationships, then it is most likely true in the parasocial realm as well.

So, one then must ask what exactly the standard for "good looks" is, and whether or not those standards are universal or culturally determined. A number of features are recognized as being universal in the realm of the objective beauty of the human form. It is generally agreed that averageness, symmetry, sexual dimorphism, pleasant facial expressions, and youthfulness are all commonly accepted components of an attractive face (Rhodes, 2006; Thomas & Dixon, 2016). How much one likes a person is also a factor when considering attractiveness (Kniffin & Wilson, 2004). Rhodes (2006) further noted that there are types of attractiveness that range from sexual attractiveness to cuteness. Motivation plays into this evaluation such that we make decisions about attractiveness based on aspects such as sexual arousal, caregiving, or competitiveness.

Kniffin and Wilson (2004) found overall that when evaluating the physical attractiveness of a person who is known socially, many other factors weigh into perceived beauty besides the classic youth, physical proportions, or symmetry factors that scholars acknowledge. Women weigh the nonphysical factors more when evaluating men than do men when evaluating women, with many individual differences occurring among members of both sexes. Prosocial orientation and social status are both additional factors that enhance the perceived attractiveness of the other person.

In a study of heterosexual speed dating (with 3-minute speed dates being the behavior of interest), the conclusion was that having an attractive face was the most important factor in being chosen for a second date, and having an attractive speaking voice was the second most important factor. When looking at women, facial attractiveness, vocal attractiveness, and being slim were the most important influences, whereas looking at men, facial attractiveness and height were important factors in being chosen for a second date. Other factors measured and considered were education, income, and personality. Men tended not to factor in education, personality, and income when considering potential second dates with women, whereas women did care, to a lesser extent than physical attractiveness, about income and personality (Asendorpf et al., 2011).

The relevance of this study is in equating a 3-minute exposure to someone on a speed date to seeing someone in a media program. In both cases, the object of interest is unknown to the person experiencing the exposure to the other person. Just as the evaluation of a speed date will be based on a quick and limited exposure to the person, initial exposure to a mediated personality will likely be similar to that same 3-minute criteria. And just as the speed dater is deciding on a second date, the audience member decides whether or not to continue watching a particular mediated figure after relatively limited exposure to that persona. Observing the typical "channel surfer," one can see how quickly the decision is made to continue watching or move on to something else (Klotz, 2011; Lim & Kim, 2011; Mapaye, 2013; Voorveld & Viswanathan, 2015).

WHAT DOES ALL THIS MEAN IN THE CONTEXT OF THE PSRR?

It is not difficult to see how the previously described factors could enhance our understanding of the mechanisms involved in both PSR and PSRR. Consider an example of a group of popular actors who have been identified as being both sexually and personally attractive to the television-viewing public. For example, actors from the movie franchise *The Hobbit* were consistently evaluated by fans as both physically attractive and prosocial positive people. Their personalities, philanthropy, and kindness toward fans contributed to the overall favorable impression that fans had of them (see the section titled "Aidan Turner and Poldark").

Parasocial Attachment

PSA theory suggests that the viewer finds comfort in the proximity of these favorite celebrities. There is an ongoing debate in the literature on physical attractiveness regarding whether being good enhances perceived beauty or perceived beauty enhances the sense that someone is "good" (Dion et al., 1972; Frederick et al., 2015; Gross & Crofton, 1977). However, as is the case in face-to-face social relationships, once the attachment object has been deemed to be attractive, whether goodness enhances beauty or the other way around becomes a purely academic question. The fan/audience member will hold to their evaluation that the object of the PSRR is an attractive, worthy, and good person. This has been found in multiple fan groups (Stever, 2019).

EXPLORING FURTHER: THE CRUSH

Research on the type of attraction known in popular culture as a "crush" has repeatedly been the object of research scrutiny (Belu & O'Sullivan, 2019; Fisher, 1998, 2004; O'Sullivan et al., 2022). Given that this is a defining feature of the PSRR, it is important to explore studies that have been done on crushes. Defined as an interpersonal attraction to someone with whom we seek contact, this is similar to the concept of proximity seeking that has already been discussed.

One acknowledged function of a crush is that it focuses mate-seeking behavior toward a single individual. This is particularly true during adolescence. For years, it was assumed that crushes were mostly characteristic of adolescence, but more recent findings suggest that the crush is a lifelong phenomenon (Tukachinsky Forster, 2021). Various definitions characterize a crush as lighthearted and juvenile, most often an infatuation that is not known to the object of the crush, and most often is love for someone you know you can't have in a real relationship. It is also described as an unreciprocated and unfulfilled longing that is not intended to lead to actual mating. Studies have found no gender differences in the likelihood of having a crush. Most often, those who report having crushes also report that they have no intention of acting on their feelings (Mullinax et al., 2016). Of particular relevance to the discussion in this chapter is the finding that among individuals reporting crushes, 41% of singles and 66% of those in a relationship indicated that the object of their crush was "a fantasy target, such as a celebrity" (O'Sullivan et al., 2022, p. 419). The main reason given for not pursuing a relationship with a "crush" was not wanting to jeopardize the current relationship or hurt the current partner in some way.

An important finding was that having a crush was "not predicted by poor relationship quality concerning commitment, intimacy, sexual satisfaction, and relationship satisfaction" (Belu & O'Sullivan, 2019, p. 8). This is consistent with my observation that when fans have a crush on a favorite celebrity or favorite character, this is not an indication that their current relationship is in any way dissatisfying or that the person is seeking to end a current relationship. Fantasy is fantasy, and its connection to real life is tenuous at best.

A study found that parasocial crushes were the least likely of a range of behaviors of a romantic partner to be considered infidelity. Those behaviors ranged from actual physical infidelity, cybersex with a stranger, and watching pornography to the lowest rated behavior, which was fantasizing about a celebrity crush (Adam, 2019). However, the idea that such crushes might be perceived at all as disloyal by romantic partners is probably a good explanation for the previous finding that people tended not to talk about their celebrity crushes to their romantic partners (O'Sullivan et al., 2022).

THE NARRATIVE AS IT RELATES TO PSRRS

Related to the concept of PSEs is the idea of narrative persuasion. A principal form of para-communication for actors is the acting performance itself. An actor's ability to convey passion or romance in a story translates into PSRRs for many viewers. Narratives or stories are a powerful means of engaging viewers in a way that is memorable and persuasive (Tal-or & Cohen, 2016). Transportation is central in completely engaging a viewer in a narrative such that the viewer experiences that narrative in a personal way, connecting themself to the characters in that story and making it seem very real. Part of the PSE is driven by such transportation into the world of the admired figure, experiencing that world in a way that feels personal and intimate. This places the PSR in a powerful position to engage the viewer in a way that encourages a sense of connection and attachment. PSA is the comfort and sense of safety and security that a person feels when in proximity to the attachment persona (Stever, 2013). The particular power of actors and their characters in a story world inspires a particularly intense form of PSR based on this sense of being part of a story with that actor and their characters.

AIDAN TURNER AND *POLDARK*

In March 2021, the *Irish Mirror Newspaper* reported that Captain Ross Poldark (Aidan Turner; Figure 7.2) "topped the *Mirror*'s poll of British women's top choices for who they fantasize about in bed. Trailing behind him were the likes of Daniel Craig, Brad Pitt, and David Beckham" (Twigger, 2021). The BBC series *Poldark* dominated British television from 2015 through 2019, as evidenced by as many as 8 million weekly viewers ("*Poldark* (2015 TV Series)," 2023 in *Wikipedia*). This was a time when streaming, DVDs, and other recorded programming tended to dominate viewers' habits, and traditional weekly television shows airing at their set time were struggling to find an audience. This program aired in the United States beginning in 2015 as well. Since that time, viewership has grown to include most of the countries in Europe and many beyond Europe. For example, France got access to *Poldark* beginning in late 2019, and as a result, many viewers binge-watched the show during the pandemic in 2020.

Figure 7.2 Aidan Turner.
Source: Jaguar PS/Shutterstock.com.

What exactly is *Poldark*, and what are the reasons why it so captivated the fantasies of viewers, particularly (although not limited to) women? *Poldark* tells the story of Ross Poldark, a man who returns to Cornwall in the 1790s after fighting in the Revolutionary War to find that his father is dead, his girlfriend is engaged to another, and his prospects are limited. The show tells the story of his struggles to find love, as well as his fight to help the poor and those who are treated unjustly.

In an era in which internet coverage is presumed, *Poldark* seems to have thrived by using more traditional tabloid and print media marketing to dominate the public consciousness with a program that was a remake of an equally successful version of the same story made in the 1970s. Based on the books of Winston Graham (1945/2015), *Poldark* had drawn as many as 17 million UK viewers per week in the 1970s.

The star of the 2015 show, Aidan Turner, certainly came into the program with a well-established fan base, having had success in a number of television series and movies, most notably *The Hobbit* and *Being Human*. Still, no one could have predicted the extent to which this program would inhabit the hearts and minds of women, particularly in the United Kingdom, for the years it aired (2015–2019) and beyond. In 2016, Turner's image and persona so dominated UK television that he was presented at the National Television Awards ceremony with the Impact Award, which had been created expressly for him and his role in *Poldark*. Later that same year, he received the annual *GQ* award for best TV actor.

Turner was marketed as a "sex symbol" from 2015 to 2019, the years this program was first aired on television in the United Kingdom. Examination of the marketing campaign shows connections between visual rhetoric and the principles of evolutionary psychology that explicate the mechanisms of attraction in a case such as this one, all of this supporting the thesis that the brain is hardwired to be attracted to the familiar and attractive face and voice that are repeatedly encountered and followed on media.

One complication involved in the study of female response to a male favorite actor is the overall cultural attitude that pathologizes fandom in women, particularly those in the mid-life and older stages of development. As stated by Anderson (2012), "Dominant cultural politics characterize . . . female fan behavior in adulthood as pathological" (p. 239). Anderson used her study to closely examine the basis and consequences of shaming women who are fans, forcing many of them into a kind of "closet" fandom. Karhulahti and Välisalo (2021) had a similar finding in their study, identifying what they called "fictophilic stigma," an embarrassment from being attracted to a fictional character, causing the person to find people online with whom to discuss this attraction because talking about it in person was too difficult.

Tukachinsky Forster (2021) also found that having a romantic attraction to a celebrity or fictional character is stigmatized, and thus it is difficult to discuss some aspects of fandom, particularly those that involve romantic attraction and sexuality. In addition, it is frequently the case that a woman's interest in male celebrities is assumed to be romantic and sexual even when it might not be (Esmonde et al., 2018).

By recognizing that the progression of affection audience members feel for a fictional character can mimic and be very similar to the same romantic feeling for a real person in one's day-to-day life, it becomes easier to understand why so many women "fall in love" with parasocial romantic figures in the media (Tukachinsky Forster, 2021).

Looking at the way *Poldark* was conceptualized, cast, and marketed gives further evidence that using the natural responses of women to romantic characters as a way to ensure the success of this program was at the heart of how the program was developed and publicized at the beginning of the show in 2015. There are two ways *Poldark* capitalizes on women's mating strategies: using narrative tropes to provide context and providing appealing visual rhetoric.

Rupp and Wallen (2008) found that the "creation of a social scenario" made visual sexual stimuli more appealing to women because they could project themselves onto it. One of the ways the *Poldark* story accomplished this was to use five prominent romantic tropes or story themes that are common in romantic narratives. It was easy to find lists of these themes on websites that have been developed for writers of romance novels (e.g., https://eviealexanderauthor.com/150-romance-novel-tropes). The five themes identified for this program were the alpha hero; love triangle; rich versus poor: unequal social status; emotional scars; and honorable marriage. Ross Poldark, the main character in this series, is portrayed as an alpha hero involved in a complex love triangle with two women. His wife, Demelza, is of a lesser status, both socially and economically, and comes into the story as an abused daughter with emotional scars. Ross Poldark's sense of honor forces him to marry her. Indeed, as an act of conscience, he marries her the day after bedding her. These tropes work because they "co-opt some pre-existing cognitive preferences and mechanisms" (Dubourg & Baumard, 2022) by establishing the protagonist as an ideal partner who pursues justifiable goals.

Another way to tap into the female mating brain is to use visual rhetoric, the study of the ways images are used to persuade in a narrative (Stafford et al., 2003). *Poldark* is a powerful example of the use of visual imagery to create iconic symbols that were associated with the show. The most prominent iconic image for this program was a picture of Ross Poldark standing shirtless in a field holding a scythe. This became an iconic representation of the masculine sex appeal of the main character. This was far from the first time this actor had appeared shirtless, indeed almost fully nude, in previous work, so why did this particular photo become such a cultural symbol? One argument is that the media so prominently featured this photo on the covers of tabloids and magazines that one could hardly walk into a store in the United Kingdom in 2015 without being greeted by this image on the cover of some publication. So powerful was this persuasive image that at the National Television Awards in the United Kingdom that year, Turner was presented with the already mentioned Impact Award, an award created expressly to recognize the power of that iconic image. In total, during the years of this program and also his earlier work (*Being Human* and a few others), he was on the cover of 56 magazines, with 79 articles, 30 pictorials, and 20 interviews (https://www.IMDB.com).

Subsequent to that 2015 episode, as reported in the news media (e.g., *The Daily Mirror*, June 1, 2018), fans made no secret that they wanted more images of Ross Poldark with no shirt on. The program obliged with regularity, showing the character emerging bare-chested from the sea, working in the copper mine, and in bed with his wife. There were plenty of scenes that elicited romantic images in addition to the shirtless ones. He was also often shown riding his horse along the sea cliffs through a sweeping seascape of cinematography par excellence.

At the show's outset, early in 2015, *The Daily Mail* asked, "Why is Poldark the perfect hunk . . . experts reveal why he makes women swoon" (Rainey, 2015). This reflects the overall coverage the program received from the local daily and weekly UK papers. One article included an interview with Michael Price (2017), an evolutionary psychologist at Brunel University, who stated,

> The most important predictor of male attractiveness is a V-shaped upper body: A lower waist-to-chest ratio indicates health and fitness—little excess fat around the waist and good, but not over-the-top, muscle mass. This has an evolutionary explanation. In the past, men did not have access to weights, gyms, or steroids. If you look at men in a hunter–gatherer society, you don't see bodybuilders. So, women may perceive muscles that are too big as abnormal and unattractive. A healthier, more physically fit man would have been a better mate because he would have been better able to obtain food, to hunt, to offer protection and fight for the interests of his mate, and to provide physical labor. Being healthy, he would also be more likely to survive for a long time.

For a discussion of male attractiveness and waist-to-chest ratio (WCR), see Swami and Tovée (2005). They did a cross-cultural comparison between Britain and Malaysia, finding that in urban settings, WCR was the best predictor of perceived attractiveness, whereas in rural settings, body mass index was the better predictor. For the Ross Poldark character, the audience would be the urban group and would focus more on the WCR, as Price (2017) indicated.

CONCLUSION

The PSRR is a prominent and common type of PSR, despite being stigmatized for both women and men, particularly those who are in middle age and old age. The triggers for PSRR have their basis in both evolutionary psychology and a study of romantic narrative tropes that prompt both emotional and cognitive responses to the romantic narrative.

8

The Social and the Spiritual in Fandom and Parasocial Relationships

GAYLE S. STEVER ■

SOCIAL AND EMOTIONAL IMPACT OF FANDOM AND PARASOCIAL RELATIONSHIPS IN A VARIETY OF CONTEXTS

Not all fandom involves a parasocial relationship (PSR), and not all PSRs are part of a fan experience. Fandom is an intense interest in something and is a concept most frequently associated with media phenomena. We've already discussed PSR as the connection between a fan and a persona, whether real or fictional. Having said that, clearly these two concepts are related and overlap in important ways. Many fans have PSRs, and many PSRs launch the individual into participation in a fandom. My own initial intention in 1988 to study superstar fans very quickly directed me into the area of parasocial theory. The questions in this chapter in particular should be understood within the framework of that connection between these two constructs.

What is the role of the PSR in the social life of a person? If social life is a combination of different kinds of social activity that all work together to help that person feel a sense of connection and personal completion, then how do PSRs with favorite persona factor into that combination?

Distinctions have been made among the various kinds of relationships that are possible with parasocial figures. For example, Tukachinsky (2011) separated parasocial romantic relationships from parasocial friendships. Just as there are a wide variety of social relationships, there are also a wide variety of PSRs. Friends, romantic partners, co-workers, mentors, role models, and other members of one's social life, both positive and negative, have counterparts in the parasocial realm.

Parasocial Experiences. David C. Giles and Gayle S. Stever, Oxford University Press. © Oxford University Press 2024.
DOI: 10.1093/oso/9780197647646.003.0009

When discussing PSRs of various types, there has been an assumption by many (myself included at one time) that when an audience member "loves" a celebrity, that attraction is romantic in nature. The Greeks called romantic love *eros*, which is the origin of words such as erotic, to describe sexual attraction. However, the Greeks also used the word *storge* to describe a kind of love characterized by a deep affection for friends, family members other than the romantic partner, pets, companions, or colleagues. To distinguish these in PSRs, reference will be made to romantic attraction versus deep affection, with the former representing eros and the latter representing storge.

Two ideas have been explored in an attempt to measure the role of PSRs in the social life of audience members. The first is the idea of the sociometer—that each individual has a repository of social needs which are met in various ways and that PSR is one of the ways in which an individual's social vessel is filled. The second is the idea of collective effervescence, which emphasizes the shared experience of being in a group and experiencing something as a collective.

THE SOCIOMETER THEORY

Leary and colleagues (1995) suggested that self-esteem is a product of the value placed on an individual in connection with the important people in their lives. If people are valued by others, they come to view themselves as having value. If one is effective in social relationships and is accepted by others, positive self-esteem is the result. If one is rejected, the opposite is true.

Conversely, self-esteem becomes a barometer for the success of a person's relationships. If one perceives rejection, self-esteem is threatened, and the individual strives to regain a balance that moves self-esteem back into a more positive valence. According to Leary et al. (1995), there are five main types of relationships factored into this kind of assessment: (a) macro-level (i.e., communities), (b) instrumental coalitions (i.e., teams or committees), (c) mating relationships, (d) kin relationships, and (e) friendships.

Historically, seeking inclusion and avoiding exclusion have been important evolutionary functions that promote the survival of an individual (Ainsworth, 1989; Allen et al., 2022; Baumeister & Leary, 1995; Bowlby, 1979). For the purposes of our discussion on parasocial experiences (PSEs), the sociometer theory relates in several very specific ways. The clearest association is in the fact that fans seek connection with favorite celebrities and their fan groups because celebrities have high status, and presumably, a connection with a high-status individual will serve to boost individual self-esteem. These connections fall into the macro-level connections as well as instrumental coalitions, as fans often group into team-like communities whose members are united in their pursuit of both information about and the work of the favored celebrity.

This is operationalized in the way that audience members reason, "I like X, X just did this important work which is getting critical acclaim, and I now benefit from association with that success." Forming friendships with others who also

Social and Spiritual in Fandom and PSRs 137

associate with that success equates to further reinforcement of the positive value of such an association. This can be observed on a daily basis on social media, where fans post about, tweet, or discuss their favorite celebrities with other fans. Such fandoms can break down into rival factions that seek to have the "best" connection to or representation of that celebrity by putting up rival websites, blog pages, or other forms of support for that celebrity. It has been observed that the more popular the celebrity, the more fans will seek attention from that celebrity and might view other fans with the same goal as rivals.

In 1990, when I was at the very beginning of my studies in fandom, Brent Spiner, who played Commander Data on *Star Trek: The Next Generation*, had not recognized any single fan group as "official." The result was fierce competition among several groups who wanted that recognition. However, if a celebrity did choose a group to be official in some sense, the rivalries were far less pronounced as in the case of the *Star Trek: Deep Space Nine* actors, many of whom recognized one fan club as official and communicated with the *Star Trek* audience through that group. The social status afforded to the person who successfully obtained such recognition was considerable and highly sought after in every fandom I have studied over the years. I observed this in the fan groups of actors and singers alike when I began my work in 1988 and have continued to do so right up until the present.

COLLECTIVE EFFERVESCENCE

In his book *Awe*, Keltner (2023) described *collective effervescence*, a term introduced by French sociologist Emile Durkheim. The term refers to a kind of physical exuberance we feel while part of a collective that is celebrating some aspect of the life of that group. As such, this is one of the eight wonders of life that inspire awe. Durkheim (1912, p. 218) stated, "Once the individuals are gathered together, a sort of electricity is generated from their closeness and that quickly launches them to an extraordinary height of exaltation."

Gabriel et al. (2020) pointed out that while Durkheim saw effervescence as something special and part of the sacred, in the context of everyday life, this experience is far more common than was originally conceptualized. They pointed out that this is present at relatively common events and that participants in their studies reported having this experience as often as once a week.

In the life of fan culture, collective effervescence, as a result of the PSRs experienced with a favorite celebrity, is important to explore. In my own experience of participant observation in fan groups, I have experienced collective effervescence in a wide variety of settings. In live concerts, media conventions, charity events, or other large fan-related gatherings, this is a common and easily observed phenomenon. What is not quite as obvious is the times when collective effervescence is felt in situations when I am still sitting at home alone and reading fan pages on my laptop computer.

Let's say that a favorite actor has just debuted in a new television drama. The first reviews are in, and they are more than favorable. TV magazines have just given it five stars, and critics are saying great things about it. Fans post these reviews, comments, and ratings on the shared fan pages, and the response from the fan group is joyous.

Or a favorite singer has just released a new album that got a lukewarm promotion from the record label, and unexpectedly that album begins to break all sales records for an album of this type. Fans share in the joy of the artist and feel that sense of vicarious triumph within the collective of supporters.

Or your favorite feature film has been nominated for a huge number of awards, and it's Oscar night, and the film is winning in all categories!

The first example described both the debut of Aidan Turner's new TV series, *The Suspect*, which occurred in the United Kingdom in September 2022, and the subsequent release of a second series, *15/Love*, in July 2023. In each case, by the end of the first week, it was clear that each of these programs was doing very well, with five-star ratings from the *TV Times* and top five ratings based on the number of viewers who were watching. The second example occurred in October 2007 when Josh Groban released his *Noel* album. The record label barely promoted it, but the fans did a great deal of promotion. The album broke sales records week after week, and records for holiday albums previously held by Elvis Presley were broken. In the third example, in 2004, when *The Return of the King* was nominated for 13 Oscar awards and swept them all, fans were jubilant participants in a celebration for a film they had supported from the day they learned it was being made.

In each of these examples, there was not just one collective gathering to celebrate success. In each case, as a participant observer in a network of fans, it was easy to perceive a sense of joy and celebration and, yes, collective effervescence in how fans expressed joy among themselves at creative expression being celebrated by society at large.

Duffett (2015) placed some emphasis on Durkheim's concept of effervescence, the focus on the social force of the collective of people who follow a given celebrity or media program. Collective effervescence (Lorenzo, 2017; Pham, 2015) is emerging as a recognized aspect of fan behavior as exhibited by individual members of fan collectives. Sharing feelings with others who have the same feelings for the parasocial object is a part of this collective effervescence. An appreciation for someone for whom everyone has a deep affection becomes a way that fans bond with and feel closer to friends who also share that affection. This also becomes an avenue to other common interests and feelings. Another way of saying this is that fantasy is fun, and sharing fantasies with others is fun, a source of hedonistic entertainment. Sometimes, the shared emotions also involve either romantic attraction (eros) or deep affection (storge), and that mutual attraction to a celebrity also creates bonds among fans.

This construct is proposed as a framework for understanding how any kind of small collective gathering gives meaning, a sense of connection, and joy to life. Social media fan forums are examples of such collectives of like-minded individuals who admire the same celebrity. This enthusiasm for the favorite celebrity is an additional influence on the "parasocial perception" of their artist (see Chapter 4) and how they have interacted with various individual fans. Fans draw

Social and Spiritual in Fandom and PSRs

inferences about how their own encounter might happen should they have one by looking at the experiences of others, which contributes to Mudita, which is described below.

MUDITA

Mudita is a word from Sanskrit and Pali with no known English counterpart. It means sympathetic or unselfish joy or joy in the good fortune of others (Casioppo, 2020; Eisenberg, 2002). Why is this mentioned here in the context of PSE and things such as collective effervescence? Because during my work as a participant observer in various fan groups, I see this kind of reaction on a daily basis. Fans converge on a blog or Facebook page, and one fan reports that they were able to meet the favored celebrity. There is almost always a sense of shared joy from the community at the success of the group member in having this encounter. The fan having the encounter shares a story or photo as a way to allow the other group members to share vicariously in the experience. Although there is occasional jealousy, in most cases, that is not the pervasive tone of the discussion that ensues.

Another example of this kind of shared joy comes from one of the actors from *The Hobbit*, Dean O'Gorman (Zoom interview, April 19, 2023), who shared the following thought with me when speaking about appearing at fan conventions:

It's fun because I get to meet up with other people from *The Hobbit*, and when we're together, we bond, and the fans enjoy that. The fans like to see it when we look like we're having a good time . . . because we are!

This comment reflects Mudita on many levels, the most obvious of which is that fans experience joy in watching their favorite actors having a good time, which, from my observations, is absolutely true. Also, clearly, the actors experience a reciprocal kind of joy in realizing that they are allowing the fans a window into their enjoyment in the relationships they have with fellow actors.

I suggest that this mutual joy is at the heart of collective effervescence, shared joy in the company of other like-minded people, fans, and celebrities alike. I have observed this phenomenon at the dozens of *Star Trek* and science fiction conventions that I have attended during the past 30 years.

FANDOM AS COMPARED TO FORMS OF RELIGIOUS EXPRESSION

The term "celebrity worship" has come into common use since Maltby and McCutcheon and others coined the term in 2002. The use of the word "worship" encourages the implicit connection that might exist between fandom and forms of religious or spiritual expression.

It would be difficult to discuss topics such as Mudita and collective effervescence without mentioning the scholarly work that draws parallels between fandom and religion. Although most of the fans I have discussed this idea with take exception to the notion that they in any way "worship" their favorite celebrity, an opinion with which I concur, there are definite parallels between the terminology used in fandom and the terminology used about religion.

Olsen (2021) began his discussion on this subject by first offering his own definition of fandom. He observed that popular culture, religion, and spirituality are all topics that influence one another in current thinking. A common problem in trying to define fandom is that it is something most people think that they just intuitively understand and thus do not attempt to define it at all. Another problem is that fandom takes so many different forms, with some fans engaging in it purely for the opportunity to socialize with other fans, whereas other fans want to form a connection or bond with the celebrity object of interest (which is far more possible than most believe; Stever, 2016). For yet others, the purpose of being a fan is to interact with the text itself rather than with celebrity producers or other fans. For Jenkins (2018), the engagement of either a text or a team (in the case of sports) is the primary activity. Others recognize that it is the emotional connection formed with a celebrity persona that is primary (Gray et al., 2007; Stever, 2013). Social media has led to fan activity becoming more mainstream, although this activity has existed for as long as there have been media.

Single-text fandoms that focus on one specific media phenomenon which forms a connection within the group of fans are common on the internet and social media. Examples of this abound, and those I have encountered in my own work include Grobanites (Josh Groban), Trekkies/Trekkers (*Star Trek*), The Armitage Army (Richard Armitage), Cumberbitches (Benedict Cumberbatch), Little Monsters (Lady Gaga alias mother monster), Gyllenhaalics (Jake Gyllenhaal), and many, many others. This group naming is conducive to forming a following that becomes as devoted to the group as to the celebrity. It is in this context that parallels with religion are very often made.

The most obvious term used in both religion and fandom is the already mentioned "worship." An entire body of scholarly work supports the thesis that large percentages of the general population engage in celebrity worship (e.g., Maltby et al., 2003, 2004). One of the difficulties in assessing this parallel is that different people have different views about the existence of God and the place God has in our world and cultures. For the person who believes in God, the notion of celebrity worship elicits a very different reaction than it does for the person who is agnostic or atheist.

Caughey (1984) found similarities between imaginary social relationships, his term for PSRs, and the relationships that Indigenous people from various cultures have with their gods. The entire real–not real dimension has a different place in religion versus celebrity worship. Celebrities are real people, although some people maintain a PSR with celebrities who are no longer living. Elvis, Michael Jackson, Prince, Whitney Houston—many celebrities no longer with us have devoted fan followings. The PSR with a fictional character has a completely different place on that real–not real continuum.

One of the commonalities between religion and fandom is the concept of devotion. One can be devoted to either a favorite celebrity or a favorite media program in ways that mimic devotion to a deity. Such commonalities are discussed by various scholars, including Olsen (2021), Malluhi (2018), Elliott (2021), and Hills (2002).

Malluhi's (2018) thesis placed a particular emphasis on the concept of devotion. He proposed that fandom parallels religion in its emotional elements, its community elements, and its form. He noted that fandom is meeting some of the needs that used to be met for people by their religious affiliations, most notably the need for community. Fans will often use the word "religion" in reference to a favorite media enterprise, meaning that their devotion to that media form would remind one of religious devotion in its many elements. Fans form communities around their media favorites, a phenomenon that is easily observable not only online but also in the wider world of entertainment in general. Fan clubs are a staple of both media stars and programs, and many individuals organize their social and personal lives around their membership in such a community.

Contrary to what some may think (e.g., Malluhi, 2018), fandom and fan clubs are not new to the internet era. One can now see some of the same fan activities on the internet that I observed during the 1980s and early 1990s before most people had internet access. Fans networked in groups very similar to the ones observed on the internet, but the methods of communication were clunkier and, in most cases, more expensive. For this reason, earlier pre-internet fandoms were somewhat limited by elements such as age and income. Most of the fan groups I observed organized themselves around pen pal lists, and they corresponded through regular mail or telephone (which in the 1980s was quite costly if it involved long distance). They traveled in order to meet up with other fans at fan events such as conventions and concerts.

Malluhi (2018) concluded his thesis by saying, "This research has not shown that fandom is a religion; rather, it showed that it has particular structures which resemble religion; that there are fan experiences that resemble religious experiences; and that it serves the same needs as religion" (p. 60).

Elliott (2021) agreed that there is a striking similarity between fan devotion and religious devotion. He suggested that fan devotion is better thought of as sacred rather than religious. Fans will often travel to iconic sites that are associated with the fandom, much as religious followers will engage in pilgrimages to sacred sites. I observed this firsthand in the *Poldark* fandom, as one of the fans' favorite things to do was travel to Cornwall, where the program was filmed. Indeed, even 4 years after filming had stopped, fans were still visiting Cornwall. Similarly, during my study of Michael Jackson fans from 1988 to 1992, fans would travel to Los Angeles to visit his residences, studios, and even the elementary school named after him. *Star Trek* fans will travel to Hollywood to visit its filming locations. *Harry Potter* fans travel to various places associated with its films and stories (e.g., King's Cross Station in London). *The Lord of the Rings/Hobbit* fans travel to New Zealand to visit the places where those films were made. There is no lack of examples to illustrate this point.

One concern expressed by some scholars and summarized by Elliott (2021) is that equating fandom with religion feeds negative stereotypes about fans, portraying fandom as irrational and extreme. Elliott expressed further concern about scholars who write about fandom as a religion: "It is not always clear what kind of comparison is being made. Are scholars arguing that pop culture fandoms are religions, are similar to religions, or are substitutes for religions?" (p. 2). He calls into question the use of words such as religious, sacred, spiritual, and cult, without defining them adequately. Elliott makes the argument that among these words, "sacred" is the one that most accurately describes most fan experiences.

Matt Hills (2002) has stated that fans often appropriate discourse from both religion and cults when describing their own experiences as fans. He preferred the term *neo-religiosity* with respect to fandom and advocated for the term *cult fan* when talking about the fan experience. Ward (2011), Rojek (2007), and Porter (2009) are all scholars who have written about fandom in the context of religion, using terms such as *para-religion* (Ward) or *implicit religion* (Porter) in their discussions.

By distinguishing religion from the sacred, Elliott (2021) argues that sacred is the more accurate term to use when talking about fandom in a religious context. Although religion always is discussed in relation to the sacred or spiritual, Elliott argues that it is possible to have the sacred in a secular rather than religious context: "The sacred is a social process of externalizing and dramatizing fundamental features of society" (p. 6). As such, many features of group identity can be described as sacred without reference to religion. For example, patriotism or national identity can be held sacred within a nation or society.

In his argument, Elliott (2021) argued that sacred means special and that for many fans, this describes exactly the nature of their fandom—the connections, interests, and symbols that are held as particularly special and unique to the group. Other aspects of the sacred often found in fan groups include inspiration, meaning, and identity, all hallmarks of fan culture.

CHARISMA

One of the things that can inspire fans to become devoted followers of a celebrity is that person's charisma. Entire books have been written trying to define "charisma" (e.g., Schiffer, 1973). It is one of the times when words seem insufficient, but while in the presence of charisma, it can be felt, and there is little doubt about that being what it is. For example, from Michael Jackson, I felt an energy and interpersonal connection that I have experienced in very few other situations. He had "sparkle" and radiated warmth, and a kind of joy in entertaining that has been unmatched in very many others I have encountered.

But recently, I was able to experience a different type of charisma, a warmth, and kindness that was exceptional in its own way. It is my belief that this kind of interpersonal connection that some form so easily to individuals in just a moment is what can set apart a favorite celebrity who has a gift for interpersonal interaction and demonstrates kindness with every breath. I see the word "kindness" twice in the previous two sentences. But if I had to choose one word to describe Aidan Turner (actor best known for *Poldark* and *The Hobbit*, among other screen credits), that would be the word.

From having heard interviews with both Turner and other celebrities who related well to their fans (Josh Groban comes to mind), I think part of what is at work is that the celebrity himself (or herself) has been in the place of admiring someone and then met that someone and been moved by it. Listening to Turner talk about meeting and working with icons like Ian McKellan; or Groban having met and worked with Paul Simon (for one example), one infers that having been in the position of "the fan," they well and truly do "get it," the experience of being in the presence of someone who inspires a bit of awe in you. Dean O'Gorman (Zoom interview, April 19, 2023) had this to say about meeting fans:

Approaching people that you think a lot of, or you like their work can be scary, so I try to be as kind and understanding towards the fans as possible because it can be intimidating even though, from my point of view, it's quite endearing when people come up and ask for autographs, I know that sometimes people can feel a bit intimidated.

In 2011, I had the unique opportunity of meeting and interacting at length with William Shatner, another celebrity who has iconic status in Western culture. He was filming a documentary about fans, and my friend Rene Auberjonois, who had done *Boston Legal* with Shatner and become good friends with him as a result, had shared with him (unbeknownst to me) about my doctoral dissertation and other research on fans. I showed up one day during a convention to have lunch with Rene (apart from the convention, which I was not attending), and the next thing I knew, I was walking around a hotel lobby with a huge microphone in front of me, camera rolling, with Shatner behind the camera directing a fan to ask me questions. I don't think any of that made the final cut in the film he was making, but the experience of being directed by Shatner for more than half an hour is one I will never forget. Despite this unlikely scenario, he completely put me at ease, and it wasn't until later that it hit me, the "What just happened?" feeling of having been directed on film by someone of his stature. So here is another example of a celebrity who had unusual interpersonal skills, making him able to interact with the public such that it had a very positive impact on his career. Indeed, the first time I met Shatner was as a 13-year-old *Star Trek* fan waiting in a long line to get his autograph and a picture taken with him. He had that same powerful charisma then, that undefinable quality that makes you never forget the encounter.

All of this is challenging to include in a book that is primarily focused on "research," but it is my belief that if we don't try to describe these moments and understand their meaning, we run the risk of never really and truly understanding what it is that makes certain individuals in our culture stand out with this thing we call "charisma." One of the most baffling aspects of this concept is that no two people I have described here as charismatic are at all alike in the way they exhibited the quality. Michael Jackson's quirky magnetism, Aidan Turner's thoughtful kindness, Shatner's putting one at ease, Groban's friendliness and disarming manner are all different versions of charisma, yet they are easily recognized as just that. And in each case, it translates into a kind of relationship between fan and celebrity that has a big impact on the fan and defines in many ways the career of that celebrity. Each of these men is memorable in his own way. I have seen women with this quality; for example, Madonna certainly had it when I saw her in concert from my front-row seat. Clearly, Taylor Swift is another celebrity with charisma.

I also suspect that many of my *Star Trek* and other actor friends have this kind of charisma, but once you get to know someone in a regular social relationship and are no longer part of "the public," it is harder to get that same feeling from them (although I know that others do). So, is charisma a part of the magic that comes from knowing someone at a distance and thus experiencing them in an idealized form, which is at the heart of the definition of PSEs? Perhaps. The *Star Trek* actors I am privileged to number among my friends all have terrific interpersonal skills, are kind and friendly, and have many fans. But in the "getting to know them" process of friendship, some of that "magic" is lost. I recall Rene Auberjonois, whom we lost to cancer in late 2019, and the force of nature he was when meeting his fans. I spent many an hour sitting next to him, watching him sign autographs for and greet his many fans. I could say the same for Nana Visitor, Alexander Siddig, Armin Shimerman, Aron Eisenberg, Max Grodenchik, Andy Robinson, Chase Masterson, J. G. Hertzler—all actors I have been privileged to know as friends. Each has a wonderful quality that could be defined as charismatic, to which their fans will attest. This observation does suggest that charisma is a thing best observed and understood at a distance.

CELEBRITY WORSHIP

This discussion would not be complete without further mention of one of the most pervasive discussions in audience psychology since 2002—celebrity worship. Maltby and colleagues (2004) set out to describe levels of celebrity worship using a Celebrity Attitude Scale and factor analysis in order to delineate the aspects of celebrity worship that might be related or clustered. They came up with three types of celebrity worship using this process.

Entertainment–social celebrity worship described behavior that is typical of fans and, in fact, is arguably not "worship" at all (Stever, 2011). This lowest level of "celebrity worship" has entertainment–social value and is reflected through items like "My friends and I like to discuss what my favorite celebrity has done" (McCutcheon et al., 2016, p. 162). Intense personal celebrity worship is defined by items like "I have frequent thoughts about my favorite celebrity, even when I don't want to" (p. 161). This level reflects individuals' intense and compulsive feelings about a celebrity, similar to the obsessional tendencies of fans often referred to in the literature (e.g., Dietz et al., 1991).

Borderline pathological celebrity worship is the most extreme expression of celebrity worship and is shown in items such as "If I were lucky enough to meet my favorite celebrity, and he/she asked me to do something illegal as a favor I would probably do it" (McCutcheon et al., 2016, p. 161). It is in this third level that pathological attitudes and behavior are most often found.

Intense personal celebrity worship characterizes 15–20% of samples taken from both general population samples and fan samples, and borderline pathological celebrity worship characterizes approximately 3–5% of samples taken (Stever, 2011). These were recognized as having serious connections to problematic audience behaviors (Maltby et al., 2003, 2004). The early celebrity worship literature conflated celebrity worship with fandom, an error that was pointed out by Stever (2011) when samples of behaviorally identified fans were given the celebrity worship instrument and were found to not show any more tendencies to celebrity worship than the general population samples that had been studied by the celebrity worship scholars. "Fan" and "celebrity worshipper" were distinct and very different constructs, a distinction that is better reflected in more recent work (e.g., Hitlan et al., 2021; Maltby & Day, 2017; McCutcheon et al., 2016).

TO CONSIDER

The language we use to describe things comes laden with emotions and personal meanings. After having read this chapter, a few reviewers took grave exception to anyone drawing any kind of parallel between fandom and religion. Religion, for those people, was about the worship of a deity, and anything less was disrespectful. In the same manner, using the word "sacred" in a secular context was not pleasing to some people.

But the reality is that in a culture where diverse opinions about all manner of things, including religion and worship, are common, the application of these words to groups that have organized around a "fandom" is an idea that is worthy of being considered. Certainly, there are fan groups that espouse values and philosophies—groups such as *Star Trek* fans or Tolkien/*Lord of the Rings* fans. Hills' (2002) application of the term "cult fan" recognizes that those who follow and advocate for a worldview that has been proposed by a fictional universe are not so terribly unlike a religious group in that they propose ways to behave, a vision of the future, or an idea about how people should act. Those unfamiliar with a particular media and fan group are not in a place to particularly judge whether or not those values and beliefs are justified.

Religion most often denotes an organized belief system with patterns of interaction that usually involve some type of intermediary, wise man, priest, or monk. The term spirituality works better because it denotes our need to understand the way the world works and to feel connected to others through a common set of understandings. There is no intermediary in fan groups, which sets them apart from religious groups. Therefore, the logical conclusion is that fandoms share some aspects of religion but lack others.

It is also important to recognize that the 21st-century culture that is dominated by media is increasingly more becoming a culture of celebrity, as is witnessed by the percentage of people who exhibit intense personal celebrity worship. If one in five individuals believes that their favorite celebrity is their soul mate, as is reflected in available data (Stever, 2011), the implications for that in the bigger picture of social relationships and community life are enormous. Lynn McCutcheon recently recounted that the percentages of samples taken more recently, since 2022, show an increase in intense personal and borderline pathological celebrity worship, which is also a point of some concern (Haupt, 2023).

FANDOM VERSUS PARASOCIAL RELATIONSHIPS

In this chapter, concepts are applied to fandom and discussed with the assumption that they will also apply to those who are engaged in PSRs. The difference between being a fan and having a PSR is one that cannot be quantified or "factored" or easily measured. Surely there is overlap, which creates problems in distinguishing the two constructs.

Being in a PSR means that one carries on an imaginary interaction with the person or character apart from consuming any media. Caughey (1984) called it imaginary social interaction, and that's actually, in some ways, a better term for it. During a media interaction, parasocial interaction (PSI) is one's sense of actually connecting with the character in a personal way in the moment. Direct address (the media persona speaking directly to the camera) enhances PSI.

Parasocial attachment (PSA) is when one seeks out a connection with the persona, either with vicarious or actual proximity seeking, to derive comfort from the relationship.

Being a fan involves a set of activities or behaviors characteristic of a follower of a celebrity persona, either the celebrity or perhaps the character they portray or even the program in which they've appeared. Beyond the imaginary interaction, fans often seek out the other work of that celebrity. On fan pages on social media, an exchange of information about how to find that work is common. The exchange of images is another commonly shared fan activity.

Before the internet and streaming were available, fans would exchange media on VHS videotapes. For example, I received many hours of Michael Jackson performances early in my research from 1988 to 1992, and I also received many photographs that other fans had and would reproduce.

Proximity-seeking behavior (integral to PSA) is actually very similar to other fan activities. Seeking out new work or looking for live performances to attend are common. In addition, the fan can extend a connection with that persona by writing their own stories about that persona. Finding like-minded others to share the love of the actor or character is also common.

What do fan groups do? They attend live events together, share stories with one another, discuss performances, and swap tales about previous encounters with their favorite celebrity. Seeking out new source material is primary.

Already mentioned was that some authors write as if all these fan undertakings started with the internet, but nothing could be further from the truth. I saw every one of these activities beginning in 1988, well before most people had internet access. It was more difficult to network with other fans back then, but people were doing it. For example, writing fan fiction is documented at least as far back as the 1960s (Verba, 2003), and fans exchanged stories by running them off on old-style ditto machines and mailing them to other fans. The "fanzine" was a publication of a collection of stories that would then be exchanged with costs covered by the participant (no one making a profit). The mimeographed stories and fanzines stopped being produced once most people were on the internet, and websites such as fanfiction.net and AO3 replaced the fanzine.

Ultimately, distinguishing between PSR and fandom only becomes a major issue when one is trying to measure either for the purposes of quantitative research. In qualitative studies, the overlap and the inability to separate them out become crystal clear (Stever, 1994, 2009). One problem, however, is that the scholarly communities that study fandom and those that study parasocial theory often are not the same groups of scholars. By not integrating the work from each group, much is lost in the quest to understand why people develop such an investment in media personalities and why those relationships and connections are so important to media viewers.

CONCLUSION

Although it has been my observation based on my years as a participant observer that most fans don't "worship" their favorite celebrities, one can't deny that there is a subset of fans who engage in this behavior. The majority of fans do not idolize their favorite celebrities in this way. For most fans I've met, the connection to their favorite celebrity symbolizes a special relationship with someone like a family member or close friend. They admire, respect, and revere them but mostly don't worship them.

My dear friend, the late Rene Auberjonois, used to tell me that programs like *Star Trek* are actually modern mythology. The characters represent universal archetypes who resonate in that way with their followers. This might be the best way to look at the interface between fandom and religious thought.

9

Fans Meet Celebrities

Cameo and Conventions

GAYLE S. STEVER ■

It has been argued that the original conception of parasocial interaction (PSI) was specific to media personae who communicate directly with the audience, breaking, as it is called, the fourth wall (Konijn & Hoorn, 2017). In a discussion of the article that conceptualized both PSI and parasocial relationships (PSRs; Horton & Wohl, 1956), it is pointed out that the original identifying characteristic of PSI involved direct address where the persona talks to the audience as if the communication was personal and private. The person on camera even incorporates a conversational style, including the gestures and other characteristics of an in-person conversation that we recognize in direct social conversations. Media is used this way to create an illusion of intimacy. Since 1956, it has been generally recognized that we form PSRs with all manner of media personalities, not just the ones who break the fourth wall. This chapter introduces a new form of social media, called Cameo, that conforms to that original conceptualization of PSI as perfectly as might be possible.

Alperstein (2019), in his discussion of mediated social connections with celebrities, asks an important question: "What happens when communication that used to be one-way becomes interactive?" (p. viii). He argued in his discussion that with the advent of digital media, the possibility of engaging a celebrity in a social exchange without ever leaving one's own home had become possible; indeed, for those active on social media, it was no longer unusual. As a student of John Caughey (1984), Alperstein writes extensively about imaginary social relationships, Caughey's term that parallels the PSR idea. One of his foci has been how fans fantasize about celebrities and include them in the inner worlds of imagination. He also observes that given the opportunity, fans will attempt to interact with them. In Chapter 3, we have already discussed various types of social media and the potential created for interaction on platforms such as YouTube, Facebook,

---

Parasocial Experiences. David C. Giles and Gayle S. Stever, Oxford University Press. © Oxford University Press 2024.
DOI: 10.1093/oso/9780197647646.003.0010

Twitter, and Instagram. In addition, we discussed the ways that influencers or microcelebrities emerge from these types of platforms.

The foundation of a PSR is PSI, when the media consumer relates to a media message personally, responding to it as they would a regular social message. If someone on television asks a question of "the audience," the viewer answers it. If someone on the program makes a mistake, the viewer castigates them a bit (and then perhaps forgives them). The dropped football, the missed opportunity, saying the wrong thing . . . the viewer responds even though they are quite aware that the message was not intended for them personally and the onscreen personality cannot hear them. In PSI, it is not so much what the viewer thinks as it is how they respond to the message. This is at the heart of interaction in general.

What if the mediated message was actually personal and intended for that individual viewer? On the Experience of Parasocial Interaction (EPSI) questionnaire (Hartmann & Goldhoorn, 2011), one of the items states, "While watching the clip, I had the feeling that [name] was aware of me." In Chapter 4, more was shared about the mutual awareness celebrities and audiences have for each other as a social group, with followers relating to and being responded to by the celebrity. But on Cameo, a website created specifically for celebrity-to-fan direct communication, PSI is taken to a whole new level. A message is created and sent by the celebrity to a viewer at their request. The belief that the celebrity is aware of the audience member is actually true with Cameo.

It should be noted that, with the administration of the EPSI questionnaire (Hartmann & Goldhoorn, 2011), which is the best measure of PSI in current research, the viewer's perception that the messages were personal and intended for them was, overall, quite low. On a 7-point scale, the means were all approximately 3 or lower. The highest was 3.24 for the item "(name) knew I paid attention to him/her." In evaluating that item in particular, it doesn't seem like a big stretch for the viewer to presume that the presenter would know they would pay attention, the point being that there is little reason to presume that viewers, for the most part, are not grounded in reality. Thus, viewers overall appear to be quite aware of the fact that any feeling they have of being addressed directly is an illusion.

One of the hallmarks of 21st-century media has been the almost continuous appearance of new forms of social media, beginning in 2003 with the creation of Myspace and continuing to 2004 with the introduction of Facebook and then Twitter in 2006. YouTube was another prominent addition in 2005. Near the beginning of the second decade of the century, Instagram (2010), Pinterest (2009), TikTok (2014), and other platforms began to emerge and even supersede some of the earlier ones. It was in this climate of new social media that Baron App Inc. introduced Cameo in 2016.

CAMEO AND PARASOCIAL INTERACTION

Cameo is a website designed to allow celebrities to create videos to share with fans who make online requests. It can be considered a performance created for a single or very small group of recipients. An important defining feature of this service is that while the viewer gets a very personalized message from the celebrity, in most cases, the celebrity gets relatively little information about the viewer. The exception to this might be in the case of a single user who sends multiple requests to the same celebrity. Because of the structure of this platform, the interaction is most decidedly parasocial between most users and celebrities. There are two other features of Cameo: the direct message (where for a small fee, a user can send a text message to the celebrity); and live video chat. These are less frequently used features of Cameo, and this discussion will focus mainly on the personalized video that a user can receive from a celebrity.

This fee service has several defining features. Basically, a person can send a request to a celebrity asking for a video that addresses an occasion, a question, or some other situation. The most common requests are birthday shout-outs, other occasions such as anniversaries or holidays, the "pep talk," or a question. The requester has 250 characters for their request, and for an additional $12, they can add another 400 characters.

After receiving the video, the requester can send a "reaction video." This is discussed further below. In addition, the requester gives feedback, including a five-star scale rating and a short reply to the video. Fees for a Cameo vary from $5 to $1,000 and up. The actors interviewed for this chapter had fees in the $45 to $150 range. As such, Cameo is an affordable way for an audience member to reach out to a favorite celebrity. It offers a unique and novel type of interaction for a fan of a particular celebrity. The actors I interviewed while writing this chapter were actively receiving Cameo requests and had been for a period of 2–4 years.

A celebrity becomes eligible to be listed on Cameo when they have 20,000 or more Instagram followers. Cameo grew rapidly during the COVID-19 pandemic because it accommodated social distance restrictions, meaning that because it was not possible to meet people in person, this was a way that fans could still have a personalized interaction with their favorite celebrities (Kircher, 2020). In 2020, Cameo topped *Fast Company's* list of the "World's Most Innovative Social Media Companies" and was listed as one of the "World's 50 Most Innovative Companies." During a pandemic research study, a survey of 166 study participants found that as mediated social activity increased, parasocial closeness with a favorite celebrity became stronger and more meaningful, particularly as face-to-face social engagement decreased (Bond, 2021). Given these circumstances, Cameo and services like it (Kim et al., 2023) have the potential to be a powerful source of fan–celebrity PSI that could serve to strengthen PSRs.

As discussed in previous chapters, PSI is the sense an audience member feels while consuming media that they are being addressed personally. The focus of PSI research has been the feeling of actual involvement in an interaction with a performer during media exposure (Hartmann & Goldhoorn, 2011). In terms of understanding PSI and PSRs and the factors that strengthen parasocial experiences, Cameo has one of the hallmarks of PSI automatically built into its platform. All the Cameo videos sent to users employ "direct address," meaning simply that the celebrity speaks to the requester looking directly into a camera (often using a smartphone). Several studies have shown the efficacy of direct address in creating a sense of PSI far more effective than the typical media message where people on the screen talk to each other but not to their audiences.

Much has been said in parasocial research about the power of direct address (Cohen et al., 2019; Dibble et al., 2016; Hartmann, 2016; Hartmann & Goldhoorn, 2011). A study of PSI using 255 viewers watching a journalist found that when direct address was employed, messages were more credible, the experience was more intense, and the enhanced vitality of the PSI increased the enjoyment of the experience for the viewer (Atad & Cohen, 2024). Furthermore, Cummins and Cui (2014) recapped their findings as follows: "In summary, scholarship suggests that gaze initiated by a media performer should serve to cue attention, influence perception formation, and aid in the 'simulacrum of conversational give and take' Horton and Wohl (1956) first described" (p. 725). Direct address and the performer's gaze are powerful cues during PSI, both defining features of Cameos.

It has been argued that interactive mediated communication is still parasocial. The argument is that even if a celebrity responds to a tweet or other social media message, the uneven relationship between celebrity and fan and the lack of access the fan has to the celebrity mean that the relationship is still parasocial (Hartmann, 2008). As I argue in this chapter, this is absolutely true in almost all cases with respect to Cameo.

TALKING WITH DEAN O'GORMAN

In the summer of 2022, I began a case study of fans of *The Hobbit* films, adding to my work since 1988 on fan–celebrity interactions and relationships. I have followed four *Hobbit* actors who had active public fan discussion forums (among fans, not including the celebrity) on Facebook: Richard Armitage, Aidan Turner, Lee Pace, and Dean O'Gorman. O'Gorman (Figure 9.1) was the only one of the four on Cameo; from his fans, I learned about this relatively new service. New Zealand actor O'Gorman played Fili the Dwarf, a role that made him more visible internationally. His career, beginning at the age of 11, is impressive. Since *The Hobbit*, he has had numerous screen credits, including *The Almighty Johnsons*, *Trumbo*, *Pork Pie*, *Under the Vines*, and *After the Party*.

Using Cameo, I reached out to O'Gorman, asking if he would be willing to answer some questions relative to my research in fan studies. He said yes, and in a series of Cameo videos (some recounted throughout this book), he answered my questions about his preferred ways to connect with fans, his impressions about what meeting him meant to them, when he realized he had fans, and whether he has ever been a fan himself. If so, did that affect how he interacted with his fans?

Figure 9.1 Dean O'Gorman.
Source: Markus Wissmann/Shutterstock.com.

As a new user of the platform, I was startled at how quickly I came to feel like I had met O'Gorman and how powerful it was to have him speak directly to me and answer my questions through the Cameo videos. I really did not have any expectation that a series of 2-minute videos would foster a sense of connection to or sense of "knowing" someone. The fact that I had this experience, as someone who, for years, has studied PSI and its effects, made me consider what this would be like for someone who had been a long-term fan of the celebrity in question. Indeed, I met and chatted with several fans who also did Cameos with O'Gorman, and I sensed they also felt they had come to know him, although several of those people had also met him at science fiction/fantasy conventions.

After our initial series of four Cameos, I had the opportunity to interview O'Gorman (April 19 and June 7, 2023). He explained that the kind of service celebrities provide fans is unique. "You represent something to someone, and they want to meet you." Considering the field of parasocial experience, there really is no one else who can help the audience member realize the dream of, for example, meeting their favorite character from a movie. The important point here is what the character represents to that person and why that character is meaningful to them. Speaking further on that subject, O'Gorman said,

> I do know that when I meet lots of fans at a convention, it seems to me that they're not meeting me, they're meeting the image of me, and so sometimes it's important for me to sort of maintain the image for them. If they see a

character as heroic or funny, then sometimes I want to live up to that image just for them because obviously me and my characters are very different.

SOCIAL MEDIA AS SELF-HELP

We live in a culture which ascribes various motivations to celebrities, many of them based on an assumption that they do what they do only for fame and money. It has been my experience speaking with various actors that this is not true in many cases. In this context, Cameo appears to be a form of "self-help," an insight that was articulated nicely by one of my university students who wrote a paper on the subject (Martini, unpublished manuscript). She argued that self-help is written and consumed for the purpose of helping the audience member or book consumer improve their mood, hopefully experiencing eudemonia in the process. Media with its potential for mood enhancement has been recognized in published research as well (Chang, 2023). So, when the viewer reaches out on Cameo to a favorite celebrity, they are engaging in a form of self-help wherein they are seeking a meaningful experience with someone they admire. That the experience can be mood-enhancing is clear from the reactions and comments to Cameo videos that are expressed on every account I looked at.

O'Gorman went on to say, "They meet me, and they have ideas about me, and I'm always really respectful and nice to people, and I can see that it means things to people, and I'm happy to do that." He defined his role on Cameo specifically in this way: "I don't need to get to know the person, I just try to see that the experience I'm giving them is something they will enjoy or need." This reinforces the premise that Cameo is entirely parasocial, as the requester is not typically seen or heard by the celebrity. Indeed, often the requester is a friend or family member of the person for whom the Cameo is being made. But the Cameo video creator, namely the celebrity, views their role as a service provider to someone who seeks an experience, and Cameo represents a variety of experiences for its users.

O'Gorman went on to further explain his reasons for initially getting on Cameo and the kinds of connections that are possible with fans he's met in various ways:

I think conventions are the best way to interact with fans. It's a good format, you meet lots of people, and it's a good way to connect with people. Failing that, Cameo is not bad. I haven't really been traveling much since COVID, so Cameo seems to be quite a good way to do it in lieu of traveling overseas. Friends emailed me, encouraging me to get on Cameo, and initially, I've always had that sort of reaction that self-promotion was never cool when I was young, so I had to remove a bit of that baggage about putting myself out there. It is nice when people ask if you can say happy birthday to someone or make other requests. That's really nice. I do like that. I feel like you can give back to people. It's something specific to celebrities. Anyone can do nice things for people, but the fan relationship is quite specific.

NANA VISITOR

After interviewing O'Gorman, I realized that my friend of almost 30 years, Nana Visitor (Figure 9.2), was also on Cameo. I reached out to inquire as to what Cameo means to her (interview conducted over Zoom, April 28, 2023). Visitor is best known for her role as Kira Nerys on *Star Trek: Deep Space Nine*, although she has a long list of other screen credits as well as being an experienced Broadway musical star, having played Roxie Hart in *Chicago* as well as other prominent Broadway leads.

In speaking about Cameo, she had this to say:

> Cameo originally wanted me to just do a 30-second "Happy Birthday" or whatever the occasion was, and that was all. That felt to me like it just would become a transaction, a dopamine hit for someone. I couldn't do it that way. I got heavily into Cameo during the pandemic. That was also when I started my Instagram account, which I won't monetize, I won't advertise. That's information. I wanted to do something honest. At 65 I feel like I can give life experience on Instagram because of my particular life, the trauma that I've had, and my way of recovery was information. I read a lot of psychology, and it's helped me. When something really helps me, I cannot help but want to give it to others.

Visitor's Instagram account has a large collection of short videos that give life advice, philosophical perspectives, and other sorts of self-help information for the

Figure 9.2 Nana Visitor, René Auberjonois, and Terry Farrell.
Source: Sam Aronov/Shutterstock.com.

Fans Meet Celebrities

viewer. This speaks again to social media as a form of self-help, something both Visitor and O'Gorman alluded to in my conversations with them.

Just as O'Gorman had compared the Cameo experience to meeting fans at conventions, Visitor also saw the parallels between the two experiences. She had this to say

> This is what I've found about going to conventions. When people come up to me, most of the time, it's not about them seeing me. It's about me seeing them. We've had that relationship where they've seen me. Now they want to complete the circle. They want me to know what I did and what the effect was. So, I understand it's not really about me at all. It's about me bearing witness to their experience with what I've done. That's what convention meetings are.

Talking about conventions, O'Gorman had a related comment:

> Initially, you meet people who are fans of you who say, "I liked you in this thing." But then I think as people sort of age up or grow with you, there are some people that I've met through conventions and life, and they've become more interested in what I'm up to as a person than just work-wise and so the connection becomes less about celebrity and more about interest in a person. But the connection is made initially through the work.

Both actors speak here about the connection, which is purely parasocial, that the viewer has made with their work, but then by meeting the celebrity at a convention, the potential is there to turn it into something more, what Visitor called completing the circle.

Does Cameo serve that same purpose? To the extent that the celebrity can learn something about the recipient of the video, there is the potential for connections to be made. This is particularly true when, as Visitor mentioned, doing multiple Cameos for the same person. It is significant to me that both these actors and many others (see the Richard Armitage quote in Chapter 4) say they don't like the word "fan." The strong sense one gets is that these actors are meeting individual persons and not "fans." Relating para-communication and the resulting parasocial perception (see Chapters 2 and 4) contributes to the idea that "parasocial to social" is a continuum, and whenever two people are involved in that connection, there is potential to move the relationship along that continuum, closer to the social end with each encounter.

As the discussion in Chapter 7 on parasocial attachment describes, we as humans are "hard-wired" or predisposed to be attracted to familiar faces, voices, and ultimately the persona of those we've met, no matter how we've met them. If that parasocial attachment is formed, the next logical step is proximity seeking, and although most often that is virtual, the many fans who pursue meeting their favorite celebrities at conventions act on a basic human impulse to bring that relationship from the parasocial into the social realm.

Although some express fear that this could lead to stalking and celebrity worship, that has not been my observation. Most people meeting a celebrity at a convention are respectful, many fulfilling the kind of dream or need that both O'Gorman and Visitor described. During my research, I have witnessed hundreds of hours of celebrity–fan meetings and sat with numerous celebrities while they were working in autograph lines. My experience and observations have convinced me that the danger is minimal. (For a list of these events, see Stever, 2019.)

That is not to say that troublesome situations don't develop. Looking at the celebrity worship literature (McCutcheon et al., 2016), 3–5% of the general public have developed troubling connections with their favorite celebrities, what McCutcheon and others call borderline pathological celebrity worship. But in our enthusiasm to talk about the troubling cases, it is important to not forget about the 80% or more of average everyday people who are forming the kinds of positive connections described by both O'Gorman and Visitor.

ROBERT PICARDO

My third actor interview regarding Cameo was conducted on May 7, 2023, with Robert Picardo (Figure 9.3) at a science fiction convention in Philadelphia, playfully called "Gays in Space: Galactic Diversity and Inclusion Convention." It was organized by a group of LGBTQ fans who advocate for diversity in Hollywood and the aerospace industry. Actors from *Star Trek* and *The Orville* met fans in traditional autograph and photo-op settings and while doing question-and-answer sessions. Picardo, best known for playing the EMH (Emergency Medical Hologram) on *Star Trek: Voyager*, was a guest at this convention. He joined Cameo in December 2019, just before the pandemic. Reflecting on his reasons for joining, he had this to say:

> I wasn't sure if I'd like it. It feels mercenary. But you have to accept the fact that real fans of science fiction not only want to meet the actors, but they want to have souvenirs. They want a remembrance of their encounter, so science fiction fans are used to the culture of buying autographs, and often they buy other memorabilia as well. It's not something that they feel bad about, in fact, what I discovered early on when I joined the *Star Trek* franchise is that they don't like it if you don't come to conventions. They get a little angry at the actors who don't make themselves available. So, it's quite the opposite of them judging you negatively for being involved in a financial transaction when you meet. That was made clear to me some 30 years ago.

What kinds of messages was Picardo asked to create for fans?

> I decided to join Cameo and do what they called video shout-outs, messages from your favorite celebrity. Sometimes the message is for themselves, but, more often than not, it is a gift for a family member, and the ones that I love the most are the ones within a family where the parent or grandparent or

Fans Meet Celebrities

Figure 9.3 Robert Picardo.
Source: Kathy Hutchins/Shutterstock.com.

uncle or older brother got the person ordering the Cameo interested in *Star Trek*. It was their mother or uncle or whomever who sat down and got them interested in *Star Trek*. They are taking that shared experience full circle. I have said to those fans that I am proud to be part of the glue in your relationship with your family member.

Sometimes they specifically ask me to reference my character on *Voyager* to act as if I am still in character. I make terrible fun of myself. Holograms are not supposed to age, so of course, I look exactly as you were used to seeing me 20 years ago. Or I'll say, "Holograms are not supposed to age. How did I miss that memo?" I apologize for getting older. I make fun of myself. But I try to get to the core of whatever they have asked me to give to their loved one. The hardest ones are the pep talks where someone is in a very difficult time in their life. Sometimes they are suffering from addiction and they're struggling with sobriety. The other hard ones are "My father was diagnosed with stage 4 colon cancer. Can you cheer him up."

I do my best to create a narrative with whatever information they have given me that is personal. You're looking directly at the camera, you say their name, you look directly at the lens. I try to have fun with that. For example, they might say, "Please pretend to be the doctor and scan him and say, 'You're in pretty good shape, but you need to lay off the potato chips.'" And I do what they tell me.

They've given me personal details, and the person watching it is unaware that you've been given those details, so it can trigger an emotional reaction. I have gotten reaction videos where people are weeping. Occasionally my "handler" at Cameo would say, "Bob, I had to send this to you."

The key is to try to make it heartfelt. I always talk for at least 2 minutes. Our obligation is really only 30 seconds. So, I talk for 2 to 3 minutes, sometimes more. There are stories they might hear at conventions, but maybe they don't get to go to conventions, so I will talk about a favorite episode or a funny anecdote from the set. It peaked, of course, during the pandemic and the aftermath because the science fiction audience that was used to going to conventions and had a certain amount of discretionary income that was going wanting, so it peaked really in 2021. Then it fell off significantly. I'm very happy I did it during the pandemic, both for the income but also because it was a way of fulfilling a passion that fans have during that time. My deal with myself was to do the best job I could possibly do, not take it for granted and treat each one the best way I could. It was my way of feeling like I was earning that money.

DENISE CROSBY

Denise Crosby (Figure 9.4) is an actor who starred in *Star Trek: The Next Generation* as security chief Tasha Yar. She is the granddaughter of Bing Crosby and daughter

Fans Meet Celebrities

Figure 9.4 Denise Crosby.
Source: Markus Wissmann/Shutterstock.com.

of singer/actor Dennis Crosby, so she grew up associated with a show-business family. She was raised by her mother, Marilyn Scott, who worked at Paramount Pictures. She married Ken Sylk in 1995, and in 1998, they had a son. I met her at the "Gays in Space" convention in May 2023, the same convention where I met Picardo, and we subsequently did an interview over Zoom (May 19, 2023).

There were many cutting-edge aspects to her performance, including the idea that the chief of security would be a woman. She mentioned that for the late 1980s, having a short simple hairstyle was very unusual as the 1980s were the era of "big hair" (think *Falcon Crest*, *Dynasty*, and *Dallas*). Crosby was also the producer of *Trekkies* and *Trekkies 2*, both documentaries about *Star Trek* fans, so for this reason, she is very well-informed about fandom in general. To help explain the greater meaning that *Star Trek* could have for fans, she recounted her experience while making the documentaries:

> When we shot *Trekkies 2*, we went to Serbia. No one from *Star Trek* had ever been there. Serbia had been bombed, and you could see big chunks of concrete out of the buildings. The head of their *Star Trek* club reached out via email to invite us there so that they could tell us their story. They didn't have *Trek* on TV. They were getting smuggled in VHS videotapes, and they told me that "we can get through this." *Star Trek* was one of the things that helped them get through. That was such an inspiration to me.

Young girls were inspired by her character and the way she was strong, smart, and able to have her own unique look. Women, both gay and heterosexual, were inspired by the character. Many gay women, over the years, have told Crosby that she was their first crush, and they loved her character as someone they could connect with. She has met many fans who have confessed that Tasha Yar was a character who gave them the ability to challenge a bad situation (as this is what the character had done on the show, having come from an abusive environment herself).

Crosby was approached early in 2019 to join Cameo. Her son, who is a professional athlete, encouraged her, knowing how popular the platform was becoming. Initially, she feared it might be invasive, and she still is not interested in doing live video chats, wanting to keep a cushion of privacy between herself and the public. She was one of the first *Star Trek* actors to join Cameo, and initially, it was a learning curve. Zoom was still in its relative infancy, so the idea of making these videos was very new. She has not really had repeat users, although she admitted she hasn't kept track. Sometimes fans will self-identify that they are doing a second Cameo, but that is not common for her account.

Many requests come from those who identified Tasha Yar as a favorite character. Husbands and boyfriends sometimes make requests on behalf of their wife or girlfriend. Requests seem to come from both men and women equally.

Cameo is not really a two-way street if you don't do live chat, so Crosby finds that conventions have a more direct personal element. Some fans have been going to conventions year after year for more than the 30 years that she has been attending them. She and the other actors believe that for many fans, the conventions and getting autographs are about having a few minutes face to face, with the autograph being an excuse to approach the actor and have a conversation.

Crosby's personal experiences as a fan were more with musicians, and she, at one point, got to work with Mick Jagger. Her mother worked at Paramount, so she had opportunities to meet famous people there. She reported that more people would approach her to say hello in places other than Los Angeles, as the social environment in Hollywood, in particular, is such that people just don't approach celebrities there. She's never gotten someone's autograph. With her son being a minor league baseball player, she has also been more likely to meet sports stars.

It's the casual "at home" aspect of Cameo that appeals to many people, as most celebrities do their cameo videos at home recording on their phones. Crosby shared that

> Cameos have become a new part of how we interact. It tweaks itself and improves as time goes on and has helped us find new ways to connect with the fans. It's a great tool in our tool kit for interacting with fans. What fueled me to do *Trekkies* was my observation that *Trek* fans are unique and the interactions with the celebrities are unusual. There was a great deal more to *Star Trek* fandom than the bad stereotypes.

She indicated that she would like to see the reaction videos that fans post, but apparently, Cameo does not always forward them to actors. Perhaps this is a way that Cameo could improve the experience. She did say Cameo did a great job creating an app that works well; do a good job communicating with celebrities; and if one does have a problem, a company representative is there to help. Cameo have a social conscience and include charity initiatives in their model.

CAMEO AS A FAN ACTIVITY

So far, the discussion has been about Cameo as PSI leading to a PSR. The presumption is that the Cameo is a relatively private communiqué between celebrity and audience member. But is this always the case? Cameo gives the user the option of making their Cameo public or private. Many of them are made public and, in that case, are posted on the celebrity's Cameo page. In addition, fans post them on social media. Instantly, the Cameo is reaching a wider audience of people for whom the Cameo was not originally intended.

Several activities result from this feature of Cameo. Within fan communities such as those on Tumblr, some blogs feature long lists of Cameos from the favorite celebrity. Discussions develop over aspects of Cameos, and, importantly, the posts and discussions stimulate more Cameos. Because anyone can download a public Cameo, fans "collect" them and soon accumulate dozens of Cameos from their favorite celebrity.

So now the fans' ability to immerse themselves in continuous PSI is a reality. Many Cameos are produced in the celebrity's home, as noted by Crosby. This contributes to the sense of intimacy the audience member has. Notice that I have not used the phrase "illusion of intimacy," as in this case, intimate interaction can be argued to no longer be an illusion. The celebrity is purposefully reaching out to the audience and sharing these things and interacting with the audience in a way that fosters a social connection. This facilitates a connection not only between celebrities and audiences but also among audience members who have shared Cameos. Fantasy happens in the imagination. What happens in the real world of one person reaching out to another or others cannot be categorized as fantasy. If the celebrity is doing the Cameo while portraying one of their characters (e.g., as Picardo indicated he was asked to do on occasion), that is a fantasy interaction (as Picardo's character, the EMH, is not "real"). But Picardo is real, and when he interacts with the audience as himself, this no longer creates an illusion but a reality.

This fantasy–reality distinction is a critical one, as much of the argument for PSRs as "pathological" is based on the belief that the audience member believes a relationship is real when it is not. But when interactions are forged in reality rather than in the imagination, this argument no longer holds (if it ever did).

CROSSING THE SOCIAL–PARASOCIAL LINE

As discussed in Chapter 4, some celebrities choose to reach out to their fan base, whether it be through social media, conventions, or live performances. This reaching out, described as para-communication, can involve any one of a number of activities on the part of the celebrity. Consider this account from an interview by a journalist/fan with singer and songwriter Andrew McMahon speaking about the communications he gets from his fans:

> I appreciate that there are people who are willing to share and be vulnerable with me in the same way that I am in my songs. It furthers my perception of what this relationship is, which is not a one-way thing.

When he goes on stage, he says he's not a television screen. "I feel more connected when I feel like I see them, and they see me," and his interactions with fans often double as a vibe check: Did they enjoy the show? Was there something more he could have done that would have made the experience better? (Haupt, 2023).

O'Gorman decided to reach out to his fans via Cameo for assistance with the postproduction of *Morning Hate*, a film he created about New Zealand stretcher bearers in World War I, which he wrote, directed, and is co-producing. O'Gorman, in his earlier interviews with me (April 19 and June 7, 2023), had indicated he was not aware of repeat Cameo users or of who was on the other side of the Cameos he created. That changed somewhat when he told his fans he would use Cameo funds to pay for postproduction costs. He received really positive responses from

Fans Meet Celebrities — 163

many of them through repeat Cameos, enough to make a meaningful difference in his ability to move forward with his film. In our interviews, parasocial–social as a continuum rather than a dichotomy was discussed, an idea with which he heartily agreed. No one in this process became O'Gorman's new best friend by any means, but the fans who participated got the satisfaction of supporting his project in a tangible way, and O'Gorman acquired a new appreciation for the segment of his fan base who really want to support this work. He shared with me that he now recognized the names of the fans who were on their third and fourth Cameo, and he was really touched and humbled by their support.

SOCIAL MEDIA AS OPERANT CONDITIONING

Operant conditioning is a principle of behaviorism, one that proposes that when a response to a stimulus creates a pleasurable outcome, the stimulus is reinforced and is very likely to be repeated. This can be applied to many types of social media, as getting any kind of response from a favorite celebrity can be very reinforcing or, as Visitor called it, a "dopamine hit."

Specifically, a fan's request for a Cameo is the stimulus; the celebrity's reply elicits the response, and the pleasure induced by this reply acts as reinforcement. This chain of stimulus–response–reinforcement is the backbone of behaviorism and operant conditioning. Although it is rare, one of the actors I interviewed indicated that a couple of fans fell into a pattern of many (even daily) Cameo requests such that they finally had to curtail the contact.

It has been argued that social media, in general, can be reinforcing (Lindström et al., 2021), just as smartphone use (Zhang et al., 2014; Zhao & Lapierre, 2020) and other forms of media can be reinforcing. In the early days of email, getting an email was analogous to getting a letter in the mail—a pleasurable social experience in most cases. Until email communication became routine, people found themselves checking their computers many times throughout the day. And now, the same could be said (and has been said) about text messages, social media "likes" and replies, and various other kinds of interaction via social media platforms.

Requesting and receiving Cameos from favorite celebrities is just one example of a reinforcing activity, though an incredibly powerful one. Caution needs to be observed, therefore, when engaging in this kind of parasocial activity.

CONCLUSION

Several repeating themes emerged from these actor interviews. Overall, Cameo was a way to interact with fans on a personal level while at the same time offering the protection of privacy so that there is no danger of being vulnerable to the public. With the commercialization of fan experiences, Cameo is one of several ways that fans can have contact with their favorite celebrities for a fee.

While Cameo videos are personalized to the receiver, the relationship in almost every case is still parasocial. All the actors I spoke with said that they really didn't have a chance to get to know a fan or interact with them on any kind of personal level in most cases. Conventions are a better chance to have that kind of personal give-and-take interaction. None of the actors I spoke with did the live video chat feature except for Visitor, who said that during the pandemic, she had done some live chats and, in those cases, felt like she had gotten to know the fans a bit more on a social level.

All of this suggests that Cameo will continue to be a powerful force in fostering more intense parasocial connections between celebrities and their fans. A parallel can be made between Cameo and a practice from a seemingly bygone era, that of sending fan letters to a celebrity. One similarity is that this is asynchronous communication. The two sides of the conversation are not held at the same time. Cameo has the added benefit that unlike the reply to a fan letter, you know the person responding to you is actually the celebrity because they are appearing there on camera and talking to you. But replies to fan letters often included autographed photos, representing a different kind of personal reply, but a reply, nonetheless. This is distinct from other social media replies in that sometimes celebrities don't manage their own Twitter or Instagram accounts. With increasing numbers of "scam" accounts and imposters posing as celebrities on social media, Cameo becomes even more significant in offering a situation in which one can be 100% certain that the actual artist is the one replying.

Consistent with the power of the PSI and PSR, audience members truly value these kinds of encounters, almost always rating them with five out of five stars on the Cameo app. It would seem that the full potential for this type of parasocial experience is yet to be seen. And as I spoke with the actors about their fan encounters, it became clear to me that they were finding the experience to be rewarding and the opportunity to help people in some way to be important in its own right, apart from any monetary gain they might be seeing from it. All four actors indicated that conventions have the same appeal, offering a chance to make connections with audience members and help them enjoy the kind of connection to a fantasy world that only the actors who created the characters can offer. This is true of appearances at conventions and on Cameos.

It should not be missed that although crossing the line from parasocial to social while using a platform like Cameo is not a frequent occurrence, it is possible. Celebrities who offer a live video chat on their Cameo account, as did Visitor, absolutely open the door to knowing and being known on another level that is no longer completely parasocial. Other platforms have offered similar opportunities, and particularly during the pandemic, there were online science fiction conventions that offered the online meet and greet, most often the opportunity to talk over Zoom for a limited period of time with the chosen celebrity. It would be reasonable to anticipate that as mediated exchanges become more sophisticated, this kind of opportunity will become more available for the viewer who is willing to pay for such access.

With the decision by the actor's union (SAG-AFTRA) to go on strike in July 2023, Cameo activity surged as a way to both make some money and maintain a connection to fans. Cameo is a useful platform for both celebrities and their fans (Blumberg, 2023).

The exchange of money for access raises all kinds of other questions about fan–celebrity interactions, but as Picardo mentioned in his interview, audience demand for such opportunities will be met by celebrities who are happy to fulfill those wishes while also enhancing their own earning potential. One pervasive myth in Western culture is the idea that celebrities are all wealthy, but this is most decidedly not the case, and the vast majority of actors, for example, work very hard and are never sure what their next job will be. The opportunity to meet fans while also having another income source was clearly welcomed by the actors I interviewed. The presence of more than 50,000 celebrities on Cameo suggests that this platform is popular among entertainers and sports figures.

10

Additional Concepts Applied to the Study of Audiences

GAYLE S. STEVER ■

There has been a debate in media studies as to whether or not the study of audiences is still relevant in today's media landscape (Rosen, 2006). In particular, as media convergence has taken shape with the blending of different forms of delivery (Jenkins, 2001), increasingly more audience members have also taken on the role of media creator. The advances in technology and user software have made it progressively easier for the viewer to step in and creatively use the source material from a favorite program or artist.

This means that the roles of producer and consumer have become more fluid, and the person who is sometimes the audience member, viewer, or fan might tomorrow become the blogger, video creator, fan fiction writer, photographer, visual artist, or musician (Livingstone, 2013). Livingstone explained that "in our present age of continual immersion in media, we are now continually and unavoidably audiences at the same time as being consumers, relatives, workers and—fascinating to many—citizens and publics" (p. 2). The role of media in our culture is so pervasive that at almost all times, one is either a media producer or a media consumer.

In media convergence, media resources that were previously separate merge to share resources and tasks (Jenkins, 2001). Jenkins described media convergence as a process that involved five types of merging. First, economic convergence is when one media producer controls multiple media distributors, such as Rupert Murdoch's News Corporation, consisting of the book, news, sports, and broadcast divisions. Second, organic convergence is when mixed media are combined into one activity, such as watching television while discussing the program with friends using a smartphone. Third is cultural convergence, which includes a participatory culture in which audience members become involved in some kind of production. Some examples are stories transmitted across multiple forms of media, such

Parasocial Experiences. David C. Giles and Gayle S. Stever, Oxford University Press. © Oxford University Press 2024.
DOI: 10.1093/oso/9780197647646.003.0011

Additional Concepts

as *Star Trek* television programs being made into books, games, and movies or Disney theme park rides being made into films (e.g., *Pirates of the Caribbean*). Fourth is global convergence, which refers to how media influence other countries and cultures despite distance or other barriers. Finally, technological convergence is using various devices for the same purpose, such as watching television on a smartphone or making a call on your personal computer.

A hallmark of media convergence is multitasking so that it is not unusual for a person to be engaged in multiple media activities concurrently, such as using personal computers, smartphones, or television sets simultaneously for various activities, whether those activities are related or not. Perhaps you email someone from your iPad while watching a movie on television. Maybe you are playing a game on your phone while listening to a meeting on your personal computer. This is all part of media convergence, which affects how audiences and producers interact with that media.

The transposition of the roles of producer and consumer has blurred the distinctions between these two things, with more viewers coming to know more producers and vice versa. In Chapter 4, we discussed para-communication and parasocial perception, which is just one way of thinking about the audience member's connection with and understanding of favorite producers and those producers' understanding of their audience.

Still, research on media effects on audiences is a vigorous field of study, with parasocial experiences (PSEs) being at the heart of much of that research, as we've described so far. Other concepts in audience research that might be similar to PSE, indeed related to it, include role modeling, vicarious social experience, identification, and transportation.

ROLE MODELING

Social cognitive theory, developed by Albert Bandura (2009), is a theoretical framework for understanding how thought, affect, and action are influenced by mediated messages. There are two pathways by which people are influenced by role models. The direct pathway is the more traditional idea of an in-person role model who motivates and guides the people in their lives. Through mediated pathways, viewers are linked to social and community settings that are guides for desirable change.

To develop these ideas, Bandura referred back to his theory of reciprocal causation (Bandura, 1986), where individuals in their native environments influence and are influenced by social and personal factors in their social networks. People do not just react to stimuli in their environment but, rather, interact and affect others as much as they are affected—the reciprocal part of the theory.

In a mediated environment, however, the actors on the screen are only available to be influenced indirectly. Audience members self-regulate and choose the role models they want to emulate in this situation (Bandura, 2009). In the parasocial relationship (PSR), audience members perceive the kind of relationships they want to have with media characters and are proactive in imitating those models.

VICARIOUS SOCIAL EXPERIENCES

Another way viewer–character relationships have been studied is through the lens of symbolic interactionism, the theoretical perspective which states that social life is a series of shared meanings between and among people. One way this happens is for the audience members to adopt the point of view of a television persona and, in that process, they may change their behavior as if they expected to be evaluated by the television personality (Ellis et al., 1983).

The second way is for the audience member to be the one evaluating the behavior of the television persona, using the point of view of a second character. In each of these situations, audience members are looking at themselves through the lens of another who is evaluating them in the acquired role of that other person (Ellis et al., 1983).

Take Sheldon Cooper of *The Big Bang Theory* as an example. As his fan, if I adopt the point of view of his character, someone who is extremely intelligent and judgmental of those who don't share his intelligence, I might strive to have a more analytical and intellectual perspective as if Sheldon were judging what I said or did. I might even begin to view those around me as inferior. But in the second form of role-taking, I might adopt the point of view of Leonard (his roommate and best friend) and judge Sheldon's attitudes and behaviors through that lens, now viewing Sheldon's attitude and behavior as arrogant and self-serving.

By taking either or both points of view, Ellis et al. (1983) suggested that such vicarious role-taking becomes a way to learn how to acquire an understanding of the point of view of another person, and thus media viewing becomes a way to train people in role-taking skills.

IDENTIFICATION

Identification has been defined as the psychological phenomenon whereby an audience member adopts the position of a character within a narrative (Cohen & Tal-Or, 2017). It involves taking on not only the perspective of that character but also their emotions and goals. Wishful identification can happen when the viewer aspires to be like the character in some fundamental way (Hoffner & Buchanan, 2005). Both kinds of identification can happen simultaneously with the same character.

Identification has three specific components: cognitive, emotional, and motivational. When the character's point of view is adopted, and their interpretation of events in the narrative is taken on, this is cognitive identification. Emotional identification results in the viewer being happy when the character is happy and sad when they are sad. When the viewer adopts the character's goals, this is motivational identification (Cohen & Tal-Or, 2017).

If I am watching *The Lord of the Rings*, and my goal is for the ring to be taken to Mount Doom and destroyed (which is the entire point of that story), I have taken on motivational identification with the main characters. When I accept their point of view as to the best way to accomplish this goal, I have cognitive identification. At the end of the movie, when the characters rejoice at the destruction of the ring and the subsequent crowning of the king, if I rejoice with them, that is emotional identification.

Several factors facilitate identification. The most commonly cited is similarity, also referred to as homophily. In this case, the viewer perceives the character as having a fundamental quality that is shared with the viewer. It could be as basic as age, gender, or ethnicity, or it could be more abstract, as in the case of philosophy, values, or personality. When the character has positive traits, the viewer is more likely to identify with them, and when the story is told from the point of view of a particular character, it is also more likely that the viewer will identify with that character (Cohen & Tal-Or, 2017).

Chang (2022) examined how watching a drama series can regulate the moods of audience members. Identified were three pathways to mood modification: the transportation path (combining transportation and enjoyment), the meaning path (combining transportation with feelings, reflections, and enjoyment), and the parasocial support path (combining transportation with parasocial interaction [PSI], identification, and enjoyment). In their findings, likability was a critical factor. In addition, the process was different for happy viewers compared to sad viewers. In the transportation path, shifting focus from the viewer to media content that really engaged the viewer was the mechanism whereby mood was enhanced. With the meaning path, viewers enjoy drama more when they explore the world and have meaningful reflections and feelings as a result of viewing the program. In the parasocial support pathway, people experience social support from interacting with characters, thus achieving a positive mood.

Cohen et al. (2019) performed a study to support the idea that identification and PSI are discreet processes. Indeed, they found that direct address supported PSI but did not support identification, something the mechanisms of the theory would predict. As in identification, the viewer assumes the identity of the media persona, and direct address shouldn't have much effect on that. PSI, on the other hand, is almost always enhanced by direct address and eye gaze (see Chapter 9 for more details).

Research has shown that transportation and identification are separate and distinct processes whereby audience members connect with characters in television programs (Tal-Or & Cohen, 2010, 2016). Research has also firmly established that narrative persuasion is more effective than expository persuasion, which makes understanding the nature of narrative persuasion necessary (Braverman, 2008; Murphy et al., 2013). Bandura's (2001) social learning theory suggested that stories are powerful and memorable and, as such, are a good way to get a point across to an audience. Transportation and identification are both powerful vehicles in narrative persuasion (Tal-Or & Cohen, 2010, 2016).

Wishful identification (Hoffner & Buchanan, 2005) is often seen in the context of childhood fantasies, perceived as unrealistic and unattainable. However, further examination reveals real-life situations in which wishful identification can result in achieved goals for some people. Consider the case of NASA astronaut Mae Jamison. During various *Star Trek* conventions, she told the story of having been inspired to become an astronaut by the presence of Nichelle Nichols' character (Uhura) in the original *Star Trek* series in the 1960s. Jamison was the first woman in space and, as a Black woman, saw Nichols' character as evidence that a woman like her could be an astronaut.

Or consider *This Is It*, a documentary/musical about the last show that Michael Jackson had planned for London, which never happened because he died in 2009. At the beginning of that film, numerous singers and dancers talk about their childhood yearnings to work with Jackson professionally, a dream they realized by being in this show with him. During my study of Jackson fans from 1988 to 1992, I met numerous fans who aspired to work with Jackson, and as a result, some of them ended up in the industry as entertainers.

During my interview with *Hobbit* actor Dean O'Gorman, he mentioned that as a child, he "wanted to be Luke Skywalker," much like numerous other children worldwide. Having become an actor with the chance to play similar heroic characters throughout his career (*Doom Runners*, *The Hobbit*, *Young Hercules*, to name a few), it makes one wonder how many actors enter their profession, in part, because of similar wishful identification. Indeed, Alexander Siddig (*Star Trek: Deep Space Nine*) has told me in interviews that as an actor, he feels like he's the little kid who was left out on the playground for extra recess after the bell should have rung for him to come back into the school.

TRANSPORTATION

Transportation is described as a process whereby viewers become completely absorbed in a media world and forget where they are. They often lose touch with their immediate surroundings and feel as if they are living inside the narrative. This can happen with a film, television show, game, or book.

Does transportation lead to an enhanced sense of a PSR? Tukachinsky et al. (2020) found that PSR intensity was strongly correlated with transportation into the media content ($r = .59$, $p < .001$; 10 studies included in this part of their analysis).

Research has shown that transportation into media worlds has resulted in both attitude change and behavior change. The mechanisms for transportation involve emotions and images in addition to the viewer's thoughts. With transportation, the viewer invests in the narrative being watched, both cognitively and emotionally. Because of this, media that evokes transportation can become a very powerful vehicle for persuasion (Green & Clark, 2013).

Additional Concepts

A literature review examining the relationship between narrative transportation and binge-watching found that transportation was both an antecedent and a consequence of binge-watching. Although early studies of these constructs link together the two phenomena in various ways, far more research is needed to create firm links. Binge-watching can affect mood in both positive and negative ways. Netflix has defined binge-watching as the consecutive watching of 2 to 6 episodes of the same TV show in one sitting (Navami & Thomas, 2022).

Slater et al. (2018) proposed retrospective imaginative involvement (RII), a concept that is in the same family of media effects as transportation. In RII, the viewer remembers the media consumed and remains immersed in that content long after the viewing has ended. RII is also conceptually connected to PSRs. In their study, they measured PSR-C (a PSR with the character) and PSR-P (a PSR with the person). The authors explain,

> One form of such RII with story characters is to consider alternative possibilities for a character outside of the story as presented. One may wonder, for example, what would have happened had the character made different choices, or if the character had been a somewhat different sort of person. One can imagine a character or characters in situations other than those portrayed in a movie or novel or can imagine conversing with one or more of the characters as if the reader or viewer him or herself was another story character. (p. 333)

RII conceptualizes an imaginary relationship with a character that can be like PSRs but extends the interaction with that character into the audience member's personal narrative creations in much the same way that fan fiction does.

One of the attractions of this kind of activity is that one can be a part of social experiences that are not possible in real life, described as vicarious social experiences. I will never be Aragorn rushing a pack of Orcs with my sword (*Lord of the Rings*) or Harry Potter putting a spell on my bully cousin, but through media, I can experience such events, and after consuming that media, I can imagine them and relive them in any augmented way I wish. Or, as Dave Ewoldsen put it at a shared presentation given at the American Psychological Association convention in 2022, "Think Gandalf with a lightsaber" (Gandalf is the wizard from *Lord of the Rings*, and lightsabers are a part of the *Star Wars* universe; Stever et al., 2022).

Raney et al. (2020), when discussing narrative persuasion, observed that there are several mental states people may maintain while consuming media content. They described them as automatic, attentional, transported, and reflective states. The automatic state is when you are watching something without really recognizing that it's there in front of you. In the attentional state, the viewers are well aware of what they are watching. The transported state is when viewers become so immersed in the media that they forget where they are and what they are doing. The reflexive state is when viewers are well aware of the message they are consuming but are being evaluative while watching, also simultaneously holding and considering their own beliefs. In this context, transportation is recognized as being distinct from the other processes that can also be a part of media viewing.

Sestir and Green (2010) found that in some circumstances, when traits are exhibited by a media character, the traits will be assumed by the viewer. Both transportation and identification were found to be associated with that process, suggesting that these processes have some factors in common that cause viewers to see themselves in ways that are consistent with the character they are watching and with whom they feel these bonds.

CONCLUSION

One of the earliest powers of the mind that children develop is narrative comprehension, the ability to understand a story. Through stories, children realize that knowledge can be learned from the point of view of someone else. Perspective-taking, the ability to perceive things the way others might, is another area of childhood cognitive development.

Unfortunately, there is such a focus in some schools of research on rationalism and empiricism that our understanding of narrative construction has suffered as a result (Bruner, 1991). Consequently, we have very little concrete understanding of how people go about constructing narratives in order to understand their own lives and the lives of others. This is why the strength of qualitative inquiry, which is addressed in some detail in Chapters 11 and 12 on methodology, is currently so necessary for research of this type.

Audience research is best engaged by utilizing a combination of the concepts discussed in this chapter in addition to parasocial theory, which is the general and overall theme of this book. These are not competing paradigms but, rather, concepts and theories that support one another in the overall goal of comprehending the impact of media on cognitive, motivational, and emotional development.

11
Research Methods in the Field of Parasocial Theory

DAVID C. GILES ■

A central theme to our book thus far has been the way that parasocial theory is constrained by the methods researchers use to study it. Are parasocial interaction (PSI), parasocial relationships (PSRs), and other variations on the parasocial topic just psychometric scales? Do they have any external reality? Are we just perpetuating literature around something that generates numbers? Although the topic of "research methods" sounds a bit dry (we rather tend to associate it with number-crunching on SPSS), the purpose of this chapter and Chapter 12 is to try to think round the idea of "parasocial" and how we might study it in ways that directly capture the multifaceted experience of day-to-day interaction with media figures.

We encourage people to use methods that are not designed to just allocate a number to each participant. Instead, they should allow readers to explore the many different ways that PSRs are formed, understood, experienced, and expressed, both by individual media users and by groups of people we might describe as communities (fans, YouTube users, users of any online space sharing a common purpose). Some of our preferred methods are qualitative, others quantitative or mixed; some have been used in parasocial research before, others not. Where relevant, we will try to illustrate them using our own work.

I have divided this chapter, perhaps rather unimaginatively, into qualitative and quantitative sections, largely because I think it is more useful for readers to navigate using these standard headings. I am giving slightly greater weight to the qualitative, partly because of the range of potential methods but also because the literature is so dominated by the quantitative. There is really not much more to

Parasocial Experiences. David C. Giles and Gayle S. Stever, Oxford University Press. © Oxford University Press 2024.
DOI: 10.1093/oso/9780197647646.003.0012

say about psychometric scales, and ideally, we hope to inspire researchers to think about the alternatives. So, we have deliberately left those out.

QUALITATIVE METHODS

Almost 20 years before starting this book, a colleague (Brendan Gough) and I set up a psychology journal—*Qualitative Research in Psychology*. In those days, it was difficult for people to publish qualitative research in psychology journals because few editors understood the methods or the philosophy behind them. Qualitative research was thought to be sloppy, unscientific, and for the maths-phobic alone. Real science meant recruiting, ideally, thousands of participants, running them through a pile of questionnaires, and stitching the whole lot to-gether with structural equation modeling. What on earth can you say about *anything* by interviewing a mere six participants and then drawing up some ad hoc list of themes?

Things have improved somewhat since then, with a few qualitative methods gaining considerable success, notably *thematic analysis,* for which our journal can claim some of the credit, having published the watershed paper (Braun & Clarke, 2006). According to Google Scholar, the paper had been cited in no fewer than 165,934 other papers by July 2023. Just to give you some idea of how influential that is, my best publication, Giles (2002), with a 4-year head start, had inspired a mere 1,567 citations at the same point, while there are many well-established professors out there who are still struggling to clock up 500 for any of theirs. It is true that qualitative methods have prospered more in some parts of the discipline than others, notably clinical and health psychology, but at least those of us who use them don't get sneered at quite so much.

Discourse Analysis

Discourse analysis, in its broadest sense, is based on the philosophy, in its broadest sense, of *social constructionism* (Burr, 2003). The basic idea of social construc-tionism is that everything we think we know is the result of social forces and, ultimately, ideological or political ones. Even science can be manipulated to serve the interests of the rich and powerful. In its purest form, social constructionism claims that knowledge is produced through discourse. For example, the concept of "mental illness" encourages us to medicalize people's distressing experiences (and even things that aren't actually distressing, such as benign hallucinations). From the psychiatric hospital to the DSM5 (American Psychiatric Association, 2013), we have borrowed ideas from physical health and medicine to structure our thinking around what we call "mental health." Much of this has been, we like to think, for society's benefit, but there are times, such as the overprescribing of antidepressants, when we might consider what other options we could offer people rather than chemical control of the brain (see Bentall, 2009).

A social constructionist account of the parasocial might, oddly enough, end up agreeing with some of the psychometricians: Yes, indeed, PSI is just something measured by a scale. There is no "real" experience of PSI beyond the cognitive constructs dreamed up in academic study. Clearly, this is not the position Gayle and I are advocating, but this is not to say that the study of *parasocial discourse* would be unproductive. In Chapter 6, I discussed Jacques Lacan's ideas on the priority of language in structuring human experience and how our understanding of relationships is always tied to the language we use to describe other people and what they mean to us. In a discursive model of the parasocial, it is perfectly reasonable to talk about a celebrity as a "friend" whose views we agree with, who has disappointed us, or who has given us ideas about things we might do or buy.

Alperstein (1991) captured some of these important aspects of the parasocial in his study of TV viewers discussing celebrities who had appeared in advertising. One viewer described her PSR with the *Good Morning America* host Joan Lumsden, calling her a "trusted friend" whose pregnancies she had "suffered through" and that she had bought baby food "based on her recommendation" (p. 48). When Lumsden appeared in an advertisement for the baby food, it was "like having a friend in for coffee," and her trust in the presenter encouraged her to take the company's word in a health scare, stating, "Joan wouldn't speak for a company that [used a risky chemical]" (p. 48). This rich detail goes well beyond what can be captured using a psychometric scale and allows us to see how PSRs function through the medium of language.

Discourse is not just about language. Our understanding of the social world is constructed through imagery of all kinds. As I mentioned in Chapter 3, an important way that YouTubers present themselves is through "thumbnail" images, which are assumed to be (although often are not) screenshots from the video that they represent. These thumbnails are usually designed in a way to frame the YouTuber as a particular type of performer, typically humorous. In Giles (2018), I discussed how a particular beauty guru had used a thumbnail of herself pulling a face while testing a product, and I suggested that this pose was contrived so that she could use the screenshot as an engaging, humorous representation of the review. In this way, YouTubers use a particular visual discourse that can be analyzed, making a broad assumption that this is how they build up subscriber numbers for their channels.

If you are wondering how to "do" discourse analysis, it is a challenging method because it requires a close understanding of the literature. There is a fine line between description and analysis, and sometimes it is very dependent on researchers' writing skills and ability to use a vocabulary that may be quite different from what they were trained in. (As a psychologist, it is very difficult to get away from talking about factors, variables, and effects, and it sometimes means having to rethink almost everything you've learned!) But a couple of good sources are Wiggins (2017) and Parker (1992), with the latter being a bit outdated but promoting a radical approach to discourse that is often missing from later texts.

Conversation Analysis

Conversation analysis (CA) has evolved in a field quite different from discourse analysis, and its research goals are often quite different as well. It was developed in the 1970s by Harvey Sacks, a Californian sociologist who wanted to inspire a science of conversation with a set of laws that could be applied to all kinds of talk based on regular patterns of turn-taking and structure (Sacks, 1964/1992). One of the most fruitful areas CA explored was the format of a telephone call, studied using a large "corpus" of calls to emergency services. When people called the operator, there was a typical sequence of questions and answers which, if violated, led to misunderstandings and possibly to conflict (especially for those desperate for help). Through much study of these sequences, a set of laws governing phone call openings could be identified (Schegloff, 1979).

Two questions may have occurred to you. First, what's this got to do with parasocial interaction, typically unreciprocated? Second, what use is a "science" based on 1970s landline phone calls in a digital society in which one rarely has to ask for callers' names? Both these questions are addressed in the next section, in which my colleagues and I have tried to drag CA into the 21st century.

Microanalysis of Online Data

Of course, there is an entire discipline of "human–computer interaction" that you might think would be perfectly suited to the study of the way audiences and media figures communicate in social media. However, you will struggle to find the research. A decade or so ago, I decided, along with some colleagues in the social sciences, to explore the possibility that CA could be applied to online environments, where the software sometimes organized people's comments into "conversations" and where you could identify clear turn-taking principles that mirrored those of offline talk (Giles et al., 2015). I started off looking mainly at interaction in discussion forums, particularly those to do with mental health (Giles & Newbold, 2011) and sites such as the UK-based parenting community Mumsnet (Giles, 2016). Over time, I realized how these methods could be addressed to social media, where—as discussed in Chapter 3—the distinction between celebrities and the "audience" is much more ambiguous than in the traditional media, and where direct interaction between the two can be observed (Stever & Hughes, 2013).

We called our "new" method digital conversation analysis (Giles et al., 2015, 2017), although I'm not sure that name has stuck. Traditional conversation analysts never really liked us pinching their ideas, and there are so many different environments with different structures and affordances that a one-size-fits-all method wasn't really on our agenda. But one of the principles I have been very keen to establish is the focus on the thread of exchanges in online environments generally (Giles, 2016). Much research of online communication has tended to take a "corpus" approach in which comments are extracted from their source and lumped together according to topic or terminology, whereas the spirit of CA lies in the turn-taking structure of the thread itself. This is particularly important for studying the interaction of celebrities and other users, even if the "thread"[1] is something that the researcher may have to reconstruct for analytic purposes (Giles, 2016).

Another point of departure for digital CA is in what counts as analyzable data. There has been some debate in the field over when it is appropriate for analysts to refer to such topics as gender (Billig, 1999; Schegloff, 1997; Stokoe & Smithson, 2001). Purists tend to insist that if the topic is not in the language used by conversational partners themselves, it is the researcher who is "importing" it and effectively biasing the analysis through their own agenda. But that only makes sense if your agenda is nothing more than the structure of conversation itself, and most social scientists have other things they're more interested in. In online environments, where there is so much additional information beyond the conversational exchanges themselves, you cannot usually ignore members' characteristics (such as gender). This also means that you can take into consideration social status, which online is often measured by follower numbers and, in some cases, can act as a proxy for categories like "celebrity."

A corpus-based approach can overlook these matters because the data are abstracted from the communicative environment and lose all these other attributes. But is this meaningful? I wondered this when reading a paper on the study of Twitter hashtags in which the author had conflated celebrity tweets with others in a way that seemed rather silly. Surely, if a celebrity tweets something to their followers, wouldn't it be read differently than a tweet designed to reach a handful of family and friends? I developed this argument in a study of a British celebrity who had been accused of making a racist joke (Giles, 2021) and attempted to defend himself (or apologize, if you can accept it) in response to the various accusations leveled by other users. Clearly, the interaction in these sequences was colored entirely by the status of the conversational members, one being a celebrity and the others (in most, but not all, instances) simply "members of the public" (for want of a better category).

From a parasocial perspective, of course, this type of interaction raises all kinds of questions about reciprocity and the status of relationships between the interactants. But I would argue that it's almost impossible to address these issues without some sense of the sequential order of the interaction, and this is where the basics of CA can be applied in a useful and informative way.

Talking Methods

Why talk to a handful of participants when you can blitz thousands online with psychometric scales? Evidently, a very large number of parasocial researchers have decided on a negative answer to this question because there are few instances in the literature when media audiences have been given a voice on the topic. Gayle will naturally discuss these issues in Chapter 12, along with instances of her own research, but I want to add a few extra ideas here.

First, we can differentiate between interviews, which are typically dyadic interactions between researcher and participant, and focus groups, in which several people take part in an unstructured discussion moderated by the researcher (or a third party, sometimes a member of the community involved). Both methods have been used in parasocial research, albeit infrequently. They each have their own advantages, but one often overlooked aspect of focus groups is that they may constitute a better reflection of media use (e.g., a group of housemates who watch TV together). When discussing media figures, this might allow the researcher to get a more accurate picture of what happens when these people consume media as a group. At the same time, a drawback of focus groups is that they may be dominated by particularly assertive individuals, so a mixture of both methods is perhaps the best option if resources allow.

Although we've called this book "parasocial experiences," we haven't really said much about the parasocial as *an experience*, and an obvious place to start would be experience in the phenomenological sense: the "life-world" as described by Husserl (1936/1989). In essence, this is what we've been driving at when talking about media figures as being seamlessly incorporated into our network of relationships. PSI is really about how we treat media figures as if they are part of our social network, but the implication of this is not that we are committing a cognitive error in doing so but, rather, that our *experience* of PSI is indistinguishable from our experience of social relationships. In some, probably a handful, of cases, this is pathological. We are erotomanic and actually believe our favorite pop star really is in love with us. There are also a few people who are so determined to preserve the social–parasocial boundary and their place resolutely on the social side of it that they are in denial of, say, the fact that celebrities are actually human beings (perhaps being part of some conspiracy theory or a *Truman Show*–style social experiment). But in the vast majority of cases, it is unproblematic. Yes, we know our fan object is ignorant of our existence, but we do feel as if we know them, and perhaps it's a bit fun pretending otherwise.

One way of attempting to capture this experience is through conducting an in-depth psychological interview followed by the analytic technique using the forbidding name interpretative phenomenological analysis (IPA; Smith et al., 2009). The practice of IPA is not so different from thematic analysis except that the research premises are more specific. We are trying to find out about interviewees' experiences or life-worlds, and so our coding and categorizing of the material will be tailored to this goal. As we interview more people, we build up a set of "master themes" that best capture this particular experience. In the field of PSRs, it has not, to my knowledge, been done.

Other Qualitative Methods

I want to round off the qualitative section of the chapter by considering a few other methods that are not exclusively qualitative and lend themselves to more of a "mixed method" design, except that, unlike content analysis (discussed later), the qualitative data usually constitute the primary material.

One highly relevant method, quantifiable but usually qualitative, is repertory grid technique. Repertory grids were designed by the cognitive personality theorist George Kelly as a way of testing his personal construct theory (Kelly, 1955). His idea was that individuals make sense of the social world by comparing others according to unique criteria. For one person, intelligence might be a big deal, so they divide the world into clever and not-so-clever people. Another person might rate others according to how kind or how funny they are. These are our "personal constructs." Kelly obtained participants' constructs by asking them to identify three individuals—a "triad" consisting of specific people such as a relation, a teacher, a neighbor, or whatever, or an archetypal person—and to consider which ways they were alike and unalike. He then got participants to rate other individuals on the dimension that linked each of the triads in the study. In this way, he was able to build up, for each individual, a schema of the constructs they used to organize their social experience—ultimately, another way of achieving the phenomenological goal of IPA and related methods. Some research using repertory grids has had promise in using media figures as part of participants' triads (see Chapter 5).

A more direct method of tapping into personal experience is the diary. These can be structured so that the researcher has more control over what type of data are collected, either in terms of data entry or by identifying specific data-generation points in time (in some studies, participants are contacted, either directly or by a programmed device that prompts them to write an entry). An advantage of the diary method for any kind of media research is that it can parallel the participant's everyday media usage. Because the participant is rather left to their own devices, diaries are often better for collecting quantitative information, with qualitative data playing a largely illustrative role. But they are potentially useful for building up an overview of an individual's parasocial experience across a longer time period, further capturing the broad scope of the many relationships that one maintains on a day-to-day basis. The dream diaries discussed in Chapter 5 might serve as a model for research of this type.

Psychology has tended to shy away from the kind of rich descriptive detail collected in the natural sciences and other social sciences, like anthropology, in favor of research findings that can be generalized, the long-term aim being to establish laws that govern behavior irrespective of time and place. In some fields, such as cognitive and biological psychology, there might be some sense in this, but in social psychology, and media psychology in particular, such an approach risks neglecting the impact of cultural and historical change. Some social psychologists have appealed for the discipline to be more sensitive to history in particular, advocating the collection of a "corpus" of material that documents the social world across time (Moscovici, 1984), like a zoologist identifying new organisms or a geologist documenting newly discovered rocks. Social media platforms offer multiple opportunities for building this type of corpus in the shape of single case studies, either of environments (such as a specific type of YouTuber and their audience) or of interactional phenomena (different types of comment structures). Who builds that corpus, to what objective, and how it is built are questions for negotiation, but one place to start might be the appearance of new types of media figure and their audiences.

QUANTITATIVE METHODS

Experiments

Given the predominance of experimental methods in psychology's history, it is surprising that they have been neglected in parasocial research, although they are effectively another victim of the psychometric obsession. Partly this is a matter of convenience. It is simpler, when under pressure to publish research, to recruit a large survey sample for one-time data collection than to devise experiments that require elaborate materials and repeated measures. But this would be the only way of "cultivating" PSRs in order to control and manipulate specific aspects of the phenomenon.

PSRs could be experimentally cultivated in two different ways. The first, a kind of natural or field experiment, would monitor a group of media users over time as they follow a TV series or, alternatively, a YouTuber who posts regular videos. The researcher in this study would not have any control over the media figures involved, but they would be able to chart the development of PSRs across time. To create a meaningful baseline measure, they would need to identify a suitable series or vlogger who was new to the participants and somehow ensure that the participants watch the material in roughly equal quantities and at roughly the same points in time. This would, of course, have been easier to do in the days of broadcast media than in the video-on-demand era, so it may be an idea past its time, but the vlogging option is a possibility.

The second type of design using this method would involve the production of original media content that would be specially designed by the researcher in collaboration with creative experts (maybe a group of drama students and trainee producers). Characters could be deliberately developed to elicit parasocial experiences and hypotheses tested (e.g., Would an attractive villain be made allowances for?). Generating original social media content might be more difficult, not least because there is no way of controlling the creator's relationships with other media users, although clearly, it would be a better option if cost and access to creative teams are issues. Then aspects such as presentation style, video content, and audience engagement could be manipulated to study their effects on

Research Methods in Parasocial Theory

the participants over time. This kind of design might only work if abstracted from the wider world of the social medium (i.e., with restricted access).

The pros and cons of these two idealized study designs reflect a long-standing debate in media research relating to the authenticity of materials. What are the disadvantages of creating original study stimuli? The issue is ultimately one of *ecological validity*. How much can researchers determine the kind of relationships that participants develop? Parents and teachers have spent years seeking ways to make instructional material attractive to learners and are forever frustrated by the fact that teenagers, in particular, will form "unsuitable" PSRs of their own accord rather than lapping up the desired role models on offer. To what extent can researchers really manipulate PSRs? Unfortunately, nobody has really collected the data that will be able to tell us.

Quantification of Qualitative Data

I want to finish this chapter by considering some more mixed-method designs that could be addressed to parasocial research questions. The first is content analysis, a very open-ended technique that depends entirely on the question driving data collection. At the time of writing, I am engaged in a project (with Gaëlle Ouvrein) exploring audience engagement with depression videos posted by popular YouTubers, some data from which were discussed in Chapter 3. One of the issues we have studied is the "PSI potential" of the videos—that is, the extent to which the performer elicits PSI in viewers. Following Thelwall et al. (2022), we coded things such as how much time the performer maintains eye contact with the camera, the friendliness of their style of talking, and the amount of focus on personal topics. We also coded certain features of the comments below the videos.

People often ask what the difference is between thematic analysis and content analysis. Although there are variations across both methods, the basic difference is that content analysis usually proceeds from a list of pre-existing categories. In our study, Gaëlle and I knew in advance what material to code and what to code for because our analysis was anchored in the existing literature. We knew we needed to match Thelwall et al.'s (2022) data, even if we embellished it with our own additional categories. And these were based on the findings of the previous study and on our own hypotheses about the data. Many of our categories were quantitative in nature (e.g., how much time the presenter faces the camera), but content analysis can be purely qualitative as long as you have drawn up your list of categories beforehand.

Thematic analysis, on the other hand, tends to proceed from a more open position, where the researcher has an interest in the broad topic but they do not want to prejudice the analysis by creating predetermined categories. For example, we could have studied the videos solely in terms of the topics covered by the presenters. Since they were all videos on the topic of depression, the theme "depression" would not have been much help, but rather than trying to guess in advance what material would come up, we could have just decided to code everything the presenters said and then gradually reduce those codes to a "master" list of themes that captured the majority of the videos. Then we would have an analysis that was fully grounded in the presenters' work rather than a set of prior assumptions. That isn't what we were interested in, but it would have been equally valid as a method for studying the topic.

Another way in which qualitative data can "serve" quantitative research is by providing researchers with more ecologically valid instruments for measuring behavior. The vast majority of psychometric scales measuring PSI/PSRs have been adapted from a cascade of instruments that can mostly be traced back to the Rubin et al. (1985) scale. Each time the items in the scale are adjusted to meet the demands of the sample (e.g., substituting for U.S. English) or the type of media figure under consideration (e.g., removing or rewording items that are inappropriate). Although this is standard psychometric practice, it does mean that participants are asked to respond to items that are not really grounded in anyone's language other than that of the researcher(s).

As it happens, though, the Rubin et al. (1985) scale was itself firmly grounded in the actual talk of viewers of U.S. television news. The spade-work was conducted by the sociologist Mark Levy, who was one of the first people to follow up Horton and Wohl's (1956) original study and whose first step, as a PhD student at Columbia University, was to speak to the very audience he was interested in. He aimed to collect data that "describe the nature of the parasocial interaction process" and that capture "the existence, quality, and extent of the parasocial relationship between the television news audience and the personae who appear on the newscasts" (Levy, 1979, p. 70). He did this by conducting focus groups (he called them "focused groups") with a total sample of 24 adults in the New York City area, each of whom watched at least one newscast a week. He asked them various questions about the newscasters and, from the transcript, identified 42 statements that constituted a "propositional inventory" that could be used as items in a scale. He then gave this scale to a further 240 adults meeting the same criteria.

Six years later, of course, the Rubin et al. (1985) scale was published. Although Rubin et al. cite Levy (1979), along with a couple of other PhD dissertations, as part of a "limited" literature that helped inform their scale construction, reading the Levy paper, it is clear that many of their statements are taken directly from his, including several that would be surprising if generated by researchers themselves. One such item, "I sometimes make remarks to my favorite newscaster during the newscast," reflects Levy's (p. 72) participants reporting that they sometimes address the newsreader with a "friendly salutation . . . e.g., Good evening, John" or reciprocate their signing off statement with "you're welcome" or "see you later." Another Rubin et al. item, "I miss seeing my favorite newscaster when he or she is on vacation" picks up Levy's finding that 25% of his sample claimed to be "upset" when the newsreader was absent.

Rubin et al. (1985) were able to use these other authors' work directly in their item construction because they were investigating relationships with the same kind of media figures (newscasters). But it is evident that newscasters elicit certain behaviors and cognitions that other figures would not, and almost 40 years later, it is fair to say that their scale is still best suited to PSRs with newscasters. However, the characteristics of PSRs with other figure types will be quite different, and at this point in history, it would be of enormous help to have this kind of qualitative data that could inform other psychometric scales—where and when they happen, of course, to be the method best suited to the research question.

12
View From the Road and Methods Employed

GAYLE S. STEVER ■

In Chapter 11, David discussed some of the methods he has used in his research. Although we both have engaged predominantly in qualitative research, there are clear differences in our methods, so we decided to develop separate chapters. These chapters are not an attempt to be traditional "research methods" chapters as one would find in a textbook. Instead, they summarize the methods used during the 30-plus years of our work.

PARTICIPANT–OBSERVER ETHNOGRAPHY

Participant–observer ethnography was initially developed in anthropology and is used to better understand other cultures than the one from which the researcher originated. It has been applied for a number of years to the study of fan cultures (Duits et al., 2016; Evans & Stasi, 2014; Kington, 2015; Popova, 2020) and, when used, offers a window into the world of fans and those who have formed parasocial relationships (PSRs) with either famous people or the characters they portray.

In the spirit of the qualitative perspective known as interpretivism, the goal is not objectivity because true objectivity, in any case, is considered in this approach to be a myth. Researchers always bring their own lenses through which things are observed, and it is not possible to separate oneself from those lenses. Instead, the goal is to describe what is observed in enough detail that the researcher's lenses are understood, and the perspective brought to the task is therefore understood.

The foundation of interpretivism is the interpretation of events through the shared meanings of language, conscious thought, and a belief that the positivist or empirical approach to social science is flawed. All human events are perceived through the socially constructed lens of the observer, and it is impossible to look

Parasocial Experiences. David C. Giles and Gayle S. Stever, Oxford University Press. © Oxford University Press 2024.
DOI: 10.1093/oso/9780197647646.003.0013

at the world any other way. A rich description of the social context is the key to understanding the phenomenon of interest, the key being the depth of meaning the observer brings (Alharahsheh & Pius, 2020). How the researcher has perceived and described the phenomenon of interest is at the heart of this research.

Whereas some scholars study fandoms of which they are already a part, as what have come to be called "aca-fans" (academic fans), my methodology has been to select fandoms that are potentially compatible with my interests and do a step-by-step immersion process by which the fandom comes to be understood in a personal way. I have gone through this process in my own work a number of times over more than 30 years, beginning in 1988 when I engaged the fandom of Michael Jackson, an artist with whom I initially only had marginal familiarity. From that starting point, I have been in and out of various fandoms with the goal of making a series of case study observations. It is hoped that when one has observed and participated in enough groups, the commonalities they share, as well as the unique properties each one exhibits, become increasingly clear over time.

WHAT EXACTLY DOES IT MEAN TO DO QUALITATIVE RESEARCH?

To be successful as a qualitative researcher of fan experiences, one needs to reach a level of immersion within the social setting of the fandom in order to experience the participant meanings that are derived from the setting. The best analogy I've heard is the metaphor of the river. If you want to understand life in the river, you can stand on the banks of the river and watch life from above. You can see much of what is happening at the point in the river from which you stand. If you get into a boat and float along the river, you can see even more of what is going on. But if one really wants to understand life in the river, eventually, one has to get out of the boat and swim. At a later point, one gets back in the boat and floats along, still observing, now from the position of someone who has been in the river. Finally, one gets back on the banks of the river, again remembering the experiences and trying to place them in the context of understanding as an observer. This analogy helps show that a participant is better able to grasp the significance of social activity within the fandom.

For this reason, it is necessary to study fandoms that one has enough affinity for that it will be possible to get into the water with the fans. One aspect I have observed and can readily relate to the principles of evolutionary psychology is that no matter what fandom I have chosen to study, I always find that within a few months, I have been able to become committed to that fandom. The principle of evolutionary psychology that is relevant here is the idea that we are born already hardwired to be attracted to the faces and voices of those in our environment who are familiar to us (see Chapter 7).

It would be easy to believe that only attractive media figures will be the object of fandoms, but what is overlooked is that everyone who becomes familiar to a person has the potential to acquire attractiveness (the opposite could be true if the person's behavior is decidedly unattractive). Although this has yet to be empirically tested in a controlled study, I began to realize it after 35 years of engaging with new fan groups. It was never a problem to embrace a fandom once I had become familiar with it. Although this study is waiting to be done, observation in naturalistic settings has supported the hypothesis that becoming immersed in a fan group—one that regularly shares the work, face, voice, and persona of the artist—produces affinity for that artist. I have observed this not only in myself but also in other people who became fans and then participated regularly in these groups.

VARIOUS KINDS OF QUALITATIVE INQUIRY

With respect to the various types of qualitative research, Creswell and Poth (2016) have enumerated five main approaches to the work: narrative research, phenomenological research, grounded theory research, ethnographic research, and case study research. In narrative research, the researcher focuses on a topic, analyzing data from case studies, surveys, observations, or other similar methods. Phenomenological research works with lived experiences in order to gain deeper insights into how people understand those experiences. Grounded theory involves the construction of hypotheses and theories through the collection and analysis of data. Ethnographic research involves observing and interacting with people in their natural environment. A case study is a detailed study of a specific subject, such as a person, group, place, event, organization, or phenomenon.

Two of the cornerstones of the philosophy of interpretivism are phenomenology and symbolic interactionism. In phenomenology, the researcher seeks to understand the world through direct experience. Symbolic interactionism involves the interpretation of symbols in order to discern what shared meanings there are in social groups (Alharahsheh & Pius, 2020).

Two very different approaches in qualitative research involve the understanding of words versus the understanding of behaviors, and these two types of analysis are relevant to all five of the previously mentioned qualitative research types. In the participant observation and self-study methods described below, both of which are forms of ethnography, the researcher is in a real-world setting observing behaviors. Those behaviors include words, but usually they are not analyzing the words they hear systematically.

On my March 2023 trip to London to see the play *Lemons Lemons Lemons Lemons Lemons*, I was most interested in observing the behavior of Aidan Turner fans who had come with the primary goal of seeing the play and a secondary goal of meeting him. It is from observing behavior that one can understand concepts such as being "star-struck" or "tongue-tied," both of which I witnessed fairly often in the four times in 1 week I attended the play. It is from observing the behavior of popular public figures that one gets a notion of what "charisma" might be about. Observing behavior is also how one comes to understand the security measures necessary for this type of social situation. These are just some examples of the kinds of questions that are investigated in a real-world, in-person setting.

But sometimes qualitative analysis is involved while trying to understand the words of other people. Over many years of fan research, I have transcribed interviews and had narratives written for me. I have analyzed news accounts and printed interviews with both stars and fans, using various kinds of established methods for such analysis. The most useful tools have been both grounded theory and a method my mentor and doctoral dissertation chair David Altheide (1987) called qualitative content analysis. Each of these involves a kind of text analysis in which coding schemes are developed, and themes and code words are found within the available text. This is a very different type of work than participant observation ethnography and yields different kinds of insights.

AUTOETHNOGRAPHY

Very much connected to participant observation is a related methodology called autoethnography or self-study. In autoethnography, researchers connect their personal experiences to broader cultural meanings, most often in an autobiographical style. As stated previously, this has come to be known as the researcher who is considered an aca-fan. Most often, the aca-fan is someone who studies a fandom of which they are already a part. In the case of my research, although I have not studied fandoms with which I was already involved, much of what I have done over the years qualifies in part as a form of self-study. I have referred to myself as a meta-fan, or a fan of fans, meaning that my interest in fan studies and parasocial theory is driven by an interest in the experiences of those who are the most devoted of fans. This inclination dates back to Michael Jackson when I wanted to understand what superstar mania was all about.

The process of becoming a fan in order to understand participant meanings is where autoethnography comes in. While I knew very little about Michael Jackson in 1988 when I began studying his fans, by 1992, when I was ready to move on to the next case study, I was somewhat of an expert on his work and career. I found through my interactions with various fans that if you didn't know and understand the source material, sometimes called the text of a fandom, it was difficult to interpret what fans were telling you in their various narratives, whether those were written or oral.

There have been times I went to a fan event with my only intention being to observe myself within the setting. Observing others is a valuable byproduct of attending fan events, but I always learned new things about fandom by participating and watching myself and my reactions to various celebrities whom I have had the privilege of meeting.

One of the things I realized is that, although the fandom of and for women (whether for men or sometimes even for women) is often attributed to romantic or sexual attraction (and this is then denigrated as we've already discussed in Chapter 7; Anderson, 2012), it was far more common for me to observe that

I had attained a kind of affection for that celebrity, what the Greeks called *storge* (as opposed to *eros*, the sexual romantic kind of love). Storge is what we feel for our family members and close friends, and "affection" is the closest English word I have come up with to describe this kind of attraction to someone, celebrity or not. In coming to this realization, I was able to then look at others in the fandom and understand what it was they reported feeling when they weren't necessarily romantically attracted to someone but still seemed to have a great love for that person.

Regarding celebrity attraction as a fan studies scholar, I can point to several instances over the years when my research was taken less seriously because I am a woman (again, as was discussed in Chapter 7). As an example, in 2007 and 2008, I was actively collecting data on the Josh Groban tour. One research question I sought to resolve was the prevalence of "celebrity worship," a construct measured by McCutcheon et al.'s (2002) Celebrity Attitude Scale. I gathered about 100 responses to that instrument at Groban concerts (and a further 100 at the big *Star Trek* convention in Las Vegas that year). Earlier in 2007, I used my own Celebrity Appeal Questionnaire (Stever, 1991a, 2008) in a similar fashion.

There was an employee of Groban's record company who was in charge of the VIP meet and greets and social hour before the concerts, an event that fans paid a premium for with their concert ticket. I remember him approaching me and asking, very conversationally, what percentage of my activity was as a scholar and what percentage of it was actually as a "fan." I suspect that because I "fit" the profile of the Groban fans (with respect to age and gender), my involvement was probably suspect to the close to 100% of men who were working for Groban on that tour. I was actually called on to consult with them regarding a problem fan with whom they had been dealing on an ongoing basis. My expertise appeared to be sought after and respected, so this "what are you really doing" question took me completely by surprise. My observation is that this is an occupational hazard for fan studies researchers, particularly true for women, so one must be prepared when taking on participant–observer status.

Back to Chapter 7, where we addressed the stigma associated with women in fandoms, I can personally attest to the veracity of that concern. It happened to me from 1988 to 1992 while on the Michael Jackson tours, and again when I moved into *Star Trek* fandom from 1992 to 2008 and beyond (but the most active years were the earlier ones). Again, it was assumed that because you were female and some of the actors whose fans you were interviewing were attractive men, you were really there for that and not for a professional, scholarly reason. Personally, after 30 years, I have become immune to that perception (meaning I no longer let it bother me), but I mention it here for other scholars trying to do this kind of research. The tendency among female fan studies scholars is to joke about it, but in the final analysis, not being taken seriously is not funny, especially when considering the many years invested in this work (35 and counting for me).

Good examples of the numerous participant–observer activities I engaged in are the two already mentioned in this chapter: the trip to London in March 2023 to see the play *Lemons Lemons Lemons Lemons Lemons* and the live performance of Aidan Turner, whose fandom I had been participating in since the summer of 2022. Unlike other fandoms I studied, no quantitative or qualitative data were collected directly from the fans. When it became necessary, I was careful to tell people who I was and what I do in my studies, but I wasn't interested in "data" at that particular time in my work. I was more interested in gathering greater insight into the concepts presented in Chapter 4, specifically para-communication and parasocial perception. How were Turner and some of his fellow actors communicating with their fan base, and how were those communications being perceived? Some of my observations are included in that chapter.

Upon observation of my reactions to fandoms and referring back to information shared about evolutionary psychology and attachment, I conclude that because of the human proclivity to be attracted to familiar faces and voices, we are somewhat (metaphorically) "hardwired" to feel attracted to those familiar people. When you start out investigating a rather random selection of actors and their fans and end up feeling this sense of "storge" or affection for each of them (as I found myself doing), this is the kind of experience that leads to speculation and consideration as to what it is that fuels fan interest in a given parasocial object.

Being on Facebook pages and websites for four different male actors from the cast of *The Hobbit*, again, chosen by me for participant observation using criteria that had little to do with my personal preference, I began to see and absorb an infinite number of pictures of the actors, most often of their faces. Although I had seen *The Hobbit* movies when they were first released in 2012–2014, and all four men were attractive and represented characters I enjoyed in the films, I hadn't joined any fandoms up to that point. It was the repeated exposure to both these images and also their previous work (because getting up to speed on their prior work was part of the process) that formed the basis of any affection I found myself feeling for these men. In the process of "getting to know" actors and their work, is this what typically happens? I won't jump to that conclusion, but it is one I have often considered. It is important, however, for both researchers and fans to differentiate eros from storge (romantic attraction for affection). This is a salient inquiry for both men and women, but because of the stigmatization of female fandom, I have found it to be a bigger issue for women.

In my participation with Cameo (see Chapter 9), I felt the strong pull of parasocial interaction (PSI). And this is despite initially approaching that task to learn about the service and get questions answered from the celebrity's point of view. The power of direct address was at work there, and I was not immune to it. Cameo is becoming a popular form of social media, and a good deal of the power it will exert over fans comes from the power of direct address, which involves both the face and the voice of the celebrity. This is something researchers need to watch carefully. We already live in a society in which 15–20% of sampled groups report intense personal celebrity worship symptoms (Stever, 2011). Will this become more the case as this type of interaction on social media becomes more available? Are individual differences in vulnerability to celebrity worship something we must monitor and be concerned about? Most fan attractions are normal fun social attractions, but the research literature clearly shows that a small percentage of people engage in a level of celebrity worship that can be troublesome for that individual.

Another question would clearly be, "Is the affection the fan feels for the actor or the character?" In our Cameo chat, Dean O'Gorman related the following:

> When I meet fans at a convention, it seems to me that they're not meeting me, they're meeting the image of me. Sometimes it's important for me to maintain the image, if they see a character as kind of heroic, or funny, then sometimes I want to live up to that image just for them, because obviously me and my characters are very different, and they don't know me, they just know my characters.

If the actor has portrayed numerous characters in their career (and most of them have), is it the affection for all that actor's characters or only some of them? Other actors have reported that fans will confuse the actor with the character, as in Alexander Siddig's (of *Star Trek: Deep Space Nine*) experience of fans asking him for medical advice because he played a doctor, something that many television doctors recount.

Finally, does repeat exposure to a person's face make it inevitable that the viewer will form an attachment of some kind to that person? The combination of face and voice can be even more powerful from the standpoint of what we know from evolutionary psychology. Infants are hardwired in a sense to be attracted to familiar faces and voices, and this tendency for attraction is adaptive, given that the evolutionary imperative is for survival and reproduction and thus never leaves us. Of all the questions I've encountered in this field of research, this is the most intriguing one—one that I hope other researchers will take up and investigate.

QUANTITATIVE METHODS IN THIS AREA OF STUDY

In discussing the measurement of PSI and PSR, there was a point in the 1970s when two schools of thought were influential. The first was emphasized by Rosengren et al. (1976), stating that PSI occurred specifically during media viewing. The second, described by Nordlund (1978), defined media interaction as taking place within the viewer in an ongoing PSR but also included concepts such as identification. As measurements were developed, Nordlund's idea became more influential. This is because the emphasis on measures during the 1980s was mainly on PSRs and not on PSI, as originally defined by Horton and Wohl (1956).

Early prominent instruments included the Parasocial Interaction Scale (PSI Scale; Rubin et al., 1985), which had two versions—one with 20 items and the abbreviated version with 10 items. This questionnaire integrated items from Levy's (1979) scale, which he developed to measure attraction to newscasters. Using the PSI Scale, studies showed that duration, history of viewing, and amount of viewing were not important factors leading to PSI. This instrument included identification as part of the scale, whereas later measures and studies considered identification to be a separate construct. Called the PSI Scale, the measure was actually closer to measuring PSRs because the items asked about the viewer's liking of a character and other items that imply a longer term relationship with a media figure. The PSI Scale had good internal reliability and supported a single-factor model of PSI and PSRs.

Auter and Palmgreen's (2000) Audience–Persona Interaction Scale measured PSI, PSRs, and other concepts, including identification. It challenged PSI as a unitary construct and supported four factors rather than just one: identification, interest, interaction with characters, and a factor concerning a favorite character's problem-solving abilities.

Tukachinsky's (2011) scale differentiated parasocial friendship from parasocial love, successfully identifying items that discriminated between the two concepts; this was supported by factor analysis. The scale showed internal reliability and construct validity, demonstrating that not all PSRs can be evaluated similarly. Also, in 2008, Schramm and Hartmann developed a measure called the PSI Process Scale, which returned to an emphasis on measuring PSI rather than other aspects of parasocial theory.

Since then, there has been a return in parasocial theory to an emphasis on PSI. Hartmann and Goldhoorn (2011) developed the Experience of Parasocial Interaction Scale (EPSI). This instrument was designed to specifically examine PSI as distinct from PSRs and measure the impact of a media performer who directly addresses the camera and audience compared to one who does not. The instrument successfully differentiated these concepts, affording researchers a distinct measure for those who wish to study PSI rather than PSRs. Both Cummins and Cui (2014) and Dibble et al. (2016) conducted studies that supported the reliability and validity of the EPSI. Its greatest strength is that it is a very specific measure that separates the construct of PSI from PSRs and focuses on the direct verbal and bodily addressing of the performer to the audience in such a way that they break the fourth wall and address the audience members as if they were present. These works on PSI recognize that the viewer understands that the interaction is an illusion, so there is no emphasis on pathology in recognizing the viewer's reaction to the performer. This instrument and the studies using it specifically focus on performers who intentionally address the audience as opposed to performances in which the audience is not addressed directly, and yet the viewers still react as if they are part of the conversation (Stever, 2017).

In fan studies, surveys and questionnaires are often employed to try to quantify the various aspects of attraction to a parasocial object or celebrity. In 1988, I wanted to come up with a way to quantify attraction to Michael Jackson, and although I intended to use qualitative methods, my mentors advocated for a multiperspectivist approach, also called the mixed methods approach, wherein both quantitative and qualitative methods are employed in the same study.

The Celebrity Appeal Questionnaire (Stever, 1991a) was a series of Likert scales using adjectives that described Jackson's potential appeal—adjectives that I had gleaned from lists provided by my many students who were asked to define the constructs I was trying to operationalize. I had several discussion group sections during the term I was working on this, and each section was given a main construct and asked to list adjectives to correspond to that construct. For musicians, the terms I ended up with were talented, artistic, creative, musical, and entertainer. For sex symbols, the words were sexy, attractive, good-looking, strong, appealing, and well-dressed. For hero/role model, the terms were helpful, honest, generous, caring, wise, and courageous. I had started with hero and role model as separate constructs, but the adjectives generated for each of these ended up being almost identical, so the concept became hero/role model for the duration of the study. At the head of the questionnaire was "How big a fan of Michael Jackson are you?" with a 10-point Likert scale offered for them to indicate their answer. The hero/role model scale and the sex appeal/romantic scale were the factors that best predicted how big a fan the person was, although the talent scale was a good predictor as well.

The Celebrity Attitude Scale, already discussed in Chapter 8, was designed to measure a concept called celebrity worship. While the borderline-pathological scale specifically focused on abnormal fan obsession, the intense-personal scale and the entertainment-social scale identified characteristics that are related to PSRs and PSA (McCutcheon et al., 2002). Some have interpreted the scales in a way that pathologized normal fandom. More work is needed to discover the implications of the various levels of celebrity worship because it is not clear whether celebrity worship is a construct separate from PSRs and PSA or whether it is a subcategory of them.

CONCLUSION

By employing multiple perspectives and mixed methods in the work concerning fan studies and parasocial experiences, one is more likely to come to the heart of the phenomenon one is striving to understand. Certainly, this has been the case in both my work and the work of other scholars with whom I have discussed these issues. Multiple lenses afford a greater understanding of the phenomena and behaviors of interest in this very fascinating area of study.

Ultimately, we research to ask questions, and it is hoped that our questions are meaningful and significant. The most important question in parasocial research is, Why do audience members form strong attachments, connections, or relationships with figures in media, most of whom they have never met and are not likely to meet? I suggest three answers:

1. Certain personality types are more predisposed to forming PSRs than others. In Jungian terms, those are the intuitive and introverted types of people (Stever, 1991b, 1995), which makes sense because these personality types prefer to process things internally and think in terms of possibilities or the theoretical.
2. Storytelling is an important part of human life, and humans connect to stories (Beach, 2010). Therefore, feeling a connection to a character in

a story is a natural extension of human beings as storytellers and story receivers. This is the power of the narrative.

3. Evolutionary psychology suggests that we as human beings are hardwired to be attracted to the familiar faces and voices of other human beings, and we form attachments to those who are familiar. The goals of survival and reproduction are served by forming attachments, and a part of the brain that processes these images and sounds cannot easily tell the difference between the face seen in person and the one seen through media.

These three findings stem from both my work and the work of others, as referenced. But more needs to be done to understand the power of the PSR, particularly for some individuals more than others.

13

Summary and Conclusions

GAYLE S. STEVER AND DAVID C. GILES ∎

In this book, we have explored fundamental canonical applications of psychological theory (e.g., psychoanalytical theory, ethological theory, evolutionary psychology, and attachment theory) as they relate to the study of parasocial experiences. Of necessity, we have focused on the ones that were the most engaging to us, as growth in this area has led to a very large number of studies that might be reviewed (Liebers & Schramm, 2019). This chapter summarizes the key themes and discussions we have offered here in our narrative.

PARASOCIAL AND SOCIAL AS A CONTINUUM

One major theme throughout the book is the idea that parasocial and social are not a dichotomy but, rather, should be conceptualized as a continuum. At the one end are relationships that are purely parasocial, where the parasocial object has not been engaged in any way. Sometimes, that is because the persona is fictional and does not actually exist. Sometimes, the person is a celebrity and entirely outside of the realm of possible interaction.

But, particularly since the advent of social media, researchers have realized that parasocial relationships (PSRs) can have varying degrees of reciprocal interaction, thus moving them toward the center of the parasocial–social scale. Have you tweeted your favorite celebrity and gotten a reply? Did they favorite your post? Did you meet them at a convention, and then at the next one, they recognized you from the previous meeting? These are all examples of varying degrees of reciprocity. Add to this idea the aspects of real social relationships that one might engage in within the imagination, and the lines blur even more.

Sometimes, a fan intersects with some aspect of the celebrity's life, and extended interaction is possible. Conversely, sometimes a person in someone's real social life does not reciprocate social behavior in such a way that the social relationship mimics aspects of the PSR. Also, a social relationship can become parasocial if

Parasocial Experiences. David C. Giles and Gayle S. Stever, Oxford University Press. © Oxford University Press 2024.
DOI: 10.1093/oso/9780197647646.003.0014

Summary and Conclusions

someone known becomes famous and you no longer have access to communication with them.

POPULAR (MASS) CULTURE OR HIGH CULTURE?

There has been a long-standing debate juxtaposing high culture with popular or mass culture, which dates back as early as the ancient Greeks (Brantlinger, 2016). Anything followed by or esteemed by the masses was deemed unenlightened. In the realm of both the study of fans and PSRs, this dichotomy has an important effect on which fan groups are stigmatized and which interests are considered "legitimate" and "cultured." During the past decade or so, the emphasis on parasocial as suspect and potentially connected with social dysfunction has everything to do with the objects of those PSRs. If you went to the opera and followed opera singers, that was "cultured," but if you went to science fiction conventions and followed those stories and characters, the media treated those interests as questionable.

In the 18th and 19th centuries, those who followed artists were called patrons. Today, they are more likely to be called fans. But as we bring our discussion of parasocial experiences to a conclusion, it is appropriate to consider this source of stigmatization of PSRs. Certain celebrities/famous people have been looked upon as "worthy" of serious consideration and interaction, whereas others are part of a category that was relegated by Daniel J. Boorstin (1971) to being "well-known for being well-known."

That the distinction is largely an artificial one can be illustrated simply by looking at the actors who were interviewed for this book: Dean O'Gorman, Nana Visitor, Denise Crosby, Alexander Siddig, Robert Picardo, Andrew Robinson, and Armin Shimerman. By their association with science fiction/fantasy franchises, it would be tempting to label these artists as part of popular culture rather than high culture, if that's even a valid dichotomy anymore (Edensor, 2020). But at a closer look, we have Shimerman, who has taught drama and Shakespeare at the University of California, Los Angeles for many years; Robinson, who originated the Master of Fine Arts for the University of Southern California and taught many years for that program; Visitor, who not only has had an extensive acting career but also did many leads on Broadway; and O'Gorman as the quintessential renaissance man and not only an actor but also a photographer, painter, and filmmaker. We could go on, but the point is that each of these actors has strong connections to classical culture in every sense of the word. So, do they have "fans," or do they have "patrons"? The distinction becomes important when the word "fan" relegates a person to the various stigmas that have been discussed throughout this book (see Chapters 4 and 7 for examples).

When one speaks of PSRs, the connection that forms most often is with popular culture, but it is just as possible to have a PSR with figures from high culture as from popular culture. There are enormous implications for that distinction.

SOCIAL MEDIA AND PSRS

As time passes, technological innovation changes the media, and the media affords new opportunities for human behavior. At no time has this been more evident than in the first two decades of the current century, and psychology cannot ignore the impact of these powerful cultural forces. The parasocial interaction (PSI) of the 1950s radio audience was quite different to the contemporary behavior of social media users, and the relationships between the media figures and individual audience members (and communities) have changed the nature of what we consider "parasocial." In Chapter 3, we examined these developments and their implications for parasocial theory.

PARA-COMMUNICATION AND PARASOCIAL PERCEPTION

Parasocial theory needs to be enhanced to better include concepts that are not well developed—for example, para-communication (including EPSI, the experience of PSI; Hartmann & Goldhoorn, 2011) and parasocial perception (Riles & Adams, 2021). Celebrities are diverse and unique individuals, and many of them are highly invested in their side of the PSR. Although PSRs are defined as "non-reciprocated," there is reciprocity with the audience as a group that many celebrities engage in.

Some scholars take exception to the idea of a PSR as a relationship, arguing that it takes two to make a relationship, and thus the relationship is an illusion. In Chapter 4, it is argued that the celebrity (when a real person) is most often an active participant in their relationship with fans and the public. Para-communication involves the ways they communicate with their audience, and parasocial perception is the way the audience views the celebrity's reaction to and relationship with the audience, most often thought of as "the fans." As such, it becomes an actual relationship with the celebrity as an active participant. In Chapter 4, examples are given of celebrities who have a strong connection to and interest in their fans. This is important because social interactions come in all types, and the social interaction of a public figure with their audience is foundational to the structure of their influence. This is true for entertainment audiences, as discussed in Chapter 10, and it is also true for political figures, sports figures, and all other types of public figures. How do each of these types of figures reach out and connect with their audience? The study of para-communication and parasocial perception is foundational to this question.

THE UNCONSCIOUS AND PSYCHOANALYTICAL PERSPECTIVES ON PSR

Unless one explicitly identifies as a fan of a particular media figure, we tend to be largely unaware of our PSRs. Media figures slip into our lives and take up residence

Summary and Conclusions 197

there without us consciously inviting them in. Despite this, PSRs are typically studied as if they were "attitudes" that can be measured according to their strength on the basis of our responses to statements about a favorite figure. What might we learn about PSRs if we approach them from an implicit perspective?

One way of doing this is to analyze the dreams people have about media figures. One study using dream diaries (Caughey, 1984) found that at least 10% of our dreams feature people we do not know, mostly famous figures from fields such as music and cinema. It seems that once unconscious, we process media figures in pretty much the same way as the people we do actually know: The brain fails to make the distinction. Much the same could be said about young children, who are often believed to be unable to distinguish between "fantasy" and "reality," but "reality" is ultimately a way of buying into an adult perspective. When media figures die, their fans and admirers experience grief reactions that are unsettling and confusing: How can I, an intelligent adult, be this upset about someone I have never actually met and who has no idea who I am? Until they acquire this realist bias, children are happy to have PSRs with all kinds of weird and wonderful fantasy media figures and even invent their own companions to spend time with.

The obvious place to go for further ideas about unconscious PSI is the psychoanalytic literature. Chapters 5 and 6 do just that.

SURVIVAL AND REPRODUCTION: EVOLUTIONARY PSYCHOLOGY AND PSR

We are born with an urgency to form social relationships, and in infancy, survival depends on it. The two imperatives of evolution are survival and reproduction. Both mechanisms are at work in the realm of PSRs as our brains can sometimes perceive the distant figure as potentially either a mate or a means for survival support. Attachment relationships, including those that are parasocial, give us support, comfort, and safe haven. We strive to maintain proximity to attachment objects and experience separation distress when proximity is lost.

Humans are social, and in the absence of other activity, the brain at rest defaults to social cognition (Lieberman, 2013; Stever et al., 2021). It could be argued that this social behavior developed in humans as a support to the survival of our species. There is safety in numbers! In addition, the attachment system is present at birth, with the infant seeking proximity to a reliable caregiver. Later in adolescence and adulthood, this proximity shifts to partners who offer the same kind of support and will sometimes become sexual partners, addressing the second evolutionary imperative of reproduction.

That PSRs can be a source of comfort is clear to anyone looking closely at any gathering of fans. Fans derive comfort from the work, indeed the persona, of the distant attachment object, but they also derive comfort from other fans in a symbiotic shared affection for that parasocial persona. This was particularly true during the 2020 COVID-19 pandemic when socializing at a distance over the internet, both with parasocial objects and with other fans, was the only source of social contact some people had. The Sid City Social Club (see Chapter 4) and the Facebook fan forums for various actors (also described in Chapter 4) are examples of the social support afforded those isolated by quarantine during the pandemic.

A CAUTIONARY POINT

There are problems that can come on the celebrity worship end of the fan–celebrity interaction scale for those who become too wrapped up in the life of someone they will never meet. This is also related to the biological mechanisms that come metaphorically hardwired into the person's tendency to be drawn to familiar faces and voices of attractive distant parasocial figures. Although it isn't common, it can be a problem, particularly for those who are somewhat socially isolated and become so wrapped up in an idealized persona that they lose sight of the people who are in their immediate and present or potential social circle. More research is needed into these aspects of parasocial attachment, intense personal celebrity worship, and parasocial romantic relationships when the person unwittingly becomes too attached to someone who is not part of a real life they can ever achieve. In these cases, the relationship can become detrimental to the person who has become lost in a parasocial attachment that's gone out of control.

Throughout this book, the emphasis has been on the PSR as a normal extension of media enjoyment and imagined social encounters that are positive and inspirational. This is because the potentially problematic aspects of fandom and PSRs have been overemphasized in both the research literature and the media coverage of PSRs for most of the years it has been studied. But there is a small percentage of people who can get into difficulty socially if they allow themselves to become lost in infatuation or lose their ability to socialize in a face-to-face situation because all their energy is being expended in imaginary realms. Our emphasis on the positive aspects of PSR does not mean that there is not a potential downside for some audience members.

Friedman and Martin (2011) performed a study of factors contributing to longevity and found that a solid social network and helping others were important factors in a healthy and happy life. Advising and caring for others were predictors of living to old age. Inasmuch as fans participate in social networks and support the charities of their honoree/favorite celebrities, such social activity is clearly good for health and longevity. However, if PSRs are isolating a person from the more direct contacts in their everyday life, this can be problematic.

PSRS AND THE SPIRITUAL LIFE OF THE AUDIENCE MEMBERS

Parasocial relationships have a social dimension that can be thought of as both spiritual and connected to others. Fan psychology contains concepts related to parasocial theory that explain this social dimension (concepts such as collective effervescence, mudita, and the sociometer). Fandom has been addressed in scholarly literature as

Summary and Conclusions

a potentially religious, sacred, or spiritual experience in many ways, with celebrity worship being a related concept. These topics were addressed in Chapter 8.

EVOLVING FORMS OF SOCIAL MEDIA: CAMEO AND SIMILAR NEW PLATFORMS

As technology becomes more sophisticated, new avenues of social interaction change the landscape of PSR and parasocial experiences. Cameo is one such new technological platform, and this new way celebrities can connect with fans has enormous implications for PSI and PSRs. Using direct address to deliver a personalized message to an audience member, the celebrity is able to tailor a performance to a very small, sometimes single-person audience. The interaction is still parasocial because in most cases, the celebrity has little or no information about the recipient of the message.

One thing that needs further study is the sharing of Cameos on social media, which appears to enhance the connection between the celebrity and the fan, the fan and other fans, and the extended fan audience (not the actual recipient) and the celebrity. This was something I observed on Tumblr, Discord, and Facebook within the fan community there for Dean O'Gorman (e.g., from *The Hobbit*). Many Cameos were posted, and this stimulated both the number of Cameo requests he was getting and the shared connection fans felt through the sharing of those Cameos. This was doubtless not a unique activity, but further inquiry could examine the ways Cameos have been used to forge connections within fandoms. Cameo itself encourages the posting of Cameo videos on social media, which makes sense because this is good advertising for their service.

THEORETICAL AVENUES TO STUDYING THE AUDIENCE

Although PSR makes a good start at describing audience behavior and the relationships fans have with their favorite characters or celebrities, other concepts, such as identification, transportation, and vicarious social experiences, are important when examining what motivates audience behavior and what explains audience experiences. Sometimes, media role models are the only choice a person has when choosing how they want to behave. This is particularly true if the audience member is part of a marginalized group such as LGBTQ, an ethnic minority, or a person with a disability. These topics were addressed in Chapter 10.

NEW QUESTIONS FOR FUTURE RESEARCH: THE PSYCHOLOGY OF ACTING

It occurred to both of us at about the same time while writing this book that an unexplored area of research is the psychology of acting. If the audience's way of relating to characters and celebrities is critical to development, then understanding the actor's relationship or connection to a character could be equally important. What is the relationship between an actor and their character? Is it parasocial? Is it identificatory? Is transportation the mechanism by which the actor engages in the story they are telling? This dilemma is similar to the one that comes up in audience research, where the demarcation between the PSR and identification is a blurry line that seems to be in constant motion. The few articles I could find on the psychology of acting can be summarized in this comment: "Psychologists know surprisingly little about the cognitive and affective underpinnings of acting" (Goldstein, 2009, p. 6).

I asked several actor friends for their take on the question, Is the actor's relationship with a character parasocial? Armin Shimerman (*Star Trek: Deep Space Nine*) had the following to say (the first three responses are from personal emails to Stever, July 1, 2023):

> Roles and the actors that create them are one and the same. We can say that the character is not me and that is somewhat true: The collective makeup is different from the actor's real personality. But the segments of the character can be found in the actor's psychological makeup, segments that may usually be suppressed in real life or held at bay. It is not interpersonal; it is pointing out what is already there.

Andrew Robinson (*Star Trek: Deep Space Nine*) had a similar answer:

> I am the character, and I rely on my experience, humanity, and imagination to create the character within the bounds the writer has created. The character ends up becoming an aspect of my personality. Rather than a parasocial experience it's more like an interactive, inner-active one. Even with whatever observations I make and take from other human beings the character is always me.

Nana Visitor (*Star Trek: Deep Space Nine*) offered these thoughts:

> To me, the relationship to a character is like being their psychologist. Without judgement, you are looking for the threads of why behavior arises, what it leads to in terms of patterns for that person, and how they view themselves. We share the thoughts of characters and can be forever shifted by growing the synapses in our brains by thinking their thoughts, over and over.

When I asked Dean O'Gorman (*The Hobbit*; *Trumbo*) if his relationship with a character was parasocial, identification, or "something else," he had this to say:

> I don't subscribe to the idea of "a character" but rather to the idea of "behavior." And different people have different behaviors. We can all relate to behavior even if we don't partake in it. So, become the character? No. It's either

Summary and Conclusions

in you or not, I think. I think you'd have to be insane really to become the character entirely. You can train yourself to have different thoughts but the essential "you" is always going to be there. . . . I actually think the closer you get to yourself, the more the character appears different from you. Sounds confusing, paradoxical, but I believe it to be true. (Cameo response to question from Stever, July 4, 2023)

The central idea included in each of the previous answers is that the actor's relationship to their character is not parasocial. The challenge for each individual actor is to take something imaginary and act on it as if it is real (in behaviors, as both Visitor and O'Gorman suggested). These actors describe an imaginary interaction with their character, but all seem to agree that it is not parasocial but, rather, a merging of their own thoughts, behavior, and characteristics with that of the character they are portraying.

ACTING AND MENTAL HEALTH

A critical area concerning the connections actors have with their characters is the effect a character can have on an actor's mental health. The case of Heath Ledger will always be steeped in controversy because playing The Joker in *Batman* led him to have difficulty sleeping, and some even believed it caused depression, although his family has denied that part of it. But what does seem to be accepted by most is that the role caused him to be unable to sleep and that prescription sleep medications played a role in his accidental death (Ravenola, 2020).

Continuing her remarks on the subject of the actor's relationship with her character, Visitor had this to say on the subject:

I will tell you what it's like for me—and I developed a protocol recently to protect myself from it. . . . Like people who have just started practicing psychology, it's easy to lose boundaries with your "patient." Young doctors can take on their patients' trauma to the point that they have affairs, abuse drugs, become alcoholics. Sounds like some actors' paths, right? We share the thought of characters and can be forever shifted by growing the synapses in our brains by thinking their thoughts, over and over. This can be to the good or bad. I believe it leads some to suicide. So, we are bonded or blended with characters on a real physical level. (Personal email to Stever, July 1, 2023)

In a recent media interview (Simons, 2023), Aidan Turner (*Poldark*) spoke on this same subject:

I was talking to my wife the other day. She's doing a play (*The Crucible*) and it's quite dark at the moment. And she was talking about just how shaking that off is difficult because it stays with you. How do you manage your mental health through these things? Especially doing a play. You're doing that eight shows a week, and it's a three-hour—like, it's a lot. And it's going on for months and there's a lot going on. . . . You don't choose to live with it. But it's there. It's there a lot. And you try to protect yourself, I think, as an actor, to do the best you can to leave it. I don't think there's gains bringing stuff home and keeping—you know, exploring that energy outside of the set. A lot of the time, I think it's exhausting and I think you can run out of the good things really quickly.

The subject of the actor's relationship with their characters, and how it can affect them when they are not acting, is an important one to explore alongside the relationship the audience develops with those same characters. If the actor has the potential to be negatively affected by darker characters, this also suggests the idea that the audience has the same potential risk.

Visitor (Figure 13.1), in her work as an actor, has done her own research and explored these issues in some depth. She talked about these kinds of roles and had this to say:

You approach a character with compassion, acceptance, and nonjudgement. If you're going to play a character, you can't think, "I'm bad." You explore issues and emotions and "I think I'm right." We aren't just acting with our voices or emotions even. Our bodies are involved and there is a somatic connection. So, when we adopt, for example, a "power pose" with your chest puffed out, this not only makes you feel powerful, but actually changes your hormone levels, with cortisol decreasing and testosterone increasing [she cites the work of social psychologist Amy Cuddy: Carney et al., 2010; Cuddy et al., 2015]. So, we are messing, as actors, with not only our chemistry but with what pathways we're forming in our brains. (Zoom interview with Stever, July 24, 2023)

Given how important this potentially could be for actors who do this full-time and invest a lot of emotional energy into the characters they portray, Alexander Siddig (Zoom interview with Stever, July 26, 2023; (Figure 13.2) explained to me why actors need to be taught how to engage characters without losing themselves in them to such a great extent, as we discussed what had happened (described above) to Heath Ledger. Siddig talked about the major differences between the ways American actors and British actors are taught to approach their roles and contrasted what he had learned at the London Academy of Music and Dramatic Arts against the "method acting" system of Lee Strasberg, an American actor, theater director, and acting teacher, hailed as one of the founders of America's first theater collective. Strasberg believed that the actor "must somehow believe. He [sic] must somehow be able to convince himself of the rightness of what he is doing in order to do things fully on the stage" (Gussow, 1982).

By way of contrast, Siddig described his training in the British acting school tradition:

Summary and Conclusions

Figure 13.1 Nana Visitor.
Source: Sam Aronov/Shutterstock.com.

Figure 13.2 Alexander Siddig.
Source: Kathy Hutchins/Shutterstock.com.

The Strasberg method asks you to live that character. It's called emotional recall, and you basically recall all of the emotions from your life that you associate with that character, and then you try not to let that character go during any point during the time when you are preparing that character and

Summary and Conclusions

playing that character. We don't use that method at all. We're taught to do stage acting and stage acting does not allow for that sort of deep dive, that sort of embodiment of the character. This was primarily because stage actors, especially women, are doing Greek Tragedies or Shakespeare plays, and in all of these, terrible things happen to the women. There's one Greek tragedy where a mother kills her son; all the women in Shakespeare have terrible things happen to them. And you have to do this eight times a week. The Shakespeare plays are three to four hours long. So, with that, you are in a process of self-annihilation unless you have a way to protect yourself. British actors are taught to protect themselves by not taking it home, by forgetting all about it and picking it up just for the show. And part of the four weeks of rehearsal for the play is to learn how do to that. We laugh and joke and then the director says "go," and we're in. American actors (I'm generalizing, of course) can't do that. We have very different approaches, and so I don't have a deep relationship to my characters. The minute you keep it, you can't manage. You simply can't live on that precipice the whole time.

Method actors are in trouble because their conscience gets overwritten. If they are playing a serial killer or a rapist or something terrible, they find a way to override their conscience, to let them inhabit that character. So, they kind of allow the devil in. (Zoom interview with Stever, July 26, 2023)

As we discussed the parasocial or not parasocial question about actors and characters, Siddig agreed with the others quoted above that it's not parasocial:

I like the identification and transportation models better than the parasocial one for actors, and identification is key. The best actors, whether they are playing villains or good guys, always elicit identification postures from the audience. You can't help liking those actors and being fascinated by them. (Zoom interview with Stever, July 26, 2023)

FURTHER EXAMPLES

Visitor (Zoom interview with Stever, July 24, 2023) cited several cases in which actors have recounted that playing a difficult role had negative psychological consequences for them in their personal lives. One example was Shelley Duval in *The Shining* (1980), where she confronted Jack Nicholson's character on a staircase while holding a baseball bat. The scene took 127 takes. Duvall recounted later that she was in and out of ill health because the stress of that role was so great (Jackson, 2021). Then there was Adrian Brody in *The Pianist* (2002), where during filming, he dropped 30 pounds, sold all his belongings, spent 4 hours per day learning to play piano, and broke up with his girlfriend. This is a frequently cited case of method acting that went too far (Macaluso, 2020).

But Visitor, expressing the perspective of the method actor, believes that "if you are pretending, if your body isn't engaged, if there's a part of you that is separated from the character, it looks presentational, because it is. You aren't telling the truth of that character" (Zoom interview with Stever, July 24, 2023). In such cases, she believes that an actor can set up protocols and sacred spaces that separate the actor from the character. As an example, she cites her own performance on Broadway in *Chicago: The Musical* (2001):

> There's a wonderful thing the doorman does after the last performance. Everyone leaves the theater, and she [the doorman] waits in her little space until everyone is gone. She then turns on the ghost light on the stage and says, "be there as long as you want." And that is a protocol, a ritual, that helps folks think "this is over." We add these things for ourselves as actors, so that going into the flow state of being an actor is a ritual and coming out of it is as well. Each day you start out with "this is the space where this character lives. It's not my life." Then after the final take, you mentally imagine a better ending for your character so that you leave them [and yourself] in that better place.

ANOTHER PERSPECTIVE: ACTING AS BEHAVIORISM WOULD SEE IT

In a Zoom interview by Gayle with Dean O'Gorman (August 4, 2023; Figure 13.3), several issues and possible research topics became clearer. Each of the three actors who spoke with Gayle on this subject (Visitor, Siddig, and O'Gorman) had a unique perspective on the craft of acting, and that in itself suggests that multiple perspectives are needed to explore these questions.

In contrasting the audience's relationship with characters on screen to what the actor's connection is, O'Gorman had this to say:

> You as a real person have much more complexity than the idea of a person, which is essentially what a "character" is. I think the word "character" is a word like "electricity" or "mother nature." It's a phrase or a word we hear often, but what does that mean? I think "character" is based much more on an audience perception of behavior, as opposed to the internal perspective of the actor. There's definitive physical characteristics like "the character is this age; they came from this country. . . ." There are these parameters, and they aren't really too negotiable. But in terms of the internal world of the character, they can only be seen through action. People think they can see emotions and thought processes, but what they are seeing is physical movements. And that isn't to say it doesn't come from an internal place, but some actors aren't emotional, but they know how to portray emotions.

Summary and Conclusions

Figure 13.3 Dean O'Gorman.
Source: Featureflash Photo Agency/Shutterstock.com.

The actor's relationship with the character is externally perceived, whereas the audience member's relationship with the character is mostly internal. That makes these two things very different and, thus, they need to be studied very differently. This perspective on acting is very much related to principles of behaviorism, where what's going on inside someone's head can't be studied; rather, the actor's behavior is where an understanding of character development and that actor's connection to the character come from. O'Gorman continued,

> The camera only sees what's there. The camera only sees what is physically there. The face is doing the job conveying the thought. So, the question becomes, "How does emotion manifest itself in behavior?"
>
> "Character" is really just the observation of habit. My friend and I would talk and say things like "my character wouldn't do this" and "my character wouldn't do that," based on my ideas of this "person." But actually, you can be seemingly random in character choices because the audience will then stitch that together in terms of their own narrative.

This suggests that there is a role to be played in understanding the audience's relationship to a character by exploring the audience's own narratives that they bring to the viewing of the story. Such a narrative analysis could be very useful when trying to understand PSRs, indeed, all manner of parasocial experiences.

One of the emphases, according to O'Gorman, comes down to the skill of the actor as much as the approach an actor takes to a character or role:

> There are actors I've worked with that I admire and really respect. I worked with Bryan Cranston (*Trumbo* [Figure 13.4]), a very good actor, a very artistic kind of guy, but he also has an extremely good sense of, well it's skill and the application of skill to present a moment in regard to the story. So, he knows how to use the camera, or he knows what beats or moments are needed in a scene to convey a story. He isn't just a spontaneous whirlwind of feelings, he's got skill involved and others, Ian McKellan, and all the other big guns that I've worked with, they have that emotional aspect . . . they are available emotionally, but they also have incredible skill that allows that emotion to be maneuvered in a way to tell the story or tell the moment or portray a moment. That's where the artistry comes in.

On the subject of how audience members come to like (or not like) a character, O'Gorman reflected on a question about his character in *The Almighty Johnsons*, a character that on the surface appeared to be unsympathetic but by the end of three seasons was much beloved by many fans of the show. Why might that have happened?

> Is that because he became more likeable or is that because you came to understand him more? As an actor you try to empathize with your character, which allows you to be much more forgiving of it. That's why actors don't perceive themselves as "bad"—they're trying to understand their

Summary and Conclusions

Figure 13.4 Bryan Cranston.
Source: Jaguar PS/Shutterstock.com.

character's perspective. When you understand, it becomes much more humanized. Liking a character, not liking a character, is all peripheral because I look out this way [gesturing from his eyes to the outside] and everyone else looks at me this way [gesturing back toward himself]. It's skill that allows emotion to be maneuvered in such a way to tell the story or tell the moment or portray a moment. I think that's where artistry comes in. I've found that working on my voice enabled me to have more control over my feelings than trying to remember my dog dying or something. The rest was to enjoy it. Looking at the shape and craft in a scene was really enjoyable. I paint and take photos and stuff and there's the artistic part but there's also the practical aspect to it, and I like that. I'm a practical guy, building things and mixing colors, and the practical aspect is really interesting to me.

These interviews with professional actors suggest ideas that could be addressed in future studies of the nature of human interaction with fictional characters. Does the actor's approach to their character result in a positive or negative impact on the actor's own life? Does the method by which an actor engages a character affect that impact? With O'Gorman, Visitor, and Siddig, three different approaches that all clearly are highly effective, as evidenced by their powerful acting performances, suggest that there isn't just one way to understand a topic of this complexity.

A similar area of inquiry could be the nature of an author's interaction with the characters they create. Very little has been done to explore either one (e.g., acting or writing fiction) of these areas.

PSRS AND METHODS OF INQUIRY

Psychologists need to be open to learning from people from all walks of life. Gayle's interviews with actors for this book, for example, greatly enhanced understanding about how audience members might relate to characters parasocially, in contrast to the people who portray those characters.

O'Gorman spoke about studying with Kim Gillingham, who uses dreams as a way to develop a scene, using the work of Robert Thurman and Jungian dream analysis:

> I love my dreams. I always find them really interesting and if you read a scene, especially an audition, and you think "that doesn't feel very right" but if you imagine that scene as a dream, you don't have to justify it, because dreams have their own logic. You're having a dream and you're flying a banana. . . . You never question the fact that you're flying a banana. It's all within the reality of the dream. I've had dreams that include celebrities, it's a relationship with the idea of a person that seems so real when you've never met them. It's weird, isn't it?

The idea that the feeling while in a dream state that your relationship with a celebrity feels very real because of the nature of dreams goes straight back to the PSR and how the unconscious reveals that relationship in a way that the conscious mind cannot. This puts a spotlight on the unconscious imagination as expressed in dreams and how that could enlighten how we think about PSRs, an idea that David develops in Chapter 5.

A variety of methods are useful when studying audience behavior and the connections that people feel with both celebrities and fictional characters. The last part of this chapter is an example of how, when we know very little about an area (e.g., the psychology of acting), the best way to start out is with a grounded theory approach, where narratives are collected and then repeating themes are coded within those narratives. This grounded theory approach is the best approach in an area where little research has been done (Glaser & Strauss, 2017). By talking with professional actors and then looking at their answers, the ideas that need to be investigated can be identified.

Much of the deeper understanding of fan psychology and PSR comes through qualitative methods. During the writing of this book, Gayle was participating in a newer (for her) fan group, and that participation enlightened her thinking throughout the writing process. Jenkins (1992) talked about continued interaction with fans when he was writing his book and asking fans their thoughts about various concepts in fandom. Following a similar procedure, we are indebted to the fans listed in the Acknowledgments section of this book, as each of those people shared their connections to their favorite characters and celebrities and whether what we were saying in these pages resonated for them. Field research will continue to be at the heart of understanding both fandom and the parasocial experience.

NOTES

Chapter 1

1. Unfortunately, I no longer seem to have my old paper copy of the review, so I am unable to quote directly.
2. As of July 2023, Twitter is now known as "X."

Chapter 3

1. Much as we might scoff at such apparently antiquated research, Griffith (1957) reports a thoroughly convincing UK study in which regular TV viewing was found to increase the likelihood of being prescribed glasses in children older than 10. Whatever happened to this line of inquiry? Have our eyes since evolved to cope with it?
2. Recent research (Schwartz, 2015) suggests that the scale of the "panic" following the Welles show has been somewhat exaggerated, even if evidence from some audience members indicates considerable, if limited, alarm.
3. Many *Lonesome Gal* episodes can be downloaded from YouTube. The line here is taken from the February 1, 1951, broadcast "In the Still of the Night" (from 7 minutes, 34 seconds; https://www.youtube.com/watch?v=Gwr2vBBY7JI&list=PLg3i3Dm9hkhjWj6_UOyP4cTVeTQh0lXwW).
4. There is, naturally, only a very small academic literature on the medium. Researchers whose first language is English tend to add a second "k" for orthographic consistency ("TikTokkers"); those with non-English-speaking backgrounds often spell it TikTokers. It is a bit like parasocial versus para-social, perhaps, although the use of a hyphen seems unrelated to linguistic preferences.
5. The "official" time limit in July 2023 was 3 minutes, although some online sources claim that it is still possible to upload 10-minute films after the limit was considerably increased in 2022 in an attempt to compete with longer form media such as YouTube (Stokel-Walker, 2022). In its early years, TikTok was competing with Vine (whose limit was a mere 6 seconds), but increasingly creators were given various options for longer videos. Like any successful social medium, however, its fundamental success can be attributed to its unique cultural affordances, and what drove traffic to the site in the first place was the short form. Like Twitter expanding its tweet limit, TikTok has gambled on its own unique identity by trying to hoover up the opposition.

214 Notes

6. Notably, Mr. Beast also has a following of more than 80 million on TikTok, barely half his YouTube number, thereby illustrating the difficulty of classifying social media celebrities by medium alone.

7. This figure actually represents something of a decline from a peak of 9.89 million in January 2021, the earlier statistic being, presumably, a pandemic-related anomaly.

8. Inevitably, sexual content, resembling the early internet phenomenon of "Webcam girls" (Giles, 2018), has resurfaced in Twitch. This seems to be a matter of some sensitivity for the platform, forcing it to regulate the content in a special "Pools, Hot Tubs and Beaches" category in which outright nudity is restricted (Cross, 2021).

9. I use the term "community" rather loosely here since these are potentially only ad hoc communities brought together in responding to a single video. Of course, subscribers to the creator's channel may well have a history of interacting in other comment streams, and longer term observation would be necessary to ascertain how established that community is. I didn't feel I could make that assumption for this one-off analysis.

CHAPTER 5

1. Once again, this raises the issue of how much we can learn about PSRs from study participants' identification of a single "favorite" figure (unless, as in fandom research, the individual has a particular interest in one figure—but even fans are liable to have more than one favorite figure).

2. Among these, Nepal was found to have a remarkably low incidence of IFs reported (5% of the sample). Among the various limitations of this otherwise interesting and valuable study, children were only asked about current IFs, so one imagines the overall prevalence is somewhat higher.

3. Of course, this is only one study, and one cannot expect it to cover too much ground. In addition to various other limitations noted by the authors themselves, the data collected on imaginary activity in childhood far outweighed those on parasocial activity in adolescence, relying, like so much parasocial research, solely on the Rubin et al. (1985) scale completed for one "favorite" figure.

4. *Perro* = dog, *hijo* = child (generically masculine).

5. Those who imagined conflict with Jones were also more likely to visit his Infowars website, which might seem surprising, although the report mentions that some of the large sample never visited the site (no actual figure is given), so it may simply be a statistical artifact.

CHAPTER 6

1. The mother's breast occupies a prominent role in psychoanalytic writing and theory from the early to the mid-20th century. Modern readers are often distracted from the essential points of psychoanalytic theory by what they view as old-fashioned sexism and homophobia. But this risks throwing out the baby with the bathwater. Better try to "translate," where appropriate, old-fashioned, sexist, or elitist assumptions in a way that one would expect a contemporary writer to communicate them. Of course, the father's bottle or any other source of nourishment might perform the same role as the mother's breast (as Winnicott himself suggests at one point).

Notes 215

2. Indeed, one questions what such an "Aha" moment would represent for the infant, who is still grappling with a myriad of perplexing questions about existence, self, and others, in addition to the physics of mirrors and reflective surfaces.

3. A late anthology of various texts and transcripts by Lacan and others was published under the title *Television* (Lacan, 1990), but this refers purely to the transcript of a discussion broadcast on French TV in the early 1970s between him and his colleague Jacques-Alain Miller. Lacan curiously titled the write-up "Télévision," although like most psychoanalytic thinkers in the postwar period, he never seemed to consider media a significant influence on childhood development.

4. Home to what is now the University of Gloucestershire in the south-west of England.

5. The saga of Hilda Ogden's lost raincoat in 1970s *Coronation Street* was a little more dramatic than it might seem at first glance, given that her attempt to replace it was scuppered by her husband running off with their savings. Not to mention the eternal problem of the weather in Manchester, which would certainly have troubled viewers in the North West of England.

CHAPTER 11

1. Twitter very usefully organizes certain strings of replies into a "conversation" (or at least it used to). YouTube comments sections have the appearance of a thread, but the messages may be organized in ways (i.e., not always chronologically) that make turn-taking difficult to address. To confuse matters further, with digital data, you also need to consider that readers may all be seeing different displays of the same information depending on the device they're using. So, it is not an exact science. But was CA ever?

REFERENCES

INTRODUCTION

Adams-Price, C., & Greene, A. L. (1990). Secondary attachments and adolescent self concept. *Sex Roles, 22*(3), 187–198.

Bretherton, I. (1992). The origins of attachment theory: John Bowlby and Mary Ainsworth. *Developmental Psychology, 28*(5), 759–775.

Duffett, M. (2013). *Understanding fandom: An introduction to the study of media fan culture.* Bloomsbury.

Erickson, S. E. (2022). Book review: *Parasocial romantic relationships: Falling in love with media figures,* by Riva Tukachinsky Forster. *Journalism and Mass Communication Quarterly, 99*(1), 341–343. https://doi.org/10.1177/10776990211042589

Ferris, K. O. (2005). Threat management: Moral and actual entrepreneurship in the control of celebrity stalking. *Sociology of Crime, Law and Deviance, 6*, 9–29.

Groszman, R. (2020, September). Revisiting parasocial theory in fan studies: Pathological or (path)illogical? *Transformative Works and Cultures, 34.*

Hartmann, T. (2008). Parasocial interactions and paracommunication with new media characters. In E. A. Konijn, S. Utz, M. Tanis, & S. B. Barnes (Eds.), *Mediated interpersonal communication* (pp. 191–213). Routledge.

Hills, M. (2015). From para-social to multisocial interaction: Theorizing material/digital fandom and celebrity. In P. D. Marshall & S. Redmond (Eds.), *A companion to celebrity* (pp. 463–482). Wiley.

Jenkins, H. (2006). *Fans, bloggers, and gamers: Exploring participatory culture.* New York University Press.

Jensen, J. (2002). Fandom as pathology: The consequences of characterization. In L. A. Lewis (Ed.), *The adoring audience* (pp. 9–29). Routledge.

Maltby, J., Day, L., McCutcheon, L. E., Houran, J., & Ashe, D. D. (2006). Extreme celebrity worship, fantasy proneness and dissociation: Developing the measurement and understanding of celebrity worship within a clinical personality context. *Personality and Individual Differences, 40*, 273–283.

Maltby, J., Houran, J., & McCutcheon, L. E. (2003). A clinical interpretation of attitudes and behaviors associated with celebrity worship. *Journal of Nervous and Mental Disease, 191*(1), 25–29.

Paravati, E., Naidu, E., Gabriel, S., & Wiedemann, C. (2020). More than just a tweet: The unconscious impact of forming parasocial relationships through social media. *Psychology of Consciousness: Theory, Research, and Practice, 7*(4), 388–403.

Riles, J. M., & Adams, K. (2021). Me, myself, and my mediated ties: Parasocial experiences as an ego-driven process. *Media Psychology, 24*(6), 792–813.

Rojek, C. (2015). *Presumed intimacy: Parasocial interaction in media, society, and celebrity culture.* Wiley.

Shabahang, R., Bagheri Sheykhangafshe, F., & Yousefi Siakoucheh, A. (2019). Prediction of interpersonal cognitive distortions based on the worship of celebrities and parasocial interaction with them. *Quarterly Journal of Child Mental Health, 6*(1), 163–175.

Stever, G. S. (2013). Mediated vs. parasocial relationships: An attachment perspective. *Journal of Media Psychology, 17*(3), 1–31.

Stever, G. S., & Lawson, K. (2013). Twitter as a way for celebrities to communicate with fans: Implications for the study of parasocial interaction. *North American Journal of Psychology, 15*(2), 597–612.

Tsiotsou, R. H. (2015). The role of social and parasocial relationships on social networking sites loyalty. *Computers in Human Behavior, 48*, 401–414.

Tukachinsky Forster, R. T. (2021). *Parasocial romantic relationships: Falling in love with media figures.* Rowman & Littlefield.

Wiemer, E. C., Riles, J. M., & Tewksbury, D. (2022). Artists and attributions: How music platform implementation affects parasocial experiences and support intentions. *Journal of Broadcasting & Electronic Media, 66*(2), 300–319.

Chapter 1

Ajzen, I., & Fishbein, M. (1975). A Bayesian analysis of attribution processes. *Psychological Bulletin, 82*(2), 261–277.

Ajzen, I., & Fishbein, M. (1980). *Understanding attitudes and predicting social behaviour.* Prentice Hall.

Costa, P. T., Jr., & McCrae, R. R. (1988). From catalog to classification: Murray's needs and the five-factor model. *Journal of Personality and Social Psychology, 55*(2), 258–265.

Dibble, J. L., Hartmann, T., & Rosaen, S. F. (2016). Parasocial interaction and parasocial relationship: Conceptual clarification and a critical assessment of measures. *Human Communication Research, 42*(1), 21–44.

Giles, D. (2000). *Illusions of immortality: A psychology of fame and celebrity.* Bloomsbury.

Giles, D. C. (2002). Parasocial interaction: A review of the literature and a model for future research. *Media Psychology, 4*(3), 279–305.

Giles, D. C. (2003). *Media psychology.* Hillsdale, NJ: Lawrence Erlbaum Associates.

Giles, D. C. (2018). *Twenty-first century celebrity: Fame in digital culture.* Emerald.

Green, M. C., & Brock, T. C. (2000). The role of transportation in the persuasiveness of public narratives. *Journal of Personality and Social Psychology, 79*(5), 701–721.

Harrington, C. L., Bielby, D. D., & Bardo, A. R. (2011). Life course transitions and the future of fandom. *International Journal of Cultural Studies, 14*(6), 567–590.

Hartmann, T., & Goldhoorn, C. (2011). Horton and Wohl revisited: Exploring viewers' experience of parasocial interaction. *Journal of Communication, 61*(6), 1104–1121.

References

Hills, M. (2016). Returning to "becoming-a-fan" stories: Theorising transformational objects and the emergence/extension of fandom. In L. Duits, K. Zwaan, & S. Reijnders (Eds.), *The Ashgate research companion to fan cultures* (pp. 9–21). Routledge.

Hills, M. (2019). When the Pet Shop Boys were "imperial": Fans' self-ageing and the neoliberal life course of "successful" text-ageing. *Journal of Fandom Studies, 7*(2), 151–167.

Horton, D., & Wohl, R. (1956). Mass communication and para-social interaction: Observations on intimacy at a distance. *Psychiatry, 19*(3), 215–229.

Kiesler, S., Siegel, J., & McGuire, T. W. (1984). Social psychological aspects of computer-mediated communication. *American Psychologist, 39*(10), 1123–1134.

Levy, M. (1979). Watching TV news as para-social interaction. *Journal of Broadcasting, 23*(1), 69–80.

Maltby, J., Houran, J., Lange, R., Ashe, D., & McCutcheon, L. E. (2002). Thou shalt worship no other gods—unless they are celebrities: The relationship between celebrity worship and religious orientation. *Personality and Individual Differences, 32*(7), 1157–1172.

Marwick, A., & boyd, D. (2011). To see and be seen: Celebrity practice on Twitter. *Convergence, 17*, 139–158. http://dx.doi.org/10.1177/1354856510394539

McCutcheon, L. E., Ashe, D. D., Houran, J., & Maltby, J. (2003). A cognitive profile of individuals who tend to worship celebrities. *Journal of Psychology, 137*(4), 309–322.

Perse, E. M., & Rubin, R. B. (1989). Attribution in social and parasocial relationships. *Communication Research, 16*(1), 59–77.

Rubin, A. M., Perse, E. M., & Powell, R. A. (1985). Loneliness, parasocial interaction and local television news viewing. *Human Communication Research, 12*(2), 155–180.

Sandvoss, C. (2005). *Fans: The mirror of consumption*. Polity.

Siegel, J., Dubrovsky, V., Kiesler, S., & McGuire, T. W. (1986). Group processes in computer-mediated communication. *Organizational Behavior and Human Decision Processes, 37*(2), 157–187.

Slater, M. D., Ewoldsen, D. R., & Woods, K. W. (2018). Extending conceptualization and measurement of narrative engagement after-the-fact: Parasocial relationship and retrospective imaginative involvement. *Media Psychology, 21*(3), 329–351.

Stevenson, N. (2009). Talking to Bowie fans: Masculinity, ambivalence and cultural citizenship. *European Journal of Cultural Studies, 12*(1), 79–98.

Stever, G. S. (2009). Parasocial and social interaction with celebrities: Classification of media fans. *Journal of Media Psychology, 14*(3), 1–39.

Stever, G. S. (2013). Mediated vs. parasocial relationships: An attachment perspective. *Journal of Media Psychology, 17*(3), 1–31.

Stever, G. S. (2016). Meeting Josh Groban (again): Fan/celebrity contact as ordinary behavior. *International Association for the Study of Popular Music Journal, 6*(1), 104–120.

Stever, G. S. (2020). Evolutionary psychology and mass media. In T. K. Shackelford (Ed.), *The Sage handbook of evolutionary psychology: Applications of evolutionary psychology* (pp. 398–416). SAGE.

Stever, G. S. (2021). Processes of audience involvement. In *Understanding media psychology* (pp. 183–204). Routledge.

Stever, G. S., & Hughes, E. (2013, September). What role Twitter? Celebrity conversations with fans [Paper presentation]. International Communication Association, Transforming Audiences Conference, London.

Stever, G. S., & Lawson, K. (2013). Twitter as a way for celebrities to communicate with fans: Implications for the study of parasocial interaction. *North American Journal of Psychology, 15*(2), 597–612.

Tukachinsky, R., & Stever, G. (2019). Theorizing development of parasocial engagement. *Communication Theory, 29*(3), 297–318.

Waters, R. H. (1934). The law of effect as a principle of learning. *Psychological Bulletin, 31*(6), 408–425.

Wise, S. (1984, January). Sexing Elvis. *Women's Studies International Forum. 7*(1), 13–17).

CHAPTER 2

Abrams, Z. (2023, June). The science of friendship. *Monitor on Psychology*, 42–49.

Aguiar, N. R., Richards, M. N., Bond, B. J., Brunick, K. L., & Calvert, S. L. (2019). Parents' perceptions of their children's parasocial relationships: The recontact study. *Imagination, Cognition and Personality, 38*(3), 221–249.

Bandura, A. (1986). *Social foundations of thought and action*. Prentice-Hall.

Bennett, W. L., Wells, C., & Freelon, D. (2011). Communicating civic engagement: Contrasting models of citizenship in the youth Web sphere. *Journal of Communication, 61*(5), 835–856.

Bond, B. J., & Calvert, S. L. (2014a). A model and measure of US parents' perceptions of young children's parasocial relationships. *Journal of Children and Media, 8*(3), 286–304.

Bond, B. J., & Calvert, S. L. (2014b). Parasocial breakup among young children in the United States. *Journal of Children and Media, 8*(4), 474–490.

Broom, T. W., Chavez, R. S., & Wagner, D. D. (2021). Becoming the king in the north: Identification with fictional characters is associated with greater self–other neural overlap. *Social Cognitive and Affective Neuroscience, 16*(6), 541–551.

Browne Graves, S. (1999). Television and prejudice reduction: When does television as a vicarious experience make a difference? *Journal of Social Issues, 55*(4), 707–727.

Caughey, J. L. (1984). *Imaginary social worlds: A cultural approach*. University of Nebraska Press.

Cohen, J. (2001). Defining identification: A theoretical look at the identification of audiences with media characters. *Mass Communication & Society, 4*(3), 245–264.

Cohen, J. (2004). Parasocial break-up from favorite television characters: The role of attachment styles and relationship intensity. *Journal of Social and Personal Relationships, 21*(2), 187–202.

Cohen, J. (2013). Audience identification with media characters. In P. Vorderer & J. Bryant (Eds.), *Psychology of entertainment* (pp. 201–216). Routledge.

Cohen, J., & Tal-Or, N. (2017). Antecedents of identification. In F. Hakemulder (Ed.), *Narrative absorption* (pp. 133–153). Benjamins.

Curry, M. (2010). *But did we have a good time? An examination of the media massacre of Michael Jackson* [Essay]. https://www.montclair.edu/writing-studies/wp-content/uploads/sites/35/2019/06/Curry105Winner09_10.pdf

Djikic, M., & Oatley, K. (2014). The art in fiction: From indirect communication to changes of the self. *Psychology of Aesthetics, Creativity, and the Arts, 8*(4), 498–505.

References

Eder, J. (2006). Ways of being close to characters. *Film Studies, 8*(1), 68–80.

Erickson, S. E. (2022). Book review: *Parasocial romantic relationships: Falling in love with media figures*, by Riva Tukachinsky Forster. *Journalism & Mass Communication Quarterly, 99*(1), 341–343. https://doi.org/10.1177/10776990211042589

Erickson, S. E., Harrison, K., & Dal Cin, S. (2018). Toward a multi-dimensional model of adolescent romantic parasocial attachment. *Communication Theory, 28*(3), 376–399.

Eyal, K., & Cohen, J. (2006). When good friends say goodbye: A parasocial breakup study. *Journal of Broadcasting & Electronic Media, 50*(3), 502–523.

Giles, D. C. (2018). *Twenty-first century celebrity: Fame in digital culture*. Emerald Group.

Hu, M. (2016). The influence of a scandal on parasocial relationships, parasocial interaction, and parasocial breakup. *Psychology of Popular Media Culture, 5*(3), 217–231.

Hu, M. (2023). Parasocial relationship dissolution and deterioration. In R. Tukachinsky Forster (Ed.), *The Oxford handbook of parasocial experiences*. Oxford University Press.https://doi.org/10.1093/oxfordhb/9780197650677.013.6

Kaufman, G. F., & Libby, L. K. (2012). Changing beliefs and behavior through experience-taking. *Journal of Personality and Social Psychology, 103*(1), 1–19.

Meyrowitz, J. (1994). The life and death of media friends: New genres of intimacy and mourning. In S. Drucker & R. Cathcart (Eds.), *American heroes in a media age* (pp. 52–81). Hampton Press.

Oatley, K. (1995). A taxonomy of the emotions of literary response and a theory of identification in fictional narrative. *Poetics, 23*(1–2), 53–74. https://doi.org/10.1016/0304-422X(94)P4296-S

Oliver, M. B., Bilandzic, H., Cohen, J., Ferchaud, A., Shade, D. D., Bailey, E. J., & Yang, C. (2019). A penchant for the immoral: Implications of parasocial interaction, perceived complicity, and identification on liking of anti-heroes. *Human Communication Research, 45*(2), 169–201.

Raney, A. A., Janicke-Bowles, S. H., Oliver, M. B., & Dale, K. R. (2020). *Introduction to positive media psychology*. Routledge.

Richards, M. N., & Calvert, S. L. (2016). Parent versus child report of young children's parasocial relationships in the United States. *Journal of Children and Media, 10*(4), 462–480.

Sestir, M., & Green, M. C. (2010). You are who you watch: Identification and transportation effects on temporary self-concept. *Social Influence, 5*(4), 272–288.

Shackleford, K., Oatley, K., Green, M., & Stever, G. (2022, May 26–30). *Engagement with fictional characters and media personalities* [Paper presentation]. The 72nd Annual ICA Conference, One World, One Network, Paris.

Stever, G. S. (2009). Parasocial and social interaction with celebrities: Classification of media fans. *Journal of Media Psychology, 14*(3), 1–39.

Stever, G. S. (2016). Meeting Josh Groban (again): Fan/celebrity contact as ordinary behavior. *International Association for the Study of Popular Music Journal, 6*(1), 104–120.

Stever, G. S., & Lawson, K. (2013). Twitter as a way for celebrities to communicate with fans: Implications for the study of parasocial interaction. *North American Journal of Psychology, 15*(2), 597–612.

Tsioulcas, A. (2019). *Michael Jackson: A quarter-century of sexual abuse allegations*. NPR.https://www.npr.org/2019/03/05/699995484/michael-jackson-a-quarter-century-of-sexual-abuse-allegations

Tukachinsky, R. (2011). Para-romantic love and para-friendships: Development and assessment of a multiple-parasocial relationships scale. *American Journal of Media Psychology, 3*(1–2), 73–94.

Tukachinsky, R., & Stever, G. (2019). Theorizing development of parasocial engagement. *Communication Theory, 29*(3), 209–320. https://doi.org/10.1093/ct/qty032

Tukachinsky Forster, R. (2021). *Parasocial romantic relationships: Falling in love with media figures*. Rowman & Littlefield.

Tukachinsky Forster, R., & Click, M. A. (2023). Beyond friendship: A call for research on non-amicable parasocial relationships. In R. Tukachinsky Forster (Ed.), *The Oxford handbook of parasocial experiences* (pp. 375–392). Oxford University Press.

Weta. (2015). *The hobbit: The art of war*. Harper.

CHAPTER 3

Abidin, C. (2016). Visibility labour: Engaging with influencers' fashion brands and #OOTD advertorial campaigns on Instagram. *Media International Australia, 161*(1), 86–100.

Abidin, C. (2017). #familygoals: Family influencers, calibrated amateurism, and justifying young digital labour. *Social Media + Society, 3*(1), 1–15.

Altman, I., & Taylor, D. (1973). *Social penetration theory*. Holt, Rinehart & Winston.

Banks, J., & Bowman, N. D. (2016). Avatars are (sometimes) people too: Linguistic indicators of parasocial and social ties in player–avatar relationships. *New Media & Society, 18*, 1257–1276.

Bennett, J. (2011). *Television personalities: Stardom and the small screen*. Routledge.

Betancourt, R. (2016). Genre as medium on YouTube: The work of Grace Helbig. *Journal of Popular Culture, 49*(1), 196–223.

Bird, S. E. (2011). Are we all produsers now? Convergence and media audience practices. *Cultural Studies, 24*(4–5), 502–516.

Clement, J. (2023, 31 May). *Active streamers on Twitch worldwide in 2023*. Statista. https://www.statista.com/statistics/746173/monthly-active-streamers-on-twitch/#:~:text=In%20May%202023%2C%20Twitch%20had,channels%20have%20milli ons%20of%20viewers

Cowan, N. (2015). George Miller's magical number of immediate memory in retrospect: Observations on the faltering progression of science. *Psychological Review, 122*(3), 536–541.

Cross, T. (2021, June 29). Twitch's hot tub drama demonstrates the difficulty of policing sexual content. *VideoWeek*. https://videoweek.com/2021/06/29/twitchs-hot-tub-drama-demonstrates-the-difficulty-of-policing-sexual-content

Delbaere, M., Michael, B., & Phillips, B. J. (2021). Social media influencers: A route to brand engagement for their followers. *Psychology & Marketing, 38*, 101–112.

Duffett, M. (2013). *Understanding fandom: An introduction to the study of media fan culture*. Bloomsbury.

Freud, S. (1922). *Group psychology and the analysis of the ego* (J. Strachey, Trans.). International Psycho-Analytical Press.

Giles, D. C. (2000). *Illusions of immortality: A psychology of fame and celebrity*. Macmillan.

Giles, D. C. (2002). Parasocial interaction: A review of the literature and a model for future research. *Media Psychology, 4*(3), 279–302.

References

Giles, D. C. (2013). The extended self strikes back: Morrissey fans' reaction to public rejection by their idol. *Popular Communication, 11*(2), 116–129.

Giles, D. C. (2017). How do fan and celebrity identities become established on Twitter? A study of "social media natives" and their followers. *Celebrity Studies, 8*(3), 445–460.

Giles, D. C. (2018). *Twenty-first century celebrity: Fame in digital culture.* Emerald.

Giles, D. C. (2024). Analysing digital audiences: A case study of YouTuber depression videos. In G. Ouvrein, A. Jorge, & H. Van der Bulck (Eds.), *An interdisciplinary approach to celebrities and their audience* (pp. 19–40). Lexington Books.

Griffith, A. H. (1957). Children's vision and television. *British Medical Journal, 2*(5056), 1299–1302.

Hartmann, T., & Goldhoorn, C. (2011). Horton and Wohl revisited: Exploring viewers' experience of parasocial interaction. *Journal of Communication, 61*(6), 1104–1121.

Hayes, A. (2023, February 23). *YouTube stats: Everything you need to know in 2023!* Wyzowl. https://www.wyzowl.com/youtube-stats

Hills, M. (2016). From para-social to multisocial interaction: Theorising material/digital fandom and celebrity. In P. D. Marshall & S. Redmond (Eds.), *A companion to celebrity* (pp. 101–118). Routledge.

Horton, D., & Wohl, R. R. (1956). Mass communication and para-social interaction. *Psychiatry, 19*, 215–229.

Jenson, J. (1992). Fandom as pathology: The consequences of characterization. In L. A. Lewis (Ed.), *The adoring audience: Fan culture and popular media* (pp. 9–29). Routledge.

Jin, S. A., & Park, N. (2009). Parasocial interaction with my avatar: Effects of interdependent self-construal and the mediating role of self-presence in an avatar-based console game, Wii. *CyberPsychology & Behaviour, 12*, 723–727.

Kehrberg, A. (2015). "I love you, please notice me": The hierarchical rhetoric of Twitter fandom, *Celebrity Studies, 6*(1), 85–99.

Konok, V., Korcsok, B., Miklósi, A., & Gácsi, M. (2018). Should we love robots? The most liked qualities of companion dogs and how they can be implemented in social robots. *Computers in Human Behavior, 80*, 132–142.

Lee, K. M., Peng, W., Jin, S., & Yan, C. (2006). Can robots manifest personality? An empirical test of personality recognition, social responses and social presence in human–robot interaction. *Journal of Communication, 56*(4), 754–772.

Leith, A. P. (2021). Parasocial cues: The ubiquity of parasocial relationships on Twitch. *Communication Monographs, 88*(1), 111–129.

Levy, M. R. (1979). Watching TV news as para-social interaction. *Journal of Broadcasting, 23*, 69–80.

Lim, W. M., Kumar, S., Verma, S., & Chaturvedi, R. (2022). Alexa, what do we know about conversational commerce? Insights from a systematic literature review. *Psychology & Marketing, 39*(6), 1129–1155.

Lou, C., & Kim, H. K. (2019). Fancying the new rich and famous? Explicating the roles of influencer content, credibility, and parental mediation in adolescents' parasocial relationship, materialism, and purchase intentions. *Frontiers in Psychology, 10*, 25–67.

Marshall, P. D., Moore, C., & Barbour, K. (2015). Persona as method: Exploring celebrity and the public self. *Celebrity Studies, 6*(3), 288–305.

Marshall, P. D., Moore, C., & Barbour, K. (2020). *Persona studies: An introduction.* Wiley.

Martínez, C., & Olsson, T. (2019). Making sense of YouTubers: How Swedish children construct and negotiate the YouTuber Misslisibell as a girl celebrity. *Journal of Children and Media, 13*, 36–52.

Marwick, A., & boyd, D. (2011). To see and be seen: Celebrity practice on Twitter. *Convergence, 17*(2), 139–158.

Marwick, A. E. (2013). *Status update: celebrity, publicity and branding in the social media age*. New Haven: Yale University Press.

McLuhan, M. (1964). *Understanding media: The extensions of man*. MIT Press.

Miklósi, Á., Korondi, P., Matellán, V., & Gácsi, M. (2017). Ethorobotics: A new approach to human–robot relationship. *Frontiers in Psychology, 8*, Article 958. https://doi.org/10.3389/fpsyg.2017.00958

Miller, G. (1956). The magical number seven, plus or minus two: Some limits on our capacity for processing information. *Psychological Review, 63*, 81–97.

Mori, M. (2012, June 12). The uncanny valley (K. F. MacDorman & N. Kageki, Trans.). *IEEE Spectrum*. https://spectrum.ieee.org/the-uncanny-valley (Original work published 1970)

Naveh-Benjamin, M., & Ayres, T. J. (1986). Digit span, reading rate, and linguistic relativity. *Quarterly Journal of Experimental Psychology Section A, 38*(4), 739–751.

Newman, J. (2016). Stampylongnose and the rise of the celebrity videogame player. *Celebrity Studies, 7*(2), 285–288.

Ouvrein, G., Pabian, S., Giles, D., Hudders, L. & De Backer, C. (2021). The web of influencers: A marketing-audience classification of (potential) social media influencers. *Journal of Marketing Management, 37*(13–14), 1313–1342.

Ramadan, Z., Farah, M., & El Essrawi, L. (2021). From Amazon.com to Amazon. love: How Alexa is redefining companionship and interdependence for people with special needs. *Psychology & Marketing, 38*(4), 596–609.

Rathje, W., & Murphy, C. (1992). *Rubbish! The archaeology of garbage*. HarperCollins.

Rihl, A., & Wegener, C. (2019). YouTube celebrities and parasocial interaction: Using feedback channels in mediatized relationships. *Convergence, 25*(3), 554–566.

Rojek, C. (2001). *Celebrity*. Reaktion.

Rubin, A. M., Perse, E. M., & Powell, R. A. (1985). Loneliness, parasocial interaction and local television news viewing. *Human Communication Research, 12*(2), 155–180.

Rubin, R. B., & McHugh, M. P. (1987). Development of parasocial interaction relationships. *Journal of Broadcasting & Electronic Media, 31*, 279–292.

Schwartz, A. B. (2015). *Broadcast hysteria: Orson Welles's war of the worlds and the art of fake news*. Hill & Wang.

Sherrick, B., Smith, C., Jia, Y., Thomas, B., & Franklin, S. B. (2023). How parasocial phenomena contribute to sense of community on Twitch. *Journal of Broadcasting & Electronic Media, 67*(1), 47–67.

Skjuve, M., Folstad, A., Fostervold, K. I., & Brandtzaeg, P. B. (2021). My chatbot companion: A study of human–chatbot relationships. *International Journal of Human–Computer Studies, 149*, Article 102601.

Stever, G. S., & Hughes, E. (2013, September 2–3). What role Twitter? Celebrity conversations with fans [Paper presentation]. Social Media: The Fourth Annual Transforming Audiences Conference, University of Westminster.

References

Stoldt, R., Wellmann, M., Ekdale, B., & Tully, M. (2019). Professionalising and profiting: The rise of intermediaries in the social media influencing industry. *Social Media + Society*, *5*(1), 1–12.

Stokel-Walker, C. (2022, February 21). TikTok wants longer videos—whether you like it or not. *Wired*. https://www.wired.co.uk/article/tiktok-wants-longer-vid eos-like-not?utm_source=twitter&utm_medium=social&utm_campaign=onsite-share&utm_brand=wired-uk&utm_social-type=earned

Taylor, M. (1999). *Imaginary companions and the children who create them*. Oxford University Press.

Thelwall, M., Stuart, E., Mas-Bleda, A., Makita, M., & Abdoli, M. (2022). I'm nervous about sharing this secret with you: YouTube influencers generate strong parasocial interactions by discussing personal issues. *Journal of Data and Information Science*, *7*(2), 31–56.

Tolbert, A. N., & Drogos, K. L. (2019). Tweens' wishful identification and parasocial relationships with YouTubers. *Frontiers in Psychology*, *10*, Article 2781.

Tsay-Vogel, M., & Schwartz, M. L. (2014). Theorizing parasocial interactions based on authenticity: The development of a media figure classification scheme. *Psychology of Popular Media Culture*, *3*, 66–78.

Turner, G. (2004). *Understanding celebrity*. SAGE.

TwitchTracker. (2023). *Twitch statistics & charts*. https://twitchtracker.com/statistics

Wedgwood, S. (2017, October 24). "I view the hurtful messages as sadism": What it's like to be Instagram famous. *The Guardian*. https://www.theguardian.com/technology/ 2017/oct/24/instagram-influencers-hurtful-messages-sadism-famous

CHAPTER 4

Babcock, M. K. (1989). The dramaturgic perspective: Implications for the study of person perception. *European Journal of Social Psychology*, *19*(4), 297–309.

Dibble, J. L., Guzaitis, M., Tukachinsky Forster, R. R., & Downey, S. E. (2023). Methods and measures in investigating PSEs. In R. Tukachinsky Forster (Ed.), *The Oxford handbook of parasocial experiences* (pp. 70–121). Oxford University Press.

Dibble, J. L., Hartmann, T., & Rosaen, S. F. (2016). Parasocial interaction and parasocial relationship: Conceptual clarification and a critical assessment of measures. *Human Communication Research*, *42*(1), 21–44.

Dietz, P. E., Matthews, D. B., Van Duyne, C., & Martell, D. A. (1991). Threatening and otherwise inappropriate letters to Hollywood celebrities. *Journal of Forensic Sciences*, *36*(1), 185–209.

Ferris, K. O. (2001). Through a glass, darkly: The dynamics of fan–celebrity encounters. *Symbolic Interaction*, *24*(1), 25–47.

Ferris, K. O. (2007). The sociology of celebrity. *Sociology Compass*, *1*(1), 371–384.

Greene, A. L., & Adams-Price, C. (1990). Adolescents' secondary attachments to celebrity figures. *Sex Roles*, *23*(7), 335–347.

Hartmann, T. (2008). Parasocial interactions and paracommunication with new media characters. In E. A. Konijn, S. Utz, M. Tanis, & S. B. Barnes (Eds.), *Mediated interpersonal communication* (pp. 191–213). Routledge.

Hartmann, T. (2023). Three conceptual challenges to parasocial interaction: Anticipated responses, implicit address, and the interactivity problem. In R. Tukachinsky

Forster (Ed.), *The Oxford handbook of parasocial experiences* (pp. 51–68). Oxford University Press.

Hartmann, T., & Goldhoorn, C. (2011). Horton and Wohl revisited: Exploring viewers' experience of parasocial interaction. *Journal of Communication, 61*(6), 1104–1121.

Horton, D., & Wohl, R. (1956). Mass communication and para-social interaction: Observations on intimacy at a distance. *Psychiatry, 19*(3), 215–229.

Hu, M. (2023). Parasocial relationship dissolution and deterioration. In R. Tukachinsky Forster (Ed.), *The Oxford handbook of parasocial experiences* (pp. 147–170). Oxford University Press.

Jenkins, H. (2012). *Textual poachers: Television fans and participatory culture.* Routledge.

Johnson, L. E. (2022, July 29). The best part of a Josh Groban concert (it isn't the singing). *Deseret News.* https://www.deseret.com

Knipe, M. R. (2022). Virtual community during a pandemic: A case study. *Journal of Fandom Studies, 10*(2–3), 111–133.

Konijn, E. A., Utz, S., Tanis, M., & Barnes, S. B. (2008). Parasocial interactions and paracommunication with new media characters. In E. A. Konjin (Ed.), *Mediated interpersonal communication* (pp. 191–213). Routledge.

Lowery, M., & Lloyd, K. (2022). *What we found together: Essays on community during the pandemic.* Sidcity.net.

Maltby, J., Houran, J., & McCutcheon, L. E. (2003). A clinical interpretation of attitudes and behaviors associated with celebrity worship. *Journal of Nervous and Mental Disease, 191*(1), 25–29.

Manusov, V., & Spitzberg, B. (2008). *Attribution theory.* SAGE.

Martin, M. C., & Cohen, E. L. (2023). "Welcome to the stream, Vykaryous4Eva!": The effect of vicarious interaction on parasocial relationships with a live streamer. *Technology, Mind, and Behavior, 4*(3). https://doi.org/10.1037/tmb0000114

McCutcheon, L. E., Ashe, D. D., Houran, J., & Maltby, J. (2003). A cognitive profile of individuals who tend to worship celebrities. *Journal of Psychology, 137*(4), 309–322.

Riles, J. M., & Adams, K. (2021). Me, myself, and my mediated ties: Parasocial experiences as an ego-driven process. *Media Psychology, 24*(6), 792–813.

Stever, G. S. (2009). Parasocial and social interaction with celebrities: Classification of media fans. *Journal of Media Psychology, 14*(3), 1–39.

Stever, G. S. (2011a). 1989 vs. 2009: A comparative analysis of music superstars Michael Jackson and Josh Groban, and their fans. *Journal of Media Psychology, 16* (1), 281–303.

Stever, G. S. (2011b). Celebrity worship: Critiquing a construct. *Journal of Applied Social Psychology, 41*(6), 1356–1370. http://dx.doi.org/10.1111/j.1559-1816.2011.00765.x

Stever, G. S. (2013). Mediated vs. parasocial relationships: An attachment perspective. *Journal of Media Psychology, 17*(3), 1–31.

Stever, G. S. (2016). Meeting Josh Groban (again): Fan/celebrity contact as ordinary behavior. *International Association for the Study of Popular Music Journal, 6*(1), 104–120.

Stever, G. S. (2017). Evolutionary theory and reactions to mass media: Understanding parasocial attachment. *Psychology of Popular Media Culture, 6*(2), 95–102. http://dx.doi.org/10.1037/ppm0000116

References

Stever, G. S., & Lawson, K. (2013). Twitter as a way for celebrities to communicate with fans: Implications for the study of parasocial interaction. *North American Journal of Psychology, 15*(2), 597–612.

Tukachinsky Forster, R. (2021). *Parasocial romantic relationships: Falling in love with media figures.* Rowman & Littlefield.

Verba, J. M. (2003). *Boldly writing.* FTL Publications.

Wiemer, E. C., Riles, J. M., & Tewksbury, D. (2022). Artists and attributions: How music platform implementation affects parasocial experiences and support intentions. *Journal of Broadcasting & Electronic Media, 66*(2), 300–319.

CHAPTER 5

Aguiar, N. R., Richards, N. M., Bond, B. J., Brunick, K. L., & Calvert, S. L. (2019). Parents' perceptions of their children's parasocial relationships: The recontact study. *Imagination, Cognition & Personality, 38*(3), 221–249.

Alperstein, L. (1991). Imaginary social relationships with celebrities appearing in television commercials. *Journal of Broadcasting and Electronic Media, 35,* 43–58.

Alperstein, N. M., & Vann, B. H. (1997). Star gazing: A socio-cultural approach to the study of dreaming about media figures. *Communication Quarterly, 45*(3), 142–152.

Aron, A., Aron, E. N., Tudor, M., & Nelson, G. (1991). Close relationships as including other in the self. *Journal of Personality and Social Psychology, 60*(2), 241–253.

Aron, A., Lewandowski, G., Branand, B., Mashek, D., & Aron, E. N. (2022). Self-expansion motivation and inclusion of others in the self: An updated review. *Journal of Social and Personal Relationships, 39*(12), 3821–3852.

Bakhtin, M. (1986). *Speech genres and other late essays* (W. McGee, Trans.). University of Texas Press.

Baldwin, M. W., & Holmes, J. G. (1987). Salient private audiences and awareness of the self. *Journal of Personality and Social Psychology, 52*(6), 1087–1098.

Barbieri, A. (2015, April 10). My husband was unfaithful and lied about it for years. *The Guardian.* https://www.theguardian.com/lifeandstyle/2015/apr/10/my-husband-was-unfaithful-and-lied-about-it-for-years

Bartz, J. A., Tchalova, K., & Fenerci, C. (2016). Reminders of social connection can attenuate anthropomorphism: A replication and extension of Epley, Akalis, Waytz and Cacioppo (2008). *Psychological Science, 27*(12), 1644–1650.

Bearison, D. J., Bain, J. M., & Daniele, R. (1982). Developmental changes in how children understand television. *Social Behavior and Personality, 10,* 133–144.

Bond, B. J., & Calvert, S. L. (2014). A model and measure of US parents' perceptions of young children's parasocial relationships. *Journal of Children and Media, 8*(3), 286–304.

Braithwaite, D. O., Bach, B. W., Baxter, L. A., DiVerniero, R., Hammonds, J. R., Hosek, A. M., Willer, E. K., & Wolf, B. M. (2010). Constructing family: A typology of voluntary kin. *Journal of Social and Personal Relationships, 27*(3), 388–407.

Briggs, M. (2006). Beyond the audience: Teletubbies, play and parenthood. *European Journal of Cultural Studies, 9*(4), 461–480.

Briggs, M. (2007). Meaning, play and experience: Audience activity and the "ontological bias" in children's media research. *Particip@tions, 4*(2), 1–15.

Bunce, L., & Harris, M. (2008). "I saw the real Father Christmas!" Children's everyday uses of the words real, really and pretend. *British Journal of Developmental Psychology, 26*(3), 445–455.

Calvert, S. L. (2017). Parasocial relationships with media characters: Imaginary companions for young children's social and cognitive development. In F. Blumberg & P. Brooks (Eds.), *Cognitive development in digital contexts* (pp. 93–117). Elsevier.

Caughey, J. L. (1984). *Imaginary social worlds: A cultural approach*. University of Nebraska Press.

Cavicchi, D. (1998). *Tramps like us: Music and meaning among Springsteen fans*. Oxford University Press.

Cole, T. (2001). Lying to the one you love: The use of deception in romantic relationships. *Journal of Social and Personal Relationships, 18*(1), 107–129.

Dalsimer, K. (1982). Female adolescent development: A study of *The Diary of Anne Frank. The Psychoanalytic Study of the Child, 37*(1), 487–522.

Davis, P. E., King, N., Meins, E., & Fernyhough, C. (2023). "When my mummy and daddy aren't looking at me when I do my maths she helps me": Children can be taught to create imaginary companions: An exploratory study. *Infant and Child Development, 32*(2), Article e2390. https://doi.org/10.1002/ICD.2390

Davis, P. E., Meins, E., & Fernyhough, C. (2011). Self-knowledge in childhood: Relations with children's imaginary companions and theory of mind. *British Journal of Developmental Psychology, 29*, 580–686.

Davis, P. E., Meins, E., & Fernyhough, C. (2013). Individual differences in children's private speech: The role of imaginary companions. *Journal of Experimental Child Psychology, 116*(3), 561–571.

DePaulo, B. M., Kashy, D. A., Kirkendol, S. E., Wyer, M. M., & Epstein, J. A. (1996). Lying in everyday life. *Journal of Personality and Social Psychology, 79*(5), 979–995.

Doss, E. (1999). *Elvis culture: Fans, faith and image*. University of Kansas Press.

Duck, S. (1986). *Human relationships: An introduction to social psychology*. SAGE.

Epley, N., Waytz, A., Akalis, S., & Cacioppo, J. T. (2008). When we need a human: Motivational determinants of anthropomorphism. *Social Cognition, 26*(2), 143–155.

Epley, N., Waytz, A., & Cacioppo, J. T. (2007). On seeing human: A three-factor theory of anthropomorphism. *Psychological Review, 114*(4), 864–886.

Fernyhough, C., Watson, A., Bernini, M., Moseley, P., & Alderson-Day, B. (2019). Imaginary companions, inner speech, and auditory verbal hallucinations: What are the relations? *Frontiers in Psychology, 10*, Article 1665. doi:10.3389/fpsyg.2019.01665

Fisher, J. A. (1991). Disambiguating anthropomorphism: An interdisciplinary review. In P. P. G. Bateson & P. H. Klopfer (Eds.), *Perspectives in ethology* (Vol. 9, pp. 49–85). Plenum.

Flavell, J. H., Flavell, E. R., Green, F. L., & Korfmacher, J. E. (1990). Do young children think of television images as pictures or real objects? *Journal of Broadcasting and Electronic Media, 34*, 399–419.

Foucault, M. (1988). Technologies of the self. In L. H. Martin, H. Gutman, & P. H. Hutton (Eds.), *Technologies of the self: A seminar with Michel Foucault* (pp. 16–49). Tavistock.

Frow, J. (1998). Is Elvis a god? Cult culture, questions of method. *International Journal of Cultural Studies, 1*(2), 197–210.

References

Geertz, C. (1973). *The interpretation of cultures*. Basic Books.

Gergen, K. J. (1991). *The saturated self: Dilemmas of identity in contemporary life*. Basic Books.

Gergen, M. (2001). *Feminist reconstructions in psychology: Narrative, gender and performance*. SAGE.

Giles, D. C. (2000). *Illusions of immortality: A psychology of fame and celebrity*. Macmillan.

Giles, D. C. (2003). *Media psychology*. Erlbaum.

Giles, D. C. (2013). The extended self strikes back: Morrissey fans' reaction to public rejection by their idol. *Popular Communication, 11*(2), 116–129.

Giles, D. C. (2018). *Twenty-first century celebrity: Fame in digital culture*. Emerald.

Gleason, T. R. (2017). The psychological significance of play with imaginary companions in childhood. *Learning & Behavior, 45*, 432–440.

Gleason, T. R., Theran, S. A., & Newberg, E. M. (2020). Connections between adolescents' parasocial interactions and recollections of childhood imaginative activities. *Imagination, Cognition and Personality, 39*(3), 241–260.

Goffman, E. (1959). *The presentation of self in everyday life*. Anchor.

Gola, A. A., Richards, M. N., Lauricella, A. R., & Calvert, S. L. (2013). Building meaningful parasocial relationships between toddlers and media characters to teach early mathematical skills. *Media Psychology, 16*(4), 390–411.

Grenier, J., Cappeliez, P., St-Onge, M., Vachon, J., Vinette, S., Roussy, F., Mercier, P., Lortie-Lussier, M., & De Koninck, J. (2005). Temporal references in dreams and autobiographical memory. *Memory & Cognition, 33*(2), 280–288.

Gunter, B., & McAleer, J. (1990). *Children and television*. Taylor & Francis.

Harré, R. (1983). *The singular self: An introduction to the psychology of personhood*. SAGE.

Hodge, B., & Tripp, D. (1986). *Children and television: A semiotic approach*. Blackwell.

Hoff, E. V. (2004-2005). A friend living inside me: The forms and functions of imaginary companions. *Imagination, Cognition and Personality, 24*(2), 151–189.

Hoffman, A., Owen, D., & Calvert, S. L. (2021). Parent reports of children's parasocial relationships with conversational agents: Trusted voices in children's lives. *Human Behavior & Emerging Technologies, 3*, 606–617.

Hoffner, C. (1996). Children's wishful identification and parasocial interaction with favorite television characters. *Journal of Broadcasting and Electronic Media, 40*(3), 389–402.

Honeycutt, J. M. (2003). *Imagined interactions: Daydreaming about communication*. Hampton Press.

Honeycutt, J. M. (2008–2009). Symbolic interdependence, imagined interaction, and relationship quality. *Imagination, Cognition and Personality, 28*, 303–320.

Honeycutt, J. M., Pecchioni, L., Keaton, S. A., & Pence, M. E. (2011–2012). Developmental implications of mental imagery in childhood imaginary companions. *Imagination, Cognition and Personality, 31*(1–2), 79–98.

Hornby, N. (1992). *Fever pitch*. Gollancz.

Jackson, P. R. (2010). *Here's a house: A celebration of Play School*. Kaleidoscope.

Jalongo, M. R. (1984). Imaginary companions in children's lives and literature. *Childhood Education, 60*, 166–171.

Jenkins, H. (1992). *Textual poachers: Television fans and participatory culture*. Routledge.

Kapitány, R., Nelson, N., Burdett, E. R. R., & Goldstein, T. R. (2020). The child's pantheon: Children's hierarchical belief structure in real and non-real figures. *PLoS One, 15*(6), Article e0234142.

Lasch, C. (1991). *The culture of narcissism: American life in an age of diminishing expectations*. Norton.

Lauricella, A. R., Gola, A. A., & Calvert, S. L. (2011). Toddlers' learning from socially meaningful video characters. *Media Psychology, 14*(2), 216–232.

Linton, D. (2022, November 19). "I love him so much I could cry": Adults who have cuddly toys. *The Guardian*. https://www.theguardian.com/lifeandstyle/2022/nov/19/adults-who-have-cuddly-toys-comfort-objects

Madison, T. P., Auter, P. J., Honeycutt, J. M., & Horst, R. (2022). In search of catharsis: Trump and parasocial predictors of social media use integration. *Journal of Social Media in Society, 11*(2), 122–139.

Madison, T. P., & Porter, L. V. (2016). Cognitive and imagery attributes of parasocial relationships. *Imagination, Cognition and Personality, 35*(4), 359–379.

Madison, T .P., Wright, K., & Gaspard, T. (2021). "My superpower is being honest": Perceived credibility and functions of parasocial relationships with Alex Jones. *Southwestern Journal of Mass Communication, 36*(1), 50–64.

Majors, K. (2013). Children's perceptions of their imaginary companions and the purposes they serve: An exploratory study in the United Kingdom. *Childhood, 24*, 550–565.

Majors, K., & Baines, E. (2017). Children's play with their imaginary companions: Parent experiences and perceptions of the characteristics of the imaginary companions and purposes served. *Education & Child Psychology, 34*(3), 37–56.

Marshall, P. D., Moore, C., & Barbour, K. (2020). *Persona studies: An introduction*. Wiley.

Marwick, A. (2013). *Status update: Celebrity, publicity and branding in the social media age*. Yale University Press.

Marwick, A., & boyd, D. (2011). To see and be seen: Celebrity practice on Twitter. *Convergence, 17*(2), 139–158.

Maton, K. (2010). Last night we dreamt that somebody loved us: Smiths fans (and me) in the late 1980s. In S. Campbell & C. Coulter (Eds.), *Why pamper life's complexities? Essays on the Smiths* (pp. 179–194). Manchester University Press.

McConnell, A. R., Brown, C. M., Shoda, T. M., Stayton, L. E., & Martin, C. E. (2011). Friends with benefits: On the positive consequences of pet ownership. *Journal of Personality and Social Psychology, 101*(6), 1239–1252.

Moctezuma, C. (2019, March). Psicología: Los perrhijos. *Alethéia: Revista IEU Universidad*. https://revista-aletheia.ieu.edu.mx/documentos/A_opinion/2019/3_Marzo/Art_Op_1.pdf

Moverley, M., Schredl, M., & Görlitz, A. S. (2018). Media dreaming and media consumption: An online study. *International Journal of Dream Research, 11*(2), 127–134.

Myers, W. A. (1979). Imaginary companions in childhood and adult creativity. *Psychoanalytic Quarterly, 48*, 292–307.

Nagera, H. (1969). The imaginary companion: Its significance for ego development and conflict solution. *Psychoanalytic Study of the Child, 24*, 165–196.

Pearson, D., Rouse, H., Doswell, S., Ainsworth, C., Dawson, O., Simms, K., Edwards, L., & Faulconbridge, J. (2001). Prevalence of imaginary companions in a normal child population. *Child: Care, Health and Development, 27*(1), 13–22.

References

Piaget, J., & Inhelder, B. (1969). *pi*. Routledge & Kegan Paul.

Prentice, N. M., Manosevitz, M., & Hubbs, L. (1978). Imaginary figures of early childhood: Santa Claus, Easter Bunny and the Tooth Fairy. *American Journal of Orthopsychiatry, 48*(4), 618–628.

Rubin, A. M., Perse, E. M., & Powell, R. A. (1985). Loneliness, parasocial interaction and local television news viewing. *Human Communication Research, 12*(2), 155–180.

Ruskin, J. (1857). *Modern painters* (Vol. 3). Smith, Elder.

Sampson, E. E. (1988). The debate on individualism: Indigenous psychologies of the individual and their role in personal and societal functioning. *American Psychologist, 43*, 15–22.

Sandvoss, C. (2005). *Fans: The mirror of consumption*. Wiley.

Schredl, M. (2018). *Researching dreams: The fundamentals*. Palgrave Macmillan.

Schredl, M., & Schweickert, R. (2022). Social network in the 2015 dreams of a male dreamer. *International Journal of Dream Research, 15*(1), 118–125.

Seiffge-Krenke, I. (1997). Imaginary companions in adolescence: Sign of a deficient or positive development? *Journal of Adolescence, 20*, 137–154.

Shotter, J. (1995). In conversation: Joint action, shared intentionality and ethics. *Theory & Psychology, 5*(1), 49–73.

Stevenson, N. (2009). Talking to Bowie fans: Masculinity, ambivalence and cultural citizenship. *European Journal of Cultural Studies, 12*(1), 79–98.

Stever, G. S. (2009). Parasocial and social interaction with celebrities: Classification of media fans. *Journal of Media Psychology, 14*(3), 1–39.

Tahiroglu, D., & Taylor, M. (2019). Anthropomorphism, social understanding and imaginary companions. *British Journal of Developmental Psychology, 37*, 284–299.

Taylor, M. (1999). *Imaginary companions and the children who create them*. Oxford University Press.

Taylor, M., & Carlson, S. M. (2000). The influence of religious beliefs on parental attitudes about children's fantasy behavior. In K. S. Rosengren, C. Johnson, & P. L. Harris (Eds.), *Imagining the impossible: Magical, scientific, and religious thinking in children* (pp. 247–267). Cambridge University Press.

Turner, G. (2010). *Ordinary people and the media: The demotic turn*. SAGE.

Vallat, R., Chatard, B., Blagrove, M., & Ruby, P. (2017). Characteristics of the memory sources of dreams: A new version of the content-matching paradigm to take mundane and remote memories into account. *PLoS One, 12*(10), Article e0185262.

Watkins, M. (1986). *Invisible guests: The development of imaginal dialogues*. Analytic Press.

Wigger, J. B. (2018). Invisible friends across four countries: Kenya, Malawi, Nepal and the Dominican Republic. *International Journal of Psychology, 53*(S1), 46–52.

Wise, S. (1990). Sexing Elvis. In S. Frith & A. Goodwin (Eds.), *On record: Rock, pop and the written word* (pp. 390–398). Routledge.

Wright, J. C., Huston, A. C., Reitz, A. L., & Piemyat, S. (1994). Young children's perceptions of television reality: Determinants and developmental differences. *Developmental Psychology, 30*(2), 229–239.

Yamaguchi, M., Okanda, M., Moriguchi, Y., & Itakura, S. (2023). Young adults with imaginary companions: The role of anthropomorphism, loneliness and perceived stress. *Personality and Individual Differences, 207*, Article 112159.

CHAPTER 6

Bahrick, L. E., Moss, L., & Fadil, C. (1996). Development of visual self-recognition in infancy. *Ecological Psychology, 8*(3), 189–208.

Barker, M. J. (2005). *Lord of the Rings* and "identification": A critical encounter. *European Journal of Communication, 20*(3), 353–378.

Baxter, L. A. (2004). Relationships as dialogues. *Personal Relationships, 11*, 1–22.

Bertenthal, B. I., & Fischer, K. W. (1978). Development of self-recognition in the infant. *Developmental Psychology, 14*(1), 44–50.

Bianculli, D. (2000). *Teleliteracy: Taking television seriously*. Syracuse University Press.

Billig, M. (2006). Lacan's misuse of psychology: Evidence, rhetoric and the mirror stage. *Theory, Culture & Society, 23*(4), 1–26.

Cohen, J. (1999). Favorite characters of teenage viewers of Israeli serials. *Journal of Broadcasting and Electronic Media, 43*, 327–345.

Cohen, J. (2001). Defining identification: A theoretical look at the identification of audiences with media characters. *Mass Communication & Society, 4*(3), 245–264.

Dill-Shackleford, K. E., Vinney, C., & Hopper-Losenicky, K. (2016). Connecting the dots between fantasy and reality: The social psychology of our engagement with fictional narrative and its functional value. *Social and Personality Psychology Compass, 10*, 634–646.

Emmison, M., & Goldman, L. (1996). What's that you said Sooty? Puppets, parlance and pretence. *Language and Communication, 16*, 17–35.

Emmison, M., & Goldman, L. (1997). *The Sooty Show* laid bear: Children, puppets and make-believe. *Childhood, 4*, 325–342.

Freud, S. (1922). *Group psychology and the analysis of the ego* (J. Strachey, Trans.). International Psycho-Analytical Press.

Frosh, S. (2012). *A brief introduction to psychoanalytic theory*. Red Globe Press.

Giles, D. C. (2002). Parasocial interaction: A review of the literature and a model for future research. *Media Psychology, 4*(3), 279–302.

Giles, D. C. (2003). *Media psychology*. Erlbaum.

Giles, D. C., & Shaw, R. L. (2009). The psychology of news influence and the development of media framing analysis. *Social and Personality Psychology Compass, 3–4*, 375–393.

Glaser, B. G., & Strauss, A. L. (1967). *The discovery of grounded theory: Strategies for qualitative research*. Aldine De Gruyter.

Green, M. C., & Brock, T. C. (2000). The role of transportation in the persuasiveness of public narratives. *Journal of Personality and Social Psychology, 79*(5), 701–721.

Haggbloom, S. J., Warnick, R., Warnick, J. E., Jones, V. K., Yarbrough, G. L., Russell, T. M., Borecky, C. M., McGahhey, R., Powell, J. L., III, Beavers, J., & Monte, E. (2002). The 100 most eminent psychologists of the 20th century. *Review of General Psychology, 6*(2), 139–152.

Hills, M. (2002). *Fan cultures*. Routledge.

Hodge, B., & Tripp, D. (1986). *Children and television: A semiotic approach*. Blackwell.

Holmes, S., Ralph, S., & Redmond, S. (2015). Swivelling the spotlight: Stardom, celebrity and "me." *Celebrity Studies, 6*(1), 100–117.

Jovchelovitch, S., Priego-Hernández, J., & Glăveanu, V. P. (2017). Imagination in children entering culture. In T. Zittoun & V. Glăveanu (Eds.), *Handbook of imagination and culture* (pp. 111–136). Oxford University Press.

References

233

Kelly, G, A. (1955). *The psychology of personal constructs* (Vol. 1). Norton.

Klein, M. (1946). Notes on some schizoid mechanisms. *International Journal of Psycho-Analysis, 27*, 99–110.

Konijn, E. A., & Hoorn, J. F. (2005). Some like it bad: Testing a model for perceiving and experiencing fictional characters. *Media Psychology, 7*(2), 107–144.

Konijn, E. A., Walma van der Molen, J. H., & van Nes, S. (2009). Emotions bias perceptions of realism in audiovisual media: Why we may take fiction for real. *Discourse Processes, 46*(4), 309–340.

Lacan, J. (1988). *The seminar of Jacques Lacan, book II: The ego in Freud's theory and in the technique of psychoanalysis, 1954–1955* (J. Miller, Ed.; S. Tomaselli, Trans.). Norton. (Original work published 1954–1955)

Lacan, J. (1990). *Television*. Norton.

Lacan, J. (1994). *The four fundamental concepts of psychoanalysis* (J. Miller, Ed.; A. Sheridan, Trans.). Penguin. (Original work published 1973)

Lacan, J. (2006). The mirror stage in the formation of the I as revealed in psychoanalytic experience. In *Écrits* (B. Fink, Trans.). Norton. (Original work published 1949)

Lear, J. (2010). *Open minded: Working out the logic of the soul*. Harvard University Press.

Löbler, H. (2009). My relationship to Scarlett O'Hara: Characterising para-social relationships using the repertory grid technique. *Journal of Customer Behaviour, 8*(1), 29–50.

Löbler, H., & Raschpichler, J. (2009). My relationship to Scarlett O'Hara—Characterising parasocial relationships using the repertory grid technique. *Journal of Customer Behaviour, 8*(1), 29–50.

Maccoby, E. E., & Wilson, W. C. (1957). Identification and observational learning from films. *Journal of Abnormal Social Psychology, 55*, 76–87.

Marcaggi, G., & Guénolé, F. (2018). Freudarwin: Evolutionary thinking as a root of psychoanalysis. *Frontiers in Psychology, 9*, Article 892. doi:10.3389/fpsyg.2018.00892

McCutcheon, L. E., Lange, R., & Houran, J. (2002). Conceptualization and measurement of celebrity worship. *British Journal of Psychology, 93*(1), 67–87.

Mulvey, L. (1975). Visual pleasure and narrative cinema. *Screen, 16*, 6–18.

Nelson, K. (2003). Self and social functions: Individual autobiographical memory and cultural narrative. *Memory, 11*(2), 125–136.

Nolan, D. A. (2021). Souvenirs and travel guides: Cognition, culture and grieving public figures. *Poetics, 84*, Article 101484.

Propp, V. (1968). *Morphology of the folktale* (L. Scott, Trans.). University of Texas Press.

Redmond, J., & Shulman, M. (2008). Access to psychoanalytic ideas in American undergraduate institutions. *Journal of the American Psychoanalytic Association, 56*(2), 391–408.

Rochat, P., & Striano, T. (2002). Who's in the mirror? Self–other discrimination in specular images by four- and nine-month-old infants. *Child Development, 73*(1), 35–46.

Sarbin, T. R. (1986). Narrative as a root metaphor for psychology. In T. R. Sarbin (Ed.), *Narrative psychology: The storied nature of human conduct* (pp. 3–21). Praeger.

Scherer, H., Diaz, S., Iannone, N., McCarty, M., Branch, S., & Kelly, J. (2022). "Leave Britney alone!": Parasocial relationships and empathy. *Journal of Social Psychology, 162*(1), 128–142.

Silverstone, R. (1993). Television, ontological security and the transitional object. *Media, Culture & Society, 15*, 573–598.

Spillius, E. B. (2001). Freud and Klein on the concept of phantasy. *International Journal of Psycho-Analysis, 82*(2), 362–373.

Sternberg, R. J. (1996). Love stories. *Personal Relationships, 3*, 59–79.

Sulloway, F. J. (1979). *Freud, biologist of the mind: Beyond the psychoanalytic legend.* Harvard University Press.

Tajfel, H., & Turner, J. C. (1979). An integrative theory of inter-group conflict. In W. G. Austin & S. Worchel (Eds.), *The social psychology of inter-group relations* (pp. 33–47). Brooks/Cole.

Winnicott, D. W. (1971). *Playing and reality.* Tavistock.

Woolley, J. D. (1997). Thinking about fantasy: Are children fundamentally different thinkers and believers from adults? *Child Development, 68*(6), 991–1011.

Wright, J. C., Huston, A. C., Reitz, A. L., & Piemyat, S. (1994). Young children's perceptions of television reality: Determinants and developmental differences. *Developmental Psychology, 30*(2), 229–239.

CHAPTER 7

Adam, A. (2019). Perceptions of infidelity: A comparison of sexual, emotional, cyber-, and parasocial behaviors. *Interpersona: An International Journal on Personal Relationships, 13*(2), 237–252.

Adams-Price, C., & Greene, A. L. (1990). Secondary attachments and adolescent self-concept. *Sex Roles, 22*(3–4), 187–198.

Ainsworth, M. D. S. (1978). The Bowlby–Ainsworth attachment theory. *Behavioral and Brain Sciences, 1*(3), 436–438.

Anderson, T. (2012). Still kissing their posters goodnight: Female fandom and the politics of popular music. *Journal of Audience & Reception Studies, 9*(2), 239–264.

Asendorpf, J. B., Penke, L., & Back, M. D. (2011). From dating to mating and relating: Predictors of initial and long-term outcomes of speed-dating in a community sample. *European Journal of Personality, 25*(1), 16–30.

Aslam, N. (2023, June). The understanding of place spirituality in Pakistan: An interpretative phenomenological analysis. *Research Journal Ulūm-e-Islāmia, 30*(1).

Ball, A. D., & Tasaki, L. H. (1992). The role and measurement of attachment in consumer behavior. *Journal of Consumer Psychology, 1*(2), 155–172.

Banchero, R. A. (2000). *The prediction of high school student dropouts using criteria based on attachment theory.* University of California, Santa Barbara.

Bates, J. E., Maslin, C. A., & Frankel, K. A. (1985). Attachment security, mother–child interaction, and temperament as predictors of behavior-problem ratings at age three years. *Monographs of the Society for Research in Child Development, 50*(1–2), 167–193.

Beck, L., & Madresh, E. A. (2008). Romantic partners and four-legged friends: An extension of attachment theory to relationships with pets. *Anthrozoös, 21*(1), 43–56.

Belu, C. F., & O'Sullivan, L. F. (2019). Roving eyes: Predictors of crushes in ongoing romantic relationships and implications for relationship quality. *Journal of Relationships Research, 10*, 1–12.

Bond, B. J. (2021). The development and influence of parasocial relationships with television characters: A longitudinal experimental test of prejudice reduction through parasocial contact. *Communication Research, 48*(4), 573–593.

References

Bond, B. J., & Drogos, K. L. (2014). Sex on the shore: Wishful identification and parasocial relationships as mediators in the relationship between *Jersey Shore* exposure and emerging adults' sexual attitudes and behaviors. *Media Psychology, 17*(1), 102–126.

Bowlby, J. (1969). *Attachment and loss: Vol. 1. Attachment.* Basic Books. (Rev. ed., 1982).

Bretherton, I. (1999). Updating the "internal working model" construct: Some reflections. *Attachment & Human Development, 1*(3), 343–357.

Bu, Y., Parkinson, J., & Thaichon, P. (2022). Influencer marketing: Homophily, customer value co-creation behaviour and purchase intention. *Journal of Retailing and Consumer Services, 66*, Article 102904.

Buss, D. M. (2003). *The evolution of desire.* Basic Books.

Caughey, J. L. (1984). *Imaginary social worlds: A cultural approach.* University of Nebraska Press.

Cherniak, A. D., Mikulincer, M., Shaver, P. R., & Granqvist, P. (2021). Attachment theory and religion. *Current Opinion in Psychology, 40*, 126–130.

Chivers, M. L., Rieger, G., Latty, E., & Bailey, J. M. (2004). A sex difference in the specificity of sexual arousal. *Psychological Science, 15*(11), 736–744.

Cohen, J. (1997). Parasocial relations and romantic attraction: Gender and dating status differences. *Journal of Broadcasting & Electronic Media, 41*(4), 516–529.

Cortez, C. A. (1991). Mediated interpersonal communication: The role of attraction and perceived homophily in the development of parasocial relationships [Doctoral dissertation]. University of Iowa.

Counted, V. (2016). Making sense of place attachment: Towards a holistic understanding of people–place relationships and experiences. *Environment, Space, Place, 8*(1), 7–32.

Counted, V. (2019). Religion, place and attachment: An evaluation of conceptual frameworks. In V. Counted & F. Watts (Eds.), *The psychology of religion and place* (pp. 33–48). Palgrave Macmillan.

Counted, V., & Watts, F. (2017). Place attachment in the Bible: The role of attachment to sacred places in religious life. *Journal of Psychology and Theology, 45*(3), 218–232.

Counted, V., & Zock, H. (2019). Place spirituality: An attachment perspective. *Archive for the Psychology of Religion, 41*(1), 12–25.

Dion, K., Berscheid, E., & Walster, E. (1972). What is beautiful is good. *Journal of Personality and Social Psychology, 24*(3), 285–290.

Dubourg, E., & Baumard, N. (2022). Why and how did narrative fictions evolve? Fictions as entertainment technologies. *Frontiers in Psychology, 13*, Article 786770. doi:10.3389/fpsyg.2022.786770

Erickson, E. (1959). *Ego identity and the life cycle.* New York University Press.

Esmonde, K., Cooky, C., & Andrews, D. L. (2018). "That's not the only reason I'm watching the game": Women's (hetero)sexual desire and sports fandom. *Journal of Sport and Social Issues, 42*(6), 498–518.

Eyal, K., & Rubin, A. M. (2003). Viewer aggression and homophily, identification, and parasocial relationships with television characters. *Journal of Broadcasting & Electronic Media, 47*(1), 77–98.

Fisher, H. (2004). *Why we love: The nature and chemistry of romantic love.* Macmillan.

Fisher, H. E. (1998). Lust, attraction, and attachment in mammalian reproduction. *Human Nature, 9*, 23–52.

Fisher, H. E., Aron, A., Mashek, D., Li, H., & Brown, L. L. (2002). Defining the brain systems of lust, romantic attraction, and attachment. *Archives of Sexual Behavior, 31*(5), 413–419.

Frederick, D., Forbes, M., Jenkins, B., Reynolds, T., & Walters, T. (2015). Beauty standards. In P. Whelehan & A. Bolin (Eds.), *The international encyclopedia of human sexuality* (113–196). Wiley.

Fullwood, C., Quinn, S., Kaye, L. K., & Redding, C. (2017). My virtual friend: A qualitative analysis of the attitudes and experiences of smartphone users: Implications for smartphone attachment. *Computers in Human Behavior, 75*, 347–355.

Fürst, A., Thron, J., Scheele, D., Marsh, N., & Hurlemann, R. (2015). The neuropeptide oxytocin modulates consumer brand relationships. *Scientific Reports, 5*(1), 1–11.

Graham, W. (2015). *Ross Poldark: A novel of Cornwall, 1783–1787* (Vol. 1). Sourcebooks. (Original work published 1945)

Granqvist, P., & Kirkpatrick, L. A. (2013). Religion, spirituality, and attachment. In K. I. Pargament, J. J. Exline, & J. W. Jones (Eds.), *APA handbook of psychology, religion, and spirituality (Vol. 1): Context, theory, and research* (pp. 139–155). American Psychological Association. doi:10.1037/14045-007

Gross, A. E., & Crofton, C. (1977). What is good is beautiful. *Sociometry, 40*(1), 85–90.

Hällström, T., & Samuelsson, S. (1990). Changes in women's sexual desire in middle life: The longitudinal study of women in Gothenburg. *Archives of Sexual Behavior, 19*(3), 259–268.

Hartmann, T. (2008). Parasocial interactions and paracommunication with new media characters. In E. A. Konijn, S. Utz, M. Tanis, & S. B. Barnes (Eds.), *Mediated interpersonal communication* (pp. 191–213). Routledge.

Hung, L. W., Neuner, S., Polepalli, J. S., Beier, K. T., Wright, M., Walsh, J. J., Lewis, E. M., Luo, L., Deisseroth, K., Dolen, G., & Malenka, R. C. (2017). Gating of social reward by oxytocin in the ventral tegmental area. *Science, 357*(6358), 1406–1411.

Karama, S., Lecours, A. R., Leroux, J. M., Bourgouin, P., Beaudoin, G., Joubert, S., & Beauregard, M. (2002). Areas of brain activation in males and females during viewing of erotic film excerpts. *Human Brain Mapping, 16*(1), 1–13.

Karhulahti, V. M., & Välisalo, T. (2021). Fictosexuality, fictoromance, and fictophilia: A qualitative study of love and desire for fictional characters. *Frontiers in Psychology, 11*, Article 575427.

Kirkpatrick, L. A. (1992). An attachment-theory approach to the psychology of religion. *International Journal for the Psychology of Religion, 2*(1), 3–28.

Kirkpatrick, L. A. (2012). Attachment theory and the evolutionary psychology of religion. *International Journal for the Psychology of Religion, 22*(3), 231–241.

Klein, M. (1932). *The psycho-analysis of children* (No. 22). International Psycho-Analytical Library.

Klotz, A. M. (2011). Social media and weather warnings: Exploring the new parasocial relationships in weather forecasting [Master's thesis]. Ball State University.

Kniffin, K. M., & Wilson, D. S. (2004). The effect of nonphysical traits on the perception of physical attractiveness: Three naturalistic studies. *Evolution and Human Behavior, 25*(2), 88–101.

Lewis, C. S. (1971). *The four loves*. Houghton Mifflin Harcourt.

References

Lim, C. M., & Kim, Y. K. (2011). Older consumers' TV home shopping: Loneliness, parasocial interaction, and perceived convenience. *Psychology & Marketing, 28*(8), 763–780.

Mapaye, J. C. (2013). The transmedia experience in local TV news: Examining parasocial interaction in viral viewership and the online social distribution of news. In A. B. Albarran (Ed.), *Media management and economics research in a transmedia environment* (pp. 258–276). Routledge.

Meehan, M., Massavelli, B., & Pachana, N. (2017). Using attachment theory and social support theory to examine and measure pets as sources of social support and attachment figures. *Anthrozoös, 30*(2), 273–289.

Mikulincer, M., & Shaver, P. R. (2020). Enhancing the "broaden and build" cycle of attachment security in adulthood: From the laboratory to relational contexts and societal systems. *International Journal of Environmental Research and Public Health, 17*(6), Article 2054.

Morgan, P. (2010). Towards a developmental theory of place attachment. *Journal of Environmental Psychology, 30*(1), 11–22.

Mullinax, M., Barnhart, K. J., Mark, K., & Herbenick, D. (2016). Women's experiences with feelings and attractions for someone outside their primary relationship. *Journal of Sex & Marital Therapy, 42*(5), 431–447.

O'Sullivan, L. F., Belu, C. F., & Garcia, J. R. (2022). Loving you from afar: Attraction to others ("crushes") among adults in exclusive relationships, communication, perceived outcomes, and expectations of future intimate involvement. *Journal of Social and Personal Relationships, 39*(2), 413–434.

Perse, E. M., & Rubin, R. B. (1989). Attribution in social and parasocial relationships. *Communication Research, 16*(1), 59–77.

Piaget, J. (1954). *The child's construction of reality*. Basic Books.

Pimienta, J. (2022). Attachment to manga (Japanese comics): Conceptualizing the behavioral components of manga attachment and exploring attachment differences between avid, moderate, and occasional manga readers. *Journal of Anime and Manga Studies, 3*, 174–226.

Pimienta, J. (2023). Towards an integrated and systematic theory of parasocial relationships: PSR as an attachment process. *Communication Research Trends, 42*(1), 4–20.

Poldark (2015 TV series). (2023, June 17). In *Wikipedia*. https://en.wikipedia.org/wiki/Poldark_(2015_TV_series)

Price, M. E. (2017). Entropy and selection: Life as an adaptation for universe replication. *Complexity, 2017*, Article 4745379. https://doi.org/10.1155/2017/4745379

Rainey, S. (2015, March 17). Why Poldark's the perfect hunk: That wolfish grin, a sexy scar and oh those pecs! Experts reveal why he makes women swoon. *Daily Mail.* https://www.dailymail.co.uk/femail/article-2999841/Poldark-s-perfect-hunk-Experts-reveal-makes-women-swoon.html?ito=email_share_article-top

Reeves, B., & Nass, C. (1996). The media equation: How people treat computers, television, and new media like real people. Cambridge University Press.

Regan, P. C., & Berscheid, E. (1999). *Lust: What we know about human sexual desire*. SAGE.

Restak, R. (1991). *The brain has a mind of its own: Insights from a practicing neurologist.* Harmony Books.

Rhodes, G. (2006). The evolutionary psychology of facial beauty. *Annual Review of Psychology, 57*, 199–226.

Roy, S., Ponnam, A., & Mandal, S. (2017). Comprehending technology attachment in the case of smart phone-applications: An empirical study. *Journal of Electronic Commerce in Organizations, 15*(1), 23–43.

Rubin, R. B., & McHugh, M. P. (1987). Development of parasocial interaction relationships. *Journal of Broadcasting & Electronic Media, 31*(3), 279–292.

Rudnicki, K., Ouvrein, G., De Backer, C., & Heidi, V. (2020). Intranasal oxytocin administration reduces bystanders' acceptance of online celebrity bashing. *International Journal of Bullying Prevention, 2*, 29–40.

Rupp, H. A., & Wallen, K. (2008). Sex differences in response to visual sexual stimuli: A review. *Archives of Sexual Behavior, 37*(2), 206–218.

Sable, P. (1995). Pets, attachment, and well-being across the life cycle. *Social Work, 40*(3), 334–341.

Scannell, L., & Gifford, R. (2017). Place attachment enhances psychological need satisfaction. *Environment and Behavior, 49*(4), 359–389.

Schmid, H., & Klimmt, C. (2011). A magically nice guy: Parasocial relationships with Harry Potter across different cultures. *International Communication Gazette, 73*(3), 252–269.

Seamon, D. (2014). Place attachment and phenomenology: The synergistic dynamism of place. In L. Manzo & P. Devine-Wright (Eds.), *Place attachment* (pp. 11–22). Routledge.

Sherwin, B. B., Gelfand, M. M., & Brender, W. (1985). Androgen enhances sexual motivation in females: A prospective, crossover study of sex steroid administration in the surgical menopause. *Psychosomatic Medicine, 47*(4), 339–351.

Solomon, J., & George, C. (1999). The measurement of attachment security in infancy and childhood. In J. Cassidy & P. R. Shaver (Eds.), *Handbook of attachment: Theory, research, and clinical applications* (pp. 287–316). Guilford.

Stafford, M. R., Spears, N. E., & Hsu, C. K. (2003). Celebrity images in magazine advertisements: An application of the visual rhetoric model. *Journal of Current Issues & Research in Advertising, 25*(2), 13–20.

Stever, G. S. (1991). The celebrity appeal questionnaire. *Psychological Reports, 68*, 859–866. http://dx.doi.org/10.2466/pr0.1991.68.3.859

Stever, G. S. (1994). Parasocial attachments: Motivational antecedents [Doctoral dissertation]. Arizona State University.

Stever, G. S. (2009). Parasocial and social interaction with celebrities: Classification of media fans. *Journal of Media Psychology, 14*(3), 1–39.

Stever, G. S. (2013). Mediated vs. parasocial relationships: An attachment perspective. *Journal of Media Psychology, 17*(3), 1–31.

Stever, G. S. (2017). Evolutionary theory and reactions to mass media: Understanding parasocial attachment. *Psychology of Popular Media Culture, 6*(2), 95–102. http://dx.doi.org/10.1037/ppm0000116

Stever, G. S. (2019). Fan studies in psychology: A road less traveled. *Transformative Works and Cultures, 30*. doi:10.3983/twc.2019.1641

Stever, G. S. (2020). Evolutionary psychology and mass media. In T. K. Shackelford (Ed.), *The SAGE handbook of evolutionary psychology: Applications of evolutionary psychology* (pp. 398–416). SAGE.

References 239

Stever, G. S. (2022). *Parasocial experiences: Exploring parasocial perception and para-communication: The case of* The Hobbit [Unpublished manuscript].

Stever, G. S. (2023). PSRs in adults and older adults. In R. Tukachinsky Forster (Ed.), *The Oxford handbook of parasocial experiences* (pp. 210–223). Oxford University Press.

Swami, V. (2016). *Attraction explained: The science of how we form relationships*. Routledge.

Swami, V., & Tovée, M. J. (2005). Male physical attractiveness in Britain and Malaysia: A cross-cultural study. *Body Image, 2*(4), 383–393.

Tal-Or, N., & Cohen, J. (2016). Unpacking engagement: Convergence and divergence in transportation and identification. *Annals of the International Communication Association, 40*(1), 33–66.

Thomas, J. R., & Dixon, T. K. (2016). A global perspective of beauty in a multicultural world. *JAMA Facial Plastic Surgery, 18*(1), 7–8.

Trinke, S. J., & Bartholomew, K. (1997). Hierarchies of attachment relationships in young adulthood. *Journal of Social and Personal Relationships, 14*(5), 603–625.

Tukachinsky Forster, R. (2021). *Parasocial romantic relationships: Falling in love with media figures*. Rowman & Littlefield.

Turner, J. R. (1993). Interpersonal and psychological predictors of parasocial interaction with different television performers. *Communication Quarterly, 41*(4), 443–453.

Twigger, W. (2021, March 30). *Poldark* heartthrob Aidan Turner locks lips with another man in new drama *Leonardo*. Mirror. https://www.mirror.co.uk/tv/tv-news/pold ark-heartthrob-aidan-turner-locks-23815806

Uvnäs-Moberg, K. (1998). Oxytocin may mediate the benefits of positive social interaction and emotions. *Psychoneuroendocrinology, 23*(8), 819–835.

Voorveld, H. A., & Viswanathan, V. (2015). An observational study on how situational factors influence media multitasking with TV: The role of genres, dayparts, and social viewing. *Media Psychology, 18*(4), 499–526.

Winnicott, D. W. (1953). Transitional objects and transitional phenomena—A study of the first not-me possession. *International Journal of Psycho-Analysis, 34*, 89–97.

Zhang, K., Zhang, M., & Li, C. (2021). Effects of celebrity characteristics, perceived homophily, and reverence on consumer-celebrity para-social interaction and brand attitude. *Frontiers in Psychology, 12*, Article 711454.

Zilcha-Mano, S., Mikulincer, M., & Shaver, P. R. (2012). Pets as safe havens and secure bases: The moderating role of pet attachment orientations. *Journal of Research in Personality, 46*(5), 571–580.

CHAPTER 8

Ainsworth, M. S. (1989). Attachments beyond infancy. *American Psychologist, 44*(4), 709–716.

Allen, K. A., Gray, D. L., Baumeister, R. F., & Leary, M. R. (2022). The need to belong: A deep dive into the origins, implications, and future of a foundational construct. *Educational Psychology Review, 34*(2), 1133–1156.

Baumeister, R. F., & Leary, M. R. (1995). The need to belong: Desire for interpersonal attachments as a fundamental human motivation. *Psychological Bulletin, 117*(2), 497–529.

Bowlby, J. (1979). The Bowlby Ainsworth attachment theory. *Behavioral and Brain Sciences, 2*(4), 637–638.

Casioppo, D. (2020). The cultivation of joy: Practices from the Buddhist tradition, positive psychology, and yogic philosophy. *Journal of Positive Psychology, 15*(1), 67–73.

Caughey, J. L. (1984). *Imaginary social worlds: A cultural approach.* University of Nebraska Press.

Dietz, P. E., Matthews, D. B., Van Duyne, C., & Martell, D. A. (1991). Threatening and otherwise inappropriate letters to Hollywood celebrities. *Journal of Forensic Sciences, 36*(1), 185–209.

Duffett, M. (2015). Elvis' gospel music: Between the secular and the spiritual? *Religions, 6*(1), 182–203.

Durkheim, E. (1912). *The elementary forms of the religious life* (J. W. Swain, Trans.). Free Press.

Eisenberg, N. (2002). Empathy-related emotional responses, altruism, and their socialization. In R. J. Davidson & A. Harrington (Ed.), Visions of *compassion*: Western *scientists* and Tibetan Buddhists examine human nature (pp. 131–164). Oxford University Press.

Elliott, M. A. (2021). Fandom as religion: A social–scientific assessment. *Journal of Fandom Studies, 9*(2), 107–122.

Gabriel, S., Naidu, E., Paravati, E., Morrison, C. D., & Gainey, K. (2020). Creating the sacred from the profane: Collective effervescence and everyday activities. *Journal of Positive Psychology, 15*(1), 129–154.

Gray, J., Sandvoss, C., & Harrington, C. L. (2007). Introduction: Why study fans? In J. Gray, C. Sandvoss, & C. L. Harrington (Eds.), *Fandom: Identities and communities in a mediated world* (pp. 1–17). New York University Press.

Haupt, A. (2023). In defense of parasocial relationships. *TIME.* https://time.com/6294 226/parasocial-relationships-benefits

Hills, M. (2002). *Fan cultures.* Routledge.

Hitlan, R. T., McCutcheon, L. E., Volungis, A. M., Joshi, A., Clark, C. B., & Pena, M. (2021). Social desirability and the Celebrity Attitude Scale. *North American Journal of Psychology, 23*(1), 105–114.

Jenkins, H. (2018). Fandom, negotiation, and participatory culture. A companion to media fandom and fan studies. In P. Booth (Ed.), *A companion to media fandom and fan studies* (pp. 11–26). Wiley.

Keltner, D. (2023). *Awe: The new science of everyday wonder and how it can transform your life.* Penguin.

Leary, M. R., Tambor, E. S., Terdal, S. K., & Downs, D. L. (1995). Self-esteem as an interpersonal monitor: The sociometer hypothesis. *Journal of Personality and Social Psychology, 68*(3), 518–530.

Lorenzo, R. (2017). Fandom conventions: A sociological theoretical perspective. *The Phoenix Papers, 3*(1), 1–9.

Malluhi, L. (2018). *Religious devotion to pop culture: Fandom as a new form of religiosity in a world of changing values* [Doctoral dissertation]. Hamad Bin Khalifa University.

Maltby, J., & Day, L. (2017). Regulatory motivations in celebrity interest: Self-suppression and self-expansion. *Psychology of Popular Media Culture, 6*(2), 103–112.

Maltby, J., Day, L., McCutcheon, L. E., Gillett, R., Houran, J., & Ashe, D. D. (2004). Personality and coping: A context for examining celebrity worship and mental health. *British Journal of Psychology, 95*(4), 411–428.

Maltby, J., Houran, J., & McCutcheon, L. E. (2003). A clinical interpretation of attitudes and behaviors associated with celebrity worship. *Journal of Nervous and Mental Disease, 191*(1), 25–29.

References

McCutcheon, L., Aruguete, M. S., Jenkins, W., McCarley, N., & Yockey, R. (2016). An investigation of demographic correlates of the Celebrity Attitude Scale. *Interpersona: An International Journal on Personal Relationships, 10*(2), 161–170.

Olsen, D. H. (2021). Fan pilgrimage, religion, and spirituality. In D. H. Olsen & D. J. Timothy (Eds.), *The Routledge handbook of religious and spiritual tourism* (pp. 90–110). Routledge.

Pham, V. M. T. (2015). Ethnography of Coachella: Communication within the intersections of popular culture, fandom, music, and performance. https://digital commons.calpoly.edu

Porter, J. (2009). Implicit religion in popular culture: The religious dimensions of fan communities. *Implicit Religion, 12*(3), 271–281.

Rojek, C. (2007). Celebrity and religion. In S. Redmond & S. Holmes (Eds.), *Stardom and celebrity: A reader* (pp. 171–180). SAGE.

Schiffer, I. (1973). *Charisma: A psychoanalytic look at mass society*. University of Toronto Press.

Stever, G. S. (1994). Parasocial attachments: Motivational antecedents [Doctoral dissertation]. Arizona State University.

Stever, G. S. (2009). Parasocial and social interaction with celebrities: Classification of media fans. *Journal of Media Psychology, 14*(3), 1–39.

Stever, G. S. (2011). Celebrity worship: Critiquing a construct. *Journal of Applied Social Psychology, 41*(6), 1356–1370. http://dx.doi.org/10.1111/j.1559-1816.2011.00765.x

Stever, G. S. (2013). Mediated vs. parasocial relationships: An attachment perspective. *Journal of Media Psychology, 17*(3), 1–31.

Stever, G. S. (2016). Meeting Josh Groban (again): Fan/celebrity contact as ordinary behavior. *International Association for the Study of Popular Music Journal, 6*(1), 104–120.

Tukachinsky, R. H. (2011). Para-romantic love and para-friendships: Development and assessment of a multiple-parasocial relationships scale. *American Journal of Media Psychology, 3*(1–2), 73–94.

Verba, J. M. (2003). *Boldly writing*. FTL.

Ward, P. (2011). *Gods behaving badly: Media, religion, and celebrity culture*. Baylor University Press.

CHAPTER 9

Alperstein, N. M. (2019). *Celebrity and mediated social connections: Fans, friends, and followers in the digital age*. Palgrave Macmillan.

Atad, E., & Cohen, J. (2024). Look me in the eyes: How direct address affects viewers' experience of parasocial interaction and credibility? *Journalism, 25*(4), 941–959.

Blumberg, P. O. (2023, August 2). Striking actors are turning to Cameo for extra cash. *The New York Times*. https://www.nytimes.com/2023/08/02/style/sag-aftra-strike-cameo.html

Bond, B. J. (2021). Social and parasocial relationships during COVID-19 social distancing. *Journal of Social and Personal Relationships, 38*(8), 2308–2329.

Caughey, J. L. (1984). *Imaginary social worlds: A cultural approach*. University of Nebraska Press.

Chang, C. (2023). The multiple mechanisms by which watching dramas can repair or enhance moods. *Journal of Broadcasting & Electronic Media, 67*(1), 21–46.

Cohen, J., Oliver, M. B., & Bilandzic, H. (2019). The differential effects of direct address on parasocial experience and identification: Empirical evidence for conceptual difference. *Communication Research Reports*, *36*(1), 78–83.

Cummins, R. G., & Cui, B. (2014). Reconceptualizing address in television programming: The effect of address and affective empathy on viewer experience of parasocial interaction. *Journal of Communication*, *64*(4), 723–742.

Dibble, J. L., Hartmann, T., & Rosaen, S. F. (2016). Parasocial interaction and parasocial relationship: Conceptual clarification and a critical assessment of measures. *Human Communication Research*, *42*(1), 21–44.

Fast Company. (2020, March 10). *The 10 most innovative social media companies of 2020*. Retrieved April 9, 2023, from https://www.fastcompany.com/90457904/social-media-most-innovative-companies-2020

Hartmann, T. (2008). Parasocial interactions and paracommunication with new media characters. In E. A. Konijin, S. Utz, M. Tanis, & S. B. Barnes (Eds.), *Mediated interpersonal communication* (pp. 191–213). Routledge.

Hartmann, T. (2016). Parasocial interaction, parasocial relationships, and well-being. In L. Reinecke & M. B. Oliver (Eds.), *The Routledge handbook of media use and well-being* (pp. 131–144). Routledge.

Hartmann, T., & Goldhoorn, C. (2011). Horton and Wohl revisited: Exploring viewers' experience of parasocial interaction. *Journal of Communication*, *61*(6), 1104–1121.

Haupt, A. (2023, July 13). In defense of parasocial relationships. *TIME*. https://time.com/6294226/parasocial-relationships-benefits

Horton, D., & Wohl, R. (1956). Mass communication and para-social interaction: Observations on intimacy at a distance. *Psychiatry*, *19*(3), 215–229.

Kim, M., Ko, H., Choi, J., & Lee, J. (2023). FlumeRide: Interactive space where artists and fans meet-and-greet using video calls. *IEEE Access*, *11*, 31594–31606.

Kircher, M. M. (2020, April 16). Cameo was made for the coronavirus. *Vulture*. Retrieved September 16, 2020, from https://www.vulture.com/2020/04/cameo-coronavirus-boom.html

Konijn, E. A., & Hoorn, J. F. (2017). Parasocial interaction and beyond: Media personae and affective bonding. In P. Rossler (Ed.), *The Wiley Blackwell–ICA International encyclopedia of media effects*. Wiley Blackwell.

Lindström, B., Bellander, M., Schultner, D. T., Chang, A., Tobler, P. N., & Amodio, D. M. (2021). A computational reward learning account of social media engagement. *Nature Communications*, *12*(1), 1311–1320. https://doi.org/10.1038/s41467-020-19607-x

Martini, D. (2023). *Self-help: A long-lasting genre rooted in positive media psychology* [Unpublished manuscript]. Empire State University of New York.

McCutcheon, L., Aruguete, M. S., Jenkins, W., McCarley, N., & Yockey, R. (2016). An investigation of demographic correlates of the Celebrity Attitude Scale. *Interpersona: An International Journal on Personal Relationships*, *10*(2), 161–170.

Stever, G. S. (2019). Fan studies in psychology: A road less traveled. *Transformative Works and Cultures*, *30*. doi:10.3983/twc.2019.1641

Zhang, K. Z., Chen, C., Zhao, S. J., & Lee, M. K. (2014, December). *Compulsive smartphone use: The roles of flow, reinforcement motives, and convenience*. AIS Electronic Library. oai:aisel.aisnet.org:icis2014-1416

References 243

Zhao, P., & Lapierre, M. A. (2020). Stress, dependency, and depression: An examination of the reinforcement effects of problematic smartphone use on perceived stress and later depression. *Cyberpsychology: Journal of Psychosocial Research on Cyberspace*, *14*(4), Article 3. https://doi.org/10.5817/CP2020-4-3

CHAPTER 10

Bandura, A. (1986). *Social foundations of thought and action*. Prentice Hall.

Bandura, A. (2001). The changing face of psychology at the dawning of a globalization era. *Canadian Psychology*, *42*(1), 12–24.

Bandura, A. (2009). Social cognitive theory of mass communication. In J. Bryant & M. B. Oliver (Eds.), *Media effects: Advances in theory and research* (pp. 110–140). Routledge.

Braverman, J. (2008). Testimonials versus informational persuasive messages: The moderating effect of delivery mode and personal involvement. *Communication Research*, *35*(5), 666–694.

Bruner, J. (1991). The narrative construction of reality. *Critical Inquiry*, *18*(1), 1–21.

Chang, C. (2022). The multiple mechanisms by which watching dramas can repair or enhance moods. *Journal of Broadcasting & Electronic Media*, *67*(1), 21–46.

Cohen, J., Oliver, M. B., & Bilandzic, H. (2019). The differential effects of direct address on parasocial experience and identification: Empirical evidence for conceptual difference. *Communication Research Reports*, *36*(1), 78–83.

Cohen, J., & Tal-Or, N. (2017). Antecedents of identification. In F. Hakemulder (Ed.), *Narrative absorption* (pp. 133–153). Benjamins.

Ellis, G. J., Streeter, S. K., & Engelbrecht, J. D. (1983). Television characters as significant others and the process of vicarious role-taking. *Journal of Family Issues*, *4*(2), 367–384.

Green, M. C., & Clark, J. L. (2013). Transportation into narrative worlds: Implications for entertainment media influences on tobacco use. *Addiction*, *108*(3), 477–484.

Hoffner, C., & Buchanan, M. (2005). Young adults' wishful identification with television characters: The role of perceived similarity and character attributes. *Media Psychology*, *7*(4), 325–351.

Jenkins, H. (2001, June 1). Convergence? I diverge. *MIT Technology Review*. https://www.technologyreview.com/2001/06/01/235791/convergence-i-diverge

Livingstone, S. (2013). The participation paradigm in audience research. *Communication Review*, *16*(1–2), 21–30. doi:10.1080/10714421.2013.757174

Murphy, S. T., Frank, L. B., Chatterjee, J. S., & Baezconde-Garbanati, L. (2013). Narrative versus nonnarrative: The role of identification, transportation, and emotion in reducing health disparities. *Journal of Communication*, *63*(1), 116–137.

Navami, P., & Thomas, P. E. (2022). Exploring the relationship between binge watching, narrative transportation and the affective responses: A literature review. *IIS University Journal of Arts*, *11*(1), 303–313.

Raney, A. A., Janicke-Bowles, S. H., Oliver, M. B., & Dale, K. R. (2020). *Introduction to positive media psychology*. Routledge.

Rosen, J. (2006). The people formerly known as the audience. In M. Mandiberg (Ed.), *The social media reader* (pp. 13–16). New York University Press.

Sestir, M., & Green, M. C. (2010). You are who you watch: Identification and transportation effects on temporary self-concept. *Social Influence*, *5*(4), 272–288.

Slater, M. D., Ewoldsen, D. R., & Woods, K. W. (2018). Extending conceptualization and measurement of narrative engagement after-the-fact: Parasocial relationship and retrospective imaginative involvement. *Media Psychology, 21*(3), 329–351.

Stever, G. S., Shackleford, K., & Ewoldsen, D. (2022, August 4–7). *Social interaction: Real and imagined* [Paper presentation]. The American Psychological Association convention, Minneapolis, MN.

Tal-Or, N., & Cohen, J. (2010). Understanding audience involvement: Conceptualizing and manipulating identification and transportation. *Poetics, 38*(4), 402–418.

Tal-Or, N., & Cohen, J. (2016). Unpacking engagement: Convergence and divergence in transportation and identification. *Annals of the International Communication Association, 40*(1), 33–66.

Tukachinsky, R., Walter, N., & Saucier, C. J. (2020). Antecedents and effects of parasocial relationships: A meta-analysis. *Journal of Communication, 70*(6), 868–894.

CHAPTER 11

Alperstein, L. (1991). Imaginary social relationships with celebrities appearing in television commercials. *Journal of Broadcasting and Electronic Media, 35*, 43–58.

American Psychiatric Association. (2013). *Diagnostic and statistical manual of mental disorders* (5th ed.). American Psychiatric Publishing.

Bentall, R. (2009). *Doctoring the mind: Why psychiatric treatments fail.* Penguin.

Billig, M. (1999). Whose terms? Whose ordinariness? Rhetoric and ideology in conversation analysis. *Discourse & Society, 10*(4), 543–558.

Braun, V., & Clarke, V. (2006). Using thematic analysis in psychology. *Qualitative Research in Psychology, 3*(2), 77–101.

Burr, V. (2003). *Social constructionism* (3rd ed.). Routledge.

Giles, D. C. (2002). Parasocial interaction: A review of the literature and a model for future research. *Media Psychology, 4*(3), 279–302.

Giles, D. C. (2016). Observing real-world groups in the virtual field: The analysis of online discussion. *British Journal of Social Psychology, 55*(3), 484–498. doi:10.1111/bjso.12139

Giles, D. C. (2018). *Twenty-first century celebrity: Fame in digital culture.* Emerald.

Giles, D. C. (2021). Context, history and Twitter data: Some methodological reflections. In J. Meredith, D. C. Giles, & W. Stommel (Eds.), *Analysing online social interaction* (pp. 41–64). Palgrave.

Giles, D. C., & Newbold, J. (2011). Self- and other-diagnosis in user-led online mental health communities. *Qualitative Health Research, 21*(3), 419–428.

Giles, D. C., Stommel, W., & Paulus, T. (2017). The microanalysis of online data: The next stage. *Journal of Pragmatics, 115*, 37–41.

Giles, D. C., Stommel, W., Paulus, T., Lester, J., & Reed, D. (2015). The microanalysis of online data: The methodological development of "digital CA." *Discourse, Context and Media, 7*(1), 45–51. doi:10.1016/j.dcm.2014.12.002

Horton, D., & Wohl, R. R. (1956). Mass communication and para-social interaction. *Psychiatry, 19*, 215–229.

Husserl, E. (1989). *The crisis of European sciences and transcendental phenomenology: An introduction to phenomenological philosophy.* Northwestern University Press. (Original work published 1936)

Kelly, G. A. (1955). *The psychology of personal constructs: Vol. 1. A theory of personality.* Norton.

References

Levy, M. R. (1979). Watching TV news as para-social interaction. *Journal of Broadcasting, 23*, 69–80.

Moscovici, S. (1984). The myth of the lonely paradigm: A rejoinder. *Social Research, 51*(4), 939–967.

Parker, I. (1992). *Discourse dynamics: Critical analysis for social and individual psychology.* SAGE.

Rubin, A. M., Perse, E. M., & Powell, R. A. (1985). Loneliness, parasocial interaction and local television news viewing. *Human Communication Research, 12*(2), 155–180.

Sacks, H. (1992). Rules on conversational sequence. In G. Jefferson (Ed.), *Lectures on conversation* (pp. 1–131). Blackwell. (Original work published 1964)

Schegloff, E. A. (1979). Identification and recognition in telephone conversation openings. In G. Psathas (Ed.), *Everyday language: Studies in ethnomethodology* (pp. 23–78). Irvington.

Schegloff, E. A. (1997). Whose text? Whose context? *Discourse & Society, 8*(2), 165–187.

Smith, J. A., Flowers, P., & Larkin, M. (2009). *Interpretative phenomenological analysis: Theory, method and research.* SAGE.

Stever, G. S., & Hughes, E. (2013, September). What role Twitter? Celebrity conversations with fans. In *Social media: The fourth annual transforming audiences conference,* University of Westminster.

Stokoe, E. H., & Smithson, J. (2001). Making gender relevant: Conversation analysis and gender categories in interaction. *Discourse & Society, 12*(2), 217–242.

Thelwall, M., Stuart, E., Mas-Bleda, A., Makita, M., & Abdoli, M. (2022). I'm nervous about sharing this secret with you: YouTube influencers generate strong parasocial interactions by discussing personal issues. *Journal of Data and Information Science, 7*(2), 31–56.

Wiggins, S. (2017). *Discursive psychology: Theory, method and applications.* SAGE.

CHAPTER 12

Alharahsheh, H. H., & Pius, A. (2020). A review of key paradigms: Positivism vs. interpretivism. *Global Academic Journal of Humanities and Social Sciences, 2*(3), 39–43.

Altheide, D. L. (1987). Reflections: Ethnographic content analysis. *Qualitative Sociology, 10*(1), 65–77.

Anderson, T. (2012). Still kissing their posters goodnight: Female fandom and the politics of popular music. *Journal of Audience & Reception Studies, 9*(2), 239–264.

Auter, P. J., & Palmgreen, P. (2000). Development and validation of a parasocial interaction measure: The Audience–Persona Interaction Scale. *Communication Research Reports, 17*(1), 79–89.

Beach, L. R. (2010). *The psychology of narrative thought: How the stories we tell ourselves shape our lives.* Xlibris.

Creswell, J. W., & Poth, C. N. (2016). *Qualitative inquiry and research design: Choosing among five approaches.* SAGE.

Cummins, R. G., & Cui, B. (2014). Reconceptualizing address in television programming: The effect of address and affective empathy on viewer experience of parasocial interaction. *Journal of Communication, 64*(4), 723–742.

Dibble, J. L., Hartmann, T., & Rosaen, S. F. (2016). Parasocial interaction and parasocial relationship: Conceptual clarification and a critical assessment of measures. *Human Communication Research, 42*(1), 21–44.

Duits, L., Zwaan, K., & Reijnders, S. (Eds.). (2016). *The Ashgate research companion to fan cultures*. Routledge.

Evans, A., & Stasi, M. (2014). Desperately seeking methods: New directions in fan studies research. *Participations. 11*(2), 4–23.

Hartmann, T., & Goldhoorn, C. (2011). Horton and Wohl revisited: Exploring viewers' experience of parasocial interaction. *Journal of Communication, 61*(6), 1104–1121.

Horton, D., & Wohl, R. (1956). Mass communication and para-social interaction: Observations on intimacy at a distance. *Psychiatry, 19*(3), 215–229.

Kington, C. S. (2015). Con culture: A survey of fans and fandom. *Journal of Fandom Studies, 3*(2), 211–228.

McCutcheon, L. E., Lange, R., & Houran, J. (2002). Conceptualization and measurement of celebrity worship. *British Journal of Psychology, 93*(1), 67–87.

Nordlund, J. E. (1978). Media interaction. *Communication Research, 5*(2), 150–175.

Popova, M. (2020). Follow the trope: A digital (auto) ethnography for fan studies. *Transformative Works and Cultures, 33.* https://doi.org/10.3983/twc.2020.1697

Rosengren, K. E., Windahl, S., Hakansson, P. A., & Johnsson-Smaragdi, U. (1976). Adolescents' TV relations: Three scales. *Communication Research, 3*(4), 347–366.

Rubin, A. M., Perse, E. M., & Powell, R. A. (1985). Loneliness, parasocial interaction and local television news viewing. *Human Communication Research, 12*(2), 155–180.

Schramm, H. & Hartmann, T. 2008. The PSI-Process Scales. A new measure to assess the intensity and breadth of parasocial processes. *Communications, 33*(4), 385–401. https://doi.org/10.1515/COMM.2008.025

Stever, G. S. (1991a). The Celebrity Appeal Questionnaire. *Psychological Reports, 68,* 859–866. http://dx.doi.org/10.2466/pr0.1991.68.3.859

Stever, G. S. (1991b). Imaginary social relationships and personality correlates. *Journal of Psychological Type, 21,* 68–76.

Stever, G. S. (1995). Gender by type interaction effects in mass media subcultures. *Journal of Psychological Type, 32.* 3–12.

Stever. G. S. (2008). The Celebrity Appeal Questionnaire: Sex, entertainment or leadership. *Psychological Reports, 103,* 113–120. http://dx.doi.org/10.2466/pr0.103.1.113-120

Stever, G. S. (2011). Celebrity worship: Critiquing a construct. *Journal of Applied Social Psychology, 41*(6), 1356–1370. http://dx.doi.org/10.1111/j.1559-1816.2011.00765.x

Stever, G. S. (2017). Parasocial theory: Concepts and measures. In P. Rossler (Ed.), *The international encyclopedia of media effects*. Wiley Blackwell. doi:10.1002/9781118783764.wbieme0069

Tukachinsky, R. H. (2011). Para-romantic love and para-friendships: Development and assessment of a multiple-parasocial relationships scale. *American Journal of Media Psychology, 3*(1–2), 73–94.

Chapter 13

Bandura, A. (1986). *Social foundations of thought and action: A social cognitive theory*. Prentice Hall.

Boorstin, D. (1971). *The image: A guide to pseudo-events in America*. Atheneum.

Brantlinger, P. (2016). *Bread and circuses: Theories of mass culture as social decay*. Cornell University Press.

References

Carney, D. R., Cuddy, A. J., & Yap, A. J. (2010). Power posing: Brief nonverbal displays affect neuroendocrine levels and risk tolerance. *Psychological Science, 21*(10), 1363–1368.

Caughey, J. L. (1984). *Imaginary social worlds: A cultural approach*. University of Nebraska Press.

Cuddy, A. J., Wilmuth, C. A., Yap, A. J., & Carney, D. R. (2015). Preparatory power posing affects nonverbal presence and job interview performance. *Journal of Applied Psychology, 100*(4), 1286–1295.

Edensor, T. (2020). *National identity, popular culture and everyday life*. Routledge.

Friedman, H. S., & Martin, L. R. (2011). *The longevity project: Surprising discoveries for health and long life from the landmark eight-decade study*. Hay House.

Glaser, B., & Strauss, A. (2017). *Discovery of grounded theory: Strategies for qualitative research*. Routledge.

Goldstein, T. R. (2009). Psychological perspectives on acting. *Psychology of Aesthetics, Creativity, and the Arts, 3*(1), 6–9.

Gussow, M. (1982, February 18). Lee Strasberg of actor's studio dead. *The New York Times*. https://www.nytimes.com/1982/02/18/obituaries/lee-strasberg-of-actors-studio-dead.html

Hartmann, T., & Goldhoorn, C. (2011). Horton and Wohl revisited: Exploring viewers' experience of parasocial interaction. *Journal of Communication, 61*(6), 1104–1121.

Jackson, K. (2021, October 24). "The Shining" baseball bat scene: Stanley Kubrick said Shelley Duval only had 2 good takes. *Showbiz Cheet Sheet*. https://www.cheatsheet.com/entertainment/the-shining-baseball-bat-scene-stanley-kubrick-shelley-duvall-only-2-good-takes.html

Jenkins, H. (1992). *Textual poachers: Television fans and participatory culture*. Routledge.

Lieberman, M. D. (2013). *Social: Why our brains are wired to connect*. Oxford University Press.

Liebers, N., & Schramm, H. (2019). Parasocial interactions and relationships with media characters: An inventory of 60 years of research. *Communication Research Trends, 38*(2), 4–31.

Macaluso, B. A. (2020, May 31). *15 times stars took method acting too far*. Awaken. https://awaken.com/2020/05/15-times-stars-took-method-acting-too-far

Ravenola, D. (2020, May 6). How playing the Joker changed Heath Ledger for good. *Looper*. https://www.looper.com/141474/how-playing-the-joker-changed-heath-ledger-for-good

Riles, J. M., & Adams, K. (2021). Me, myself, and my mediated ties: Parasocial experiences as an ego-driven process. *Media Psychology, 24*(6), 792–813.

Simons, R. (2023, July 18). *Aidan Turner thinks actors should leave their roles on set: "It doesn't serve anybody."* Yahoo. https://uk.movies.yahoo.com/aidan-turner-thinks-actors-leave-090640771.html

Stever, G. S., Giles, D. C., Cohen, J. D., & Myers, M. (2021). *Understanding media psychology*. Routledge.

INDEX

For the benefit of digital users, indexed terms that span two pages (e.g., 52–53) may, on occasion, appear on only one of those pages.

Figures are indicated by an italic *f* following the page number.

Abidin, Crystal, 37–38
academic disciplines, 6
aca-fans (academic fans), 185, 187
accidental fame, 36
achieved celebrity, 36
acting
 actor's relationship with
  character, 206–9
 behaviorism, 206–10
 mental health and, 201–5
 parasocial relationships and methods of
  inquiry, 210–11
 psychology of, 199–201
advice
 breastfeeding, 8
 media and behavior, 7
adviser, fan object as, 82
affective closeness, 25
After the Party, Dean O'Gorman in, 151
agape, charity, 126
AIBO (robotic puppy), Sony, 47–48
Ainsworth, Mary, 116
Alexa, 42, 47
Almighty Johnsons, The (television series),
 Dean O'Gorman in, 70–73, 151, 208
Alperstein, Neil, 148–49
alpha hero, 133
alternative universe fan fiction stories, 29
Altheide, David, 187

American Psychological Association, 171
Amnesty International, 22
Anglophile (internet-based program), 58
animals, attachment to, 118
anthropology, participant-observe
 ethnography, 184
anthropomorphic tendencies, 89
anthropomorphism, 90
 imaginative, 90
 situational, 90
 theory of, 89
app attachment, 119
Armitage, Richard, 27, 56, 140
 Facebook fan community, 151
 fan base of, 56–63
 photograph, 57*f*
Armitage Army, 59, 140
Arsenal (football team), 95, 96
ascribed celebrity, 36
attachment
 adult romantic, xi, 115
 animals/pets, 118
 anxious, 30, 88–89, 90, 116
 behavior, 116, 118, 123
 character, 26–27
 child/caregiver, xi, 3–4, 115, 116, 197
 death of Queen Elizabeth, 121–22
 definition, 120
 essentials of theory, 115–16

attachment (*cont.*)
evolutionary psychology, 123
God, 119
interpersonal, 117
media figures, 11
mediated, 119–21
parasocial, 119–21
persona, 130
place, 116–17
primary, 120, 121
secondary, 120, 121
security, 118
transitional objects, 118–19
attachment mechanisms
comfort, 3–4, 55, 116, 118–19, 120
proximity seeking, 115, 116, 146
safe haven, 3–4, 55, 116, 118–19, 120
security, 115, 116
separation distress, 115
attachment theories, 194
defining features, 115
essential elements of, 115–16
lifespan development, 3–4
psychoanalytic theories and, 114
attraction
Aidan Turner and *Poldark*, 130–34
celebrity, 188
crush, 129–30
desire and arousal, 123–24
hero/role model, 61–62, 124, 191–92
observations on, 127–28
romantic, 18
task, 61–62, 124
attributed celebrity, 36
Auberjonois, Rene, 23, 143, 147
photograph of, 154f
Audible, 60
audience
behavior, 43, 108, 111, 145, 199, 210
identification, 168–70
media figure relationships, 76
parasocial interaction, 19
parasocial relationships (PSRs) and
spiritual life of, 198–99
research, 172
role modeling, 167–68
study of, 166

theoretical avenues to studying, 199
transportation into media
worlds, 170–72
vicarious social experiences, 168
Audience-Persona Interaction Scale, 191
audience theory, impact of digital
culture, 76
authenticity, 35, 68, 69, 72, 88, 94
autoethnography, 187–90
avatars, media figures, 41–42

Bandura, Albert, 167
reciprocal causation, 167
role modeling, 167–68
Barker, Martin, 106–7
Baron App Inc., 149
Batman, 95
Batman (film), 201
Beatles, 29, 34
Beckham, David, 130
behaviorism, operant conditioning, 163
Being Human (television series), 69,
132, 133
Beltran, Robert, 23
Berlin Station (television show), 56–58
Big Bang Theory, The (television series), 21,
30, 168
"Big Five" personality theory, 7
binge-watching, 171
biology of sexuality, 124
bloggers, 38
Bond, Bradley, 85
Boorstin, Daniel J., 195
Boston Legal (television series), 143
Bowie, David, 80–81
Bowlby, John, 116
boy bands, 34
boyd, danah, 14, 46, 76
breastfeeding advice, 8
Brideshead Revisited (Waugh), 89
broadcast media, 34
parasocial theory, 11–12
Brody, Adrian, 205
Brophy, Jed, 27
Brunel University, 134
Buttigieg, Chasten, 20
Buttigieg, Pete, 20

Index   251

Cairo Time (film), 68
Calvert, Sandra, 84
Cameo, 4, 49, 52, 70, 72–73, 121, 148,
    149, 163–65
  crossing social-parasocial line, 162–63
  Dean O'Gorman, 151–53
  Denise Crosby and, 158–61
  as fan activity, 161–62
  fees for, 150
  Nana Visitor, 154–56, 164
  parasocial interaction (PSI) and, 149–51
  Robert Picardo, 156–58
  as self-help, 153
  social media, 189–90, 199
  social media as operant
    conditioning, 163
Caughey, John, 76, 77–78, 148–49
celebrities, 9
  achieved, 36
  ascribed, 36
  attributed, 36
  charisma, 142–44
  culture, 75
  dreamworld and, 77
  fans and, 60
  fans of, 12
  microcelebrities, 35
  para-communication and parasocial
    perception, 196
  parasocial breakup (PSB) and, 28–31
  social media interaction, 17
  worship, 144–45
Celebrity Appeal Questionnaire,
    188, 191–92
Celebrity Attitude Scale, 10–11, 144,
    188, 192
celebrity confessions, 44
celebrity influencers, 39
celebrity worship, 10
  borderline-pathological, 136–45, 146
  entertainment-social, 144–45
  fan-celebrity interaction scale, 198
  intense personal, 145, 146, 189–90, 198
  term, 139
celebrity worshippers, 108
celetoid, 36
character, actor's relationship with, 206–9

charisma
  celebrities, 142–44
  notion of, 186–87
chatbots, 48
Chicago (musical), Nana Visitor in, 154
Chicago: The Musical (musical), 206
childhood
  fantasy-reality distinction, 85–86
  imaginary relationships, 86–90
  imagined others, 86–90
  parasocial relationships in, 83–93
  role of fantasy and imagination, 90–93
children
  parasocial relationships (PSRs)
    of, 30–31
  puppets and, 112
classical culture, 195
cognitive psychology, real-life
    interactions, 25
Cohen, Jonathan, 30, 68, 106, 107
Colbert, Stephen, 52
collective effervescence
  parasocial relationships (PSRs), 137–39
  term, 137
Columbia University, 182
communication, social media
    platforms, 35
compensatory hypothesis, 87
computer-mediated relationships/
    communication (CMC), 13
construct of liking, 11
context collapse, social media as, 46
continuity hypothesis of dreaming,
    Schredl's, 76–77
continuity theory, media figures, 77
convergence, 166–67
conversational agents, media figures, 42
conversation analysis, qualitative
    method, 176
Cooper, Sheldon, 21, 168
correlational methods, 99
Cosby, Bill, 93
Costa, Paul, 7
COVID-19 pandemic
  Cameo and, 150, 153
  parasocial relationships (PSRs), 197–98
Craig, Daniel, 130

Cranston, Bryan, 208
  photograph of, 209f
creators, 39, 40–41, 53, 88, 100–1
Crosby, Bing, 158–60
Crosby, Denise, 195
  Cameo, 158–61
  photograph of, 159f
Crosby, Dennis, 158–60
Crucible, The (play), 60, 201–2
crush
  attraction, 129–30
  definition, 129
Cuddy, Amy, 202
cult fan, term, 142, 145
cultural influence, 32–33
Culture of Narcissism, The (Lasch), 96
Cumberbatch, Benedict, 140
Cumberbitches, 140

Daily Mirror, The (newspaper), 134
Daltrey, Roger, 77
Daniel Tiger's Neighbourhood (television
  series), 112
Davie504, 22
defective decision-making, 8
defense mechanism
  denial, 100
  repression, 100
deficit hypothesis, 87, 90
degree of reciprocity, social
  relationships, 13
Denis, Marilyn, 59
devotion
  concept of, 141
  fan and religious, 141–42
Diagnostic and Statistical Manual of Mental
  Disorders, 174
diary, qualitative method, 179
digital conversation analysis, 176–77
digital culture, audience theory, 76
direct address, 4, 52, 146, 148, 150–51, 169
Discord, 68, 199
discourse analysis, qualitative
  method, 174–75
discursive, 15
Disney, 166–67
distance relationships, 13

Doctors Without Borders, 22
dopamine, reward chemical, 126
Doss, Erika, 79
Down syndrome, 23
dreaming, continuity hypothesis of, 76–77
dreaming business dormants, 39
dream research, 77
dreams
  interpretation of, 100
  scene development, 210
  Trump in, 76–78
Duffett, Mark, 138
Durkheim, Emile, 137
Duval, Shelley, 205

Easter Bunny, 85–86
ecological validity, 181
effective reciprocity, TV viewers and, 34
effervescence, Durkheim's concept of, 138
ego-ideal, Freud, 104
Eisenberg, Aron, 144
El Fadil, Siddig, 65
Elizabeth (Queen)
  death of, 121–22
  photograph of, 122f
Elizabeth II (Queen), 29
Elmo, Sesame Street, 84–85
"elsewhere, the," definition, 103
Elvis, 10–11, 29, 86, 140–41
  copying or representing, 94–95
  fan objects as family members, 79–80
Emmison, Michael, 112
emotions, elements of behavior, 105–6
empirical, 12–13, 116, 184–85
empiricism, 172
entertainment, celebrity worship, 144–45
eros, romantic love, 18, 126, 136, 187–88
erotomania, 55, 74
ethnography
  autoethnography, 187–90
  participant-observer, 184–85
ethological theory, 194
ethorobotics, 48
evolutionary psychology, 16, 194
  attachment and, 123
  desire and arousal, 123–24
  principles of, 185

Index 253

Evolution of Desire, The (Buss), 125
Ewoldsen, Dave, 171
Experience of Parasocial Interaction
(EPSI), 43, 44
process scale, 53–54
questionnaire, 149
term, 50
Experience of Parasocial Interaction Scale
(EPSI), 10, 191
extended self, concept of, 95

Facebook, 2, 17, 30, 35, 37, 41, 72, 75–76,
139, 148–49, 189, 199
fan groups, 124
fame, 36–37
fame-by-association, 95
family members, fan objects as, 79–80
fan base, Richard Armitage, 56–63, 57f
fan objects
as family members, 79–80
as friend, 81–82
as mentor or adviser, 82
as soulmate or kindred spirit, 80–81
fan studies, social psychology and, 4
fandom(s), 10
concept of, 135
mudita, 139
para-communication and parasocial
perception in, 52–53
parasocial relationships (PSRs) vs., 4,
135–36, 146–47
religious expression and, 139–42
single-text, 140
fans
Cameo as activity, 161–62
celebrity's reaction to audience, 196
fantasy
imagined interactions, 91–93
role of imagination, 12
social and parasocial interaction, 90–93
fantasy-reality boundary, 113
fantasy-reality confusion, 98
fantasy-reality distinction,
childhood, 85–86
fanzine, 147
Farrell, Terry, photograph of, 154f
Fellowship of the Ring (film), 56

Fever Pitch (Hornby), 95
fictophilic stigma, 132
15/Love (television series), 69, 138
Figwit, 56
file selves, concept of, 94
film theory, 107
Find Your Light Foundation, 22
Fischoff, Stuart, 13
Flight of the Conchords (New Zealand
comedy duo), 56
Flintstone, Fred, 21
followers, fans as, 35
Fortnite (game), 41
Foundation (television series), 68
"fourth wall," King's character breaking, 33
Frank, Anne, 87
Freud, Sigmund, 45, 99–100, 108–9
dreamworld, 78
ego, 105
ego and superego, 104
evolutionary psychology, 114
ideal-ego, 104
"Freudian slip", 100
friend, fan object as, 81–82
Friends (television series), 30
Frodo Is Great, Who Is That?
(documentary), 56
Frow, John, 94

Galaxy Ball, 23
Game of Thrones (television series), 26, 68
Gandalf, 171
gender, language and, 110
General Hospital (soap opera), 69
Gergen, Kenneth, 94
Get Back (documentary), 29
Giles, David, x, 14, 23, 35, 36, 37, 45,
174, 175
Gillingham, Kim, 210
God, attachment to, 119
Golden Girls, The (television show), 21
Goldman, Laurence, 112
Good Morning America (television
show), 175
gossip, parasocial, 21–23
Gotham (television series), 68
Gough, Brendan, 174

254   Index

GQ (magazine), 22
Grahn, Nancy, 69
Granada Studios, 98
Grand Theft Auto (game), 41
Greek loves
  agape, 126
  eros, 18, 126, 136, 187–88
  phileo, 126
  storge, 33, 126, 136, 187–88, 189
Groban, Josh, 23–24, 138, 140, 143–44
  case of, 63–65
  fans of, 17, 22
  photograph, 64*f*
  profile of fans, 188
  research of tour, 188
Grobanites, 140
Grodenchik, Max, 144
grounded theory, 99
*Group Psychology and the Analysis of the
  Ego* (Freud), 105
Guardian, The (newspaper), 90–91
Gyllenhaal, Jake, 140
Gyllenhaalics, 140

Harold Pinter Theater, 69–70
Harry Potter (film), 26
  fans, 141–42
  place attachment, 117
Hartmann, Tilo, 50, 72
Hawn, Goldie, 77
Heifer Project, The, 22
Hertzler, J. G., 144
high culture, popular (mass) culture or, 195
Hills, Matt, 12, 15, 102, 142
Hilton, Paris, 22
Hobbit, The (films), 199
  actors from, 58–59, 189
  Aidan Turner in, 69–70
  Armitage in, 56–58
  attraction, 128
  Dean O'Gorman, 151
  Dean O'Gorman in, 70–73
  fan attraction, 124
  fandom, 27–28
  fans, 141–42
  fans of, 29
  shared joy, 139

  Turner and, 132
Hobbit, The (Tolkien), 55
  parasocial perception, 56
Hollywood icons, 46
homophily, 127, 169
Hornby, Nick, 95
Horton, Donald, xi, 8, 10, 33, 34 , –43, 51,
  54, 55, 151, 182, 190
Houston, Whitney, 29, 140–41
human-computer interaction, discipline
  of, 176
human nature, psychology, 32–33
hysteria, 34

ideal-ego, 104
identification
  audience members, 168–70
  components of, 168–69
  differentiating parasocial relationship
    (PSR) from, 24
  with the Other, 105–8
  process of, 104
  projective, 107
  psychological mechanism, 34
  similarity, 106, 107–8
  transportation and, 169–70
  wishful, 168, 170
illusion of intimacy, 20
imaginal dialogues, 93
imaginary companion (IC), 86–87, 88–89, 90
imaginary friends, 47, 86–87, 89, 95, 118
imaginary relationships, childhood, 86–90
imaginary social relationship, term, 24
imagination
  fantasy, 12
  imagined interactions, 91–93
  role in PSRs, 24–25
  social and parasocial interaction, 90–93
imagined interactions (IIs), 91–93
imagined others, childhood, 86–90
imitation, 24, 106
Impact Award, 133
implicit religion, term, 142
individual differences, 7, 89, 99,
  128, 189–90
influencers
  macro, 38

Index

mega, 38
social media, 37–39
types of, 38–39
Instagram, 17, 22–23, 42–43, 46, 62, 73, 148–49
celebrities, 164
Nana Visitor, 154–55
interaction, audience response, 34
intercommunication, description of, 37
interdisciplinary research, 6
internal working model (IWM)
attachment, 116
attachment objects, 25–26
definition, xi
narrative from, 25
parasocial attachment (PSA) and, 25
Internet Movie Database (IMBD), 70
interpretative phenomenological analysis (IPA), 178
interpretivism, 16
foundation of, 184–85
philosophy of, 186
qualitative perspective, 184
intimacy, in digital age, 54–56
intimacy at a distance, 54–56
parasocial relationships (PSRs), 58
intimate, definitions of, 54–55
invisible friend (IF), 86–89
invisible guests, 93
Irish Mirror Newspaper, 130

Jackson, Michael, 21–22, 28–29, 140–41, 142, 143–44, 188, 191
autoethnography, 187
fandom of, 185
fan objects as family members, 80
This Is It (documentary), 170
Jackson, Peter, 29, 56, 60–61
Jagger, Mick, 161
Jamison, Mae, 170
Jenkins, Henry, 79
Jones, Alex, 92
Jungian personality type, 46, 192

Kardashian, Kim, 22–23
Kardashians, 22–23
Kelly, George, 111, 179

Kennedy, John, 29
kindness, word, 142–43
kindred spirit, fan object as, 80–81
King, Jean, The Lonesome Gal (broadcast), 33–34
Kingdom of Heaven (film), 68
Klein, Melanie, 100–1, 107

Lacan, Jacques, 100–1, 109–10
Lady Gaga, 140
Lame, Khaby, 41
language, role in psychoanalytic theory, 109–11
Lasch, Christopher, 96
Late Show with Stephen Colbert, The (television show), 52
Leaving Neverland (film), 21–22
Ledger, Heath, 29, 201, 202
Lemons, Lemons, Lemons, Lemons, Lemons (play), 69–70, 186–87, 188–89
Lennon, John, 29
Let It Be (album), Beatles, 29
Letterman, David, 22–23
Levy, Mark, 8, 182
Lieutenant of Inishmore, The (play), 70
lifespan development
attachment theory, 3–4
parasocial across, 15
role of fandom in, 10
Little Monsters, 140
livestreamers, media figures, 41
London Academy of Music and Dramatic Arts, 202
loneliness, measure of social need, 90
Lonesome Gal, asking for hand in marriage, 98
Lonesome Gal, The (King's broadcast), 33–34, 43
Lord of the Rings, The (films), 55, 56, 58, 60, 169, 171
audience screening of, 106–7
fan groups, 145
fandoms, 17–18
fans, 141–42
place attachment, 117
storytelling, 26
Lowery, Melissa, 66–67, 68

Lumsden, Joan, 93, 175
lying, 88–89, 91–92

macro influencers, 38
Madison, T. Phillip, 92
Madonna, 143–44
Malluhi's thesis, 141
Maltby, John, 10–11, 139, 144
Marwick, Alice, 14, 34, 46, 76
Mary Sue fan fiction, 26
mass culture, 195
Masterson, Chase, 144
Mastodon, 63
McCrae, Robert, 7
McCutcheon, Lynn, 146
McHugh, Michael, 34, 127
McKellan, Ian, 143, 208
McKenzie, Bret, 56
McLuhan, Marshall, 32, 33
McMahon, Andrew, 162
McTavish, Graham, 28
media
    parasocial theory for broadcast, 11–12
    transitional objects and, 101–2
    See also audience
media-audience relationships,
        behaviorism, 105–6
media consumers, 75, 149, 166
media conventions, 111, 137
media effects, 167, 171
media equation argument, 32
Media Equation, The (Reeves & Naas), 125
media figure(s)
    avatars, 41–42
    conversational agents, 42
    defining new types, 36–42
    dimensions of, 36
    as family members and friends, 79–82
    fan object as friend, 81–82
    fan object as mentor or adviser, 82
    fan object as soulmate or kindred
        spirit, 80–81
    fan objects as family members, 79–80
    livestreamers, 41
    navigating the uncanny valley, 47–48
    social media influencers, 37–39
    TikTok(k)ers, 40–41

YouTubers, 39–40
media personality, 9
media producers, 166–67
media psychology, 15
    human nature, 33
    unanswered questions in, 98–99
media use, conceptualization of, 34
media violence, 34
medium is the message, 32
mega influencers, 38
memes, 37
mental health, 174
    acting and, 201–5
    stressful acting roles and, 205
mentor, fan object as, 82
method acting system, Strasberg, 202–5
MI5 (television show), 56–58
microanalysis of online data, qualitative
        method, 176–77
microcelebrities, 35, 39
    emergence of, 75–76
Midnight Films, 56
Miller, Arthur, 60
Minecraft (game), 40, 41
mirrors
    developmental theory, 103–4
    self-recognition tool, 103
Mitchell, John, 69
mixed methods, 179
modality
    concept, 83
    judgments, 111–12
modeling, 4–5, 24, 96, 99, 167–68
Monroe, Marilyn, 106
mood modification, 169
Morning Hate (film), 162–63
Morrissey, 80, 81–82
Mr. Beast, YouTuber, 35
mudita, parasocial relationships
        (PSRs), 139
multidisciplinary research, 6
multiperspectivism, 16
multisocial interaction, 43
    social media as, 49
    term, 2
Mulvey, Laura, 106
Musk, Elon, 62

Index

257

Myspace, 149

narrative, parasocial romantic
  relationships (PSRRs), 130
narrative comprehension, 172
narrative persuasion, 171–72
  idea of, 130
narrative psychology, 25
  science of storytelling, 25–27
narrative realism, fantasy-reality
  divide, 112
narrative research, approaches to, 186
*Natasha, Pierre, and the Great Comet of
  1812* (musical), 64
National Television Awards, 132, 133
neo-religiosity, term, 142
Nichols, Nichelle, 170
Nicholson, Jack, 205
Nordlund, 190
normal social interaction, 10
North and South (television show), 56–
  58, 59
notoriety, parasocial, 21–23

object relations theory, Winnicott's,
  3, 118–19
Oedipus complex, 99, 105
O'Gorman, Dean, 4, 27, 28, 29–30, 139,
  170, 195, 200–1
  Cameo, 151–53, 155, 190
  Facebook fan community, 151
  fan community, 199
  The Hobbit and *The Almighty
    Johnsons*, 70–73
  photograph of, 71f, 152f, 207f
  Zoom interview, 206–9
online data, microanalysis of, 176–77
ontology, 11, 86
operant conditioning, social media
  as, 163
Orville, The (television series), 156
"Other, the"
  the elsewhere and, 102–4
  identification with, 105–8
oxytocin, brain chemistry, 126

Pace, Lee, Facebook fan community, 151

para-communication, 2–3
  fandoms, 52–53
para-proxemics, 26–27
para-religion, term, 142
parasocial, 3
  concept of, 7
  definition of, 12–13
  researching the, 8–10
  scandal, gossip and notoriety, 21–23
parasocial and social, as a
  continuum, 194–95
parasocial attachment (PSA), xi, 2,
  115, 146
  death of Queen Elizabeth, 121–22, 122f
  definition, xi, 120
  mediated attachment, 119–21
  primary, 120, 121
  proximity-seeking behavior, 146
  quality of, 25
  secondary, 120, 121
  theory, 129
  See also attachment
parasocial attachment (PSA)
  theory, 54–55
parasocial breakup (PSB), 22
  concept of, 28–31
  definition, xi
parasocial discourse, study of, 175
parasocial experience(s) (PSEs), 1, 2–
  3, 178
  actor Aidan Turner, 69–70, 71f
  actor Dean O'Gorman, 70–73, 71f
  attachment to media figures, 10–11
  case studies, 54–73
  definition, xi
  determination of, 19–21
  fan base of Richard Armitage, 56–
    63, 57f
  Grobanites, 63–65, 64f
  inductive approach to
    understanding, 1–2
  intimacy in a digital age, 54–56
  methods for researching, 5
  mudita, 139
  parasocial and social, 17
  place attachment, 117
  positive engagement, 9

258   Index

parasocial experience(s) (PSEs) (*cont.*)
   roles of producer and consumer, 4–5
   Sid City Social Club and Alexander
      Siddig, 65–69, 66f
   sociometer theory, 136–37
   theoretical approaches, 15–16
parasocial friendship, 18
parasocial interaction (PSI), xi, 2, 44
   146, 189–90
   Cameo and, 149–51
   concept of, 8
   conception of, 148–49
   definitions of, xi–xii, 36
   direct address, 4, 52, 146, 148, 150–
   51, 169
   eye gaze, 4, 169
   individuals and media, 19
   parasocial objects and, 4
   role of fantasy and imagination, 90–93
   self-recognition and mirrors, 104
   social psychology, 76
Parasocial Interaction Scale (PSI),
   8, 190–91
parasociality, 13
parasocial perception, 2–3
   celebrity object caring for audience 55
   fandoms, 52–53
   para-communication and, 196
   term, 51–52
parasocial project, notion of, 34
parasocial relationships (PSRs), xi, 1, 2
   attachment, 116
   with baddies, 108, 113
   celebrity side of, 2–3
   in childhood, 83–93
   collective effervescence, 137–39
   continuum of social and, 194–95
   definition, xii, 50
   differentiating from identification, 24
   emergence of, 98
   evolutionary psychology and, 197–98
   extension of media enjoyment, 198
   fandom and, 135–36
   fandom vs., 4, 146–47
   language, 109–11
   method of inquiry and, 210–11
   narrative of, 111–13

   observations on attraction, 127–28
   parasocial to social transitions, 23–24
   popular (mass) culture or high
      culture, 195
   research, 9
   role of imagination, 24–25
   social media, 2
   spiritual life of audience
      members, 198–99
   term, 140–41
   unconscious and psychoanalytical
      perspectives on, 196–97
parasocial romantic relationships
   (PSRRs), 3–4
   attraction, 124–27, 128–29
   celebrity worship, 198
   definition, xi
   narrative persuasion, 130
   parasocial relationships (PSRs) and, 18
   See also attraction
parasocial theory, 2, 6–7, 9
   broadcast media, 11–12
   dimensional approach, 14
   illusion of intimacy, 20
   introducing the discursive, 15
   para-communication and parasocial
      perception, 196
   parasocial across the lifespan, 15
   research questions, 5, 10–15
   See also research methods in
      parasocial theory
participant-observer ethnography, 184–85
passionate business influencers, 39
passionate influencers, 39
passionate topic enthusiasts, 39
pathetic fallacy, 90
Peaky Blinders (television series), 68
performance, persona studies, 46
Perry, Matthew, 30
persona, study of, 36
personal construct theory, George Kelly,
   111, 179
personified objects, 86–87
pets, attachment to, 118
phantasy, 107, 108–9
phenomenology, 186
philanthropy, celebrities, 22

Index

phileo, friendship, 126
philia, brotherly love, 18
Piaget, Jean, 6
Pianist, The (film), 205
Picardo, Robert, 72, 162, 195
  Cameo and, 156–58
  photograph of, 157*f*
Pinterest, 149
Pirates of the Caribbean (films), 166–67
Pitt, Brad, 130
place attachment, 116–17
  definition, 117
Play School (BBC), 83–84
Poldark (UK television series), 30, 124, 201
  Aidan Turner in, 69–70, 130–34
  fans, 141–42
pop stars, 37, 46
popular culture, 195
Pork Pie, Dean O'Gorman in, 151
positivist, 184–85
Potter, Harry, 101
Presley, Elvis, 29, 79, 138
Price, Michael, 134
Prince, 29, 140–41
Princess Diana, 79
psychoanalytic theory, 3, 194
  attachment theories and, 114
  defense of, 99–101
  the elsewhere and the other, 102–4
  fantasy...and phantasy, 108–9
  identification with the other, 105–8
  language, 109–11
  narrative, 111–13
  transitional objects and media, 101–2
psychology
  collection of "corpus" of
    material, 179–80
  human nature, 32–33
psychology of acting, questions for future
    research, 199–201
psychometric scales, 182–83
psychometric testing, 76
puppets, fantasy-reality divide, 112

qualitative research
  autoethnography, 187–90
  case studies, 54–73

conversation analysis, 176
  describing, 185–86
  diary method, 179
  discourse analysis, 174–75
  ethnography, 184–85
  focus groups, 178, 182
  grounded theory, 99
  interpretative phenomenological
    analysis, 178
  interviewing, 174, 188
  qualitative content analysis
    (Altheide), 187
  qualitative inquiry, 210–11
  participant-observer
    ethnography, 184–85
  repertory grid technique, 179
  thematic analysis, 174, 181–82
  types of, 186–87
  See also quantitative research; research
    methods in parasocial theory
Qualitative Research in Psychology
    (journal), 174
quantitative research
  Audience-Persona Interaction Scale, 191
  Celebrity Appeal Questionnaire, 191–92
  Celebrity Attitude Scale, 192
  content analysis, 181
  Experience of Parasocial Interaction
    Scale (EPSI), 191
  experiments, 180–81
  multivariate statistics, 100
  Parasocial Interaction Scale
    (PSI), 190–91
  psychometric scales, 182–83
  See also qualitative research; research
    methods in parasocial theory
Quixote, Don, 110–11

radio stars, 37
Rathje, William, 43–44
rationalism, 172
Reagan, Ronald, 77
reciprocity, social relationships, 13
religion, word, 141
religious expression, fandom and, 139–42
repertory grid technique, qualitative
    method, 179

research, psychology of acting, 199–201
research methods in parasocial theory
  collection of "corpus" of
    material, 179–80
  experiments, 180–81
  microanalysis of online data, 176–77
  mixed method design, 179
  qualitative methods, 174–80
  quantification of qualitative
    data, 181–83
  quantitative methods, 180–83
  talking methods, 177–78
  See also qualitative research; quantitative
    research
retrospective imaginative involvement
    (RII), 171
Return, The (Shatner), 30
Return of the King, The (film), 56, 138
Robinson, Andrew, 144, 195, 200
Rojek, Chris, 36, 142
role model, 61–62, 124, 167–68, 191–92
romantic attraction, xi, 17–18, 61–62, 124,
    125, 126, 132, 136, 138, 189
romantic tropes
  alpha hero, 133
  emotional scars, 133
  honorable marriage, 133
  love triangle, 133
  rich vs. poor, 133
  unequal social status, 133
Root, Joe, 78
Rosengren, Karl, 190
"rouge test", 103
Rubin, Alan, 8
Rubin, Rebecca, 34, 127
Rupert Murdoch's News
    Corporation, 166–67
Ruskin, John, 90

Sacks, Harvey, 176
sacred, 100, 117, 137, 141–42, 145, 198–
    99, 206
Sandvoss, Cornel, 95
Santa Claus, 85–86
Save the Children, 22
scandal, parasocial, 21–23
Schredl, Michael, 76–77

Scott, Marilyn, 158–60
self, fashioning of, 96–97
self-help, social media as, 153
self-nonself boundary, 94–97
self-recognition
  mirror, 103
  smartphone/video, 101–2, 103–4, 119
self-study, autoethnography, 187–90
self-worth, 118–19
seriation task, 84
Sesame Street (television show), 85
  Elmo from, 84
sex symbol, Turner as, 132
sexual desire, 77, 125, 126
Shantaram (television series), 68
"sharenting" influencer, YouTube, 7
Shatner, William, 30, 143–44
Shepherd, David, 109
Shimerman, Armin, 144, 195, 200
Shining, The (film), 205
Sid City Social Club, 197–98
  Alexander Siddig and, 65–69
Siddig, Alexander, 61, 144, 170, 190, 195
  on character role, 202
  photograph of, 204*f*
  Sid City Social Club and, 65–69
  on training in British acting
    school, 202–5
Silverstone, Roger, 101, 102
similarity identification, 106, 107–8
Simon, Paul, 143
Simpson, Homer, 21
Siri, 42, 47, 150–51, 163, 166–67
smartphone, 101–2, 103–4, 119
soap opera, 113
soap opera audiences, study of, 11
social celebrity worship, 144–45
social cognition, 25, 197
social cognitive theory
  Bandura's, 167
  identifications, 24
social constructionism, 16, 174
social experiences, vicarious, 168
social ghosts, 79, 93
social identity theory, 107–8
social interaction, role of fantasy and
    imagination, 90–93

Index

social media, 17
  advent of, 194
  Cameo, 163, 199
  context collapse, 46
  fan groups, 124
  interactions, 17
  multisocial interaction, 49
  new platforms, 199
  as operant conditioning, 163
  parasocial relationships (PSRs), 2, 196
  parasocial theory for, 12
  reciprocity criterion, 13
  reshaping communication, 35
  as self-help, 153
  See also Cameo
social-parasocial continuum, 194–95
social penetration theory, 48
social processing, 113
social psychology
  fan studies and, 4
  parasocial interaction (PSI), 76
  self-nonself boundary, 94–97
social realism, of portrayal, 112
social relationships, degree of reciprocity, 13
sociometer theory, parasocial experiences
    (PSEs), 136–37
Sony, AIBO (robotic puppy), 47–48
Sooty Show, The (television show), 112
  audience, 112
Sootyville, 84
soulmate, fan object as, 80–81
source monitoring dysfunction, 98
Spiner, Brent, 137
Springsteen, Bruce, 80–82
  fan of, 95
  fans, 96
SPSS, 99, 173
Stampylongnose (gamer), 40
Star Trek (television series), 61, 139,
    140, 166–67
  actors, 22, 23
  Alexander Siddig and, 65–67
  fan attraction, 124
  fan groups, 145
  fandom, 17, 23, 79, 188
  fans, 141–42
  place attachment, 117

Star Trek: Deep Space Nine (*DS9*)
    (television series), 23, 137, 170, 200
  Alexander Siddig in, 65, 68, 190
  Nana Visitor, 154
Star Trek: Generations (film), 30
Star Trek: The Next Generation (television
    series), 137
  Denise Crosby, 158–60
Star Trek: Voyager (television series), 23
  Robert Picardo in, 156, 158
Star Wars (films), 26, 171
Stever, Gayle, 10–11, 145
stigma of fandom, 132, 188, 189
storge, affection, 33, 126, 136, 187–88, 189
storytelling, narrative psychology and
    science of, 25–27
Stott, Ken, 27
Strasberg, Lee, method acting system
    of, 202–5
superego/ego-ideal, 104
Superman, 109
surrogate attachment figures, 119
survival and reproduction, evolutionary
    psychology, 197–98
Suspect, The (television series), 69, 138
Sweeney Todd (musical), 64
Swift, Taylor, 143–44
Sylk, Ken, 158–60
symbolic interactionism, 186
Syriana (film), 68

Tajfel, Henri, 107–8
talk radio, 75
talking methods, qualitative
    method, 177–78
task attraction, 61–62, 124
tele-literacy, process, 102–3
Teletubbies (BBC television), 83–84
television, transitional objects and, 101–2
thematic analysis, qualitative methods,
    174, 181–82
theories of self, 94
theory of planned behavior (TPB), 7
third person effect, media research, 43–44
This Is It (documentary), 170
This Person Needs No Introduction (Netflix
    show), 22–23

Thurman, Robert, 210
TikTok, 2, 42–43, 149
TikTok(k)ers, media figures, 40–41
Tolkien, J. R. R., 17–18, 26, 29, 55–56, 70, 145
Tooth Fairy, 85–86
transitional object(s)
    attachment to, 118–19
    concept of, 101
    media and, 101–2
transportation
    binge-watching and, 171
    identification and, 169–70
    viewers into media worlds, 170–72
transported, 113
Trekkies/Trekkers, 140, 158–60, 161
triangulation, concept of, 6
Truman Show (film), 178
Trumbo, 199, 209*f*
    Dean O'Gorman in, 151
Trump, Donald, 92
    dreaming about, 76–78
Tsay-Vogel and Schwartz, 36
Tukachinsky Forster, Rebecca, 132
Tumblr, 29, 53, 120, 161, 199
Turner, Aidan, 138, 142–44
    Facebook fan community, 151
    fans of, and play *Lemons Lemons Lemons
        Lemons Lemons*, 186–87, 188–89
    The Hobbit and *Poldark*, 69–70
    photograph, 71*f*, 131*f*
    Poldark, 130–34
    relationship with character, 201–2
Turner, Graeme, 36
Turner, John C., 107–8
TV personality, 37
TV Times, 138
24 (television series), 68
Twitch, 41, 42–43, 45–46
Twitter (X), 2, 13, 17, 30, 35, 37, 42–43, 46,
    62, 63, 73, 75–76, 148–49, 177
    celebrities, 164
    fan groups, 124

uncanny valley, navigating, 47–48
Uncle Vanya (Chekov), 60
unconscious, psychoanalytical perspectives
    on PSR, 196–97

unconscious desires, 99–100
Under the Vines, Dean O'Gorman in, 151
University of California, Los Angeles, 195
University of Southern California, 195

verbal immediacy, 45–46
vicarious experience, 106
vicarious punishment, 24
vicarious reinforcement, 24
vicarious social experiences, 168
Visitor, Nana, 4, 144, 195, 200, 205
    Cameo and, 154–56, 164
    photograph of, 154*f*, 203*f*
    relationship with character, 201
    on researching character, 202

War of the Worlds (Welles' broadcast), 33
Watkins, Mary, 93
Waugh, Evelyn, 89
Welles, Orson, 33
White, Betty, 21
Winnicott, Donald, 101–2, 104
    object relations theory, 118–19
Wise, Sue, 81
wishful identification, 106, 168, 170
Wohl, Richard, xi, 8, 10, 33, 34 , –43, 51,
    54, 55, 151, 182, 190
Working Girl (film), 24
working memory, short-term, 32–33
World Cup, 108–9
worship, 147
    celebrity, 139, 144–45
    word, 139–40

Young Hercules (television show)
    O'Gorman, 72
YouTube, 2, 7, 22, 23, 32, 37, 41, 44, 75–
    76, 148–49
    celebrities and fans, 60
    fan groups, 124
    Mr. Beast, 35
YouTube personalities, 39
YouTubers, 175
    media figure, 39–40

Zoella, 22, 23
Zoom, 67–68